Berlin Contemporary

Visual Cultures and German Contexts

Series Editors
Deborah Ascher Barnstone (University of Technology Sydney, Australia)
Thomas O. Haakenson (California College of the Arts, USA)

Visual Cultures and German Contexts publishes innovative research into visual culture in Germany, Switzerland and Austria, as well as in diasporic linguistic and cultural communities outside of these geographic, historical, and political borders.

The series invites scholarship by academics, curators, architects, artists, and designers across all media forms and time periods. It engages with traditional methods in visual culture analysis as well as inventive interdisciplinary approaches. It seeks to encourage a dialogue amongst scholars in traditional disciplines with those pursuing innovative interdisciplinary and intermedial research. Of particular interest are provocative perspectives on archival materials, original scholarship on emerging and established creative visual fields, investigations into time-based forms of aesthetic expression, and new readings of history through the lens of visual culture. The series offers a much-needed venue for expanding how we engage with the field of Visual Culture in general.

Proposals for monographs, edited volumes, and outstanding research studies are welcome, by established as well as emerging writers from a wide range of comparative, theoretical and methodological perspectives.

Advisory Board
Donna West Brett, University of Sydney, Australia
Charlotte Klonk, Humboldt Universität Berlin, Germany
Nina Lübbren, Anglia Ruskin University, UK
Maria Makela, California College of the Arts, USA
Patrizia C. McBride, Cornell University, USA
Rick McCormick, University of Minnesota, USA
Elizabeth Otto, University at Buffalo SUNY, USA
Kathryn Starkey, Stanford University, USA
Annette F. Timm, University of Calgary, Canada
James A. van Dyke, University of Missouri, USA

Titles in the Series
Art and Resistance in Germany, edited by Deborah Ascher Barnstone and Elizabeth Otto
Bauhaus Bodies: Gender, Sexuality, and Body Culture in Modernism's Legendary Art School, edited by Elizabeth Otto and Patrick Rössler
Berlin Contemporary: Architecture and Politics after 1990, by Julia Walker
Photofascism: Photography, Film, and Exhibition Culture in 1930s Germany and Italy, by Vanessa Rocco
Single People and Mass Housing in Germany, 1850–1930: (No) Home Away from Home, by Erin Eckhold Sassin

Berlin Contemporary

Architecture and Politics after 1990

Julia Walker

BLOOMSBURY VISUAL ARTS
NEW YORK • LONDON • OXFORD • NEW DELHI • SYDNEY

BLOOMSBURY VISUAL ARTS
Bloomsbury Publishing Inc
1385 Broadway, New York, NY 10018, USA
50 Bedford Square, London, WC1B 3DP, UK
29 Earlsfort Terrace, Dublin 2, Ireland

BLOOMSBURY, BLOOMSBURY VISUAL ARTS and the Diana logo are trademarks
of Bloomsbury Publishing Plc

First published in the United States of America 2022
Paperback edition published by Bloomsbury Visual Arts 2024

Copyright © Julia Walker, 2022

For legal purposes the Acknowledgments on p. xi constitute an extension
of this copyright page.

Cover design: Tjasa Krivec
Cover image © Colin McPherson / Contributor / Getty Images

All rights reserved. No part of this publication may be reproduced or transmitted in any
form or by any means, electronic or mechanical, including photocopying, recording,
or any information storage or retrieval system, without prior permission
in writing from the publishers.

Bloomsbury Publishing Inc does not have any control over, or responsibility for, any
third-party websites referred to or in this book. All internet addresses given in
this book were correct at the time of going to press. The author and publisher
regret any inconvenience caused if addresses have changed or sites have
ceased to exist, but can accept no responsibility for any such changes.

ISBN: HB: 978-1-5013-6752-6
       PB: 978-1-3504-3704-3
       ePDF: 978-1-5013-6753-3
       eBook: 978-1-5013-6754-0

Series: Visual Cultures and German Contexts

Typeset by RefineCatch Limited, Bungay, Suffolk

To find out more about our authors and books visit www.bloomsbury.com
and sign up for our newsletters.

Contents

List of Illustrations	vi
Acknowledgments	xi
Introduction: Berlin, the Contemporary Capital	1
1 Bridging and Breaking—Master Planning the Spreebogen	23
2 The Reichstag's New Lightness of Being	79
3 Monumental Modernism—The Chancellery as Future Ruin	121
4 Palaces of Doubt	175
Conclusion: No One Intends To Open an Airport	221
Bibliography	237
Index	241

Illustrations

0.1	Foster + Partners. Reichstag, Berlin, 1999. View from Platz der Republik.	2
0.2	Gehry Partners, DG Bank (now DZ Bank), Berlin, 1995–2001.	7
0.3	Helmut Jahn, Renzo Piano, Hans Hollein, Rafael Moneo, et al., renovation of Potsdamer Platz, Berlin, 1992–2001.	8
0.4	Studio Libeskind, Jewish Museum, Berlin, 1988–2001.	9
0.5	Rem Koolhaas/OMA, Embassy of the Netherlands, Berlin, 1997–2003.	12
1.1	Site of the Spreebogen, early 1990s.	24
1.2	Schultes Frank Architekten, proposal for Spreebogen, Berlin, 1992.	24
1.3	Map of Berlin and Kölln, c. 1300.	27
1.4	Johann Stridbeck, *Prospect oder Weg, gegen dem Their-Garden vor Berlin*, 1691.	28
1.5	Carl Gotthard Langhans, Brandenburg Gate, c. 1798.	29
1.6	Samuel Graf von Schmettau, map of Berlin, 1764.	29
1.7	Julius Straube, map of Berlin, 1895.	30
1.8	Paul Wallot, Reichstag building, 1894.	31
1.9	Cornelis van Eesteren, "*Gleichgewicht*," proposal for Unter den Linden, 1925.	32
1.10	Otto Kohtz, *Reichshaus am Königsplatz, Berlin-Tiergarten*, 1920.	33
1.11	Karl Böttcher and Hugo Häring, *Reichstag, Berlin*, 1927.	34
1.12	Hans Poelzig, *Erweiterung des Reichstags und Neugstaltung des Platzes der Republik, Berlin-Tiergarten*, 1927.	34
1.13	Albert Speer, model for *Welthauptstadt Germania*, 1937–42.	35
1.14	Martin Mächler, *Nord-Süd-Achse mit der Neustrukturierung des Potsdamer Bahnhofsgeländes, Berlin*, 1917.	36
1.15	Inhabitants of Berlin picking potatoes in front of the Reichstag, 1947.	37
1.16	Hugh Stubbins with Werner Düttmann and Franz Mocken, Berlin Congress Hall, 1957.	38

Illustrations vii

1.17 Le Corbusier, proposal for *Hauptstadt Berlin*, 1958. 39

1.18 Alison and Peter Smithson, proposal for *Hauptstadt Berlin*, 1958. 40

1.19 Aldo Rossi, site plan for Deutsches Historisches Museum, Berlin, 1988. 42

1.20 Bundesviertel, Bonn, 2010. 43

1.21 Jean Nouvel, Emmanuel Cattani & Associés, proposal for the *Berlin Morgen (Berlin Tomorrow)* competition, 1990. 46

1.22 Zaha Hadid, *Berlin 2000*, proposal for the *Berlin Morgen (Berlin Tomorrow)* competition, 1990. 47

1.23 Peter Riemann, *Die Stadt in der Stadt–Berlin das Grüne Stadtarchipel (The City in the City–Berlin as Green Archipelago)*, 1977. 48

1.24 John Hejduk, proposal for the *Berlin Morgen (Berlin Tomorrow)* competition, 1990. 49

1.25 Studio Libeskind, model for proposal for the *Berlin Morgen (Berlin Tomorrow)* competition, 1990. 50

1.26 Robert Venturi and Denise Scott Brown, *Brandenburger Treppe*, 1990. 51

1.27 Morphosis, proposal for the Spreebogen, Berlin, 1992–3. 56

1.28 Schultes Frank Architekten, proposal for the Spreebogen, Berlin, 1992–3. 58

1.29 Superstudio, *Monumento Continuo, New York*, c. 1969. 59

1.30 Bruno Taut, *Gemeinschaften und Eigenbrödler (Communities and Loners)*, from *Die Auflösung der Städte*, 1920. 63

1.31 Rem Koolhaas, *The Berlin Wall as Architecture*, 1971. 65

1.32 Rem Koolhaas, Elia Zenghelis, Madelon Vriesendorp, and Zoe Zenghelis, *Exodus, or the Voluntary Prisoners of Architecture, The Strip, Project, Aerial Perspective*, 1972. 66

1.33 Spreebogen, Berlin, 2016. 67

2.1 Christo and Jeanne-Claude, *Wrapped Reichstag*, Berlin, 1995. 80

2.2 Ludwig Bohnstedt, *Hauptfaçade des deutschen Parlamentsgebäudes*, in Ernst Keil (publisher), *Die Gartenlaube (The Garden Arbor)*, Leipzig, 1872. 83

2.3 Paul Wallot, Reichstag building, 1882–94. 84

2.4 Paul Baumgarten, renovations to Reichstag building, 1961. 86

2.5 The Berlin Wall under construction to the east of the Reichstag, November 23, 1961. 87

2.6 Wassili Luckhardt, project for a cinema, c. 1920. 93

2.7 Rudolf Steiner, Goetheanum, Dornach, Switzerland, 1919. 94

2.8 Jean Nouvel, Emmanuel Cattani & Associés, proposal for the Reichstag, Berlin, 1992. 96

2.9 Gottfried Böhm, *Wettbewerb Umgestaltung des Reichstags*, Berlin, 1992. 97

2.10 Coop Himmelb(l)au, proposal for the Reichstag, Berlin, 1992. 98

2.11 Pi de Bruijn, proposal for the Reichstag, Berlin, 1992. 99

2.12 Santiago Calatrava, *Realisierungswettbewerb Umbau des Reichstagsgebäudes zum Deutschen Bundestag Ein 1. Preis, Regierungsviertel, Schnitt*, Berlin, 1992. 100

2.13 Foster + Partners, proposal for the Reichstag, Berlin, 1992. 101

2.14 Norman Foster (Architect) and Helmut Jacoby (Artist), *Wettbewerb Umgestaltung des Reichstags*, Berlin, 1992. 102

2.15 Foster Associates, Sainsbury Centre for Visual Arts, the University of East Anglia campus, Norwich, UK, 1978. 104

2.16 Foster + Partners, Carré d'Art, Nîmes, France, 1993. 105

2.17 Foster + Partners, models for Reichstag cupola, 1993. 107

2.18 Reichstag corridor with conserved graffiti, 2017. 109

2.19 Yevgeny Khaldei, *Soviet Flag over the Reichstag*, 1945. 110

2.20 Reichstag stair with graffiti, Berlin, 1945. 110

3.1 Schultes Frank Architekten, Federal Chancellery, Berlin, 1994–2001. 122

3.2 Stephan Braunfels, Paul-Löbe-Haus, Berlin, 1997–2002. 124

3.3 Stephan Braunfels, Marie-Elisabeth-Lüders-Haus, Berlin, 1998–2003. 125

3.4 Rudolf Reitermann and Peter Sassenroth, Chapel of the Reconciliation, Berlin, 1999–2000. 127

3.5 Sergei Tchoban and Sergey Kuznetsov, Tchoban Foundation – Museum for Architectural Drawing, Berlin, 2009–13. 127

3.6 David Chipperfield Architects, Forum Museumsinsel, Berlin, 2010–16. 128

3.7 Toyo Ito, Tama Art University Library, Tokyo, 2004–7. 128

3.8 Michael Photiadis, Venus Marble Headquarters, Athens, 2010. 129

3.9 Sep Ruf, Kanzlerbungalow, Bonn, 1964. 132

3.10 Albert Speer, Reich Chancellery, Berlin, 1937–9. 134

Illustrations ix

3.11 Hermann Henselmann and Richard Paulick, Stalinallee, Berlin, begun 1949. 137
3.12 James Stirling, Neue Staatsgalerie, Stuttgart, 1977–84. 139
3.13 O. M. Ungers, proposal for Chancellery, Berlin, 1994. 141
3.14 Ludwig Ruff, Congress Hall, Nuremburg, 1934–8. 142
3.15 O. M. Ungers, residence for the German Ambassador, Washington, D.C., 1994. 143
3.16 Krüger Schuberth Vandreike (KSV), proposal for Chancellery, Berlin, 1994. 144
3.17 Schultes Frank Architekten, proposal for Chancellery, Berlin, 1994. 144
3.18 Axel Schultes/BJSS, Kunstmuseum Bonn, 1992. 147
3.19 Louis Kahn, National Assembly Building, Dhaka, Bangladesh, begun 1962. 149
3.20 Louis Kahn, project for Hurva Synagogue, 1968. 152
3.21 Schultes Frank Architekten, proposal for Chancellery, Berlin, 1995. 154
3.22 Schultes Frank Architekten, Chancellery, Berlin 1994–2001. 156
3.23 Schultes Frank Architekten, Chancellery, Berlin 1994–2001. 157
3.24 Stephan Braunfels, Paul-Löbe-Haus and Marie-Elisabeth-Lüders-Haus, Berlin. 158
3.25 Stephan Braunfels, Pinakothek der Moderne, Munich, 1992. 159
3.26 Schultes Frank Architekten, project for the extension of the Chancellery, Berlin, 2019. 163
4.1 Spreebogen construction site, Berlin, 1996. 176
4.2 Berlin Stadtschloss, early twentieth century. 177
4.3 Heinz Graffunder, Palast der Republik, Berlin, 1974–6. 177
4.4 Schultes Frank Architekten, "Schinkel's Dream," 1994. 178
4.5 Stadtschloss, Berlin, aerial photograph taken between 1905 and 1925. 182
4.6 Karl Friedrich Schinkel, *Perpektivische Ansicht von der Galerie der Haupt, Treppe des Museums durch den Porticus auf dem Lustgarten und seine Umgebungen*, 1824. 183
4.7 National Socialist parade on the Schlossplatz, Berlin, 1936. 184
4.8 Detonation of Berlin Stadtschloss by GDR, 1950. 185

4.9   Model of East Berlin Stadtzentrum with Marx-Engels-Platz, Palast der
      Republik, Ministerium für Auswärtige Angelegenheiten, and
      Staatsratsgebäude in right foreground.   187

4.10 Palast der Republik, main lobby with "glass forms."   189

4.11 Ralf Schüler and Ursulina Schüler-Witte, Internationale
      Congress Centrum (ICC), Berlin, 1976–9.   192

4.12 Bernd Niebuhr, proposal for the Spreeinsel, Berlin, 1994.   194

4.13 Krüger Schuberth Vandreike (KSV), proposal for the
      Spreeinsel, Berlin, 1994.   196

4.14 Schultes and Frank Architekten, proposal for the Spreeinsel, Berlin, 1994.   197

4.15 Simulation of rebuilt Stadtschloss, Berlin, 1993.   199

4.16 Benjamin Foerster-Baldenius and Raumlabor, *Volkspalast: Der Berg*,
      2005. Installation, Palast der Republik, Berlin.   205

4.17 Lars Ø. Ramberg, *PALAST DES ZWIFELS (PALACE OF DOUBT)*,
      2005. Installation, Palast der Republik, Berlin.   207

4.18 KSV, Humboldt Box, Berlin, 2011.   210

4.19 Franco Stella, Humboldt Forum, Berlin, 2008–20.   211

4.20 Franco Stella, Humboldt Forum, Berlin, 2008–20.   212

5.1   Berlin Brandenburg Airport, Terminal 1. Exterior view.   224

5.2   Berlin Brandenburg Airport, Terminal 1. Interior view.   224

5.3   Johannn Heinrich Hintze, *Blick vom Kreuzberg*, 1829.   227

5.4   Ernst Sagebiel, *Flughafen Berlin-Tempelhof*, c. 1935–45.   228

5.5   Ernst Sagebiel and Adolf Kautzki, *Flughafen Berlin-Tempelhof,
      Perspektivische Innenansicht der Abfertigungshalle*, 1935–45.   229

5.6   Eagle Square, Tempelhof Airport, Berlin.   230

5.7   Refugee accommodation center in a former hangar at
      Tempelhof Airport, Berlin, 2015.   231

Acknowledgments

It is a very great pleasure to thank the many people who have been instrumental in seeing this project through to completion. First, I thank Deborah Ascher Barnstone and Tom Haakenson for their discerning, sure-handed, and supportive work as editors of the Visual Cultures and German Contexts series at Bloomsbury Academic. I am honored to be included alongside the groundbreaking work of the other authors in the series. At the press, I am grateful to April Peake for her deft editorial skill as well as her consistent positivity and good humor, especially remarkable in the throes of a global pandemic.

That Karl Scheffler's now-clichéd characterization of Berlin as a city "doomed forever to become and never to be" does not also apply to this book is due to the help and support of countless individuals and organizations. It began as a dissertation at the University of Pennsylvania under the guidance of David Brownlee, whose wisdom, wit, and friendship will always be one of the great gifts of my scholarly life. Liliane Weissberg is a model of academic commitment in her keen insight, intellectual generosity, and unflagging kindness. The same can be said of the entire Penn community, to whom I am ever grateful. In addition, my work benefited immensely from participation in the 2016 summer school of the University of Bern's interdisciplinary Walter Benjamin Kolleg, and I am thankful to the Kolleg for its support and to Bernhard Siegert for his invaluable advice on my project at a key moment in its development. I am likewise indebted to the Deutscher Akademischer Austauschdienst and the Savannah College of Art and Design's Presidential Fellowship for Faculty Development for supporting the extended travel necessary to complete this book. Furthermore, any research on the architecture of the immediate past requires the cooperation of its makers, and for opening their archives, providing documentation, and allowing their work to be reproduced herein, I humbly thank Schultes Frank Architekten, Krüger Schuberth Vandreike, Foster + Partners, Ateliers Jean Nouvel, Zaha Hadid Architects, David Chipperfield Architects, Morphosis Architects, Studio Libeskind, the Office for Metropolitan Architecture, Santiago Calatrava Architects & Engineers, Coop Himmelb(l)au, de Architekten Cie, Bernd Niebuhr, Lars Ø. Ramberg, and Michael Photiadis.

I consider myself immeasurably fortunate to call the department of Art History at Binghamton University my scholarly home—not only for its long-standing commitment to examining the many visual histories of the built environment, but also for the support and tight-knit collegiality of my compatriots there. Heartfelt thanks to Karen Barzman, Tom McDonough, Pamela Smart, John Tagg, Nancy Um, and Andrew Walkling, as well as Marcia Focht and Sylvia Skok, for providing an intellectual atmosphere that both challenges and sustains me. My special gratitude is due to Jeffrey

West Kirkwood, not only for his unfailingly brilliant feedback, but also for his unfailingly brilliant friendship, without which I would be at sea. I also thank the students—especially in my seminars on Berlin, graffiti, and architectural romanticisms—whose lively discussions have improved the quality of this book in fundamental ways. At the Binghamton University Art Museum, Diane Butler generously offered me the opportunity to explore one theme of this manuscript in the exhibition *Reclaiming Ruins* in 2015. The staff of the Bartle Library has been tireless in helping me obtain resources from every corner of the world. I am also grateful for the financial support and release from teaching responsibilities offered by university and SUNY sources, including the Institute for Advanced Study in the Humanities and the Nuala McGann Drescher Diversity Leave Program. It would not have been possible to complete this project without the support of a Harpur College Dean's research leave and faculty development grant, and the funds provided by a Harpur College book subvention award have allowed me to include the many illustrations that so enrich my text. I am grateful every day to be in an environment that encourages research so energetically.

I am no less lucky in my wider circle of friends and coconspirators in Binghamton. To Brian Wall and Wendy Stewart, Elizabeth Casteen and Frank Chang, Dael Norwood and Michelle Paul, Jessie Reeder and Kevin Boettcher, John Kuhn and Andrew Beaty, Katja Kleinberg and Ben Fordham, Meg Leja and Alex Chase-Levenson, John Havard, Paul Schleuse, Celia Klin, and Tina Chronopolous—I am grateful beyond words for your warm fellowship, your ethical engagement with the world around you, and the general atmosphere of hilarity and support you've created here. The members of my "motley crew"—Lori Schapiro, Amy Shapiro, Bridget Metzler, John Perticone, and the late Bat-Ami Bar On—remind me daily what it really means to be part of a community. I am also grateful to Roger Luther and the other board members of PAST, the Preservation Association of the Southern Tier, for giving me such a meaningful way to experience my adopted hometown; I am in a constant state of wonder at the beauty of upstate New York.

And then there are those relationships that, simply put, make things worth doing. First, Ruthie Palmer has been my top sidekick for as long as I can remember. It is a rare gift to share not only our thousands of childhood memories, but also our adult lives as researchers, writers, and teachers, with our friendship only burnished by the passage of four decades. Emily Alexander-Wilmeth makes my life a wonderful adventure, from Austin to New York to Berlin to Melbourne. My views on architecture were formed by a group of Austin-based practitioners known as the COBB, whose waggish intellect has impacted me more than they will ever know. Linda Dalrymple Henderson was my earliest art historical mentor and continues to inspire me as a scholar and a person. Pepper Stetler, Andrew Casper, Adrian Duran, and Alexandra Cardon have supported this project, and its author, since they were in their most infantile states. Erin Schoneveld is family. Dan Davis and Adam Haslett have offered not only their unstinting friendship, but also uncompensated creative therapy. Finally, words fail me when it comes to the bounty of my bond with Deanne Westerman and Matt Johnson. I will never take for granted getting to take them for granted.

Topmost among my many blessings is my beloved family, both nuclear and accrued. Jerry Hatch is a model of patience, sweetness, and support, and I am grateful to him and my late mother-in-law Darlene, as well as to Kristin Hatch and Luke, Leo, and Maxine Sykora, for letting me be a part of their family. Curran Walker was and is my first best friend, and I thank him for bringing Deniz, Connor, and Braydon into my life. Most especially, I thank Anne and Mike Walker—my mother, the writer, and my father, the architect. To quote Laura Dern: "Some say never meet your heroes, but I say, if you're really blessed, you get them as your parents." This book is dedicated to them, with my love and sincere admiration.

Finally, I thank my husband and colleague Kevin Hatch. May everyone be so lucky as to have a reader like you. To say that our writing process is merely "reciprocal" doesn't fully express my joyful good fortune in our creative partnership. In the one million household tasks, edited pages, long walks through Berlin, words of reassurance, and so much more, you do me great honor. Nothing about this project would have been a fraction as fun, challenging, exciting, and rewarding if you weren't there—and that's true of every second of my life as well.

Introduction

Berlin, the Contemporary Capital

A decade after the fall of the Berlin Wall, the international media once again had reason to train its attention on the city and its built environment. This time, however, the occasion was a celebration of construction rather than destruction, as journalists gathered in June of 1999 to observe the presentation of the Pritzker Architecture Prize to the British architect Sir Norman Foster. The prize, considered then as now to be architecture's most prestigious award, was established in 1979 by Hyatt Hotels cofounder Jay Pritzker and his wife Cindy to recognize the lifetime achievement of a significant individual figure contributing substantially to "the art of architecture."[1] The jury's selection of Foster as the 1999 laureate depended in no small part on his spectacular renovation of Berlin's Reichstag building (Figure 0.1), the past and future seat of Germany's parliament that had opened officially to widespread acclaim earlier that year. Though Pritzker conferrals are always high-profile affairs, the final event of the millennium took on heightened historical meaning, aligning a celebrated architect and the city he had helped transform into a major center for the latest developments in architecture. This alignment of architect and location was unusual: the year before, Renzo Piano had received his award at the White House; in 1997, Sverre Fehn accepted his at Frank Gehry's soon-to-debut Guggenheim Bilbao; and in 1996, Rafael Moneo was feted at Richard Meier's Getty Center in Los Angeles several months before that sprawling structure opened its doors to the public. In each of these cases, the selection committee intended the ceremony's site to provide an architecturally significant backdrop for the apotheosis of a new "starchitect" into the pantheon.[2] The tendency to use the buildings of former Pritzker winners rendered the choice of site, architect, and accolade mutually reinforcing.[3] Yet in 1999, the committee selected Berlin as the setting for the ceremony and, rather than focusing on any single building, made full use of the city's exhilarating bounty of new architecture. This expanded notion of what was being celebrated in the Pritzker festivities tells us something important about the architectural standing of the reunified capital. By the end of the 1990s, it had become widely known as "the city that let in the architects," as a writer for the London *Times* described it.[4] For the award committee, Berlin proved to be a special case in which the city itself functioned like the oeuvre of a Pritzker winner, boasting some of the most groundbreaking examples of recent architecture while also forecasting the profession's newest directions.

Figure 0.1 Foster + Partners. Reichstag, Berlin, 1999. View from Platz der Republik. hanohiki / stock.adobe.com.

This momentous (and much-hyped) Pritzker celebration offers a succinct look at the ambitions, contradictions, and challenges embodied in Berlin's political and architectural "rebuilding," twinned projects that became fully conjoined after Germany's official reunification in 1990 and the Bundestag's decision the following year to reestablish Berlin as the capital city. The rhetoric surrounding the official relocation of the *Hauptstadt* was one of optimistic speculation, and Rem Koolhaas's intentionally postcritical conception of Berlin as an urban "laboratory," which he first developed in the 1970s, was recapitulated by many architects, scholars, and officials in the early 1990s.[5] Indeed, the political aspirations of the federal government were given their most palpable expression in architecture, with Eberhard Diepgen (mayor of both West Berlin and subsequently of the reunified city) pronouncing the new capital "a workshop of unity" in the city's official guidebook.[6] Throughout these years, discussions of the city's urban projects were predicated on the implicit notion that the "return" to Berlin demanded new ways of materializing history in the built environment. In 1995, Paul Goldberger described Berlin as a large-scale architectural experiment, declaring, "London is London, Rome is Rome, Tokyo is Tokyo, but Berlin is a question mark."[7] The intensified atmosphere of risk and reward involved in the city's rebuilding went far beyond the blunt contingencies of economics and political logistics to encompass the sensitive historical questions that this wave of construction raised. The implication was that the world was breathlessly watching as the so-called "New Berlin" sprang into being—while also anxiously fearing the destruction of memory that these massive projects would entail.[8] The success or failure of Berlin's new architecture would condition the success or failure of its politics, and vice versa.

In the euphoric atmosphere surrounding reunification, architecture in the New Berlin was invested with poignant new meanings that, examined closely, reveal the high stakes and competing narratives at work in the process of rebuilding. On the one hand, architects, politicians, and city marketers made use of the enduring trope of Berlin-as-underdog—"poor but sexy," as mayor Klaus Wowereit famously described it in 2003—as part of their effort to rehabilitate a battered city that had borne the brunt of many of the twentieth century's most brutal conflicts.[9] In this context, Berlin's sophisticated new architecture (under the heading of an officially established *Baukultur*) took on the task of healing and memorializing history's urban effects, indelibly inscribing the past within the built environment.[10] On the other, Berlin's long-standing image as a city in flux (expressed most frequently via the critic Karl Scheffler's oft-quoted aphorism that the city is "doomed forever to become and never to be") supported its extravagant new building initiatives in elevating the capital to the status of a "global city," that numinous formation whose primary characteristic is its unchecked growth.[11] The image of a flux-addled city provided both a pretext and a justification for Berlin's astonishing rate of development following reunification, when it became for years the largest construction site on the European continent. For some, the skyline of more than 700 cranes that loomed over Berlin throughout the 1990s was an energizing testament to urban resilience.[12] Yet for others, the frenzy of construction seemed both compulsive and repressive, a frantic cover-up job intended to conceal the painful traces of history that marked Berlin's urban landscape. As Godela Weiss-Sussex has observed, this "myth of the fluid and fast-changing city" has been repeatedly instrumentalized to distance Berlin's current image from its multiple traumatic pasts.[13] In both perspectives, what was at stake was the city's unique historicity, and the problem of how architecture might commemorate this difficult past while also expressing the desire for a new beginning.

Perhaps nowhere was this more evident than in the government projects that form the core of my investigation here. My focus in this book is a crucial but curiously neglected component of the architecture and planning of reunified Berlin—namely, the projects designed and built for the national government and its related functions. I conduct close examinations of those structures proposed during the first two major competitions of the 1990s that were held to determine "Hauptstadt Berlin's" new form—the master plan of the government district at the Spreebogen, along with the Reichstag and Chancellery buildings it contains, as well as the Spreeinsel, the site of the German Democratic Republic's demolished Palast der Republik and the ornate Humboldt Forum soon to open in its place. These projects were more than simply new building commissions, I suggest; rather, they were tasked with managing the city's negotiation with its own history. I argue here that one of the key means of this arbitration entailed the unexpected resurfacing of avant-gardist strategies and tactics from the early years of the twentieth century in otherwise highly contemporary designs. Yet these echoes from the modernist past resurface in these new structures as dislocated and decontextualized fragments, set into motion in strange, unexpected ways. Indeed, these modernist reverberations are a hallmark of what I will describe in this book as *global contemporary architecture culture*. These projects cannot be fully understood without recourse to this larger discursive frame, and I insist here on the interdependence of national political representation and global architectural ambition.

My claim here is *both* that Berlin is a particular urban environment with unique urban conditions *and* that those conditions are illustrative of tendencies in the development of contemporary cities in general. Although my priority in this book is not periodization, I view the intensification of contemporary architecture culture—with its galaxy of star practitioners, media obsessions, and vexed relationship to both modernism and postmodernism—as coeval with Berlin's building boom. If the Cold War backgrounded the codification of modernism, as Andreas Huyssen has argued, its conclusion set the stage for the contemporary scene I describe in the following chapters.[14] Indeed, Theodor Fontane's observation that what occurs in Berlin "has a direct effect on the great events of the world" was never more keenly evident than in the last years of the twentieth century, as the international celebration of the fall of the Berlin Wall paved the way for the acceleration of multinational capitalism and globalization occurring in its wake.[15] Of course, these conditions impacted cultural production in visible ways that have clarified with the passage of time, and the neoliberal rhetoric of the removal of barriers has now come into focus as a substantial substrate for the development of global contemporary architecture.

In its expansiveness, exuberance, and triumphalism, the *language* of contemporary architecture demonstrates an institutionalized confidence in its own global horizons. Thus, my exploration here rests partly on an analysis of this language, especially when it becomes shared among officials, architects, critics, and the public. In addition to this limitless sense of reach, contemporary architecture's daring *forms* instantiate the culture's emphasis on visuality and iconicity, always digitally mediated and reproduction-ready. Therefore, I am also attuned to the repetition of certain visual ideas that occur in the architecture of the New Berlin as they do in other contemporary cities. My focus on the visual is hence not intended to characterize contemporary architecture as a style; rather, I position these visual ideas as strategies, often used to address troublesome historical questions and convey historical information to a global public. Throughout this study, I attend closely to the public faces and spaces of Berlin's new government architecture to illuminate the meanings these buildings project to various urban audiences.

Yet these conditions are the same ones responsible for the widespread if diffuse anxiety that underpins contemporary architecture culture, most evident in the tension between history and futurity that is common to many growing cities today. Consequently, themes of fragmentation and ruination recur throughout my analysis of Berlin's new government architecture, as do questions of architects' preoccupations with the inevitable forces of decay and decline at work in the urban environment.[16] Paradoxically, contemporary architecture both represses these forces and draws attention to them, and Berlin makes this ambivalence especially clear. As *New York Times* critic Herbert Muschamp reported after Foster's Pritzker win, "The smooth skin of architecture glosses over such conflicts. (In Berlin it's difficult to find where the wall stood just 10 years ago.) And I think if a design is outstanding, the odds are that I'll gloss over those tensions too."[17]

My examination of global contemporary architecture culture in this book is by no means a comprehensive exploration of contemporaneity in architecture. There is no consensus over what constitutes contemporary architecture, and only now are critics and scholars beginning to disentangle the contemporary from its modern and postmodern forebears. Despite the increasing number of classes on contemporary architecture that are now offered in departments of art history and schools of architecture, a critical examination of the contemporary as such is still taking shape. (It is worth comparing this paucity of scholarship to corresponding treatments of contemporary art, which have proliferated over the past two decades.) Until very recently, most work on contemporary architecture has taken the form of glossy monographs, hagiographic biographies, exhibition catalogs, or otherwise architect-centric examinations of architectural work itself, with little in the way of sustained critical or historical analysis. Happily, in the past few years, two important anthologies have been published that situate architecture in its contemporary context: Elie Haddad and David Rifkind's *A Critical History of Contemporary Architecture: 1960–2010*, and Swati Chattopadhyay and Jeremy White's *The Routledge Companion to Critical Approaches to Contemporary Architecture*.[18] The essays collected in these volumes have begun the work of understanding the contemporary holistically, in terms of its newly digital apparatus, its relationship to modernism and postmodernism, its imbrication with global imperialism and the military-industrial complex, its association with problems of privacy and security, its complex sense of temporality and history, and the ways in which it addresses political and environmental instability across the globe. I seek to make a modest contribution to this larger undertaking here.

I now turn back to Foster's Pritzker celebration, the details of which paint a vivid picture both of the specific architecture culture of the New Berlin and global contemporary architecture culture more broadly. The day before the ceremony, attendees (including former Pritzker winners like Hans Hollein and Gottfried Böhm, prominent architects like Richard Rogers and Helmut Jahn, and judges Ada Louise Huxtable, Jorge Silvetti, and Toshio Nakamura) were treated to a carefully curated city tour, the first stop of which was the Reichstag itself. Foster led his colleagues through the building, stopping for a lingering visit to the radiant cupola with its fountain-like cone of mirrored glass issuing from the plenary chamber below. Already, the building had received rave reviews from architecture critics around the world, along with resounding international support of the Pritzker committee for recognizing the magnitude of Foster's achievement. A writer for the Spanish daily *El País* claimed that the Reichstag renovation alone justified its architect's receipt of the award, describing Foster as "the spiritual father of the nineteenth-century building."[19] On the scene at the Pritzker ceremony, a journalist for the Argentinian newspaper *La Nación* remarked that the dome "has become the symbol of the Berlin Republic (and the) emblem of the political unity of Germany," and marveled, "but not even the most optimistic suspected that the popularity of the architect who redesigned it would be imprinted on the building."[20] On the Pritzker tour, one guest noted that Foster's luminous glass dome afforded panoramas of the city reminiscent of those painted by the Berlin architect Karl Friedrich Schinkel nearly two hundred years before. Another jokingly suggested that the dome's interior, with its funnel of mirrored glass conjuring a certain disco vibe, would make an excellent Berlin-style nightclub after working hours.[21] Despite the jests, however, the consensus of the group was dazzled admiration of Foster's deft and intelligent lightening of the historical building's saturnine countenance. (Oddly little was said about the other massive new buildings under construction next to the Reichstag, including Axel Schultes and Charlotte Frank's Chancellery and Stephan Braunfels's parliamentary offices and library.) *El País* was not the only publication to attach a salvific narrative to the architect's role in creating the building anew. In *Interior Design*, one writer dubbed Foster the building's "Bright Knight," while *Guardian* architecture critic Jonathan Glancey asserted that the building had been entirely "reborn" through Foster's efforts.[22] And at the Reichstag's official opening, Chancellor Gerhard Schröder declared that the building's incandescent air of optimism represented nothing less than "the completion of German unification."[23]

From the Reichstag, the Pritzker excursion continued south to Pariser Platz, where Gehry provided a tour of his nearly completed DG Bank building (Figure 0.2), with a documentary film crew recording his every word.[24] Tamed by the strict reconstruction regulations governing the historical city center (the work of Senate Building Director Hans Stimmann), the building's facade was restrained and formal, with its stocky piers of buff-colored limestone echoing the nearby Brandenburg Gate. However, though the bank's exterior might not have plainly announced its celebrity parentage, its interior was signature Gehry. The spacious atrium swelled upward into a glass vault whose taut diagrid skin the architect related to the scales of a fish, a metaphor he also associated with the titanium panels cladding his recently opened (and already fabled) Guggenheim Bilbao.[25] At the center of the bank's atrium rose a four-story stainless steel sculpture, its undulant surfaces irresistibly suggesting the massive skull of a prehistoric horse. Contained within the steel "skull," an oval conference room was framed by curving walls sheathed in narrow strips of burnished red oak. Some guests marveled at the virtuosic handling of these dramatic forms and praised the apparently bottomless wellspring of Gehry's visual imagination. Others teased the architect good-naturedly about the elegant craftsmanship on view in the lobby's wood-paneled walls, seemingly at odds with his early aesthetic of junkstore salvage. Gehry shrugged off the jokes with typical self-deprecation, responding wryly that everyone present knew he wasn't really a "details man."[26] Overall, the group was impressed that, despite the officious limitations of Berlin's "critical reconstruction," Gehry had found ways to push the envelope. Critic Martin Filler extolled the architect for finding subtle exterior means—the canting of the top row of windows along the building's front, for example, and the sinuous waves of its rear facade—of expressing that this was "no ordinary building," but rather "typical of the architect's work."[27] Gehry had given Berlin a true Frank Gehry building, despite the fact that it was only on the interior that he was "free to let loose."[28]

The tour bus then proceeded south, pausing at Potsdamer Platz for visitors to praise Piano's refined buildings for Daimler-Benz and critique Helmut Jahn's vast, hyperactive

Figure 0.2 Gehry Partners, DG Bank (now DZ Bank), Berlin, 1995–2001. View of interior. Christian Mueller / Shutterstock.

Sony Center, set to open the following year (Figure 0.3). Under the center's torqued, glass-and-steel canopy, a neobaroque fragment of the legendary Hotel Esplanade known as the Kaisersaal (for its use by Wilhelm II as a gentlemen's salon) had been expensively relocated and preserved, enshrined under a glass skin and thus "retroactively ennobled," in the words of the writer Peter Schneider.[29] Continuing to Jean Nouvel's Galeries Lafayette on Friedrichstrasse, the group contemplated yet another recently completed glassy cone, this one descending into the building's interior rather than triumphantly rising from its depths, as Foster's Reichstag cupola had so eloquently done. In place of the Reichstag's tasteful transparency, Nouvel (who would be awarded the Pritzker in 2008) intended his glass cone as a transmitter of fleeting images siphoned from the department store's various surfaces and provocatively deformed by the cone's reflective panes. The exterior of the building was wrapped in a sweeping glass facade that rounded the corner of Friedrichstrasse and Französiche Strasse, capturing ephemeral impressions of city life—a compelling update of Erich Mendelsohn's expressionistic Mossehaus (1921–3), lying a few blocks to the south.

Finally, the day's activities concluded at Daniel Libeskind's extension of the Jewish Museum (Figure 0.4), whose stark zigzag form (a zinc-clad, deconstructed Star of David) was already gaining fame in architecture journals around the world. Though the building had been finished only months before, it would take two laborious years for the gallery installation to be completed and the museum to open to the public. In this liminal moment before the building's new life began, the architects and critics who

Figure 0.3 Helmut Jahn, Renzo Piano, Hans Hollein, Rafael Moneo, et al., renovation of Potsdamer Platz, Berlin, 1992–2001. Aerial view. mato / Shutterstock.

had gathered in Berlin lapsed into silence as they contemplated the horror encapsulated in Libeskind's cavernous Tower of Holocaust, one of the structure's now-famous "voids."[30] Throughout Berlin's redevelopment, Libeskind remained an outspoken champion of his own adventurous approach to form (at first iconoclastic, and now perhaps all too iconic; within contemporary architecture, his buildings are among the most easily recognizable). Yet the Pritzker group's praise of his museum portended the downbeat mood to come when, like many others, Libeskind found himself disappointed at how rapidly the city's spirit of adventurousness seemed to recede. In 1995, he had declared that Berlin was an architectural "Klondike, a gold rush."[31] But upon the Jewish Museum's opening in 2001, Libeskind leveled a wholesale critique at Berlin's new architecture: "Despite the big names, the rebuilding has been lackluster. It's mediocrity on a scale probably never seen at any one time."[32]

The following evening, the Pritzker festivities resumed with the official award ceremony, held in the magnificent rotunda of Schinkel's neoclassical Altes Museum. Pritzker laureates and jurors, clad in dignified black tie, streamed through Schinkel's Ionic colonnade and took their seats beneath ancient marble statues of Hermes, Aphrodite, and Zeus. At the podium, chairman of the jury J. Carter Brown (then-director of the National Gallery of Art in Washington, D.C.) praised Schinkel's exquisite creation and lamented that Schinkel himself could not be given the Pritzker that he so eminently deserved.[33] Yet he extended his praise beyond the museum to encompass

Figure 0.4 Studio Libeskind, Jewish Museum, Berlin, 1988–2001. View of exterior. imageBROKER / Alamy Stock Photo.

the city's new architecture, saying, "Somehow the *Wirtschaftswunder* has become the *Hauptstadtswunder*."[34] Thomas Pritzker, who had become the chair of the award after his father Jay died in January 1999, claimed that a single architectural lineage connected Schinkel, Mies, and Foster.[35] Accepting the prize, Foster spoke with his usual purposefulness of the pressing tasks of architecture as he saw them: addressing social problems, responding to ecological pressures, and helping a growing population adapt to the various scenarios of crisis and conflict that characterized contemporary life.[36] Underscoring the genealogy suggested during the ceremony, the evening continued with a cocktail reception at Mies's lushly austere Neue Nationalgalerie. Finally, the partygoers repaired to the ballroom of Moneo's newly completed Grand Hyatt at Potsdamer Platz for a gala dinner. Presiding over the occasion, Thomas Pritzker joked that all should feel free to call Moneo with complaints if they found the food to be lacking. The building's transcendent architecture, he promised, would more than compensate for a disappointing meal.[37]

These events marked the culmination of a banner year for the Pritzker, which was simultaneously celebrating its twentieth anniversary with an exhibition at the Art Institute of Chicago, *The Pritzker Architecture Prize: The First Twenty Years*.[38] As one critic noted, though it displayed computer renderings, hand drawings, and models of significant buildings, the exhibition's primary purpose was to lionize the "hemi-demi-semi-gods" of architecture.[39] In recent years, the Pritzker Prize has been the target of trenchant critiques for its overweening role in defining the shape of contemporary architecture culture. Architects and critics have called attention to its failure to recognize the contributions of women and people of color, its insistence on celebrating the work of an individual rather than illuminating the deeply collaborative nature of design work, and its tendency to heroicize the "wow" buildings (to use Huxtable's term) over visually modest but socially engaged architecture.[40] Though under Martha Thorne's directorship, the award committee has made concerted efforts to broaden its purview while remaining committed to its core mission, the Pritzker still functions as an architectural kingmaker. Of course, the prize is not solely responsible for propagating contemporary architecture culture, along with its inequalities, contingencies, and blind spots. It shares this role with many other institutions and phenomena, including the increase of exhibitions on architecture taking place in museums of art, the proliferation of architecture biennials, and the substantial impact of architecture critics in determining the successes and failures of today's built environment. Architectural historians are likewise complicit in the perpetuation of this contemporary culture. It is my hope that, by outlining its contours as they emerged in postreunification Berlin, I will contribute to the current discussion of how problematic aspects of this culture might be productively reconsidered.

Twenty years later, the details of Foster's Pritzker celebration seem clearly emblematic of a coalescent contemporary architecture culture in the full flush of its global expansion. Yet it is not the only "scene" I could invoke here that draws attention to the conventions of this culture. Other episodes, equally conditioned by the starchitect's cult of personality and equally staged as highly mediated *events*, immediately spring to mind when considering the key years of the New Berlin's frenetic building activity. For example, we might remember the theatrical topping-out ceremony of Piano's Daimler-Benz complex at Potsdamer Platz, during which Daniel Barenboim, the acclaimed director of the Berlin Philharmonic, conducted a "ballet of cranes" swinging robotically to the soaring strains of the Ode to Joy from Beethoven's Ninth Symphony, which was performed live on the site by the Golden Gospel Singers. (Wearing a hard hat and standing on a scissor lift, Barenboim gamely waved the safety flags he had been given to use in place of his conductor's baton while the crane operators above him strained to follow his cues.) We might remember the opening ceremony of the same building, in which a solemn procession of construction vehicles was accompanied by 250 musicians and escorted by over a thousand construction workers marching in formation. We might remember another grand opening, of Nouvel's Galeries Lafayette, during which a large police presence was necessary simply to control the excited crowd. We might remember the dramatically public debate over Berlin's official Holocaust memorial, spearheaded by television journalist Lea Rosh, and the victorious competition entry by Peter Eisenman and Richard Serra; we might also recall Serra's later withdrawal from the project, which Eisenman carried forward and inaugurated as the Memorial to the Murdered Jews of Europe in 2005.[41] We might remember former Senator for Urban Development Volker Hassemer's decisive stint as the head of city marketing organization Partner für Berlin, during which he unveiled a number of information centers, exhibitions, press conferences, and public symposia to advertise the capital's new architecture to a global public.[42] In all of these cases, whether the projects in question were publicly funded or financed by one of the many "public-private partnerships" forged by the federal government after reunification, the tendency toward spectacle and the high-stakes nature of historical reckoning inhere.

Yet in retrospect, these spectacles take on a hectic, almost panicked air, one that has only come into view with the passage of time. In February 2013, a three-day symposium was held at the Yale University School of Architecture titled *Achtung: Berlin*. Organized by the architectural historian Stanislaus von Moos, the symposium's aim was to take stock of the results of Berlin's postreunification urban experiment. The event gathered together some of the most significant scholars of Berlin's urban culture from across disciplines (including Kurt Forster, Andreas Huyssen, and Simone Hain), as well as architects, critics, artists, and government officials. From the audience, I watched as heated discussions—over the nature of Berlin's architectural heritage, the ongoing tension between history and progress, and the suitability of the city's iconic new buildings—seemed to reopen (and, occasionally, merely to rehash) the debates of the 1990s rather than historically contextualizing the questions raised by Berlin's contemporary building boom. On the side of "innovation," Peter Eisenman critiqued the city's timidity in failing to construct his Max Reinhardt Haus, a massive crumpled arch that would have sprung from the site of Hans Poelzig's destroyed Grosses Schauspielhaus. Artist Thomas Demand denounced the destruction of the Soviet Palast der Republik in favor of a gleaming reconstruction of the historical Stadtschloss, to be known euphemistically as the Humboldt Forum. And speaking from the auditorium screen on a video conference call from Doha, Rem Koolhaas (who had won the Pritzker in 2000, based partly on his design for the Embassy of the Netherlands in Berlin, then under construction) (Figure 0.5) cynically proclaimed that Berlin's shot at becoming a center of daring new architecture was well over, since it had first caved to market pressures and then pandered to investors. On the side of "tradition," architect Léon Krier reprised his decades-old polemic testifying to the high quality of Albert Speer's architecture, while Vittorio Magnano Lampugnani justified the necessity of building restrictions to prevent an urban landscape of exceptional and yet disconnected structures. Hans Stimmann emphatically defended his doctrine of Critical Regionalism, alleging that its embrace of tradition was, in fact, fundamentally anchored in progressive politics while also attempting to forestall the loss of urban memory threatened by Berlin's wide-scale reconstruction. Many speakers on both sides of these debates reiterated the image of Berlin as a city in a state of constant flux.

Repeatedly throughout the conference proceedings, I observed the ongoing power of entrenched binaries and tropes in characterizations of Berlin's rebuilding. At the same time, I also noticed that Berlin's new government district at the Spreebogen and the colossal buildings within it were rendered strangely invisible. Though several speakers alluded to Foster's Reichstag, it received little in the way of thorough analysis. Noting the allocation of federal funds for the controversial Humboldt Forum, Demand stood alone in drawing attention to those projects spearheaded and overseen by the German government as a client. The journalist Michael Z. Wise, author of *Capital*

Figure 0.5 Rem Koolhaas/OMA, Embassy of the Netherlands, Berlin, 1997–2003. View of exterior. Eden Breitz / Alamy Stock Photo.

Dilemma: Germany's Search for a New Architecture of Democracy (a significant early examination of Berlin's new official architecture published in 1998, which to date remains the most thoroughgoing investigation of these federal projects), likewise observed this glaring omission, noting that few of the participants even mentioned that Berlin was the capital of Germany.[43] Within a wide-ranging discussion of Berlin's contemporary architecture, its actual capital buildings receded into obscurity. Yet my argument here is that, far from being irrelevant, these structures yield particular and indispensable insights into Berlin's contemporary architecture—and therefore into contemporary architecture culture more generally.

If there is a scarcity of critical work on the subject of contemporaneity in architectural history, the opposite is true of Berlin's postreunification urban culture, and I am indebted to the work of those insightful scholars whose interventions I draw upon in what follows. Wise's examination of the government district is just one example of the lively and ongoing discussion on Berlin's contemporary architecture, much of which has originated outside the field of architectural history. Examples include Brian Ladd's *The Ghosts of Berlin: Confronting German History in the Urban Landscape*, Claire Colomb's *Staging the New Berlin: Place Marketing and the Politics of Urban Reinvention*, Jennifer Jordan's *Structures of Memory: Understanding Urban Change in Berlin and Beyond*, Karen Till's *The New Berlin: Memory, Politics, Place*, and Janet Ward's *Post-Wall Berlin: Borders, Space and Identity*.[44] In very recent years, architectural historians have broadened the discourse in significant ways, particularly emphasizing how political meanings proliferate beyond simply representative architecture and underscoring the necessity of engaging other histories and narratives of modernism, including those of migration, colonization, racial discrimination, and gender inequities. These studies include Deborah Ascher Barnstone's *The Transparent State: Architecture and Politics in Postwar Germany*, Daniela Sandler's *Counterpreservation: Architectural Decay in Berlin since 1989*, Peter Christensen's *Germany and the Ottoman Railways: Art, Empire, and Infrastructure*, Itohan Osayimwese's *Colonialism and Modern Architecture in Germany*, Esra Akcan's *Open Architecture: Migration, Citizenship, and the Urban Renewal of Berlin-Kreuzberg by IBA-1984/87*, and Kathleen James-Chakraborty's *Modernism as Memory: Building Identity in the Federal Republic of Germany*.[45] Many others, including James Young and Andreas Huyssen, have examined the visual culture of contemporary Berlin in the context of memory studies.[46]

This book contributes a crucial framework to discussions of Berlin by asking what it means for architecture to lay claim to political identity at the turn of the twenty-first century. To present a new perspective on Berlin's architecture, I thus situate my discussion within larger developments in contemporary architecture. I address how national character functions in a global architectural economy, and I uncover how the modernist inheritance informs, inflects, and destabilizes claims to governmental symbolism. In this effort I tend to train my attention on the highly visible—prominent architects, well-known buildings, significant competitions, prizes, or exhibitions—not in order to shore up rehearsed ideas of their importance, but rather to critique the discursive and institutional structures that create and sustain their overexposure.[47] To uncover these often repressed mechanisms, I am aided by less visible fragments of architectural history: unrealized plans, experimental projects, artistic interventions, and unanticipated additions or alterations to extant architectural forms. Approaching Berlin's contemporary architecture in this way allows me to investigate the ideological programs, whether implicit or explicit, that are reinforced by theory and praxis as they are carried out today on a global stage.

The primary purpose of this book, therefore, is to look closely at Berlin's specific postreunification culture of architecture by examining its crucial intersections with Germany's larger political self-fashioning. Yet I also intend this study to contribute to the growing historiography of global contemporary architecture itself. With the benefit of retrospect allowed by the passage of three decades, it is clear that the "rebuilding" of Berlin demonstrates, in intensified form, many of the concerns most fundamental to global cities worldwide. Therefore, the focus of this book is narrow, but I intend the questions I raise to have transnational resonance. Indeed, the growing interdependence of the local and the global is core to contemporary architecture culture. Throughout what follows, I take seriously the notion of Berlin as a microcosm of modernity and its aftermath, as expressed by writers from Fontane to Alfred Döblin to Martin Wagner, and I propose some new understandings of how the city's recent architecture serves a similar function in our contemporary moment.

Berlin Contemporary comprises four chapter-length studies, each of which examines a significant building or urban plan constructed in Berlin under the aegis of the reunified government. Throughout, I argue that Berlin's official architecture captures in miniature, as it were, a fundamental truth about contemporary architecture across the globe, which oscillates dialectically between compulsive claims of newness and nostalgic ruminations on the past. Understanding how this dialectic played out in Berlin requires a careful diachronic examination of the city's palimpsest, which means reading its layers of accumulated buildings and plans while exhuming its many unrealized modernist futures.[48] Reading this landscape of real and imagined ruins and futures is precisely the aim of the following chapters.

Chapter 1 examines Axel Schultes and Charlotte Frank's master plan for Berlin's new government district along the Spreebogen, the curve of the Spree river that has become the administrative heart of the city. Upon winning the commission to plan Berlin's new government district, Schultes remarked, "the challenge posed by the competition was to coax the soul out of the Spreebogen, the genius loci."[49] Only by so doing, according to Schultes, could the site's new architecture "begin to link the virtues of each place together."[50] Schultes and Frank had generated public enthusiasm with a design anchored by a Band des Bundes, or band of federal buildings, spanning the Spree twice and traversing the former boundary between East and West Berlin. Supporters saw the plan as bridging the painful voids in the torn urban fabric and suturing together the formerly divided city. And indeed, Schultes and Frank's design thematized the Spreebogen's status as a collection of fragments that needed to be "linked together"—a historical zone of rupture, movement, and surveillance whose spectral presences included the former course of the Berlin Wall and Nazi architect Albert Speer's vast, unrealized north–south axis. But the Band des Bundes does more than symbolically reconnecting the city's wounded terrain. In fact, it links the contemporary Spreebogen to the many avant-garde plans that have been proposed for the area, not only those that thematize connection but also those that enact the breaking apart of urban elements. These plans range from Bruno Taut's 1920 scheme for the dissolution of the city to Rem Koolhaas and O. M. Ungers's 1977 plan to make Berlin into a "green archipelago," in which fragments of the city would effectively float in a surrounding undeveloped "ocean" of parkland. The new master plan of the Spreebogen thus reveals the site to be a constellation of transitory historical fragments that come together only briefly, and only to decay.

The second chapter examines Norman Foster's design for the Reichstag, which quickly became iconic shorthand for the New Berlin after its opening in 1999. Though most scholarly analyses of the Reichstag focus on Foster's futuristic glass-and-steel cupola, I look away from the cupola toward specific moments in the building's long life, including the artists Christo and Jeanne-Claude's celebrated wrapping of the building in 1995, Foster's visionary 1992 competition entry, and the preservation in the completed renovation of Soviet graffiti dating to the Battle of Berlin in 1945. Each of these instances demonstrates the way in which the Reichstag's present meaning has coalesced around a discourse of "lightness." In the first case, it was precisely a new "lightness of being" that Christo and Jeanne-Claude's shimmering fabric seemed to grant the building. Subsequently, for his renovation, Foster adopted a museological approach to the structure, initially proposing that it be covered with a vast translucent roof that framed the building like a ruin on display. When the project's brief shifted to a more modest undertaking, he then insisted that the "authentically" historical graffiti left by Soviet soldiers be maintained within the building, arguing that erasing these marks would be tantamount to silencing history. In both his proposal and his finished building, Foster's rhetorical strategy emphasizes indexes of the past to imbue the Reichstag with gravitas while allowing new interventions to "lighten" the building, visually and historically. Despite its long history, the trope of the ruin took on powerful new resonance during the turbulent twentieth century, during which, as Theodor Adorno observed, "scars of damage and disruption" began to function poignantly as a "seal of authenticity."[51] My analysis of these three different moments in the Reichstag's new life reveals how contemporary architecture anchors itself in historical architectural precedents in order to highlight its own contrastive lightness.

Building on the discussion of ruin-gazing begun in Chapter 2, the third chapter considers Schultes and Frank's design for the Chancellery, for which the architects drew on a mode of monumental modernism common to American and European architects working in developing nations in the middle of the century (such as Le Corbusier's designs for Chandigarh in India and Louis Kahn's National Assembly in Dhaka, Bangladesh, both of which Schultes and Frank cite explicitly). I argue that by adopting this monumental mode for the seat and residence of the Chancellor of Germany, the government intentionally and explicitly aligned itself with the political liberalization of postcolonial capitals. However, as in the case of Foster's Reichstag, the modernist aspects of the Chancellery design belie an underexamined relationship to Germany's spectral history. Kahn claimed that his design process resembled "wrapping ruins around buildings," and imagined his own buildings as ruins "in reverse" to be encountered by travelers in future millennia. In its evocation of Kahn's anthropocene monumentality, Schultes and Frank's Chancellery thus revives a tradition that was taboo in Germany after National Socialism, with its morbid anticipation of Nazi architecture in ruins a thousand years hence. If the Reichstag reveals how contemporary architecture shows a romanticist obsession with the scars of the past, then the Chancellery reveals an equally romanticist fascination with how the ravages of the future might appear—and, indeed, this tendency toward the creation of anticipatory ruins winds its way through the whole of contemporary architecture.

Finally, chapter 4 looks at the site of the Stadtschloss, the city palace that was home to the Hohenzollern dynasty before it was demolished in 1950 to make way for the insistently modernist East German Palast der Republik. Some fifty years later, in 2002, the Bundestag controversially voted to raze the Palast and rebuild the Stadtschloss as the Humboldt Forum, a new museum to showcase "non-European" artifacts drawn from ethnographic collections in Berlin. The site has thus become an arena in which the fragments of multiple palaces and their contested politics contend for architectural representation. For example, several competitions (official and otherwise) were held during the 1990s to collect ideas for the site's future use; these unrealized plans now exist as traces of the structures that have existed there. Furthermore, during the *Zwischennutzung* (interim use) of the Palast der Republik that occurred before its demolition, artists such as Thomas Demand, Olafur Eliasson, and Lars Ø. Ramberg created elegiac meditations on the Palast's short, troubled life and pointed critiques of its destruction. While sometimes invoked in analyses of Berlin's politics of reunification and in discussions of contemporary art practices, these projects in fact provide a surprisingly effective analysis of the modernist architecture that frames them. Staged against the backdrop of the slow-motion demolition of the Palast (it took five years to dismantle fully), these artworks expose more than just the memory politics that dominated aesthetic discourse in post-Wende Berlin; they also reveal, in the most poignant terms, that it is not doubt but rather *belief* that underlies global contemporary architecture culture—a fundamental belief that, even in an increasingly mediated visual world, architecture retains a powerful, if friable, authenticity.

As the book's four chapters show, and as I demonstrate in my conclusion on the recent controversies over Berlin's airports, modern architecture is itself (to paraphrase Jürgen Habermas) an "incomplete project" whose utopian social theories and techno-deterministic optimism for the possibilities of mechanization are still being worked through in the contemporary moment, now on a global scale.[52] Berlin's postreunification building boom, therefore, is symptomatic of concerns that are not limited to the new German capital. More broadly, Berlin's recent architecture illuminates how the propulsive growth that characterizes the contemporary city is always undercut by forces of entropy, decay, collapse, and ruination. Ultimately, what is on view in the New Berlin is the uneasy negotiation of the constructive procedures and techniques of statecraft on the one hand and, on the other, those of a globalized contemporary architectural practice preoccupied with staving off imminent catastrophe (whether social, political, or ecological). The modernist project and its oft-cited "failure" both haunt the contemporary, and I seek to clarify the relationship between the two. The development of Berlin has been continually unsettled by its own past in ways that reveal the essential anxiety at the core of contemporary architecture culture, and postreunification government architecture offers a particularly apt lens for its investigation.

Notes

1. "Purpose/History/Ceremony," The Pritzker Architecture Prize, Hyatt Foundation, last modified 2019, https://www.pritzkerprize.com/about. Journalists often refer to the recognition as the "Nobel Prize for architecture," and upon the announcement that Foster had won the award in 1999, *Der Spiegel* nicknamed it the "Architecture-Oscar." In "Ein Haus mit vielen Gesichtern," *Der Spiegel*, April 16, 1999, 233.
2. For the history of this neologism and its roots in architectural modernism, see Michael J. Lewis, "The Rise of the 'Starchitect,'" *New Criterion* 26 (December 2007): 4–9. For a discussion of how architecture prizes overlap with starchitect culture, including the Pritzker and the Gold Medals awarded by the American Institute of Architects and the Royal Institute of British Architects, see Jeremy White, "Starchitecture: Starchitect," in Swati Chattopadhyay and Jeremy White, eds., *The Routledge Companion to Critical Approaches to Contemporary Architecture* (New York: Routledge, 2020), 405–23 and Franz Fuerst, Patrick McAllister, and Claudia Murray, "Designer Buildings: Estimating the Economic Value of 'Signature' Architecture," *Environment and Planning A* 43 (April 2009): 166–84. For a sociological exploration of starchitect-designed buildings and their urban functions, see Leslie Sklair, *The Icon Project: Architecture, Cities, and Capitalist Globalization* (New York and Oxford: Oxford University Press, 2017).
3. The committee's selection of a building designed by a former Pritzker laureate as the setting for the ceremony has been repeated many times, starting in 1984, when Meier received his award in I. M. Pei's East Wing of the National Gallery of Art in Washington, D.C. Pei had won the award the year before, and his John F. Kennedy Presidential Library and Museum in Boston was later the setting for the Pritzker's celebration of Toyo Ito in 2013. Buildings by Frank Gehry, who won the prize in 1989, have hosted two ceremonies; in addition to Fehn's celebration in Bilbao, Thom Mayne was given the award at the Jay Pritzker Pavilion in Chicago in 2005. Finally, in 2018, Balkrishna Doshi's festivities took place at Fumihiko Maki's Aga Kahn Museum in Toronto.
4. Rachael Jolley, "The City That Let in the Architects," *The Times*, January 15, 2000, 28.
5. "Berlin is a laboratory." Rem Koolhaas, "Imagining Nothingness," in *S,M,L,XL* (New York: Monacelli Press, 1995), 200. Political scientist and urban scholar Elizabeth Strom has likewise declared the city a "laboratory." See Strom, *Building the New Berlin: The Politics of Urban Development in Germany's Capital City* (Lanham and Oxford: Lexington Books, 2001), 1–3.
6. Quoted in Svetlana Boym, "Berlin, The Virtual Capital," in *The Future of Nostalgia* (New York: Basic Books, 2001), 179.
7. Paul Goldberger, "Reimagining Berlin," *The New York Times Magazine*, February 5, 1995, 47.

8 The city was first celebrated as the "New Berlin" by a marketing campaign launched in 1997 to hail the return of the government from Bonn and to celebrate the reconstruction of Mitte, which had lain formerly in East Berlin. See Janet Ward, "Berlin, the Virtual Global City," *Journal of Visual Culture* 3 (2004): 248.
9 Gerda Frey and Anja Zwittlinger-Fritz, "Money Talks: Lassen sie uns über Geld reden ... Klaus Wowereit," *Focus Money* 46 (November 2003): 90.
10 On the subject of urban memorialization, see Karen Till, *The New Berlin: Memory, Politics, Place* (Minneapolis and London: University of Minnesota Press, 2006) and Jennifer Jordan, *Structures of Memory: Understanding Urban Change in Berlin and Beyond* (Stanford: Stanford University Press, 2006).
11 Karl Scheffler, *Berlin: Ein Stadtschicksal*, second edition (Berlin: Erich Reiss, 1910), 267. We might also think of the writer Franz Hessel's description of "a city that's always on the go, always in the middle of becoming something else." In Franz Hessel, *Walking in Berlin: A Flaneur in the Capital*, trans. Amanda DeMarco (Cambridge, MA: MIT Press, 2017), 7. These sentiments reemerged after the *Wende* in slogans such as city marketer Volker Hassemer's phrase "Berlin wird" (Berlin is becoming), part of a 1996 tourism campaign that presaged the later turn to the idea of the "New Berlin."
12 Journalists remarked frequently on this skyline of cranes, repeating their impressive number in articles published around the world. See Brian Hatton, "The Reichstag, Potsdamer Platz, and the Jewish Museum," in *Vertigo: The Strange New World of the Contemporary City*, ed. Rowan Moore (London: Laurence King, 1999), 76.
13 Godela Weiss-Sussex, "Berlin: Myth and Memorialization," in *The Cultural Identities of European Cities*, eds. Katia Pizzi and Godela Weiss-Sussex (Bern: Peter Lang, 2011), 152. See also Brian Ladd's now-canonical book *The Ghosts of Berlin: Confronting German History in the Urban Landscape* (Chicago: University of Chicago Press, 1998).
14 Andreas Huyssen, "Mapping the Postmodern," *New German Critique* 33 (Autumn 1984): 26.
15 Quoted in Gordon A. Craig, *Theodor Fontane: Literature and History in the Bismarck Reich* (New York: Oxford University Press, 1999), 176. Among many other analyses of these conditions, see Saskia Sassen, *Globalization and its Discontents: Essays on the New Mobility of People and Money* (New York: New Press, 1998); David Harvey, *Spaces of Global Capitalism: A Theory of Uneven Geographical Development* (London: Verso, 2006); and Gilles Deleuze and Félix Guattari, "1440: The Smooth and the Striated," in *A Thousand Plateaus: Capitalism and Schizophrenia*, trans. Brian Massumi (London and New York: Continuum, 1987), 474–500.
16 In this focus, my book joins such recent explorations as Daniel M. Abramson's *Obsolescence: An Architectural History* (Chicago and London: University of Chicago Press, 2016); Daniela Sandler's *Counterpreservation: Architectural Decay in Berlin since 1989* (Ithaca: Cornell University Press, 2016); Dora Apel's *Beautiful Terrible Ruins: Detroit and the Anxiety of Decline* (New Brunswick, NJ: Rutgers University Press, 2015); Donald Kunze, David Bertolini, and Simone Brott, eds., *Architecture Post Mortem: The Diastolic Architecture of Decline, Dystopia, and Death* (Farnham: Ashgate, 2013); and Ann Laura Stoler, ed.'s *Imperial Debris: On Ruins and Ruination* (Durham, NC: Duke University Press, 2013).
17 Herbert Muschamp, "Peeling Off Architecture's Tranquil Skin," *The New York Times*, June 19, 1999, B7. Muschamp is considered one of the critics most responsible for boosting starchitect culture.

18 Elie Haddad and David Rifkind, eds., *A Critical History of Contemporary Architecture: 1960–2010* (Farnham: Ashgate, 2014). Swati Chattopadhyay and Jeremy White, eds., *The Routledge Companion to Critical Approaches to Contemporary Architecture* (New York: Routledge, 2020). We might add to these volumes the several important collections of contemporary architectural theory that have appeared in recent years, including Charles Jencks and Karl Kropf, eds., *Theories and Manifestoes of Contemporary Architecture* (Chichester: Wiley-Academy, 1997); Kate Nesbitt, ed., *Theorizing a New Agenda for Architecture: An Anthology of Architectural Theory 1965–1995* (New York: Princeton Architectural Press, 1996); K. Michael Hays, ed., *Architecture Theory since 1968* (Cambridge, MA: MIT Press, 1998); and Krista Sykes, ed., *Constructing a New Agenda: Architectural Theory 1993–2009* (New York: Princeton Architectural Press, 2010).

19 Luis Fernández-Galiano, "Jay Pritzker no estará en Berlín: Foster recibe el Nobel de arquitectura," *El País*, April 12, 1999, https://elpais.com/diario/1999/04/12/cultura/923868003_850215.html. The notion that Foster's building had embodied or solidified the abstract idea of reunification, or somehow made the process official, was repeated throughout the international press. In *Architecture*, for example, Catherine Slessor reported, "Foster's conversion of the Reichstag in Berlin to house the relocated German parliament will set the seal on the country's political reunification." Slessor, "Foster Wins Pritzker," *Architecture* 88 (May 1999): 70.

20 "La pureza de la alta tecnología," *La Nación*, June 30, 1999, https://www.lanacion.com.ar/arquitectura/la-pureza-de-la-alta-tecnologia-nid207037.

21 Suzanne Stephens recounts both these anecdotes in "Berlin Proves Fitting Setting for Foster's Pritzker Fete," *Architectural Record* (August 1995): 55.

22 Julie Einspruch Lewis, "Bright Knight," *Interior Design* 70 (June 1999): 39. Jonathan Glancey, "The Eagle Has Landed," *The Guardian*, April 18, 1999, https://www.theguardian.com/theguardian/1999/apr/19/features11.g26.

23 David Hudson, "The Berlin Republic: Day One," *Der Spiegel* (online edition), April 19, 1999, https://www.spiegel.de/politik/deutschland/news-digest-the-berlin-republic-day-one-a-18370.html.

24 The DG Bank building featured prominently in Michael Blackwood's 2000 film, *Frank Gehry: An Architecture of Joy*, which traced the architect's meteoric rise over the course of the 1990s.

25 The voluptuous curves of the "fish" form at the Guggenheim were only one aspect of the building that prompted Muschamp to compare the building rapturously to "a reincarnation of Marilyn Monroe." See Muschamp, "The Miracle in Bilbao," *The New York Times*, September 7, 1997, 54.

26 Stephens, 55.

27 Martin Filler, "Norman Foster," in *Makers of Modern Architecture: From Frank Lloyd Wright to Frank Gehry* (New York: New York Review Books, 2007), 237.

28 Ibid. Gehry himself is well aware of the constricting effects of this demand for "signature" buildings. In 2005, he noted, "since Bilbao, I get called to do 'Frank Gehry buildings.' They actually say that to me. We want a 'Frank Gehry.' I run into trouble when I put a design on the table and they say, 'Well, that isn't a Gehry building.' It doesn't have enough of whatever these buildings are supposed to have." In Charles Jencks, *The Iconic Building: The Power of Enigma* (London: Frances Lincoln, 2005), 9.

29 Peter Schneider, *Berlin Now: The City after the Wall*, trans. Sophie Schlondorff (New York: Farrar, Straus and Giroux, 2014), 38.
30 Libeskind structured the design around a set of symbolic lines and voids, with the Tower of Holocaust constituting a "voided void" at the very heart of the building. See Daniel Libeskind, "Between the Lines: Extension to the Berlin Museum, with the Jewish Museum," *Assemblage* 12 (August 1990): 18–57.
31 Quoted in Rick Atkinson, "Building a Better Berlin? Critics See Too Much of Its Past in Its Future," *Washington Post*, January 8, 1995, G1.
32 Quoted in Andrew Nagorski, "Berlin," *Town and Country* 155 (April 2001): 150. Libeskind has long fashioned himself as one of contemporary architecture's renegades, and has frequently spoken of his Jewish Museum as having miraculously evaded the "conservative" impulses that eventually took control of Berlin's new architecture. In a 2015 interview, he boasted that Hans Stimmann "told me that if he had been in power just one month earlier, the building would never have received building permission." Quoted in Sophie Lovell, "Radically Modern in 60s Berlin: Interview with Daniel Libeskind," *uncube magazine*, August 1, 2015, http://www.uncubemagazine.com/blog/15835479.
33 In "The Pritzker Architecture Prize," Hyatt Foundation, pamphlet, 1999, 17.
34 Ibid., 18.
35 Ibid., 20.
36 Norman Foster, "Acceptance Speech," June 1999, The Pritzker Architecture Prize, Hyatt Foundation, https://www.pritzkerprize.com/sites/default/files/inline-files/1999_Acceptance_Speech.pdf.
37 Thomas J. Pritzker, "Ceremony Speech," June 1999, The Pritzker Architecture Prize, Hyatt Foundation, https://www.pritzkerprize.com/sites/default/files/inline-files/1999_speech_Pritzker.pdf.
38 The exhibition also traveled to the Heinz Architectural Center at the Carnegie Museum of Art in Pittsburgh later in 1999.
39 Patricia Lowry, "Pretty as a Pritzker: Architecture's Art Saluted in Limited Carnegie Exhibit," *Pittsburgh Post-Gazette*, November 4, 1999, http://old.post-gazette.com/magazine/19991104pritzker6.asp. For the same reason, Martin Filler critiqued the exhibition as "less a milestone than a millstone." Filler, "Eyes on the Prize," *The New Republic*, April 26, 1999, https://newrepublic.com/article/63912/eyes-the-prize.
40 Philip Lopate, "Her New York," interview with Ada Louise Huxtable, *The New York Times*, November 7, 2008, CY1. Here, Huxtable satirically defined a "wow" building as "eye candy ... we need something that looks 'iconic,' that's going to put our city on the map," and argued that architecture critics were more to blame for the phenomenon than architects themselves, including Frank Gehry.
41 For an analysis of the memorial's development, see James Young, "Germany's Holocaust Memorial Problem—and Mine," in *At Memory's Edge: After-Images of the Holocaust in Contemporary Art and Architecture* (New Haven and London: Yale University Press, 2000), 184–223.
42 See Claire Colomb, "The Actors of Place Marketing in the New Berlin," in *Staging the New Berlin: Place Marketing and the Politics of Urban Reinvention Post-1989* (London and New York: Routledge, 2012), 112–43.
43 Michael Z. Wise, "Achtung: Berlin: German Capital Keeps its Grip on the Architectural Imagination," *Constructs: Yale Architecture* (Fall 2013): 6. See also Wise,

Capital Dilemma: Germany's Search for a New Architecture of Democracy (New York: Princeton Architectural Press, 1998).

44 Brian Ladd, *The Ghosts of Berlin: Confronting German History in the Urban Landscape* (Chicago: University of Chicago Press, 1997); Colomb, ibid.; Jennifer Jordan, *Structures of Memory: Understanding Urban Change in Berlin and Beyond* (Stanford: Stanford University Press, 2006); Karen Till, *The New Berlin: Memory, Politics, Place* (Minneapolis and London: University of Minnesota Press, 2006); Janet Ward, *Post-Wall Berlin: Borders, Space and Identity* (New York: Palgrave Macmillan, 2011).

45 Deborah Ascher Barnstone, *The Transparent State: Architecture and Politics in Postwar Germany* (London and New York: Routledge, 2005); Daniela Sandler, *Counterpreservation: Architectural Decay in Berlin since 1989* (Ithaca: Cornell University Press, 2016); Peter Christensen, *Germany and the Ottoman Railways: Art, Empire, and Infrastructure* (New Haven: Yale University Press, 2017); Itohan Osayimwese, *Colonialism and Modern Architecture in Germany* (Pittsburgh: University of Pittsburgh Press, 2017); Esra Akcan, *Open Architecture: Migration, Citizenship, and the Urban Renewal of Berlin-Kreuzberg by IBA-1984/87* (Basel: Birkhäuser-de Gruyter, 2018); Kathleen James-Chakraborty, *Modernism as Memory: Building Identity in the Federal Republic of Germany* (Minneapolis and London: University of Minnesota Press, 2018).

46 James Young, *At Memory's Edge: After-Images of the Holocaust in Contemporary Art and Architecture* (New Haven and London: Yale University Press, 2000); Andreas Huyssen, *Present Pasts: Urban Palimpsests and the Politics of Memory* (Stanford: Stanford University Press, 2003).

47 To be sure, the buildings I examine here are only a handful of the projects spearheaded by the federal government after reunification. As Christian Welzbacher has pointed out, though most of Germany's new government buildings have received little notice, it is these largely unknown buildings that guide the country's development. Welzbacher, "The Federal Government in the Role of Builder: Public Building between Transition and Continuity, Representation, and Ethics," in *Architektur der Demokratie: Bauten des Bundes 1990–2010*, ed. Martin Seidel (Ostfildern: Hatje Cantz, 2009), 229.

48 A now-canonical analysis of Berlin as palimpsest can be found in Huyssen, *Present Pasts*.

49 Quoted in *Hauptstadt Berlin: Parlamentsviertel im Spreebogen-Internationaler Städtebaulicher Ideenwettbewerb 1993*, ed. Felix Zwoch (Berlin: Bauwelt/Birkhäuser, 1993), 49.

50 Ibid.

51 Theodor Adorno, "Situation," in *Aesthetic Theory*, trans. Robert Hullot-Kentor (London: Athlone Press, 1997), 23.

52 Jürgen Habermas, "Modernity—An Incomplete Project," in *The Anti-Aesthetic: Essays on Postmodern Culture*, ed. Hal Foster (Port Townsend, WA: Bay Press, 1983), 3–15.

1

Bridging and Breaking—Master Planning the Spreebogen

At the stroke of midnight on October 3, 1990, the arc in Berlin's river Spree known as the Spreebogen came alive with sound, color, and light as one million people gathered to celebrate the official reunification of East and West Germany. In front of the Reichstag, flags waved, fireworks burst, and the cheering of the crowd rose above the steady toll of a copy of the Liberty Bell, a Cold War-era gift from the United States to West Germany. The euphoric excitement on display at this long-awaited declaration of national unity was inextricable from the site in which the ceremonies unfolded. Swarms of revelers flowed down Unter den Linden, the city's historic main thoroughfare, streaming through the Brandenburg Gate and into the Spreebogen to bridge and unify the very area that had been broken during the country's division, fractured by the Berlin Wall and the death strip surrounding it. The collective exhilaration of this moment could only have resulted from a profound awareness of the site's various histories, many of them traumatic, as these intense memories of place mingled ambivalently with the optimism of a fresh start.

It is in this context—that is, in the feverish atmosphere of possibility surrounding Germany's newfound unity—that this chapter considers the master plan for the new administrative heart of Berlin at the Spreebogen (Figure 1.1). During the process of reunification, perhaps no area of the city was the subject of as much heightened global interest as this horseshoe-shaped bend in the river that defined the former course of the Wall and embraced the past and future home of the national government. Occupying a parcel of about 150 acres at the western edge of the historical city center, the Spreebogen lies north of the Tiergarten and slightly northwest of Unter den Linden. For many years preceding reunification, the site had been one of Berlin's most notorious voids, and it remained a painful urban record of the century's violent rifts.[1] The architect Axel Schultes, whose firm won the 1992 competition to master plan the new government quarter, claimed that the challenge posed by this wounded terrain was how "to coax the soul out of the Spreebogen, the genius loci."[2] Only by so doing, according to Schultes (who had lived most of his life in Berlin), could the site's new architecture make sense of the city's spectrum of townscapes and "begin to link the virtues of each place together."[3] In their winning competition entry, Schultes and his partner Charlotte Frank proposed that the new plan for the area take the form of an immense "Band des Bundes," or band of federal buildings (Figure 1.2), twice spanning

Figure 1.1 Site of the Spreebogen, early 1990s. Aerial view.

Figure 1.2 Schultes Frank Architekten, proposal for Spreebogen, Berlin, 1992. Schultes Frank Architekten.

the Spree and crossing the former path of the Wall, the scars of which remained deeply etched in the urban fabric. As one reporter for *Der Spiegel* described it, the Band des Bundes would "unite the tattered halves of the city," while also asserting a clear-eyed vision of the balance of powers in the new democracy.[4] This historical zone of rupture and conflict would thus be transformed into a confident embodiment of Germany's new national self-image.

To many viewers at the time of the competition, Schultes and Frank's Band seemed to be a remarkably bold statement of how, at the tail end of the ruinous twentieth century, the idea of national unity might be signified in urban form. On paper, the Band had the paradoxical quality of appearing at once monumental and fragile, stable and transient. Somehow, this master plan seemed clearly to communicate both the new nation's optimism and its awareness of the constraints on monumentality put in place by the crimes of past regimes. The overarching form of the Band, and its associated visual processes of connecting, suturing, and repairing, appeared capable of embodying the complex way in which the Spreebogen's particular history made its way into an uncertain present. In the new master plan for the government district, history would return insistently through its architects' conscious citations.

But the very assuredness of Schultes and Frank's plan masked the way that the Spreebogen's history also returns involuntarily, as architectural and urban forms from the past resurface in the Band like debris after a shipwreck. After all, this was a site, and a city, freighted with the historical baggage of some of modernity's most politically significant urban ideas.[5] From Germany's first *Gründerzeit* to the moment of reunification, Berlin's urban development rocketed forward on an accelerated cycle of construction and demolition, with dramatic spasms of urbanization followed by the repeated ravages of war and division. Berlin's tendency toward the erasure of its built environment throughout the twentieth century led the author Peter Schneider to characterize the postreunification landscape in the city center as a "tabula rasa," a slate whose very blankness seemed to hinder reconstruction.[6] In truth, Berlin, its post-Wall voids notwithstanding, was anything but a tabula rasa. Rather, the city after 1990 was a palimpsest of realized and unrealized urban plans, a zone replete with ideas competing for currency—especially at the site of the Spreebogen, the primal scene of Germany's most notorious failures of democracy. Understanding the Spreebogen today requires a careful reading of its layers of accumulated buildings and plans, and an exhumation of its many unrealized modernist futures. More broadly, I argue that the Band des Bundes demonstrates, in intensified form, history's often uncomfortable recrudescence in the contemporary city.

In its built form, the Band des Bundes has tended to frustrate, in multiple senses of that term: its many modifications since the bold gesture outlined in their competition proposal have frustrated its architects, its curiously unsettled quality has frustrated viewers, and its massive yet oddly tentative appearance has frustrated analysis. Indeed, this sense of frustration has characterized much of the reception of Berlin's building boom. As the excitement surrounding reunification subsided, and as more and more urban projects reached completion toward the end of the millennium, the architecture and planning of contemporary Berlin came under repeated critical fire. For many close observers, Berlin today represents a wasted chance to realize some of contemporary architecture's most adventurous ideas. In this chapter—and throughout this book—I seek to step back from the debate surrounding the success or failure of Berlin's new state architecture. Rather, I aim to see the debate itself, and its attendant aura of sky-high stakes, as historically situated within global contemporary architecture culture. For the questions posed by the debate over the uses and abuses of history in Berlin's new official architecture are symptomatic of far larger struggles in contemporary architecture regarding how to cope with the relentless invasion of the past into the present.

Ultimately, what is on view in the Band des Bundes, whether its architects and patrons intended it or not, is the way in which the city of today is understood to be continuously infiltrated by historical forms, theories, and procedures. This intrusiveness is specific—and it is also instructive. At least in theory, the utopian aims of modern architecture and urban planning demanded the suppression of history and its tyrannical claims to authority. In contrast, the most reactionary of postmodern architecture treated history as a shopping mall's worth of formal delights and expressive possibilities, to be hand-selected by the designer of discerning taste. But the particular infiltration of the past exhibited in Schultes and Frank's Band is typical of broader tendencies in global contemporary culture, saturated as it is with anxiety over history's proper place in the present world. Thus, rather than as a decisive and monumental form, the Band des Bundes might be better understood as an analytical device, revealing the inexorability of history in contemporary architecture culture and proposing how one might deal with this sometimes unwelcome guest.

History of the Site

The 200-page brief for the Spreebogen design competition, complete with maps, photographs, charts, and lengthy historical information, offers just one demonstration of this infiltration of history into the present.[7] Circulated internationally to nearly 2,000 architects and planners, its abundant material emphasized the site's complex history. Repeatedly, the program underscored the necessity of understanding that past to allow for the "integration" of new architecture into the cityscape.[8] By the early 1990s, it was clear that designing the new Spreebogen meant mining the manifold layers of its past to uncover how its present form should take shape. Thus, many architects who participated in the competition found themselves researching the very origins of the city of Berlin. Its medieval core consisted of two close-lying towns, Berlin and Kölln, both of which had been founded in the thirteenth century and remained small, eastward-lying villages until the sixteenth century (Figure 1.3). At that time, the Hohenzollern dynasty began its rise to power from margraves to emperors and Berlin-Kölln, along with other towns in the region of Brandenburg east of the Elbe, began its urban expansion. Under Friedrich Wilhelm, the Great Elector who ruled from 1640 to 1688, Berlin-Kölln's status grew from a regional outpost to an important center of military, financial, and political activity. Beginning in 1658, fortifications were built

Bridging and Breaking—Master Planning the Spreebogen　　27

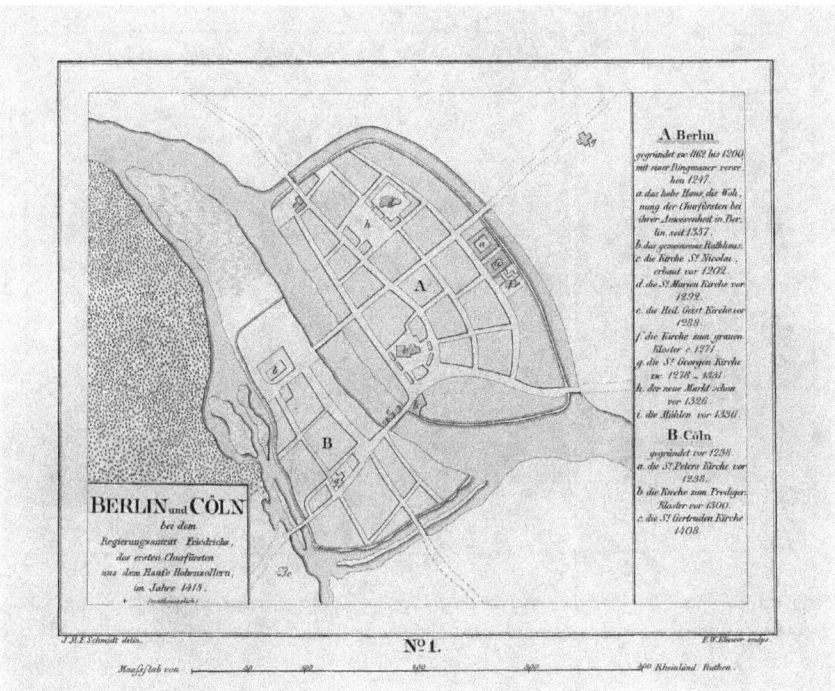

Figure 1.3 Map of Berlin and Kölln, c. 1300. From J. M. F. Schmidt, *Historischer Atlas von Berlin in VI Grundrissen nach gleichem Maßstabe von 1415 bis 1800*, Berlin: Simon Schropp & Kamp, 1835.

around the city, and the woodland area to the west of the city walls was enclosed and stocked with animals to serve as a royal hunting ground, known as the Tiergarten. (It would eventually be opened to the public in 1740 by Friedrich Wilhelm II, the son and successor of the Great Elector.)

In 1647, Friedrich Wilhelm ordered that the bridle path that connected the royal palace to the Tiergarten be paved and planted with rows of linden trees to create a ceremonial boulevard between the fortified town and the hunting grounds. At its completion, the boulevard was 1.5 kilometers long and 60 meters wide, with a central pedestrian pathway bordered by rows of trees and a carriageway on each side. Eventually named "Unter den Linden" for the shade provided by the landscaping, this thoroughfare was a central gathering point used for parades and other official functions (Figure 1.4). By the nineteenth century, it also provided a spine through the expanding city, linking its newly prosperous western districts with the central and eastern working-class areas. At once a main traffic artery and an open public space, this short boulevard has defined much of Berlin's subsequent urban development; over the years its axis has been extended westward, but its original contours remain the same today,

Figure 1.4 Johann Stridbeck, *Prospect oder Weg, gegen dem Their-Garden vor Berlin*, 1691. View of "Lindenallee," the later boulevard Unter den Linden in Berlin. Watercolor, 16.2 x 25.1 cm. Berlin State Library.

and it still provides the essential urban link between the eastern and western sections of the city. In 1925, the architect Max Heinrich described Unter den Linden as Berlin's "backbone" and "main nerve," and the urban significance of this strong axial presence in an otherwise multinodal town has persisted despite centuries of urban development.[9] In some ways, Unter den Linden acts as a band in the same manner as Schultes and Frank's master plan, linking together otherwise isolated urban areas and providing notional and actual links between disparate sites. For centuries, Unter den Linden terminated in the west at the city's customs wall, which would remain in place until 1860. In 1788, their meeting point was marked by the construction of Carl Gotthard Langhans's Brandenburg Gate (Figure 1.5), which served not only as a customs checkpoint but also as the monumental entry to the imperial axis of the city. Thus, from its origin, the Brandenburg Gate signified a border territory; only after passing through this liminal space could city dwellers move northwest into the Spreebogen.

Though seventeenth-century maps show the Spreebogen as a topographical feature, the site was not represented as a distinct urban element until the well-known map of 1757 published by Prussian field marshal Samuel von Schmettau (Figure 1.6), demonstrating the site's persistently marginal position on the fringe of the historical city center.[10] During the nineteenth century, the Spreebogen remained as undeveloped land just outside the customs fortifications (for which the Brandenburg Gate was one of eighteen points of entry), serving primarily as a military training field. The city's

Bridging and Breaking—Master Planning the Spreebogen 29

Figure 1.5 Carl Gotthard Langhans, Brandenburg Gate, c. 1798. Aquatint by D. Berger after Lütke. From Hermann Schmitz, *Berliner Baumeistervom Ausgang des achtzehnten Jahrhunderts*, Berlin: Ernst Wasmuth, 1914, p. 160. The Getty Center for the History of Art and the Humanities, Santa Monica, California.

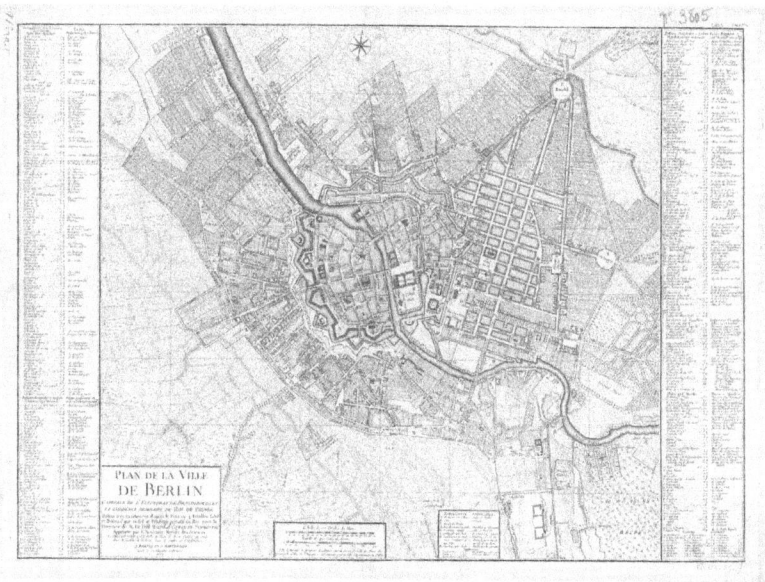

Figure 1.6 Samuel Graf von Schmettau, map of Berlin, 1764. Copper engraving, 55.0 x 51.0 cm. National Library of France, Gallica. As the map is oriented S–N, the Spreebogen is visible in the bottom right corner.

ongoing westward expansion, as well as a surge in public traffic to the Tiergarten, placed the site in an increasingly central location in the mid nineteenth century. In response to its new centrality, the landscape architect Peter Joseph Lenné modified the entire area, transforming the Tiergarten into a landscaped park, altering the course of the river to form a more symmetrical arch, and laying out a hierarchical network of roadways and bridges (Figure 1.7). Lenné also acknowledged Berlin's rising economic status in his creation of the Humboldthafen, the harbor leading northward out of the arc that intersected with the railways paralleling the river. By the century's end, partly due to its strengthened infrastructure, the land contained inside the arc had been developed into a middle-class residential area known as the Alsenviertel. The construction of the Reichstag building (Figure 1.8), completed in 1894, gave the area a new official character, and more and more government workers and parliamentarians took up residence in the Alsenviertel. Stretching toward the Kroll Opera House on its western edge, the Königsplatz was anchored by a monumental victory column celebrating Prussia's military prowess. Yet despite its increasing vitality, the Spreebogen remained symbolically remote from the historic core of the city around the city palace (Stadtschloss), reflecting the tension between the democratic Reichstag and the dynastic Hohenzollerns.

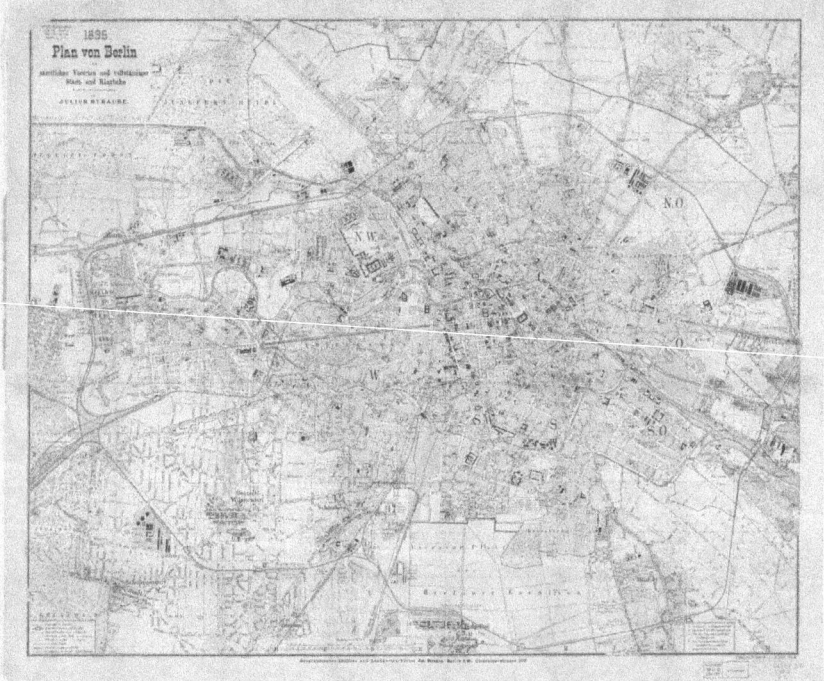

Figure 1.7 Julius Straube, map of Berlin, 1895. Chromolithograph, 62.8 x 78.0 cm. Harvard College Library. The map shows the Spreebogen and Humboldthafen at its approximate center; the newly completed Reichstag is visible at the bottom right of the arc.

Figure 1.8 Paul Wallot, Reichstag building, 1894. Aerial view, with Königsplatz in foreground and Alsenviertel at top left.

Indeed, what Schultes and Frank would have found when they began to research the site was that political unification was a fantasy that had haunted the Spreebogen throughout modernity. From the late nineteenth century to the end of the twentieth, the site's political importance grew along with the fortunes of the numerous states that governed from Berlin during this condensed time period. However, this political volatility itself meant that urban plans for the Spreebogen accumulated rapidly but with little realization. Competitions to revamp the Königsplatz and the little-loved Reichstag came to nothing, and the Königsplatz remained an ill-defined green space with no distinguishable boundary along its southern edge. While architects and planners lamented the lack of equilibrium in the city, the asymmetry between east and west reflected larger administrative realities. Despite the Reich's claims to democracy, the Prussian state—and its Hohenzollern representatives—maintained the crux of power at the Stadtschloss in both a political and an urban sense.

This spatial dispersal of government functions meant that, in contrast to other European capital cities, Berlin lacked a clear, central area for government use. Planners sought throughout the twentieth century to find ways of uniting these distant spaces, and the Prussian state sporadically hosted competitions to solve the seemingly intractable problem of the marginalization of its own elected representatives. From 1908 to 1911, a volley of competitions explicitly targeted the growing city and the need to balance the urban emphasis between the site of the royal palace and the increasingly active government area. For a 1908–10 competition for a master plan for Greater

Berlin, for example, the architect Bruno Möhring (along with economist Rudolf Eberstadt and transportation engineer Richard Petersen) submitted a scheme in which the Spreebogen embraced the "Forum of the Reich," an imperial square inspired by French baroque models.[11] Here, the ministry of war would sit opposite the Reichstag, symbolizing "the army and the people, the true bearers of German greatness and power, unified in the monuments of architecture."[12] In retrospect, the *ancien régime* savor of Möhring's plan appears willfully oblivious, attempting as it does to head off the built expression of modernity while failing to realize that its most concentrated effects would occur in the violent world war of the next decade.

During the Weimar Republic established after the war (1919–33), government support for construction efforts in Berlin flowed in the direction of infrastructural and social projects (for example, Cornelis van Eesteren's proposal to replace Unter den Linden's baroque architecture with a series of modernist towers connected by low-rise horizontal strips) rather than toward monumental expressions of the state (Figure 1.9).[13] Only at the Spreebogen, by then considered the place of democracy's

Figure 1.9 Cornelis van Eesteren, *"Gleichgewicht,"* proposal for Unter den Linden, 1925. Het Nieuwe Instituut, Rotterdam, Netherlands. Collection Het Nieuwe Instituut/Collection Van Eesteren-Fluck & Van Lohuizen Foundation, Amsterdam/Archive: EEST 8.66-2.

birth in Germany, was any kind of official representation envisioned.[14] As early as 1920, Otto Kohtz proposed an immense glass-and-steel "Reichshaus" for the site (Figure 1.10), a modern stepped pyramid that would testify to Germany's industrial might.[15] In 1926, the government renamed the Königsplatz as the Platz der Republik, and systematically, if bootlessly, sought proposals for modernist expressions of republican ideals. In Hugo Häring's 1927 proposal (Figure 1.11), the Platz der Republik in front of the Reichstag was to be surrounded by grandstands for public events, turning the former imperial square into a "Forum of the Republic."[16] Häring clustered government functions within high-rise buildings dispersed around the square, creating a modernist office complex reminiscent of the administration center in Le Corbusier's 1922 project for a Contemporary City for Three Million Inhabitants (which had been circulated in German architectural journals as the "Stadt der Gegenwart" shortly after its publication in France). However, whereas Le Corbusier's project married a highly rational grid plan with an almost picturesque emphasis on siting and green space, Häring organized his plan along a strong central axis. His intention was to undermine the imperial city planning that then defined Berlin's cityscape, such that his new north–south boulevard, cutting opposite the directionality of Unter den Linden, would inscribe "a distinct and clear line through this axis of the rulers."[17] Hans Poelzig's project of 1929 (Figure 1.12) similarly placed government offices in slabs that radiated into the curve of the Spree and visually lightened the bulky, Wilhelmine Reichstag. Like many Weimar architects, Häring and Poelzig saw the efficiency of the clean-lined slab building as inherently democratic in both address and content. Here, avant-garde

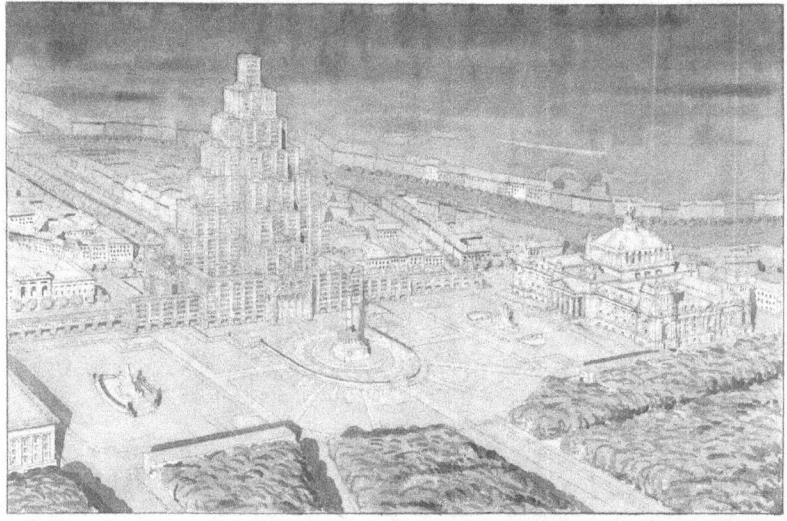

Figure 1.10 Otto Kohtz, *Reichshaus am Königsplatz, Berlin-Tiergarten*, 1920. Watercolor pencil on paper, 51.1 x 76.0 cm. Architekturmuseum der Technischen Universität Berlin.

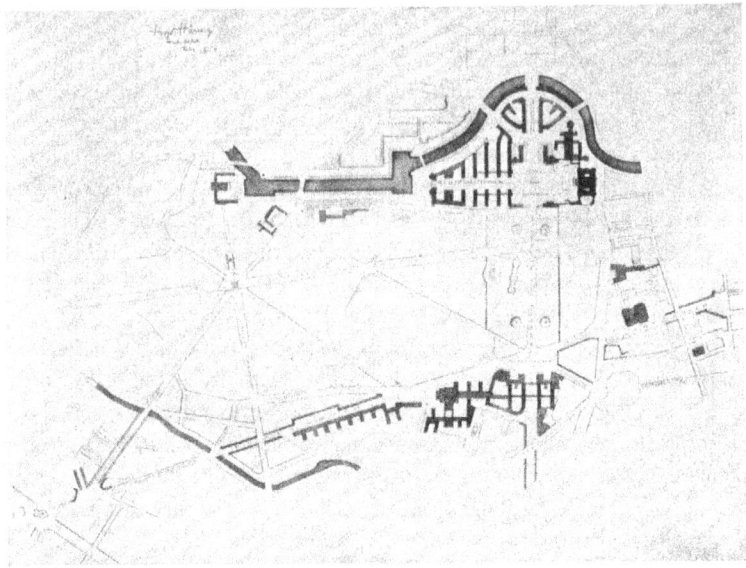

Abb. 2. Studie für die Bebauung der Gebäete nordlich, östlich und südöstlich des Tiergartens von Hugo Häring.

Figure 1.11 Karl Böttcher and Hugo Häring, *Reichstag, Berlin*, 1927. Ink on paper, 56.3 x 88.0 cm. Published in *Zentralblatt der Bauverwaltung*, 1927. Architekturmuseum der Technischen Universität Berlin.

Figure 1.12 Hans Poelzig, *Erweiterung des Reichstags und Neugstaltung des Platzes der Republik, Berlin-Tiergarten*, 1927. Charcoal on transparent paper, 115.8 x 144.4 cm. Architekturmuseum der Technischen Universität Berlin.

architecture offered a bracing corrective to the Spreebogen's former political marginalization, positioning it instead as a gleaming City Crown in line with the visions of Bruno Taut.

Yet these and other modernist plans put forward to develop the area were halted with the beginning of National Socialist rule in Germany. Under the Third Reich, the site was the target of repeated violence against the existing urban fabric, beginning with the Reichstag fire of 1933, which Hitler used as a pretext to suspend civil liberties. Infamously, this moment produced one of the most indelible proposals for the Spreebogen site: Albert Speer's plan to make over Berlin into the Welthauptstadt Germania, the seat of the Third Reich, with an immense north–south axis that would have stretched for 5 kilometers through the city (Figure 1.13). This broad boulevard was based on a 1917 proposal by Martin Mächler (Figure 1.14); but whereas Mächler's

Figure 1.13 Albert Speer, model for *Welthaupstadt Germania*, 1937–42. CPA Media Pte Ltd / Alamy Stock Photo.

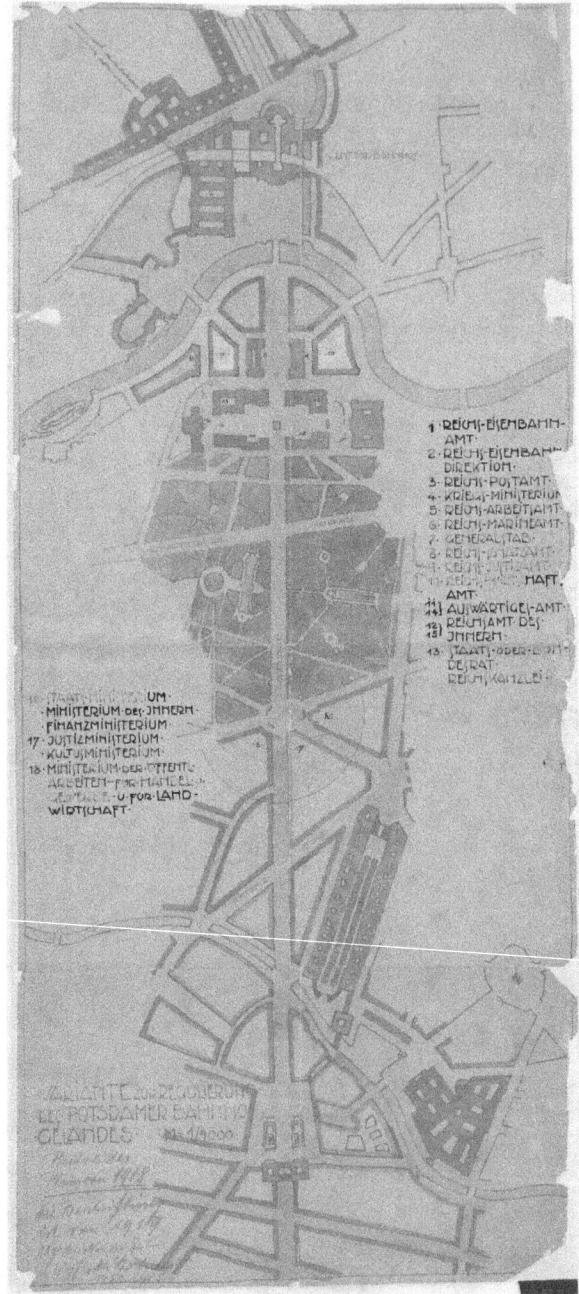

Figure 1.14 Martin Mächler, *Nord-Süd-Achse mit der Neustrukturierung des Potsdamer Bahnhofsgeländes, Berlin,* 1917. Pencil, colored pencil, and watercolor ink on blueprint, 91.6 x 42.0 cm. Architekturmuseum der Technischen Universität Berlin.

scheme had emphasized the pragmatic urban matters of economics and circulation, Speer imbued his own with aggressive symbolic content. The road was framed by symmetrical civic buildings, providing a classicizing backdrop for lines of troops during the regime's constant parades and military exhibitions. At the northern terminus, embraced by the Spreebogen, Hitler and Speer envisioned a colossal domed hall that would have been the largest building in the world, spacious enough for 180,000 people and so vast that Speer worried that clouds would form inside the dome. The Nazis' nightmarish visions of grandeur achieved little but destroyed much as buildings, streets, and parkland were demolished to make way for this steroidal cityscape. The Spreebogen was cleared to make way for the Great Hall, including most of the residences in the Alsenviertel, and plans were put in place to change the course of the river yet again to accommodate the oversized structure.[18] However, due to increasing wartime pressures on manpower and finances (the project was meant to be subsidized by the spoils of subjugated territories), Hitler halted construction in 1943.[19] What was left was a windswept terrain that would become only more desolate after the devastating effects of the last years of the war.[20]

After 1945, the vacant Spreebogen projected a distinctly ghostly atmosphere that was somewhat different in tone than the areas of the city that remained cluttered with rubble. The trauma of recent history was inescapable in the bombed-out streets and collapsed buildings of the historical city center, but despite its relative emptiness, the traces of the Spreebogen's past remained nonetheless disquietingly present. To the south, the Tiergarten lay stripped of many of its trees as war-ravaged Berliners cut them down for use as fuel. The Reichstag, its dome scorched and sagging and its interior laden with graffiti left by Soviet soldiers during the Battle of Berlin, loomed over the Platz der Republik like a battered human form. Until 1949, the stricken population used the vacant land to grow vegetables for sustenance (Figure 1.15).

Figure 1.15 Inhabitants of Berlin picking potatoes in front of the Reichstag, 1947. dpa picture alliance / Alamy Stock Photo.

Though the Spreebogen lay technically in the British sector of the city, as early as the late 1940s, it was virtually off-limits for political use due to its closeness to the border between Allied- and Soviet-occupied city zones. Therefore, the site's barren landscape became the stage set for Cold War cultural salvos from both East and West.[21] Immediately after the war, the Soviets erected a memorial to their war dead along the site's southern perimeter. Later, for the 1957 Interbau, the United States constructed the Berlin Congress Hall, designed by the American architect Hugh Stubbins in collaboration with Germans Werner Düttmann and Franz Mocken, on the western edge of the Platz der Republik (Figure 1.16). A gift to West Germany to recognize the ongoing friendship between the two democracies, the Congress Hall was a powerfully visual piece of political propaganda. Throughout the Cold War, its soaring concrete roof sheltered U.S.-sponsored exhibitions (such as a show of photography of everyday

Figure 1.16 Hugh Stubbins with Werner Düttmann and Franz Mocken, Berlin Congress Hall, 1957. View of building under construction.

life in America) and hosted John F. Kennedy during his 1963 visit to Berlin.²² As West Berlin reoriented increasingly toward the Kurfürstendamm, the Spreebogen—and the Brandenburg Gate at its southeastern edge—ambivalently functioned as both the center of the city as a whole and the bare, contested border between its halves.

The urban schemes that were proposed in the postwar years, especially the results of West Germany's 1958 *Hauptstadt Berlin* competition, sought to heal the wounds of Speer's north–south axis and to bridge the deepening chasm between East and West. As the area had famously been the site of tense confrontations between Soviet and Allied forces from 1945 onward, *Hauptstadt Berlin* was compensatory, aiming to cool this particularly hot spot within the larger Cold War.²³ As would its 1990s counterpart, the brief emphasized the necessity of international participation and the avoidance of expressions of monumentality and nationalism.²⁴ Like the process of the *Hauptstadt Berlin* competition itself, the submissions were based on a fantasy of future reunification while also aiming to repair the damage sustained to the city during the war. Hans Scharoun and Wils Ebert's plan shared with many of the other proposals an insistence that only wide-scale demolition could help prepare the landscape for the new Berlin. Here, the Spreebogen area served as a bridge between the inner city and the northern suburbs, occupying the northwest corner of the newly reorganized urban center. Le Corbusier's entry (Figure 1.17) drew on his city plans from the 1920s, such as the Contemporary City, the Plan Voisin, and the Radiant City, in which the urban environment was divided and separated into specific functional zones. However, he tempered his vision in Berlin with the lower structures and relaxed hierarchy of forms that characterized his other late-career urban schemes. Though it is impossible to reduce to a single type the provocative and multifaceted plans produced for *Hauptstadt Berlin*, they reveal as a whole the profession's tendency in the postwar years to supplant history with technology as a source of formal inspiration. Thus, modernism—or at least "modernism" as it had been codified by the *Congrès internationaux d'architecture moderne* (CIAM)—seemed to be a safe language with which to address Berlin's complex history.²⁵

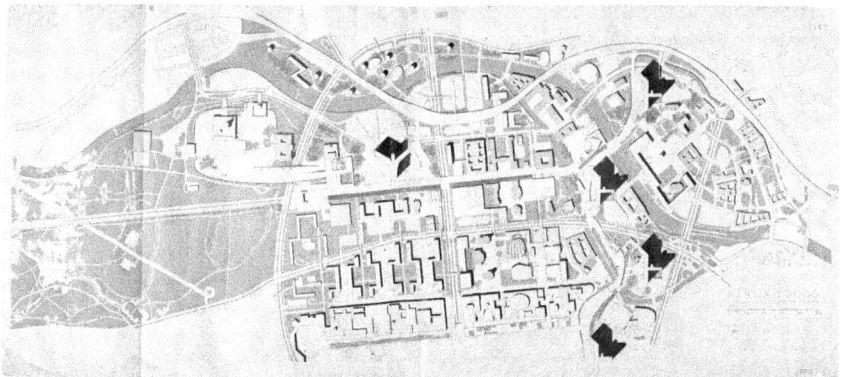

Figure 1.17 Le Corbusier, proposal for *Hauptstadt Berlin*, 1958. Fondation Le Corbusier. © F.L.C. / ADGAP, Paris / Artists Rights Society (ARS), New York 2020.

In fact, many of the proposals drew on avant-garde plans from the 1920s, like Häring's or Poelzig's, in which slab buildings were surrounded by ample green space and motor traffic was strictly separated from pedestrian zones. Alison and Peter Smithson's proposal (Figure 1.18) remade the devastated core of the city into a multileveled, bustling city center bedecked with undulating slab buildings. In their vision, the Spreebogen would again take up its role as a government district (as it did in most of the competition entries), with a sleek, disc-like civic building hovering in front of the Reichstag that paid homage to Berlin's expressionist legacy and served as a beacon on the skyline. The infrastructure around it—highways and train stations, as well as helipads and escalators leading to subterranean urban spaces—would provide

Figure 1.18 Alison and Peter Smithson, proposal for *Hauptstadt Berlin*, 1958. Frances Loeb Library, Harvard University Graduate School of Design. Courtesy of the Frances Loeb Library, Harvard University Graduate School of Design.

the technological energy that the Smithsons saw as the lifeblood of a vibrant downtown. In an accompanying film produced in collaboration with John McHale, Peter Smithson described the need to disregard "historic spaces" in favor of the "specific poetry" of machine-mediated human movement.[26] Indeed, all of the competition entries, including the winning submission from Friedrich Spengelin, Fritz Eggeling, and Gerd Pempelfort, had at their foundation a nearly compulsive assumption that annihilating the old urban fabric was necessary to make way for the new.[27] Here, coming to terms with history meant superseding it with captivating visions of a bright, if chimerical, future.

But like so many before them, these architects would not see their plans realized. On the morning of August 13, 1961, Soviet guards began to close the border between East and West Berlin starting just south of the Spreebogen at the Brandenburg Gate. What had previously been an invisible if nevertheless official boundary between East and West was made all too visible in the coming years, as the military of the German Democratic Republic (GDR) cut a wide swath through the heart of the city to build what they termed an "anti-fascist protective rampart." Running along the eastern edge of the Spreebogen, the no-man's-land that surrounded the Wall's multiple barriers disrupted movement and charged the area with a new, deadly ideological content. From the 1960s through the 1980s, the Spreebogen became not only the actual site of the city's political division, but also the international image of the Cold War, with its interminable face-offs across boundaries. News of failed attempts to traverse the Wall, many of which took place at the Spreebogen and sometimes resulted in fatalities, were met with fear and anger in the West and taken as evidence of the barbarism of the GDR. Upon the fall of the Wall in 1989, jubilant Berliners crowded the Spreebogen, filling the former void of the death strip with lively human activity as befuddled East German troops stood by.

In general, in the postwar years as with the half-century preceding them, the Spreebogen accumulated the historical baggage of critical events and momentous urban plans. In 1988, Aldo Rossi won a competition for the German Historical Museum near the Reichstag, which formed one part of a larger government plan to develop the area (Figure 1.19). Rossi's striking design, using materials he believed to be fundamental to Berlin's architectural heritage—its industrial red brick, the white marble of Karl Friedrich Schinkel's Altes Museum, and brightly colored vernacular ceramic tiles—has become one of Berlin's most legendary fragments, having been shelved after the fall of the Wall.[28] Aside from a handful of additions and alterations, the site remained undeveloped during the country's years of division. By the time of the 1992 Spreebogen competition, the area had returned to a relatively placid green field, punctuated only by groves of trees and its few remaining structures: the Reichstag, the Congress Hall, and the Swiss Embassy, a chance survivor of Nazi demolition and Allied bombing, lying between them. Overall, despite the absence of visible debris, the site bore the unmistakable quality of a ruin, a once-inhabited area that had been reclaimed by "nature's revenge," as Georg Simmel described such places.[29]

In some ways, then, the Bundestag after reunification was trapped between two *terrains vagues*: on the one hand, the Spreebogen, whose serene meadows belied its turbulent

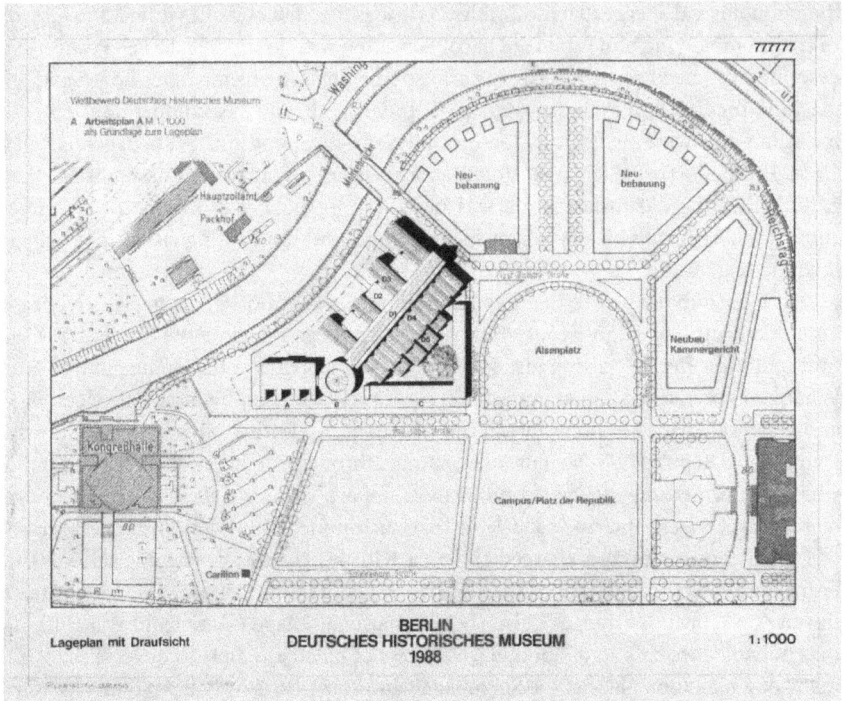

Figure 1.19 Aldo Rossi, site plan for Deutsches Historisches Museum, Berlin, 1988. Reprographic copy on plastic film with transfer lettering, 78.4 x 96.3 cm. Canadian Centre for Architecture. Aldo Rossi fonds, Canadian Centre for Architecture, © Eredi Aldo Rossi / Fondazione Aldo Rossi.

history, and on the other, the noncommittal architecture and urbanism that characterized the provisional capital of Bonn.[30] When the Bundesrepublik moved its functions to that provincial western town in 1949, it operated initially out of already existing buildings. For example, the Bundestag's first sessions took place in the modernist Pedagogical Academy, quickly modified for the purpose by Hans Schwippert, who was the first to attach the word "transparency" to this modest official architecture.[31] As Bonn's state architecture and urbanism developed, it remained a curiously unprepossessing version of the modernist language of form that sought to follow the ethos of transparency laid out in Adolf Arndt's well-known speech "Democracy as Building Client."[32] What traditions were there seemed safely anchored in the natural landscape of the Rhineland, tending toward the meandering and pastoral and away from anything that could be construed as nationalistic or monumental (Figure 1.20).[33] Axel Schultes, who had spent time in the "Hauptdorf" while designing the new Bonn Kunstmuseum (1985–92), analogized this casual, haphazard townscape to "cows in a pasture."[34]

Given the Spreebogen's overburdened history, it is clear why relocating the government from Bonn to Berlin was an unnerving prospect, let alone the idea of

Figure 1.20 Bundesviertel, Bonn, 2010. Aerial view.

transferring the capital's functions to the Spreebogen itself. The Bundestag's move back to Berlin would officially mark the fifth time the city would become the capital of a German state during the twentieth century. Returning to Berlin meant leaving sleepy, rural Bonn, with its relaxed architecture and urbanism, and confronting a still-palpable urban legacy of fascism, destruction, and division. Therefore, to reoccupy the Spreebogen would entail addressing the site's particular scars, including the spectral contours of Speer's north–south axis and the bleak no-man's-land that still traced the river's curve, running south toward Potsdamer Platz. After a series of tense debates, the Bundestag's vote to return to Berlin was finalized by a narrow margin of 337 to 320. In the face of this decision, though strong resistance to the very idea of Berlin as the new federal capital remained, most representatives averred that any development of the historically burdened Spreebogen site would need to be accomplished transparently, openly, and internationally.

Imagining the City: *Berlin Tomorrow*

In the sense of urgency attending its public milieu, the Spreebogen competition was in good company with other initiatives held concurrently to reimagine the unified city. In the years immediately following reunification, competitions sponsored both by the government and by private institutions were underway for an astonishing range of Berlin's most important areas, including Potsdamer Platz, Alexanderplatz, the Friedrichstadt Passagen, and the Spreeinsel. The hotly contested nature of these sites, their high international visibility, and the headlong speed with which their plans unfolded created an atmosphere of virtually unparalleled public engagement in shaping the city. Insightful and rigorous scholarship on the *Planungskultur* of Berlin's postreunification years has helped to clarify the individuals, organizations, and pressures both economic and political that were involved in Berlin's rebuilding.[35] My purpose in what follows is not to add to these thorough discussions of the very real forces shaping the New Berlin. Rather, I seek to isolate one example of how Berlin's building boom unfolded in a highly public, and intensely mediated, context of what Jürgen Habermas has termed "communicative action."[36] By looking at the urban project *Berlin Tomorrow*, I aim to illuminate how architects proposing to intervene in Berlin's fraught present found themselves at the center of a larger debate over how to deal with history's incursion into public awareness in the 1990s. More broadly, however, it is important to note the extent to which urban planning in contemporary cities worldwide relied on precisely the visual format of Schultes and Frank's Band des Bundes—that is, a collection of ideas and concepts communicated through visual schema, designed to synthesize the old and the new and to captivate the imagination of a mass audience.

In the same month during which hordes of people crowded the Spreebogen to celebrate reunification, Vittorio Magnano Lampugnani, then-director of the Deutsches Architekturmuseum (DAM) in Frankfurt, met with the architecture critic Michael Mönninger to discuss the future image of Berlin. This propitiously timed meeting resulted in the sprawling, influential project *Berlin Tomorrow: Ideas for the Heart of a Great City*, which unfolded across a range of media throughout 1991. *Berlin Tomorrow* invited architects from around the world to submit urban schemes for the city to a multiplatform initiative carried out in partnership with the *Frankfurter Allgemeine Zeitung* (FAZ), one of the most widely circulating daily newspapers in the country. Seventeen firms participated, including established international figures (Aldo Rossi, Norman Foster, and the firm of Venturi Scott Brown) as well as rising contemporary stars like Zaha Hadid and Daniel Libeskind.[37] Like many architects from around the world active in the early 1990s, these figures eagerly pursued the opportunity to gain a foothold, however prospective, in the process of designing the New Berlin. Even before the Bundestag had officially resolved to move the capital of reunified Germany from Bonn back to the nation's former capital, the delirium of rebuilding was already well underway.

As one manifestation of this delirium, *Berlin Tomorrow* operated in a late-twentieth-century realm of urban design that we might describe as imagining the city. This subcategory of urban planning, to which the Spreebogen competition and Schultes and Frank's master plan belong as well, bears distinctively contemporary characteristics. In its factual, physical form, urban planning demands the complex negotiation of policy, permissions, and codes, and involves concrete questions of land use and ownership, zoning and development, microecologies and macroeconomics. For architects and planners to imagine the city, on the other hand, means for them to conceive new urban and social forms and to propose new perceptual experiences through architecture and urbanism.[38] Methodologically, this mode depends on research just as exhaustive as the more practical version must undertake. But as opposed to the hard data necessary to carry out urban planning, the tools used to imagine the city—the rendering, the photomontage, the model, the collaged map—intentionally allow for incompleteness and abstraction.[39] Disseminated through exhibitions, catalogs, and mass media, the visual documents of this process of imagining the city make appeals both to planning experts and to amateur audiences, attempting to foster public interest and to be universally comprehensible.[40] The viewer is thus interpolated as a participant, and asked to assemble his or her own unitary urban image from fragments of visual data. As Esra Akcan has argued, we might consider these unbuilt projects as part of an alternative "history of possibility," brimming with critical potential for the architectural historian.[41]

As one of many initiatives aimed at imagining the city, *Berlin Tomorrow* made a significant impact even in the oversaturated planning scene of the 1990s. Exhibited at the DAM and in a companion show at the Berlinische Galerie in the first half of 1991, printed as a series of articles in the FAZ and in a special issue of the English-language journal *Architectural Design*, and compiled into a catalog published in several different languages, the architects' visionary plans made their way around the world. These city "ideas" reflect the exhilarated urban sensibility that characterized many of the debates, competitions, and exhibitions that unfolded in Berlin during the early part of the 1990s, in which the government's official imperative was "growth, growth, growth."[42] For a brief moment, anything seemed possible. Flush with investment capital and creative energy, reunified Berlin appeared to be a realm of boundless possibility fueled by the euphoria of wide-scale construction. Excitement about the New Berlin was at its most heightened state, and at the dawn of its rebirth, the city was poised between fantasy and reality. Thirty years hence, however, what seems most clearly on view in *Berlin Tomorrow* is how it reveals that contemporary cities more generally have been built on these twinned poles, suspended between the id-like limitless freedom of global capitalism and the reality principle of construction costs, local resistance, and disappointing schemes. Indeed, years before Frank Gehry's Guggenheim Bilbao, we see the so-called Bilbao Effect being attempted in Berlin, with similar faith in architecture to attract international acclaim and money in the direction of the city that houses it: as the saying goes, "if you build it, they will come."[43] Above all, *Berlin Tomorrow* reveals the possibilities and limitations of contemporary architecture culture, displaying its conditions as it took international hold.

Both the organizers and the architects involved in *Berlin Tomorrow* left their reflections intentionally detached from real analyses of feasibility and implementation, focusing instead on the overall image of the new capital. Their idea was that provocative and sweeping plans could combat the negative effects of small thinking and nostalgia on the future of Berlin. Though a handful of the submissions were neotraditionalist, morphological city studies, other results were thus satisfyingly arcane; as a journalist for the *Berliner Morgenpost* later noted, "many of the international stars sketched extravagant, high-flying ideas that had more to do with art than with real building."[44]

But Lampugnani was at pains to minimize his expectations of tangible outcomes. Instead, he sought to establish the tone of the project as primarily imaginative: "The concern is not initially to measure the proposals by what is and what is not possible in Berlin today."[45] He asked the public instead to understand the designs "as fragmentary programmatic manifestoes, as collected ideas and concepts, as initial attempts at solutions; *not* as fully fledged solutions."[46]

Berlin Tomorrow was intended to be a visionary brainstorming platform aimed at using the full range of architectural means current in the 1990s to imagine the possibilities of the New Berlin. The scope of the proposals makes clear that what was at stake was to rethink how a viewer might participate in making sense of the city, from Jean Nouvel's streetscape of Times Square-style screens blinking around the clock, to Zaha Hadid's plan to reinvigorate the "dead zone" immediately adjacent to the former course of the Berlin Wall by leaving it as a contemplative blank space, to Herzog & de Meuron's proposal to condense city functions into four vast slab buildings of varied proportions distributed in vacant lots surrounding the Tiergarten (Figures 1.21 and 1.22). As with many of the proposals for the Spreebogen competition, the contributions to *Berlin Tomorrow*, whether historicist or progressive in stylistic

Figure 1.21 Jean Nouvel, Emmanuel Cattani & Associés, proposal for the *Berlin Morgen (Berlin Tomorrow)* competition, 1990. ©Artists Rights Society (ARS), New York / ADAGP, Paris.

Figure 1.22 Zaha Hadid, *Berlin 2000*, proposal for the *Berlin Morgen (Berlin Tomorrow)* competition, 1990. Acrylic on cartridge paper, mounted on gatorfoam, 225 x 192 cm. © Zaha Hadid Foundation.

terms, made visible the procedures and methods their designers had undertaken to research the history of the city.

Lampugnani's use of the word "solutions" reveals that he considered *Berlin Tomorrow* an experiment in reflecting how a contemporary subject might regard the scattered residue of history as it lingered obdurately in the urban fabric. O. M. Ungers's proposal, *Urban Islands in a Metropolitan Sea*, built on an earlier study completed in collaboration with Rem Koolhaas, Hans Kollhoff, Arthur Ovaska, and Peter Riemann during the 1977 Berlin Summer Academy for Architecture at Cornell University.[47] The results of the academy were published in a 1978 pamphlet, titled *The City within the City: Berlin as Green Archipelago*, containing plans to reconfigure Berlin as what Ungers labeled "islands-in-the-city."[48] The results were something like a paranoid-critical rendition of the 1944 Morgenthau Plan, which had proposed the "pastoralization" of Germany as a way of preventing further military aggression. In this green archipelago, decay and depopulation were taken as facts of urban life in the late twentieth century, not as problems to be fought (Figure 1.23). Ungers and his colleagues proposed that

Figure 1.23 Peter Riemann, *Die Stadt in der Stadt–Berlin das Grüne Stadtarchipel (The City in the City–Berlin as Green Archipelago)*, 1977. UAA Ungers Archiv für Architekturwissenschaft.

cities should work with these tendencies rather than against them, and take measures to ensure that cities retained their most essential metropolitan qualities.

To that end, they planned to identify and emphasize Berlin's "urban islands," those areas that had remained vital and vibrant, allowing the rest of the city to go to pasture and become a "natural lagoon." The Spreebogen would be among these new, resuscitated islands. The city of Berlin would thus become a group of enclaves (much in the way that West Berlin was itself an enclave), city fragments "liberated"—Ungers's word—from the falsity of a unified urbanism. *Urban Islands in a Metropolitan Sea* similarly allowed Berlin's fragments to rise up, in blatant defiance of top-down urban planning.

Bridging and Breaking—Master Planning the Spreebogen   49

In this project, expansion is merely the obverse of decay, as both inevitably result from the city's unremitting state of flux. Indeed, the contemporary city represses its own decay, insisting instead on the spurious optimism of speculation and development. By pointing out the artificial stasis in which most urban theory suspends urban conditions, Ungers's islands reveal decay as immanent in the city, which necessarily insists on its own constant renewal.

Ungers's proposal thus pointed to the despotic nature of the master plan itself, as did John Hejduk's gnomic *The Potsdam Printer's House and Studio* (Figure 1.24). According to Hejduk, his project was contributed "as a plea in opposition to super/

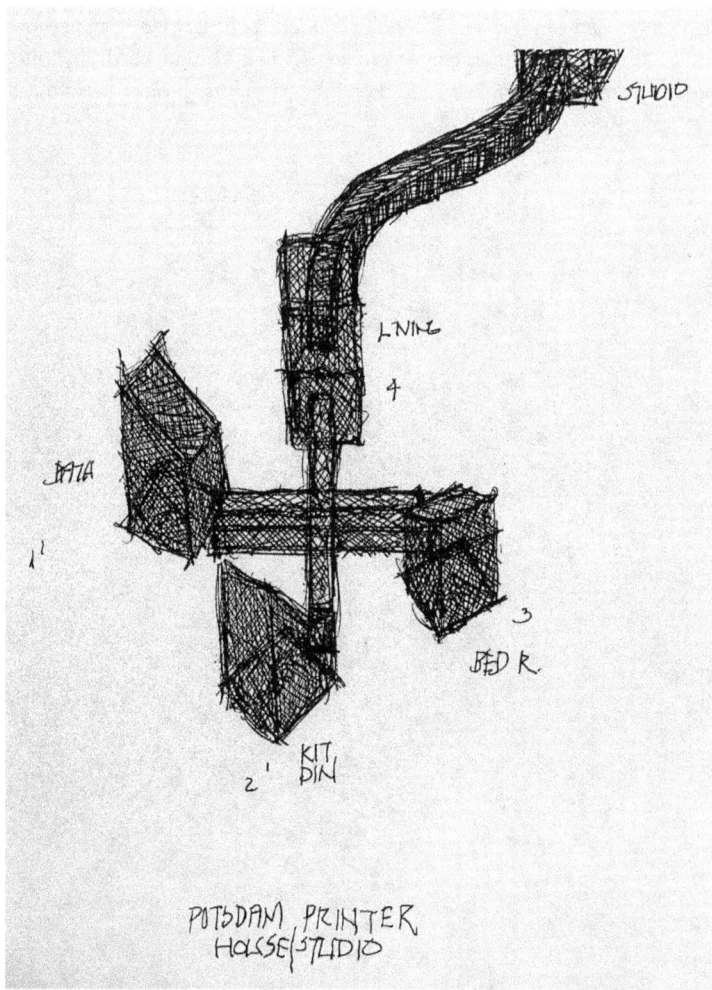

Figure 1.24 John Hejduk, proposal for the *Berlin Morgen (Berlin Tomorrow)* competition, 1990. Ink on paper, 28 x 22 cm. Canadian Centre for Architecture.

master/grand/planning, which has destroyed so many significant places."⁴⁹ The surrealist plan, associated with Hejduk's larger "Berlin Masque," consists of five volumes with specific individual programs, four of which are arranged in a rough diamond and joined by two corridors crossing at the center. The fifth volume lies at the end of another corridor that ambles toward the implied north of the site. No matter how inward and multiple Hejduk's references are here, the project irresistibly suggests the historical silhouette of Potsdamer Platz, theoretically placing the fifth volume somewhere near the Brandenburg Gate.

In fact, the former borderland around the Brandenburg Gate and Pariser Platz provided grist for a number of proposals that suggested how one might mend this torn urban fabric without erasing the marks of history. Daniel Libeskind's proposal to transform Unter den Linden into *Über den Linden*, as he named it, pulled trajectory lines out of the historical boulevard and extrapolated them vertically into space, dwarfing the nearby gate (Figure 1.25). For Libeskind, this project drew out existing

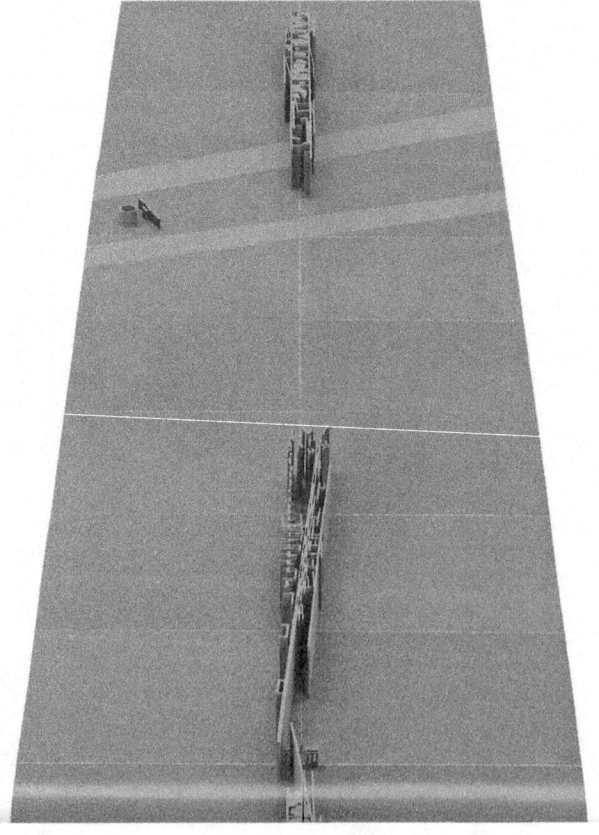

Figure 1.25 Studio Libeskind, model for proposal for the *Berlin Morgen (Berlin Tomorrow)* competition, 1990.

historical traces and set them in friction against older urban expressions of power. Not only did *Über den Linden* transmogrify the imperial axis of the Hohenzollerns into a dynamic, contemporary megaform, but it also enacted a deconstructivist cut, slicing through the former course of the Wall and Speer's north–south axis.[50] This process of design allowed Libeskind to build a bridge between East and West, uniting and connecting the two formerly separate halves while commemorating the former separation of the city—a tactic shared with other proposals, such as Robert Venturi and Denise Scott Brown's *Brandenburg Stair* (Figure 1.26), which marched up and over the neoclassical gate to form a monumental bridge, also itself a gate, across the former boundary. (Venturi and Scott Brown had long been interested in the effects of bridging, as their sustained examination of the Las Vegas Strip attests.)

These proposals implicitly rejected the modernist conception of the city as consecrated by CIAM: that is, a dense, efficient metropolis created and inhabited by rational technocrats whose planning is governed by a *Leitbild*, or guiding image.[51] Instead, they experimented with the late-twentieth-century notion of the urban environment as primarily a site of visual information, theorized in such texts as Kevin

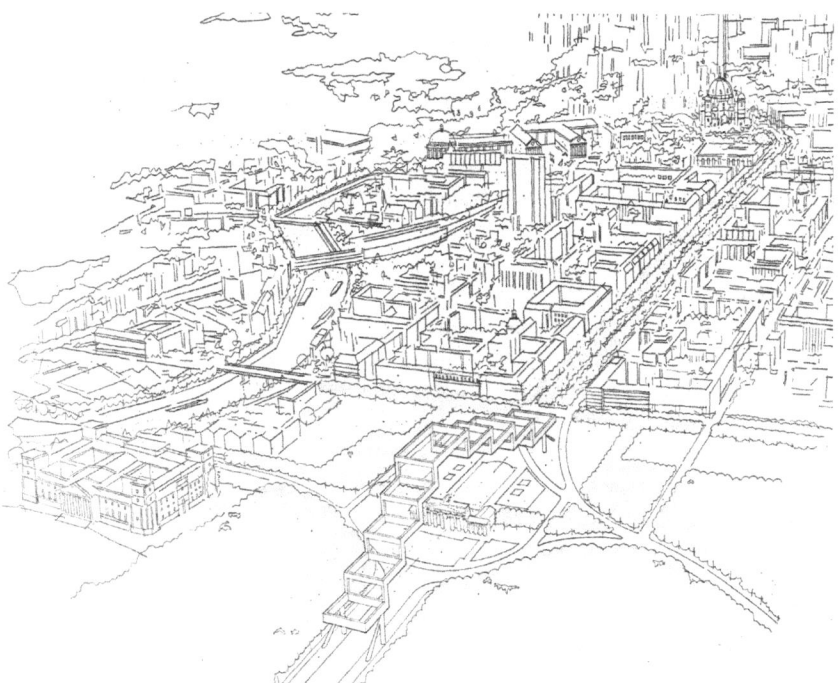

Figure 1.26 Robert Venturi and Denise Scott Brown, *Brandenburger Treppe*, 1990. In Carsten Krohn (Hrsg.), *Das ungebaute Berlin: Stadtkonzepte im 20. Jahrhundert*, Berlin: DOM Publishers, 2010, pp. 278–80. Architectural Archives, University of Pennsylvania by the gift of Robert Venturi and Denise Scott Brown.

Lynch's *The Image of the City*, Colin Rowe's *Collage City*, and Venturi, Scott Brown, and Steven Izenour's *Learning from Las Vegas*, which presented the city as a sensorial experience rather than a petrified urban form.[52] Ultimately, much like the Band des Bundes, *Berlin Tomorrow* is best understood as a medium of urban ideas. At a key moment in time, it introduced the public to new perceptual experiences of the city into which history, and historical fragments, might be fitted—if not exactly assimilated.

"A New Architectural Allegory"

In official state contexts even more than in commercial ones, planning debates following reunification played out on a public stage. As the international audience attuned to the Spreebogen's new master plan brought heightened scrutiny to the project, the Bundestag made clear from the beginning that consensus for the master plan would be reached openly and democratically ("transparency" remaining a powerful concept, if no longer the prevailing architectural metaphor that it had been in Bonn). Even before the competition opened, the Berlin Senate formed an advisory council known as the *Stadtforum*, whose open meetings provided the public an opportunity to air its opinions on the government's plans for the new federal district. At the same time, the Senate published and widely circulated a series of reports on city planning and architecture. Besides encouraging community participation in the process and fostering an atmosphere of openness around federal planning activity, these gestures, for some critics, offered the government a certain amount of protection against what they envisioned as inevitable blowback. They would merely provide the framework to build international consensus around a master plan, thus democratically enacting the will of the people.

In addition to its emphasis on public participation, the other overriding theme running through the Spreebogen competition proceedings was how to negotiate between Berlin's urban history and its future. While wholesale historical reconstruction seemed dangerous, not to mention impossible (how could a single period of Berlin's multilayered history even be chosen?), it was no longer tenable to wipe clean the urban slate and begin anew, as earlier competitions had done. Instead, it seemed a balance would have to be struck between respecting past precedents and proposing new forms, thus placing history and the present in a fragile equilibrium. Despite the range of positions espoused by architects, planners, and critics on how to rebuild Berlin, they nearly uniformly point to the necessity of *Vergangenheitsbewältigung*, or coming to terms with the past, in architecture as in the larger social and political context.[53]

But how that struggle might manifest in Berlin's urban environment was a subject that split the profession down the middle. On the one hand, proponents of so-called "Critical Reconstruction" (including Lampugnani, Senate Building Director Hans Stimmann, and the well-known Berlin architects Josef Paul Kleihues and Hans Kollhoff, among others) claimed that Berlin's rebuilding should draw on existing urban attributes that had withstood the test of time. This group of architects often found their anchor in Aldo Rossi's *The Architecture of the City* (1964), which argued that cities could be studied to discover typologies, styles, and urban contours that had endured through the centuries. In particular, Stimmann, who remained in his position from 1991 to 2006, contended that Berlin's future depended on reconstructing it as a "European city," which meant staving off the armies of glassy, idiosyncratic skyscrapers that were invading many contemporary downtowns.[54] To accomplish this historical consistency, he set architectural height limits and build-to lines in the city according to "traditional" parameters (which, for him, meant the classicizing commercial buildings of the 1920s), as well as advocating a return to stone as a material.[55] Stimmann's position, which he had espoused vehemently since the 1980s IBA (Internationale Bauaustellung), came increasingly to be associated with political conservatism.[56]

On the other side stood many of the giants of late-modern, high-tech architecture. This faction championed the view that the city's metamorphosis depended on its willingness to take architectural risks, forging new urban experiences that were appropriate to the time. Including Richard Rogers, Rem Koolhaas, and Daniel Libeskind (who argued against critical reconstruction passionately, claiming that Stimmann's approach "simply erase(d) fifty years of Berlin's history" in pursuit of "a more carefree age"), these architects embraced an ethos of fragmentation and experimentation.[57] Often associated in the press with left-leaning politics, these architects loosely shared a devotion to contemporary techniques, materials, and forms, as well as an interest in post-structuralist theories and digital technologies.[58] This fight between tradition and originality was one that had been brewing in international architectural circles for decades; by the early 1990s, it had escalated into a showdown between apparently incommensurable architectural philosophies with no possibility of resolution.[59]

The fervor on both sides of this ongoing dispute has obscured that a single premise underlies the entire discussion: in the contemporary city, history refuses to be ignored. From Kollhoff to Koolhaas, these architects unanimously, if unconsciously, believe that contemporary architecture's primary task is to deal responsibly with the remnants of history; the open question is merely what research methods and technical means might be employed to do so.[60] Yet these deeper commonalities have gone largely unrecognized, leading to what Huyssen has described as a "stifling architectural debate" between historicism and progressivism that does little to address the ambiguities of the New Berlin.[61]

This false dichotomy is one that has permeated discussions of the Spreebogen competition, contributing to the sense of frustration I described above. But the problems raised by Berlin's "architectural debates" go far beyond that city's boundaries.[62] Unacknowledged thus far is that the wider issue of how cities across the globe might contend with their own histories has characterized contemporary urban discourse overall. In some cases, new and old urban fabric are positioned artificially as opposites to be reconciled; in other cases, a superficial continuity running through the urban palimpsest is drawn out, often with grand metaphysical claims regarding the durability of tradition. But too few architects, planners, critics, and theorists have examined the processes of selection involved at every stage of design in this post-postmodern historical turn, nor have they confronted the often procrustean measures taken to grapple visibly with "history" in an urban context. The difficulty of escaping the historicist/progressive binary suggests that architectural historians would do well to find more subtle ways to probe the role of history at the Spreebogen, and in the contemporary city more generally.

Running from 1992 to 1993, the Spreebogen International Competition for Urban Design Ideas was the largest urban planning competition ever held, casting a vast net across the globe. "Throughout the world, from Egypt to Cyprus, the international urban planning ideas competition for the parliamentary and government district around the Reichstag building has aroused great interest," announced the *Neues Deutschland* (formerly the official party organ of East Germany) in July of 1992.[63] The final tallies reflected an astounding level of participation: 1,912 firms requested the brief, 835 submissions were entered, and a jury of twenty-three international representatives—architects, politicians, planners, and critics—convened to form the jury that reviewed these proposals in February of 1993.[64] To cope with this bewildering number of proposals, the jury met twice in Berlin for four days each, and each juror was given small reproductions of the plans bound into two dense volumes. Following this process, the models and drawings for all 835 submissions were displayed at an enormous exhibition in the former East German Council of State building, where the jury also met to make its selections. Despite the uncertain timeline for the transference of political functions from Bonn to Berlin, the reach of the competition demonstrates both the national and international excitement over the possible image the new democracy could take. Its staging across a range of venues, furthermore, shows us how this bit of political theater was meant to fan the flames of eager new developers and investors.[65] Unlike some competitions in the 1990s, in which the vast majority of competitors hailed from Europe or the United States, the Spreebogen claimed genuinely global participation, attracting submissions from fifty-four countries including Israel, Venezuela, India, South Africa, and Barbados.

As with the popularity of *Berlin Tomorrow*, this heady rush of global participation demonstrates the architectural euphoria that followed in the wake of reunification. The Spreebogen was consistent with other concurrent competitions in that its initial headlong pace seemed to stall quickly into eddies of doubt and controversy over every conceivable aspect of the building project at hand. The exhaustive brief drawn up for the Spreebogen called for a master plan of the area that would include buildings for the parliament offices, a chancellery, a press office, a press club, the German Parliamentary Association, and new accommodations for the Bundesrat. The guidelines of the competition specified a mixed-use zone at the government quarter, requiring that new residences, businesses, transit, and cultural sites be established along with government functions. Along with this diversity of use, the brief emphasized the importance of urban integration and historical connection. The idea, according to the Bundestag, was to find "exemplary solutions to the problem of bringing together the two halves of the city at this place marked by the deep historical division between East and West Berlin."[66] According to Bundestag President Rita Süssmuth,

The new quarter in the Spreebogen should become an integrated part of the unified city of Berlin. For this to happen, not only must the Spreebogen's urban texture and urban spaces acquire meaningful links with the adjacent neighborhoods, but the architectural expression of its new building must also be convincingly integrated into the Berlin cityscape. Integration of the parliamentary quarter along these lines would also correspond to the self-awareness of the German Bundestag as an open and accessible parliament close to the people.[67]

The influx of submissions reflected a striking range of firm profiles, suggesting just how seductive Berlin's postreunification promise of opportunity appeared. Proposals arrived from some expected international firms—Foster + Associates, Murphy/Jahn, and Coop Himmelb(l)au were all represented, for example—but smaller, unknown groups from around the world tossed their hats into this promising ring as well. As in the Reichstag competition (see Chapter 2), the submissions as a whole might be more revealing in their similarities rather than in their differences, and in what those similarities disclose about official contemporary planning. Most notably, we might observe the way in which the overwhelming majority of schemes made an effort to eschew the language of traditional official urban plans, often jettisoning symmetry, strong axes, and hierarchical groupings of buildings.

For example, the Los Angeles-based firm Morphosis, headed by Thom Mayne, aimed to avoid what they saw as the historical means of representing government: "the courtly language of classical forms with powerful symmetries means to emphasize the moral authority of the State."[68] Instead, the firm's plan (Figure 1.27) drew together elements of the collision, imperfection, and heterogeneity that, in their view, were characteristic of global contemporary culture. Using existing elements of the Spreebogen landscape—the topography of the river's path and the emerging spur of the Humboldthafen, as well as the rectangles of the Platz der Republik and the Reichstag—Morphosis created a geometric schema of a series of arcs swooping evocatively around the perimeter of the site. These calligraphic arcs would then translate into two types of "walls:" building walls and landscape walls. Rather than isolating government functions in stiff, block-like buildings, they would instead be housed in curved slabs raised on Corbusian pilotis, thus maintaining the public space at the pedestrian level. These buildings took the form of "undulating, ribbonlike low rise buildings," while landscape walls of pathways and garden elements would give shape to the site and regulate circulation.[69] This arrangement, according to Anthony Vidler, contested the very form of governance, offering instead an arrangement that "deconstructs the bureaucratic infinities and closures of modern life."[70]

Morphosis's intention was to body forth an alternative idea of political unity while refusing to aggrandize the state itself. As they wrote, "All of this challenges the isolation, autonomy, and monumentalization of government."[71] Other competitors, like the Portuguese firm ARX, explicitly referred to the post-structuralist notion of the city-as-text in their competition materials, positioning the viewer as a "reader" navigating Berlin's voids. Stressing the necessity of historical research, ARX employed a recognizably deconstructivist syntax in their project to comment on the obsolescence

Figure 1.27 Morphosis, proposal for the Spreebogen, Berlin, 1992–3. Morphosis.

of the centralized, hierarchical state and its outdated planning.⁷² As the architects stated, "This notion of center, related to the specificity of the program, which tries to define a new center for Germany, is also a typical romantic ideal of past centuries."⁷³

What these plans had in common was their commitment to the use of a late modernist idiom, however fractured and nonhierarchical, that reflected the methods of critical investigation at the core of their design processes—that set of contemporary artistic practices that Hal Foster has described as "ethnographic."⁷⁴ For her firm's proposal, the German architect Dagmar Richter, then a faculty member at the University of California Los Angeles (UCLA), gathered historical maps of the site to detect the spatial orders that had developed along axes of power. Richter's research studio of UCLA students then extrapolated these maps into conceptual models that provided the basis for her plan.⁷⁵ As with the work of Morphosis and ARX, Richter avoided expressions of "stasis, timelessness, and authoritarian comfort," aiming instead at "a formal transformation of the signs latent in these maps" to express "simultaneous realities at all times."⁷⁶ But Richter, like many others involved in the competition, found the discourse surrounding the competition to oscillate between two blinkered positions: on the one hand, the tired modernism/transparency/democracy axiom, and on the other, the cluster of associations that Stimmann and his cohort had gathered around the idea of Europeanism, which she saw as a form of conservative power-brokering. In a 1996 essay published in *Assemblage*, she assailed these stultifying polemics, arguing that the truly original thinking of some of the competition proposals was dead in the water of this theoretical morass.[77]

As Richter's frustration indicates, an air of disappointment set in nearly immediately after the conclusion of the competition, shared equally among architects, critics, and jurors. The dissatisfaction was manifold, rooted, in the first place, in a sense that such a massive and expensive process (overall, it cost the Bundestag 4 million deutsche marks) should have produced stronger results. Charles Jencks declared the entire process a "fiasco," arguing that the absence of compelling responses for "an exceptionally auspicious site and program, undoubtedly the most significant in the world today" was evidence of the pervasive confusion that characterized the architectural profession worldwide in the 1990s.[78] Writing in *The Atlantic*, the critic Ellen Posner dismissively grouped the proposals into

> ... grids, semi-circles, skyscrapers, groups of small low buildings, polite classically inspired schemes, arrangements of oddly angled shards, a few nihilistic and apocalyptic entries, several anthropomorphic designs, and one that looked like a serving of eggs and vegetables.[79]

Here, Posner collapsed the historicist/progressive dichotomy, reducing the range of responses to a glib taxonomy of contemporary architecture. In this derisive system of classification, Posner suggests that contemporary architecture as a whole prizes form over content, resorting continually to a few, predictable stylistic ploys. (Amplifying her argument, Jencks acidly chimed in: "No bananas, no cocktail sticks?"[80])

Not surprisingly, both Posner and Jencks exaggerate the weakness of the competition submissions. Yet it would be difficult to deny that, taken together, the proposals appear eager to sidestep questions of political representation and meaning, opting more frequently to reflect contemporary architectural processes—or, as in the case of the proposals from Morphosis and ARX, to meditate on the nature of statecraft itself. According to jury members, discussions of these plans often mirrored this palpable anxiety, taking the form of apprehensive debates over what counted as monumentality at the end of the twentieth century. Jurors from within the Bundesrepublik were especially concerned to avoid anything that seemed like an overaggressive or monumental representation of the new democracy, leaning repeatedly toward the most modest and self-effacing proposals. It was foreign jury members, including New York-based architects Richard Meier and Karen Van Lengen, who swayed them in the direction of a more assertive statement.[81] After much discussion, eight proposals were selected as the prizewinners. Of these eight, five were oriented along a clear east–west axis, and four recommended a return to the "traditional" urban planning ideals that had defined the area, proposing new symmetry for the Platz der Republik and networks of bridges and pathways radiating into the arc of the Spreebogen. Out of the premiated choices, Schultes and Frank's plan slowly accumulated approval among the jury and among the vocal parties in Berlin; Bonn's representatives were more reluctant to endorse it but were gradually swayed.[82] Eventually, after reconvening for one final discussion, the jury voted in favor of awarding it first prize, with 16 for and 7 opposed.[83]

Figure 1.28 Schultes Frank Architekten, proposal for the Spreebogen, Berlin, 1992–3. Bundsarchiv-Bildarchiv, Berlin.

Though the vote was hardly unanimous, transcripts of the jury's discussions suggest that Schultes and Frank's proposal garnered more unequivocal enthusiasm than any of the hundreds of other submissions at hand (Figure 1.28).[84] Perhaps one of its attractions was that it made a forceful statement that was nonetheless difficult to classify, as its critical reception attests, having been labeled variously as "hypermodern," "supermodern," "postmodern," "classical," "romantic," and "baroque." In the context of Berlin's planning politics, it seemed to lie neither quite to the "left" nor "right" of the debate, but, in many ways, to bridge concerns expressed by both sides. In the master plan, the Band des Bundes appears as a long, rectilinear urban strip bound by curved ends, 1.5 kilometers long and 110 meters wide. The Band would run perpendicular to the footprint of the Reichstag building, twice crossing the Spree with footbridges. Offices for the parliament and its committees were housed in the buildings to the east, balanced visually and symbolically by the Chancellery and Chancellor's garden to the west. A public park lay to the north, and the redeveloped Alsenviertel and new central train station would ensure plenty of lively quotidian traffic through the area. To the south, the Platz der Republik would take new form, defined by the Reichstag and a new building for the Bundesrat. In keeping with the guidelines of the competition, the architects did not specify the forms or materials of the individual buildings in the Band, but they suggested that the buildings be constructed from concrete and glass, thus creating a provocative play between lightness and monumental solidity.

For some critics, Schultes and Frank's design represented the triumph of modernism at a site where modernist schemes had continually failed to materialize. The slab buildings of the 1920s reappear in their proposal arranged like dominos into one monumental row, in a Weimar-inspired composition of dynamic, abstract geometry. Likewise, the plan's indebtedness to the 1960s has been repeatedly pointed out, given its obvious evocations of the architecture of Louis Kahn (the architect whose influence Schultes most frequently cites) and the concrete forms of later Le Corbusier.[85] Indeed, it shares with these precedents the powerfully raw sensation of what William Curtis described as "the ancient in the modern."[86] At the same time, however, the Band recollects the experimental megastructures of the 1960s, such as Superstudio's *Continous Monument* (Figure 1.29).[87] The Italian group Superstudio termed their concept "an architectural model for total urbanization," and their satirical idea was that this gridded superstructure would eventually cover the entire surface of the globe, eliding urban difference and providing a uniform standard of living worldwide with a single architectural act. Certainly, these twentieth-century plans seem embedded in the very concept of the Band. However, others have observed that Schultes and Frank relied on many of the same planning principles—a strong emphasis on symmetry, axes and axial links, a clustering of government buildings into one more or less single-use area, and formally landscaped open spaces for gatherings and recreation—as did many

Figure 1.29 Superstudio, *Monumento Continuo, New York*, c. 1969. Color crayon, felt tip pen, photomontage, 71.5 x 102 cm. Musée National d'Art Moderne, Centre Georges Pompidou, Paris. © CNAC/MNAM, Dist. RMN-Grand Palais / Art Resource, NY.

planners from the nineteenth century who proposed designs for the Spreebogen, from Lenné to Schinkel. Yet the Band des Bundes is not a pastiche of these earlier plans; rather, their forms bob to the surface of the Band-like fragments floating in a primordial soup, defying easy stylistic classification. As Janet Ward has observed, the Band "provides the formerly divided Berlin with a bridge across the former border: an act of which the sociologist of modern urbanity, Georg Simmel, would have been proud" (Ward's claim was echoed by mayor of Berlin Eberhard Diepgen, who described it as a "harmonic solution" that spanned East and West with a "bridging form.")[88]

Once Schultes and Frank's proposal was announced as the competition winner, its reception was predictably divided. The parliamentarian Peter Conradi, who had trained as an architect and was closely involved in the Bundestag's architectural decisions, deemed it excessively monumental and pompous—or "Speer quer," as he described it (roughly translating to "Speer crisscross").[89] On the other hand, the *Washington Post* praised how the "simple arrangement" provided a clear "link between two halves of the city."[90] "The linear flow," continued the author, "is faintly suggestive of Washington's Mall," thus aligning the plan with other democratic spaces.[91] And whereas Conradi had interpreted the Band des Bundes as an arrogant statement of nationalist intentions, a writer for the Italian architecture magazine *Domus* described it as "the most reassuring solution" for its cancellation of the site's most painful history: "Schultes collects the main buildings in an ordered linear band arranged with an east-west orientation along the hypothetical chord of the arc, thus denying the north-south axis of Speerian memory."[92] Interestingly, critics and boosters of the plan saw in it a striking clarity: on the one hand, its detractors perceived it as an overblown, Wilhelmine stronghold, while on the other, its supporters saw it as elegant, organized, and transparently simple.

But Schultes concisely stated during the competition that he had no interest in attempting to communicate a single narrative or idea with the Band des Bundes.[93] In a presentation to the Bundestag, he quoted Aldo Rossi, saying, "In our times, our capacity for synthesis is broken; we can only offer fragments."[94] Given this fragmentation, Schultes suggested that what was needed for the government district was not a single idea but rather what he called a "Spreebogen convention," an urban lingua franca assembled from the site's historical detritus.[95] It was only within this convention, he argued, that a viewer could make the connections necessary to "link the virtues of each place together."[96] To counterpose the somewhat fortress-like appearance of the Band, the architects intended to place a "Bürgerforum" for public gatherings at its center. This open, public forum, Schultes felt, would be the most important place in the federal district. It was to contain a variety of public spaces, including a library, a cafe, and a sort of amphitheater in which citizens could demonstrate or simply hang out, all in the name of, as Schultes put it, "heal(ing) themselves of the malady of being German."[97] The forum would also provide a necessary break in the linearity of the form, creating rupture and ambiguity rather than a powerful, unified message.

In order to understand how history resurfaces in the Band des Bundes as a set of linkages, we might first attend to Schultes's claim that the goal of the plan was to "pour [the Spreebogen's] historical and spatial dimensions into the mold of a new architectural allegory."[98] The notion of allegory addresses questions of cohesion, of the conflicting impulses to come together or unify and the opposite, to disperse. In describing his firm's proposal to the jury, Schultes made clear his preoccupation with architecture's structural relationship to language, a notion that had been invigorated by many postmodern theorists, from Charles Jencks to Peter Eisenman. For Schultes, architecture explores not only what the built environment says but also analyzes its means of signification. In his text for the competition, Schultes played with the multiple significances of the word *Bund*: most obviously, it refers to the German federation, but it also indicates a link or a bond between disparate objects or concepts. (It is worth noting that such semantic layering is characteristic of allegory in both its classical and postmodern guises.) He further claimed that the political body of the Bund would offer the "missing link" needed to create coherence both in politics and urbanism.[99] In other words, the German Bund would provide the linguistic connection necessary for the Spreebogen to be a legible text.

To Schultes, allegory is the key formal device governing his and Frank's master plan. Even more significantly, it is the mode in which the plan of the Spreebogen discloses its historical and political past, as its meaning is continuously deferred or absent. The Band des Bundes is not self-contained, but rather communicates by drawing a link with something unlike itself: the *allos*, or other, leading to this layered plan in which the ghosts of Spreebogens past push their way into the present. Schultes summons allegory for its open-endedness and denial of the very possibility of straightforward interpretation. This application of the term conjures Walter Benjamin, whose writings Schultes regularly cites in his own.[100] According to Benjamin, it is the "common practice" of allegory "to pile up fragments ceaselessly, without any strict idea of a goal," in the very way in which Schultes's plan accrues images from the past with no resolution.[101] In Benjamin's conception of allegorical structure, "history does not assume the form of the process of an eternal life so much as that of irresistible decay. Allegory thereby declares itself to be beyond beauty."[102] Allegory presented itself, in Benjamin's thinking, at times of profound political disquiet, and therefore proffered the most accurate literary representation of real-world experience. It seems likely that Schultes and Frank found the trauma of reunification to be just such a moment. Benjamin characterizes literary allegory in architectural terms in a way that would almost certainly resonate with Schultes, born in war-torn Dresden in 1943 and raised among the rubble in Berlin: "Allegories are, in the realm of thoughts, what ruins are in the realm of things."[103]

It is telling, then, that Schultes would describe his firm's master plan as an allegory of unification rather than as a symbol, with the high-modernist implications of fullness and resolution attending the latter. In Schultes and Frank's plan, unity, whether political, historical, or urban, is manifested as a desire rather than as reality. The Band des Bundes does not represent a mythical post-Wende German state, but rather invokes the yearning subtending the very idea of unification. Viewed allegorically, the Band makes its own fragility clear, showing that the connections it makes are delicate and contingent; the Bund is the "missing link" that is nonetheless temporary and vulnerable to the vagaries of history. Schultes invokes allegory not to show the inviolability of reunification, but rather its frailty. He refers to the Spreebogen's past not to create a heroic narrative culminating in the present, but rather to show the process of breakages through which the present has been reached. Schultes and Frank's master plan shows us that, in his view, the only form possible at the Spreebogen is one that exposes the site's various ruptures instead of overlaying it with a false veneer of unity. It is only in this manner that the Spreebogen's multiple histories can be "linked together."

Bridging and Breaking

But when it comes to architecture, the device of allegory is one that is difficult to pin down, Schultes's eloquent efforts notwithstanding. What Schultes and Frank's plan offers, ultimately, is a diagnosis of history's assiduous infiltration into the New Berlin and a structure, both linguistic and architectural, for how urban planning might begin to cope with that fact. But beyond its designers' intentions, what the Band des Bundes reveals is a quandary that planners are charged with the task of unraveling in even those contemporary cities with apparently less Gordian histories than Berlin's. This condition is the way in which certain elements of history endure, requiring that bridges be constructed between them for temporal coherence; and the way in which other historical elements constantly rise up, disrupting and breaking those bridges. Schultes and Frank's Band des Bundes shows us how contemporary architecture attempts to make historical meaning, not as a contained and unified symbol, but as a fragmented collection of discrete objects. Unconsciously, then, the Band invokes not only the plans described above; that is, the officially sanctioned fragments of the Spreebogen's past included in the competition materials, and those from outside imposed by its architects. It also engages a history of planning in Berlin that thematizes the bridging and breaking of urban form across time's inconsistent path.

We might return here to Ward's tantalizing suggestion that the true function of the Band is as a *bridge*. As Simmel explained it in his 1909 essay "Bridge and Door," the bridge is not only an architectonic form, but is more importantly an organizing function whose purpose is to order the external world. As evidence of the human "will to connection," the bridge acts simultaneously to unite and to distinguish the matter in which it intervenes.[104] Furthermore, it suspends those operations in permanent flux, such that meaning constantly vibrates between connectivity and dissolution. Simmel notes, "Only to humanity, in contrast to nature, has the right to connect and separate been granted, and in the distinctive manner that one of these activities is always the presupposition of the other."[105] The bridge, therefore, is human-centric, if not exactly humanist; it is an externalization of human volition onto the nonhuman world.

The bridge is distinct from other linear forms; unlike a boulevard, it does not necessarily create space, and unlike an axis, it does not create hierarchical arrangements. At the same time, it is not simply an encompassing urban-architectural arrangement analogous to the megastructure, the superblock, or the linear city. Rather, its primary function is to place historical fragments in tentative and temporary relation to one

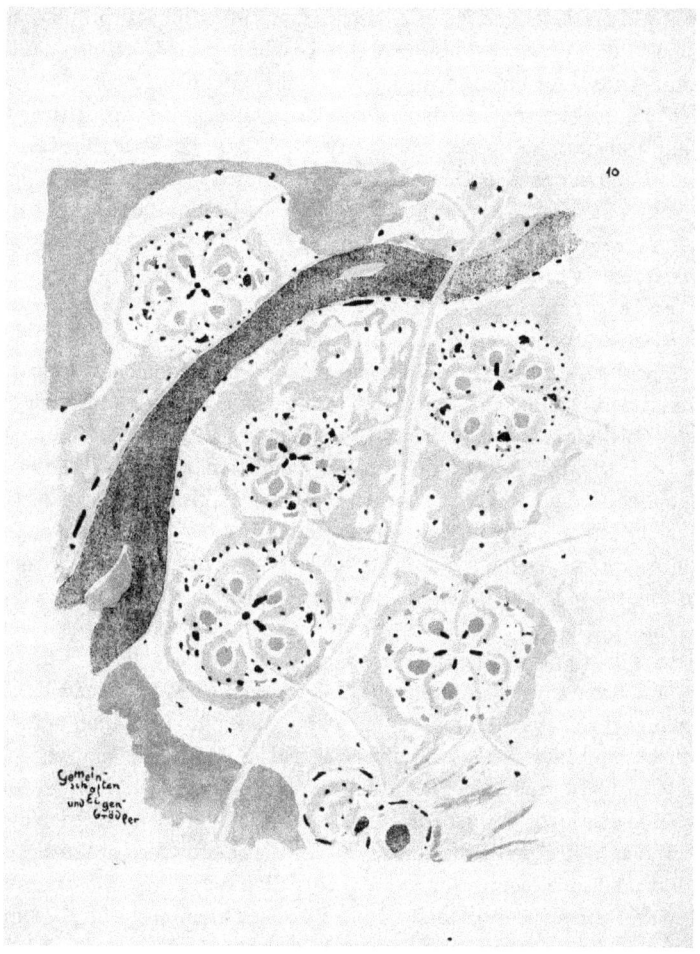

Figure 1.30 Bruno Taut, *Gemeinschaften und Eigenbrödler (Communities and Loners)*, from *Die Auflösung der Städte*, 1920.

another, manifesting Simmel's "will to connection" in the built environment. Understanding the Band des Bundes as a bridge calls our attention to the fragments poised within the uniting form and places it in conversation with a host of historical plans that deal with these coincident effects of bridging and breaking. In so doing, an alternative history of urban planning emerges as present in the Band, one that includes not only the utopian Weimar plans described above but also those that reverse their constructive course, chief among them Bruno Taut's *Die Auflösung der Städte* (*The Dissolution of the Cities*) of 1920 (Figure 1.30). This short treatise included thirty drawings, many rendered in vibrant color, in which Taut illustrated the end of the metropolis and the dissemination of urban functions into a natural, primordial setting. We might also start to see how historical "bridges" in Berlin—Unter den Linden itself, for example, whose breadth and span Schultes and Frank's Band invokes, as well as van Eesteren's 1925 project and Libeskind's *Über den Linden*—float to the surface in the Band, while also anticipating their own decay.

To understand the cycle of growth and decay suggested by the Band-as-bridge and its implications for Schultes and Frank's master plan, it is productive to turn to a few specific projects from this alternative history of planning in Berlin. One of the most significant voices against empty historicism and the "Europeanization" of the city is Rem Koolhaas, whose firm, Office for Metropolitan Architecture (OMA), has been among the most prominent actors in the New Berlin. Indeed, the theme of decay runs throughout Koolhaas's work as a theorist, architect, and planner.[106] Looking back on his career, it emerges that Berlin's impact on Koolhaas's thinking was formative, instilling in him a sense of decay as both an inevitable natural process and a savage ordering force. Koolhaas's childhood was spent in Rotterdam and Amsterdam, amid the wreckage of the war. Showing a linguistic preoccupation similar to Schultes's, his first professional pursuits were not architecture but rather journalism and filmmaking. "In a script," he says, "you have to link various episodes together, you have to generate suspense and you have to assemble things—through editing, for example. It's exactly the same in architecture. Architects also put together spatial episodes to make sequences."[107]

Koolhaas's first encounter with Berlin came as a student during the required Summer Study course of the Architectural Association (AA), the mandate for which was a prolonged analysis of a single architectural object. In opposition to the favored Greek villages and Italian villas, Koolhaas elected to visit Berlin, arriving in August 1971, ten years to the month after the initial construction of the Berlin Wall. Seeing the Wall triggered a series of "reverse epiphanies" that Koolhaas documented in his project *The Berlin Wall as Architecture* (Figure 1.31), which he presented at the AA upon his return (and published later in his seminal collection *S,M,L,XL*).[108] He painstakingly researched the formal history of the Wall and illustrated his project with photomontages that irresistibly recalled the precedents of the avant-garde. (For example, a souvenir postcard of the Brandenburg Gate with a collaged airplane plainly evokes a photomontage with a giant dirigible made by Ivan Leonidov for his Linear City project.) In his study, Koolhaas sought not to condemn the Wall in political terms, but rather to read it against the grain as architecture, noting especially its high-modernist ability to make a maximum of architectural impact with a minimum of intervention; in the Wall, less was much, much more. He was struck by how its materiality—so monolithic in the imagination of the "free world," a part of which it cordoned off and confined—was anything but, integrating functioning buildings that happened to lie in its path, incorporating ruins when it encountered them, ranging from concrete slab to bricks to tangles of barbed wire in some of its most far-flung sections. He noted with amazement that some portions of the Wall comprised nothing but piled-up garbage—heavily guarded, of course.

Koolhaas's close reading led him to argue that bridging and breaking, or construction and decay, were not opposing forces. Rather, they were two sides of the same coin,

Figure 1.31 Rem Koolhaas, *The Berlin Wall as Architecture*, 1971. Reproduced in Rem Koolhaas and Bruce Mau, *S,M,L,XL: O.M.A.*, 1997. Used with permission of Rem Koolhaas, from *S,M,L,XL: O.M.A.*, Rem Koolhaas and Bruce Mau, 1997; permission conveyed through Copyright Clearance Center, Inc.

inherent in any act of architecture. "*The Berlin Wall was a very graphic demonstration of the power of architecture and some of its unpleasant consequences*," he argued. "Were not division, enclosure (i.e. imprisonment), and exclusion ... the essential stratagems of *any* architecture?"[109] He points out that, "in narrowly architectural terms, the Wall was not an object but an erasure, a freshly created absence ... it was the first demonstration of the capacity of the void—of nothingness—to 'function' with more efficiency, subtlety, and flexibility than any object you could imagine in its place."[110] He noted that in the Wall's decade-long life to that point, it had "provoked and sustained an incredible number of events, behaviors, and effects," from routine daily procedures to unplanned, deadly standoffs.[111] He was fascinated by the way in which the wall functioned as "a vast system of ritual," noting that it "was a *script*, effortlessly blurring divisions between tragedy, comedy, melodrama."[112] Finally, he concluded provocatively that "[t]he greatest surprise" was that "the Wall was heartbreakingly beautiful."[113]

Koolhaas's indecorous take on the Wall is often trotted out by journalists in interviews or newspaper profiles in order to demonstrate that the architect's provocateurist tendencies were present even at the beginning of his career.[114] But the more salient issue here is how he offers a different slant not only on the Wall, but also on the Band des Bundes itself. Koolhaas's descriptions of the Wall's architectural force

Figure 1.32 Rem Koolhaas, Elia Zenghelis, Madelon Vriesendorp, and Zoe Zenghelis, *Exodus, or the Voluntary Prisoners of Architecture, The Strip, Project, Aerial Perspective*, 1972. Cut-and-pasted paper with watercolor, ink, gouache, and color pencil on gelatin silver photograph, 40.6 x 50.5 cm. Museum of Modern Art, New York. Gift of Patricia Phelps de Cisneros. Takeo Ohbayashi Purchase Fund, and Susan de Menil Purchase Fund. Digital Image © The Museum of Modern Art/Licensed by SCALA / Art Resource, NY.

show us that Schultes and Frank confronted an impossible fragment bobbing to the surface of their own project. After all, the Wall achieved the ambitions pursued by much contemporary architecture. It was effective and efficient, it was modernist in material and execution; but at the same time it was visually powerful, becoming a global architectural icon that remains indelible today for those imagining the city of Berlin. By exposing the Wall's qualities qua architecture, Koolhaas reveals architecture's inability to cope with it as history. Koolhaas would continue to explore the Wall's perverse architectural potency in later projects, such as *Exodus, or the Voluntary Prisoners of Architecture*, completed in 1973, in which city dwellers would consent to living in "a prison on the scale of a metropolis," in Terence Riley's words (Figure 1.32).[115] Ultimately, we might see Koolhaas's impish take on the wall as a reflection on the way in which architecture necessarily proceeds from entropy to order—and back, inevitably, to entropy.

That entropy brings us back to the Band des Bundes—and back to Schultes's desire for a "new architectural allegory." For in essence, Schultes and Frank got the allegory they never wanted, one that narrates, as Craig Owens described the "allegorical impulse," "its own contingency, insufficiency, lack of transcendence."[116] As Owens noted, such an impulse "tells of a desire that must be perpetually deferred," a prognosis that has been borne out in the Band des Bundes as it exists today (Figure 1.33).[117] Since its completion in 2006, Schultes and Frank's design has been met with what can only be described as general disappointment. Few Germans have expressed satisfaction with it, and critics are divided between those who claim that the Band des Bundes is too imposing to be appropriate to Germany's charged history and those who find it bewilderingly aloof about its claims to national identity. Certainly, the master plan as it was built has a curiously unfinished quality, the result of a series of budgetary cuts and politically motivated alterations to the original scheme. For example, there was strong government pressure to raise the parapet of the Chancellery above the other buildings, significantly recasting the architects' original vision of the Band's equilibrium of powers. The Bundesrat is now housed in a neoclassical early-twentieth-century building nearby, leaving the Platz der Republik as an ill-defined clearing that awkwardly cedes to the Tiergarten, despite the efforts of landscape architects to delimit it. The Chancellery and its garden, both of which Schultes also designed (see Chapter 3), cross the Spree but with a far shorter enclosing wall than originally planned, so that it is challenging to detect the garden except in an aerial view; and Stephan Braunfels's Marie-Elisabeth-Lüders-Haus, the building that forms the easternmost section of the Band, stops

Figure 1.33 Spreebogen, Berlin, 2016. Aerial view.

abruptly well short of Friedrichstrasse, where Schultes and Frank originally intended it to terminate.[118] Perhaps most importantly, the Bürgerforum has all but disappeared as an architectural space and is now present only as an uncertain caesura in the Band between the Chancellery and the Paul-Löbe-Haus, with landscaped *allées* of trees, fountains, and vehicle traffic running through it.

When plans for these changes were finalized in 2001, Schultes defended his firm's original concept against a barrage of bad press, asserting that his feelings during the Spreebogen project hovered between "frustration and elation," more frequently tending toward the former.[119] Though the glassy shed of the central railway station, by Gerkan, Marg & Partners (gmp) was considered an infrastructural and architectural triumph, the rest of the area seemed surprisingly vague. The architecture critic Rainer Haubrich spoke with Schultes about his unrealized hopes for the project, reporting that Schultes could only "appeal to the imagination of the audience to imagine this Band at its best, and complain again that the 'heart' of his 'political-architectural concept,' the 'forum' between the Chancellery and the Bundestag blocks, has now been silently deleted."[120] Haubrich concluded that, at the Spreebogen, "only the void will rule."[121]

These frustrated plans stand in contrast to the coherence of the mixed-use area around the station, the subject of a 1994 master plan by O. M. Ungers. In 2020, the Danish firm 3XN unveiled their design for the area's final element, a faceted glass office block facing Washingtonplatz, to be known as the Berlin Cube. Yet as late as 2018, the breakages of Schultes and Frank's master plan continued. After years of equivocation, the Bundestag finalized its plans for traffic circulation in the area, with a road passing north through the Band before veering east toward Konrad-Adenauer-Strasse and the Kronprinzenbrücke. Though a road was laid during the Band's construction, it was for years presented as a temporary stopgap pending the completion of the tunnel under the Spree connecting the Landwehrkanal to the neighborhood of Moabit. The Bürgerforum has become yet another void haunting the Band. Dogged by the brutal effectiveness of the Wall, the Band des Bundes as built feels uncomfortably slack.

Schultes had imagined his design as a legible—at least, legibly allegorical—text; but in the built Band des Bundes, Schultes and Frank's own original proposal has become one more fragment of the past palimpsestically pushing its way into the present reality.[122] Famously, Benjamin was a proponent of allegory as a mode that reflected history's dialectical complexity. Schultes implicitly adopts this position in his written defense of the Band, but it is an impossible one to sustain. Finally, rather than writing its own history, his and Frank's plan becomes yet another of the Spreebogen's unrealized futures. In Benjamin's terms, master plans function as "the expression of an Idea," rather than as lived experience.[123] The master plan inherently exists beyond the view from the ground, perceptible only from a vantage point outside itself (from above, from the page). In theory, the pedestrian will experience or intuit the logic of a master plan without access to this totalizing view, but in fact, the pedestrian is always blind to the totality of the plan and its unbuilt pasts. Once within the master plan, the viewer cannot see the fragments infiltrating from below.

Notes

1 Andreas Huyssen has characterized as "voids" those absences in the city that were compulsively filled or erased during the postreunification building boom in order to make over Berlin into an easily consumable, image-driven capital city. See Huyssen, "The Voids of Berlin," in *Present Pasts: Urban Palimpsests and the Politics of Memory* (Stanford: Stanford University Press, 2003), 49–71.
2 Quoted in *Hauptstadt Berlin: Parlamentsviertel im Spreebogen-Internationaler Städtebaulicher Ideenwettbewerb 1993*, ed. Felix Zwoch (Berlin: Bauwelt/Birkhäuser, 1993), 49.
3 Ibid.
4 "Palast oder Dampfer," *Der Spiegel* (December 19, 1994), 172.
5 As Carol Anne Costabile-Heming phrases it in her essay on Berlin's postreunification building projects, "the very essence of Berlin seems to emerge from the remnants of the past that surreptitiously come into view from various corners." Costabile-Heming, "Berlin's History in Context: The Foreign Ministry and the *Spreebogen* Complex in the Context of the Architectural Debates," in *After the Berlin Wall: Germany and Beyond*, eds. Katharina Gerstenberger and Jana Evans Braziel (New York: Palgrave Macmillan, 2011), 232.
6 In this passage, Schneider describes architect Renzo Piano's struggle to define Potsdamer Platz, lying in the "wasteland at the heart of the city," before which the architect was "stumped by the task of creating urban life from this *tabula rasa*." Peter Schneider, *Berlin Now: The City after the Wall*, trans. Sophie Schlondorff (New York: Farrar, Straus and Giroux, 2014), 34.
7 See *Internationaler Städtebaulicher Ideenwettbewerb Spreebogen. Band 1: Bericht der Vorprüfung*, eds. Bernd Faskel and Günter Strey (Berlin: Oktoberdruck, 1993).
8 Rita Süssmuth, "Preface of the President of the German Bundestag," in Zwoch, 7.
9 Quoted in Sonja Dumpelmann, *Seeing Trees: A History of Street Trees in New York City and Berlin* (New Haven: Yale University Press, 2019), 223.
10 For a discussion of military maps of Berlin, including those produced by the engineer La Vigne in the seventeenth century, see David Buisseret, *The Mapmaker's Quest: Depicting New Worlds in Renaissance Europe* (Oxford: Oxford University Press, 2003), 135–8.
11 Wolfgang Sonne, "Ideas for a Metropolis: The Competition for Greater Berlin 1910," in *City of Architecture, Architecture of the City: Berlin 1900–2000*, eds. Thorsten Scheer, Josef Paul Kleihues, and Paul Kahlfeldt (Berlin: Nicolai, 2000), 74.
12 Quoted in Sonne, 73.
13 The title of van Eesteren's 1925 proposal was "Gleichgewicht," or "equilibrium," resonating with the later goals of the Band des Bundes. Though it was awarded first prize in a 1925 competition, the project as a whole for the rebuilding of Unter den Linden did not advance.
14 Christoph Asendorf, "Berlin: Three Centuries as Capital," in *Power and Architecture: The Construction of Capitals and the Politics of Space*, ed. Michael Minkenberg (New York and Oxford: Berghahn Books, 2014), 144.
15 As Dietrich Neumann points out, the evolution of the skyscraper in Germany was not straightforwardly modernist, since it often aligned with conservative desires to express the strength of German identity after World War I. Adolf Behne, among other critics,

cautioned against the drive toward monumental height and advised that high-rise buildings and axial planning were yet another expression of political imperialism, their modern materials notwithstanding. See Dietrich Neumann, "The Unbuilt City of Modernity," in *City of Architecture, Architecture of the City: Berlin 1900–2000*, 166–7.
16 Quoted in Sonne, "Berlin: Capital under Changing Political Systems," in *Planning Twentieth Century Capital Cities*, ed. David L. A. Gordon (New York: Routledge, 2006), 199.
17 Ibid.
18 Die Drei Rulands, a subversive cabaret act, satirized these megalomaniac plans by singing, "Yes, through Berlin it still flows, the Spree; but from tomorrow it'll run through the Charité," referring to the hospital north of the Spreebogen that had been established by Friedrich I. Kate Connolly, "Story of Cities #22: How Hitler's Germania Would Have Torn Berlin Apart," *The Guardian* (April 14, 2016), https://www.theguardian.com/cities/2016/apr/14/story-of-cities-hitler-germania-berlin-nazis.
19 For more on the detailed, if speculative, financial planning of Germania, see Wolfgang Schäche, *Architektur und Städtebau in Berlin zwischen 1933 und 1945–Planen und Bauen unter der Ägide der Stadtverwaltung* (Berlin: Gebrüder Mann, 1991).
20 Despite the cessation of construction activities, the GBI (Generalbauinspektor, both Speer's title and the name of the ministry of building) continued to bludgeon forward with plans for Berlin to be continued after the conclusion of the war. Architects to the political and aesthetic left continued their work on paper as well; only a few days before Germany surrendered to the Allies, Otto Kohtz produced a new draft of a project for the Spreebogen—ongoing since 1937—in which a dense field of elegantly stepped slab buildings were clustered inside the arc of the river.
21 For more discussion of how Berlin was used as a stage to enact Cold War face-offs through design and architecture, see Greg Castillo, *Cold War on the Home Front: The Soft Power of Midcentury Design* (Minneapolis: University of Minnesota Press, 2010).
22 Emily Pugh, *Architecture, Politics, and Identity in Divided Berlin* (Pittsburgh: University of Pittsburgh Press, 2014), 54.
23 In yet another Cold War deployment of culture in the form of architecture, the results of the competition were widely published, including in the lavish volume *Berlin: Ergebnis des Internationalen städtebaulichen Ideenwettbewerbs Hauptstadt Berlin* (Stuttgart: Krämer, 1960).
24 Hans Stephan, "Rebuilding Berlin," *The Town Planning Review* 29 (January 1959): 226.
25 CIAM itself would splinter only two years later after years of infighting and generational disputes. Several of the participants in the *Hauptstadt Berlin* competition, including the Smithsons, had become powerfully dissident voices against CIAM's doctrinal approach to urbanism and were instrumental in its planned dissolution by their group (known as Team X) at the 1959 congress in Otterlo. See Eric Mumford, "CIAM '59 in Otterlo and the End of CIAM," *The CIAM Discourse on Urbanism, 1928–1960* (Cambridge, MA: MIT Press, 2000), 258–66. For a discussion on the complex nature and legacy of modernism in Berlin in the 1940s and 1950s, see Francesca Rogier, "The Monumentality of Rhetoric: The Will to Rebuild in Postwar Berlin," in *Anxious Modernisms: Experimentation in Postwar Architectural Culture*, eds. Sarah Williams Goldhagen and Réjean Legault (Cambridge, MA: MIT Press, 2000), 165–90.
26 Quoted in Stephen Barber, *Berlin Bodies: Anatomizing the Streets of the City* (London: Reaktion Books, 2017), 238–9.

27 See Florian Urban, "Recovering Essence through Demolition: The 'Organic' City in Postwar West Berlin," *Journal of the Society of Architectural Historians* 63 (September 2004): 354–69.
28 See Diane Ghirardo, *Aldo Rossi and the Spirit of Architecture* (New Haven: Yale University Press, 2019), 127. Schultes and Frank took third prize in the 1988 competition.
29 In Simmel's words, "This is the fascination of the ruin, too; but in addition, the ruin has another one of the same order: the destruction of the spiritual form by the effect of natural forces, that reversal of the typical order, is felt as a return to the 'good mother,' as Goethe calls nature. Here the saying that all that is human 'is taken from earth and to earth shall return' rises above its sad nihilism." Georg Simmel, "The Ruin," in *Georg Simmel, 1858–1918: A Collection of Essays, with Translations and a Bibliography*, ed. Kurt H. Wolff (Columbus: Ohio State University Press, 1959), 262. I will discuss ruins more fully in Chapter 3.
30 In 1995, Ignasi de Solà-Morales defined the term *terrain vague* as describing those spaces that are marginal to the "legitimized" city, its "Unincorporated margins, interior islands void of activity, oversights" as well as its "residual spaces, its folded interstices." On the eve of their redevelopment, both Potsdamer Platz and Alexanderplatz appear in his essay as exemplary of this type of space, which he claims is characteristic of the contemporary city. In such spaces, he argued, architects and planners must consider carefully a fundamental problem: "How can architecture act in the *terrain vague* without becoming an aggressive instrument of power and abstract reason?" He concludes that architectural interventions must respect and acknowledge fragmentation and estrangement. Ignasi de Solà-Morales Rubió, "Terrain Vague," in *Anyplace*, ed. Cynthia C. Davidson (Cambridge, MA: MIT Press, 1995), 118–23.
31 Deborah Ascher Barnstone, *The Transparent State: Architecture and Politics in Postwar Germany* (New York: Routledge, 2005), 108.
32 Adolf Arndt, *Demokratie als Bauherr* (Berlin: Gebrüder Mann, 1961). Barnstone explores Bonn's insistence on this modernist idiom. See especially "Transparency in German Architecture before and after the War," 27–60.
33 Samuel Sadow details Bonn's postwar development in "Provisional Capital: National and Urban Identity in the Architecture and Urban Planning of Bonn, 1949–79" (PhD dissertation, CUNY Graduate Center, 2016).
34 Quoted in Zwoch, 49.
35 See, for example, Francesca Rogier, "Growing Pains: From the Opening of the Wall to the Wrapping of the Reichstag, *Assemblage* 29 (April 1996): 40–71; Klaus von Beyme, "Hauptstadtplanung von Bonn bis Berlin," in *Stadt als Erfahrungsraum der Politik. Beiträge zur kulturellen Konstruktion urbaner Politik*, ed. Wilhelm Hofmann (Berlin: LIT, 2011), 13–33; Elizabeth A. Strom, *Building the New Berlin: The Politics of Urban Development in Germany's Capital City* (Lanham, MD: Lexington Books, 2001); Janet Ward, *Post-Wall Berlin: Borders, Space and Identity* (Basingstoke: Palgrave Macmillan, 2011); and Claire Colomb, *Staging the New Berlin: Place Marketing and the Politics of Urban Reinvention Post-1989* (London and New York: Routledge, 2012).
36 Jürgen Habermas, *The Theory of Communicative Action*, trans. Thomas McCarthy (Boston: Beacon Press, 1984).
37 The architects represented in the show were Mario Bellini, Coop Himmelb(l)au, Norman Foster, Giorgio Grassi, Vittorio Gregotti, Zaha Hadid, John Hejduk, Jacques

Herzog/Pierre de Meuron/Rémy Zaugg, Josef Paul Kleihues, Hans Kollhoff, Daniel Libeskind, Jean Nouvel, Aldo Rossi, Denise Scott Brown/Robert Venturi, Manuel de Solà-Morales, Bernard Tschumi, and Oswald Mathias Ungers.

38 As Itohan Osayimwese has compellingly shown, the public channels of the city imaginary, especially exhibitions and expositions, were important vectors of social meanings in the early twentieth century, particularly important in disseminating racist and colonialist narratives to their viewership and promoting essentialist ideas of cultural difference. See Osayimwese, "Expositions in German Colonialism and German Architecture," in *Colonialism and Modern Architecture in Germany* (Pittsburgh: University of Pittsburgh Press, 2017), 21–60.

39 It is worth acknowledging, as the sociologist Rob Shields has noted, that all urban planning takes place through the means of "representations" (maps, drawings, models) that are far from objective representations of "reality": "If representations are souvenirs which serve to remind us of the city on the other hand they replace or stand in for the city. Representations are treacherous metaphors, *summarizing* the complexity of the city in an elegant model ... (they also) *displace* the city completely so that one ends by not dealing with the physical level of direct social exchange and brute arrangements of objects but with a surrogate level of signs. This arrangement of signs is a simulacrum which presents itself as 'reality.'" In my discussion, I seek not to overturn this claim, but simply to draw a distinction between the representations that Shields describes and those that are explicitly imaginative and do not present themselves as "reality." Rob Shields, "A Guide to Urban Representation and What to Do about It: Alternative Traditions of Urban Theory," *Re-Presenting the City: Ethnicity, Capital and Culture in the 21st-Century Metropolis* (London: Palgrave, 1996), 229.

40 For more on the newly public environment of planning in the 1990s, see Patsy Healey, "Planning through Debate: The Communicative Turn in Planning Theory," *The Town Planning Review* 63 (April 1992): 143–62.

41 Esra Akcan, "Stop VI: Open History in the Past Subjunctive Tense," in *Open Architecture: Migration, Citizenship, and the Urban Renewal of Berlin-Kreuzberg by IBA-1984/87* (Basel: Birkhäuser-de Gruyter, 2018), 298–335.

42 Strom, 119.

43 The critic and historian Witold Rybczynski coined the term "Bilbao Effect" in an article of the same name published in *The Atlantic* in September 2002. Numerous writers have defined it in brief by quoting the cryptic proclamation made famous by the popular 1989 film *Field of Dreams*, implying that a city's survival under the economic conditions of neoliberalism depends on its architecture's ability to attract international tourism. It is especially frequently invoked in discussions of the New Berlin.

44 Rainer Haubrich, "So wollten Architekten 1990 die Stadtmitte gestallten," *Berliner Morgenpost*, May 12, 2009, https://www.morgenpost.de/berlin/article104123563/So-wollten-Architekten-1990-die-Stadtmitte-gestalten.html.

45 Vittorio Magnano Lampugnani, "An Exhibition of Pictures," *Architectural Design* 92 (1991): 11. It is worth noting that Lampugnani would later become a strong proponent of Critical Reconstruction (or what he termed "New Simplicity"), which might temper our reading of his visionary rhetoric here. He begins the introduction to *Berlin Tomorrow*'s exhibition catalog by exalting "Berlin, that mythical metropolis of the 20s, immortalized in the literature of Walter Benjamin and Franz Hessel," shoring

up later critiques of Critical Reconstruction as defining *Berlinische Architektur* exclusively in terms of one period and style. Lampugnani, "Einleitung," in *Berlin Morgen: Ideen für das Herz einer Groszstadt*, eds. Vittorio Magnano Lampugnani and Michael Mönninger (Stuttgart: Gerd Hatje, 1991), 8.
46 Ibid.
47 As previously noted, Kollhoff's work was also featured in *Berlin Tomorrow*, and Ovaska submitted a proposal to the Spreebogen competition in 1992. Both projects thematize the "urban fragments" they pondered at Cornell.
48 For the contents of the pamphlet along with insightful commentary, see Florian Hertweck and Sébastien Marot, *The City in the City—Berlin: The Green Archipelago* (Zürich: Lars Müller, 2013).
49 John Hejduk, "The Potsdam Printer's House/Studio," in *Architectural Design* 92 (September 1991): 49.
50 Kenneth Frampton defines the megaform as a primarily horizontal form with a strong topographical character aimed at the densification of the urban landscape. See Kenneth Frampton, *Megaform as Urban Landscape: The 1999 Raoul Wallenberg Lecture* (Ann Arbor: University of Michigan Taubman College of Architecture + Urban Planning, 1999).
51 For a discussion of the role of the *Leitbild* in modernist German planning and its later critique, see Christopher Klemek, *The Transatlantic Collapse of Urban Renewal: Postwar Urbanism from New York to Berlin* (Chicago: University of Chicago Press, 2011).
52 Kevin Lynch, *The Image of the City* (Cambridge, MA: MIT Press, 1960). Colin Rowe, *Collage City* (Cambridge, MA: MIT Press, 1978). Robert Venturi, Denise Scott Brown, and Steven Izenour, *Learning from Las Vegas* (Cambridge, MA: MIT Press, 1972).
53 Jeffrey Herf elucidates the discourse of *Vergangenheitsbewältigung* in *Divided Memory: The Nazi Past in the Two Germanys* (Cambridge, MA: Harvard University Press, 1997).
54 Karen E. Till, *The New Berlin: Memory, Politics, Place* (Minneapolis: University of Minnesota Press, 2005), 45.
55 Tensions over "traditional" rebuilding reached their apex with the adoption of Stimmann's Planwerk Innenstadt (Inner-City Plan) in 1999, a sweeping—and, in many critics' eyes, reactionary—scheme for the development of the neighborhood of Mitte.
56 Naraelle Hohensee has insightfully analyzed how various political meanings came to be assigned to architectural form beginning in the 1980s. See Naraelle Hohensee, "Building in Public: Critical Reconstruction and the Rebuilding of Berlin after 1990" (PhD dissertation, CUNY Graduate Center, 2016). See also Florian Hertweck, *Der Berliner Architekturstreit: Architektur, Stadtbau, Geschichte und Identität in der Berliner Republik 1989-1999* (Berlin: Gebrüder Mann, 2010) and Karin Lenhart, *Berliner Metropoly: Stadtentwicklungspolitik Im Berliner Bezirk Mitte Nach Der Wende* (Opladen: Leske + Budrich, 2001).
57 Quoted in Brian Ladd, "Capital of the New Germany," in *The Ghosts of Berlin: Confronting German History in the Urban Landscape* (Chicago: University of Chicago Press, 1997), 233.
58 The perceived political alignment of both "camps" is itself facile, reflecting what Dietmar Schirmer has described as a "naïve interpretation" of architecture's political meaning. According to Schirmer, this interpretation is characterized by a "routine application of some simple and well-established schemata" to identify "architectural

attributes more or less explicitly with political forms of domination and their legitimating ideologies." See Schirmer, "Politik und Architektur, Ein Beitrag zur politischen Symbolanalyse am Beispiel Washingtons," in *Sprache des Parlaments und Semiotik der Demokratie: Studien zur politischen Kommunikation in der Moderne*, eds. Andreas Dörner and Ludgera Vogt (Berlin: Walter de Gruyter, 1995), 310.

59 On the intensity of these rivalries in Berlin, see Werner Sewing, "Berlinische Architektur," *ARCH+* 122 (June 1994): 60-9.

60 Consider, for example, Koolhaas's claim regarding the design for his Dutch Embassy, in which "every move through (the building) reveals Berlin's history." Quoted in Samira Chandwani, "Koolhaas Speaks On 'Global' Style," *Cornell Daily Sun*, April 26, 2005, http://www.cornellsun.com/vnews/display.v/ART/2005/04/26/426ddebcc1992.

61 Andreas Huyssen, "After the War," *Harvard Design Magazine* (Winter/Spring 2000): 1–5.

62 For more on Germany's specific debates, see Gavriel D. Rosenfeld, "The Architects' Debate: Architectural Discourse and the Memory of Nazism in the Federal Republic of Germany, 1977–1997," *History and Memory* 9 (Fall 1997): 189–225.

63 "Weltweites Interesse am Spreebogen-Wettbewerb," *Neues Deutschland*, July 7, 1992.

64 Zwoch, back cover.

65 "Go East, Young Man!," *The Banker*, May 1, 1992, 50.

66 Süssmuth, in Zwoch, 7.

67 Ibid.

68 Thom Mayne, *Morphosis: Buildings and Projects, 1993-1997* (New York: Rizzoli, 1999), appendix 11.2.

69 Arthur Lubow, "How Did He Become the Government's Favorite Architect?," *The New York Times Magazine*, January 16, 2005, 28–33.

70 Anthony Vidler, "Death Cube 'K': the Neoformations of Morphosis," in *Warped Space: Art, Architecture, and Anxiety in Modern Culture* (Cambridge, MA: MIT Press, 2000), 212.

71 Mayne, appendix 11.5.

72 ARX itself was international in its composition, as several members of the team were American and one of its founding members, Takashi Yamaguchi, was a Japanese-born and -trained architect who had spent his early career working for Tadao Ando. Their Spreebogen proposal was published in an issue of *ANY*, including a selection of the faxes submitted by the members of ARX during the competition. See *ANY: Architecture New York* 3 (November/December 1993).

73 Zwoch, 62.

74 Hal Foster, "The Artist as Ethnographer," in *The Return of the Real: The Avant-Garde at the End of the Century* (Cambridge, MA: MIT Press, 1996), 171–204.

75 See Dagmar Richter, Claire Zimmerman, and Anthony Vidler, *XYZ: The Architecture of Dagmar Richter* (New York: Princeton Architectural Press, 2001), 83–8.

76 Dagmar Richter, "Spazieren in Berlin," *Assemblage* 29 (April 1996): 74.

77 Ibid. Richter's was one of several proposals originating from the United States that was covered extensively in architectural journals; another was New York-based Asymptote Architecture's proposal in Hani Rashid and Lise Anne Couture, "Analog Space to Digital Fields: Asymptote Seven Projects," *Assemblage* 21 (August 1993): 24–43. The twelve proposals from New York firms were also displayed at a 1993 exhibition at the Goethe House titled *Berlin: Designing a Capital for the 21st Century*.

78 Charles Jencks, *The Architecture of the Jumping Universe* (London: Academy Editions, 1995), 18.
79 Ellen Posner, "Hell's Capital," *The Atlantic Monthly*, July 1, 1994, 95.
80 Jencks, 19.
81 See Karen Van Lengen, "Scheme for New Berlin Government Center Awaits Approval," *Architecture* 82 (September 1993): 28–31.
82 Ladd, 227.
83 Galetti, 224.
84 See *Internationaler Städtebaulicher Ideenwettbewerb Spreebogen. Band 3: Protokoll des Preisgerichts*, eds. Bernd Faskel and Günter Strey (Berlin: Oktoberdruck, 1993).
85 Schultes frankly acknowledged this influence: as he put it, "Louis Kahn or Corbusier will see to this place alright." In Axel Schultes Architekten, *Spreebögen Wettbewerb und Überarbeitung* (Berlin: Aedes Galerie für Architektur und Raum, 1993), exhibition catalog, 13. I discuss Schultes's reliance on Kahn's work in detail in Chapter 3.
86 See William J. R. Curtis, "The Ancient in the Modern," in *Architecture in India*, eds. Raj Rewal, Jean-Louis Verét, and Ram Sharma (Paris: Association Française d'Action Artistique, 1985).
87 Sonne, "Specific Intentions—General Realities: On the Relation between Urban Forms and Political Aspirations in Berlin during the Twentieth Century," *Planning Perspectives* 19 (2004): 301.
88 Janet Ward, "Recapitalizing Berlin," in *The German Wall: Fallout in Europe*, ed. Marc Silberman (New York: Palgrave Macmillan, 2011), 90. Eberhard Diepgen, "Preface of the Governing Mayor of Berlin," in Zwoch, 9.
89 Quoted in Nino Galetti, *Der Bundestag als Bauherr in Berlin: Ideen, Konzepte, Entscheidungen zur politischen Architektur (1991–1998)* (Berlin: Droste, 2008), 225–6.
90 Rick Atkinson, "Building a Better Berlin: Critics See Too Much of Its Past in Its Future," *The Washington Post*, January 8, 1995, G4.
91 Ibid.
92 "Berlino: I concorsi per lo Spreebogen e il Reichstag," *Domus* 748 (April 1, 1993): 4.
93 Though Schultes and Frank conceived the Spreebogen proposal together, I refer throughout what follows to Schultes, who is the outspoken representative and theorist of the firm, as his many essays attest.
94 Zwoch, 49.
95 Ibid.
96 Ibid.
97 Quoted in Wise, 62.
98 Zwoch, 49.
99 Ibid.
100 See, for example, Axel Schultes, "Das Elend des Berliner Feuilletons: am Beispiel des Berliner Stadtschlosses," in *Zur Sprache bringen: Kritik der Architekturkritik*, eds. Ulrich Conrads, Eduard Führ, and Christian Gänshirt (Münster: Waxmann, 2003), 108. Indeed, Benjamin's theory maintained a privileged status in European architectural schools in the 1960s and 1970s (the years of Schultes's training), with many students fascinated by the way in which the author had seemed to anticipate

the disasters of the twentieth century. For a discussion of this status, see Gevork Hartoonian, *Walter Benjamin and Architecture* (London: Routledge, 2010).
101 Walter Benjamin, *The Origin of German Tragic Drama*, trans. John Osborne (London: New Left Books, 1977), 178.
102 Ibid.
103 Ibid.
104 Georg Simmel, "Bridge and Door," trans. Mark Ritter, *Theory, Culture & Society* 11 (February 1994): 6.
105 Ibid, 5. Bernhard Siegert has described the significance of Simmel's analysis to understanding the bridge, and the door, as cultural techniques: "What Martin Heidegger, drawing on Georg Simmel, suggests about the bridge also counts for the door: 'the bridge does not just connect banks that are already there. The banks emerge as banks only as the bridge crosses the stream.'" Both forms, according to Siegert, crucially "articulate space in such a way that it becomes a carrier of cultural codes." Bernhard Siegert, "Doors: On the Materiality of the Symbolic," trans. John Durham Peters, *Grey Room* 47 (Spring 2012): 8–9.
106 See, for example, his 2002 essay "Junkspace." Rem Koolhaas, "Junkspace," *October* 100 (Spring 2002), 175–90.
107 "Evil Can Also be Beautiful: Interview with Rem Koolhaas," *Der Spiegel*, March 27, 2006, http://www.spiegel.de/international/spiegel/spiegel-interview-with-dutch-architect-rem-koolhaas-evil-can-also-be-beautiful-a-408748.html.
108 Rem Koolhaas, "Field Trip: A(A) Memoir (First and Last . . .)," in *S,M,L,XL* (New York: Monacelli Press, 1995), 225.
109 Ibid, 226.
110 Ibid.
111 Ibid.
112 Ibid, 222.
113 Ibid.
114 For example, Tim Adams, "Metropolis Now," *The Observer*, June 25, 2006.
115 Terence Riley, *Envisioning Architecture: Drawings from the Museum of Modern Art*, ed. Matilda McQuaid (New York: The Museum of Modern Art), 166. The double slab of the Wall would resurface in Koolhaas's later work, such as the "travelator" in OMA's project for Welfare Island (1975–6) and their "strips" for the park of La Villette in Paris (1982), as well as many others that take the form of a band or bridge.
116 Craig Owens, "The Allegorical Impulse: Toward a Theory of Postmodernism," *October* 12 (Spring 1980): 80.
117 Ibid.
118 The destruction that would have been necessary to carry out Schultes and Frank's Band as designed, especially to the Friedrichstadt, seemed all too redolent of Speerian demolition tactics. The Band was, however, recently extended to the street line of Luisenstrasse, after a years-long delay. For a discussion of the debate over the Friedrichstadt, see David Clay Large, *Berlin* (New York: Basic Books, 2000), 619–20.
119 Rainer Haubrich, "Hier Regiert die Leere," *Die Welt*, January 31, 2001, http://www.welt.de/print-welt/article431126/Hier-regiert-die-Leere.html
120 Ibid.

121 Ibid.
122 The connections between architecture and literature strengthen through this process of layering. As Owens suggests, "In allegorical structure, then, one text is *read through* another, however fragmentary, intermittent, or chaotic their relationship may be; the paradigm for the allegorical work is thus the palimpsest." Owens, 80.
123 Benjamin, 161.

2

The Reichstag's New Lightness of Being

On June 17, 1995, more than a hundred hard-hatted workers ascended to the top of Berlin's Reichstag building, then rappelled down the facade trailing billowing sheets of silver polypropylene in their wake. A throng of viewers watched raptly from the ground while this balletic performance unfolded and the structure morphed from an awkward ruin into an evanescent but unified sculpture. Over the course of the next two weeks, the adoring crowd remained constant as hordes of visitors crowded the Platz der Republik in front of the building, picnicking, tossing frisbees, or simply gazing at the colossus that had been rendered oddly insubstantial by shimmering fabric. Never in its century-long life had the building seemed lighter, either in form or in message.

Christo and Jeanne-Claude's wrapping of the Reichstag (Figure 2.1) has now become a standard chapter in the narrative of post-1990 Berlin—thanks in part to the fundamental ambiguity of the gesture, with its meaning as pliable as the fabric itself. For Bundestag president Rita Süssmuth, the completion of the long-standing project symbolized a fresh start for German democracy. For the 5 million viewers who saw the work in person during its brief existence, it created a jubilant atmosphere and a sense of ease seldom experienced in self-conscious Berlin. For the artists, it was a tribute to the city and its visitors, auguring—so they hoped—a "lighter" future for Germany.[1] And for the British architect Norman Foster, who would begin his renovation to make the building over into the seat of the new reunified German parliament the day after the project ended (Figure 0.1), the wrapping served as an auspicious prelude to his own efforts by establishing the appropriate atmosphere for the building's renaissance.[2] "The mood of the period in which it was wrapped was just unbelievable," he recalled in 1999. "It was an extraordinary experience, a signal for the transformation, the rebirth, of the Reichstag."[3]

Despite *Wrapped Reichstag*'s near-universal positive reception, its enormous media exposure, and its canonical status in art history, the work has lost none of its critical edge in the intervening decades. Indeed, Christo and Jeanne-Claude's refusal to assign a definite meaning to the project allows it to remain alive in our own day, and invites us to probe it for what it might reveal about what the Reichstag signified in the historical moment following reunification. Ultimately, the wrapping points to the key strategy at the heart of Foster's renovation, which entailed posing lightness and both its opposites, weightiness and darkness, as antithetical conditions that could only be mediated by architecture. In the 1990s and still today, this mediation of historical weight,

Figure 2.1 Christo and Jeanne-Claude, *Wrapped Reichstag*, Berlin, 1995. Germany Images David Crossland / Alamy Stock Photo.

attainable exclusively through spatial experience, was precisely the kind of effect that contemporary architecture aimed to achieve.

Twenty years after its completion, Foster's Reichstag, particularly his effulgent glass cupola, has become fully iconic of the New Berlin. So iconic has it become, in fact, that its historicity has been pushed out of view. *Wrapped Reichstag* is one of several lenses through which a reframing of this overly visible building becomes possible, allowing us to look past its familiarity and instead train our attention on its abiding strangeness. Making use of these lenses, this chapter will offer a new look at the building, focusing on its distinctively contemporary approach to history and historical architecture. Such an approach requires looking at the building obliquely—looking past the cupola, as it were, to other events in the building's postreunification history that are ephemeral, invisible, or hard to see. Thus, in addition to *Wrapped Reichstag*, I will also examine Foster's remarkable unbuilt competition proposal from 1992, as well as one of the most audacious decisions made during the renovation, which was to preserve and showcase the graffiti scrawled on the building's walls by Soviet soldiers during the Battle of Berlin in the spring of 1945. My argument here is that these different iterations of the building are not merely serial views onto the same object, but rather are fundamentally interrelated instances of how its current significance has coalesced around a discourse of lightness. The Reichstag's very multiplicity of iteration itself, its existence as an accumulation of images transmitted across different media, is one important characteristic that the structure shares with other examples of iconic contemporary architecture. This accrual of its different imagistic manifestations, not just its static, material presence, is what communicates the impression that the building has finally—so to speak—lightened up.

Of the buildings and plans included in this study, the Reichstag has by far attracted the most scholarly and critical attention. Foster's renovation has been examined thoroughly and perceptively, especially in terms of its commitment to continuing the rhetoric of architectural transparency established during the Bundestag's exile in Bonn.[4] In *The Transparent State: Architecture and Politics in Postwar Germany*, Deborah Ascher Barnstone examines the dictum that "transparency equals democracy," which had been explored by the German avant-garde in the early years of the twentieth century, codified in West Germany in the postwar years, and enshrined in the official buildings constructed in its provisional capital. In architecture, the political ideology of transparency has most often been expressed through the materiality of glass, which renders buildings visually penetrable and phenomenologically open. The use of large expanses of transparent glass in architecture amassed meanings during the twentieth century that connected it, however loosely, with moral clarity, progressive social values, neoliberal economic policies, and permeable borders. Foster's glass cupola thus extends the ideology of transparency established in Bonn (most notably in Hans Schwippert's Bundeshaus of 1949 and Günter Behnisch's Bundeshaus of 1992) while aiming to revitalize the concept for the Berlin Republic.[5] As we will see, transparency intersects with lightness in crucial ways, especially in relation to glass as a favored material, but it is not philosophically synonymous with it. Rather, lightness as an architectural objective depends on an antipodean tension with the inherent massiveness of architecture, and its achievement requires the architect's skillful visual negation of that massiveness.

As well as in its enunciation of political transparency, Foster's Reichstag has also been insightfully discussed in its relationship to expressionist architecture, especially the utopian fantasies Bruno Taut conceived in collaboration with the writer Paul Scheerbart. As several scholars have noted, Foster's Reichstag alluringly evokes Taut's crystalline forms, both those that were realized (his visionary Glashaus of 1914 at the exhibition of the Deutscher Werkbund in Cologne) and those that remained imaginary (the quixotic proposals outlined in *Alpine Architektur* and *Die Stadtkrone*).[6] These analyses focus on the most visible aspect of the Reichstag's renovation as it was completed: its dazzling glass-and-steel dome. In looking away from the dome, I seek to add to this discussion by determining how expressionistic thinking about lightness in particular recurs in Foster's project. In addition, examining some of the less visible fragments of the building's postreunification life reveals that Foster's scheme for "lightening" the building was holistic and depended not only on the highly visible, techno-utopian dome. Rather, the dome was to be the visual culmination of a carefully choreographed, diagetic demonstration of historical renewal, a lightening with both architectural and philosophical resonance. Further, I will argue that, in exhibiting its own perpetual movement toward lightness, the refurbished building makes claims to a cycle of continual national unburdening.

By putting certain physical marks of the past on display—the aforementioned graffiti as well as bullet holes and battle-scarred walls—the Reichstag self-consciously pits its historical gravity against its contemporary lightness. This practice does not simply equate to opening a transparent window onto history, nor does it merely balance necessary contemporary additions against historical remnants. More importantly, it shows a distinctly contemporary romantic fascination with the ravages of the twentieth century, in which architecture is often deployed to frame "authentic" encounters with that past. Although recent architecture is often critiqued for its radical ahistoricity—the way in which it seems to ignore urban and historical context in favor of an insistent *newness*—the Reichstag offers compelling evidence against this widespread misunderstanding about contemporary architecture culture.[7] In fact, global architecture since 1990 evinces a near obsession with history, and more often than not appoints the architect to fulfill the role of historian.[8] Foster's renovated Reichstag demonstrates that the very idea of historical transparency belongs to the contemporary. The contemporary architect's concern, therefore, is not only design, but also the amassing, selection, and distillation of historical information.

In the Reichstag, as in Berlin's other official state buildings, architecture is called upon to project the character of the nation through certain prominent features that emphasize the distance between the past and the present. To function as the seat of parliament for reunified Germany, the new Reichstag had to narrate its own weighty history while also positioning itself at a bearable remove from that trauma. Indeed, the pursuit of lightness in architecture is one that had preoccupied German architects from the eighteenth century onwards, and had taken on new urgency during the turmoil of the twentieth. But while this discourse of lightening has a specifically German heritage, it is also important to identify this rhetoric as a primary gambit of global contemporary architecture, most evident in the realm of adaptive reuse. In projects roughly simultaneous with Foster's work at the Reichstag and proportional in their international visibility, such as Herzog & de Meuron's Tate Modern in London (2000), historical traces are similarly presented in diachronic dialogue with new interventions, pitting plainly new architectural "updates" against the ruined, decaying, or stylistically outmoded.[9] Like many high-profile projects of adaptive reuse underway at the end of the millennium, Foster's Reichstag renovation depends on the tension between the new and the old, and relies on the dyads born of this tension—not only lightness and its opposites but also the visible distinctions between sleek and patinated, soaring and earthbound, machine-made and handcrafted, intact and disintegrated—to communicate its message. In many cases, such works underscore these dyads by transgressing cherished modernist principles, maintaining nonstructural fragments and nonfunctionalist ornament. In the specific case of Foster's Reichstag, these showily nonmodernist techniques are part of a larger concerted effort on the part of official functionaries to signal Germany's political transformation through architecture. Yet they are also symptomatic of a phenomenon that extends far beyond this German context, and that is in fact one of global contemporary architecture's most salient characteristics: the playing off of "history" against "the present."

"A building that could not decide what it wanted"

During the first meeting of the newly elected Reichstag in 1871, a central point of discussion was the construction of a new building to signal the importance of the parliament, and of democracy in general, in the newly unified German empire.[10] A competition was held in 1872, receiving a surprisingly international range of submissions for the time. In fact, presaging the high visibility of the renovation that would occur over a century later, the London-based journal *The Architect* reported: "more than an ordinary degree of interest is being taken by the profession in this competition."[11] The English architect George Gilbert Scott won second place with a characteristically neo-Gothic design surmounted by a towering ribbed dome, but first prize went to Ludwig Bohnstedt's scheme (Figure 2.2), in which colonnaded wings were anchored by a massive triumphal arch behind which hovered a shallow cupola. This Renaissance-revival design was shelved when disputes over land ownership paused the project for a decade. Eventually, a new competition was held in 1882, receiving another barrage of historicist proposals from architects around the continent (including a classicizing scheme anchored by a large rotunda by the Viennese Otto Wagner that presaged some of the strict geometry of his later Jugendstil designs). The competition was won by the Frankfurt architect Paul Wallot, whose design demonstrated the stylistic tumult that eclecticism had produced on the European

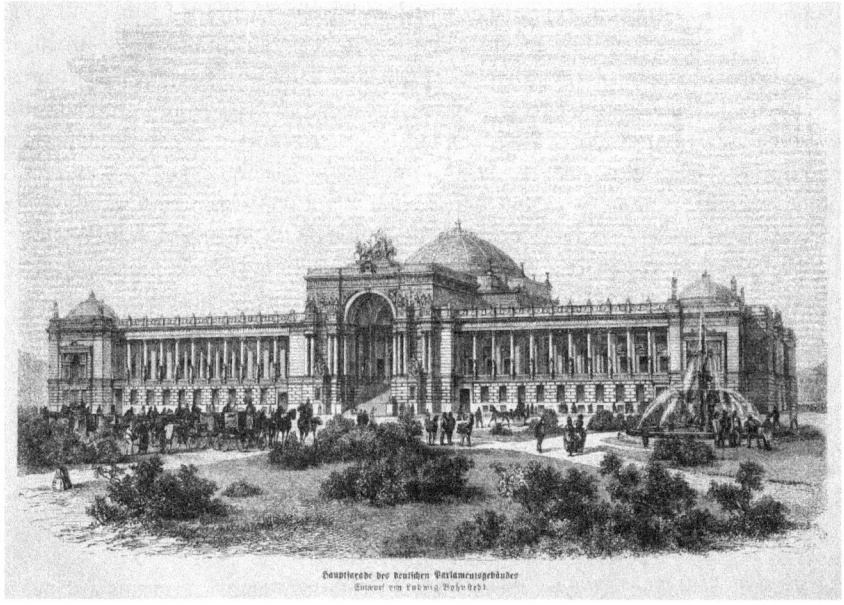

Figure 2.2 Ludwig Bohnstedt, *Hauptfaçade des deutschen Parlamentsgebäudes*, in Ernst Keil (publisher), *Die Gartenlaube (The Garden Arbor)*, Leipzig, 1872.

Figure 2.3 Paul Wallot, Reichstag building, 1882–94.

continent during the nineteenth century. Over the course of its completion, the Reichstag developed beyond Wallot's initial design into a cluttered composition of baroque details piled atop Renaissance massing (Figure 2.3). In the finished building, which finally opened in 1894, square towers marked the four corners of the structure, whose wings surrounded a central plenary chamber flanked by two inner courtyards. The hefty columned entrance and staircase projected forward from the facade and stout sculptural figures adorned the parapet. In a labored effort to synthesize modernity and history, Wallot ultimately topped this mélange with a segmented iron-and-glass dome springing from a square base.[12] These attempts at synthesis notwithstanding, the industrial materials of the dome seemed hopelessly at odds with the rest of the building, especially the heavy allegorical ornament and its emblems of German unification. This stylistic heterogeneity, according to the Reichstag historian Michael Cullen, created

> a building that presented a different appearance on nearly every façade and yet another different one in the cupola. It was a building that could not decide what it wanted. Or rather, it was supposed to be an expression of imperial unity and at the same time a monument of parliamentarism, but it became merely an example of the deep division in the German Empire and of a parliament's powerlessness to become master in its own house.[13]

As a result of this eclecticism, the historical Reichstag's architecture unconsciously reflected the political difficulty of unification.[14] In contrast to the *Volkisch* narratives espoused by the government, which promoted the idea of a natural identity underpinning and justifying German unification, Wallot's Reichstag presented a visual discord that revealed all too plainly the myth of a cohesive German identity at the time of its first *Gründerzeit*. Kaiser Wilhelm II did not aid the new edifice's public image, declaring it "the height of tastelessness" and dismissing the whole institution—both building and parliament— as "the imperial monkey house."[15]

Over the course of the twentieth century, the Reichstag's architectural reputation did not improve. Though it invoked several historical languages, it seemed to speak none of them fluently, and its audience was put off by its blustering polyglotism. Lacking stylistic clarity, it failed to reach the status of beloved structures close by, such as Karl Friedrich Schinkel's Altes Museum, Friedrich August Stüler's Neues Museum, and Carl Gotthard Langhans's Brandenburg Gate, or even to gain the rueful affection acquired by less distinguished buildings like Julius and Otto Raschdorff's Berlin Cathedral. But although the Reichstag did not rise in architectural esteem, it nonetheless collected considerable historical baggage. It acted as a built bookend for the volatile Weimar Republic, proclaimed from its balcony on November 9, 1918 and ended by the calamitous fire of 1933 that enabled Hitler's dictatorial power grab. After the fire, the collapsed dome was reglazed but the building was only partially restored, a physical reminder of the utter futility of the Reichstag as a governing body under National Socialism. Despite later popular misunderstanding, Hitler never ruled from the building and the Reichstag was banished to the nearby Kroll Opera House after 1933. Hitler was somewhat more positively disposed to the Wilhelmine building than his predecessors, yet he only maintained the building so that it could ultimately cower in the shadow of Albert Speer's domed Volkshalle for Germania. In Hitler's mind, this aggressive juxtaposition would demonstrate how the Third Reich had dwarfed Germany's original imperial aspirations, since the Volkshalle's volume was to be fifty times that of its neighbor.[16] Despite Hitler's relative indifference to the Reichstag, the Soviet army associated it indelibly with the enemy. Soviet soldiers took particular aim at the building during the Battle of Berlin, after which, scarred and exhausted, the building slumped in a state of ruin for fifteen years. The dome was finally demolished in 1954, having been declared a public hazard.

The postwar years saw little resolution for the Reichstag's use. In January of 1961, the architect Paul Baumgarten refurbished the structure as the hopeful future home of the Bundestag, which was by then meeting in Bonn (Figure 2.4). Baumgarten's project was part of a wave of preemptive architecture and urbanism that anticipated the needs of a reunified, reconstructed country.[17] Though the building's contentious site would make its use impossible for many decades to come—construction of the Berlin Wall began in August of the same year, directly to the east of the building (Figure 2.5)— Baumgarten nonetheless envisioned a progressive Reichstag that expressed the same ideals as Bonn's government structures. His scheme for the Reichstag called for the removal of much of the ponderous sculptural ornament on the building and the stabilization of the interiors for use by the Bundestag. In essence, Baumgarten's renovation embedded a Bonn-style modernist building within the hull of the Reichstag, its glass-walled plenary chamber echoing the transparency of the Bundestag's then-current home. The renovation gutted the Reichstag's damaged interior and covered its

Figure 2.4 Paul Baumgarten, renovations to Reichstag building, 1961. Interior view. Bundsarchiv-Bildarchiv, Berlin.

ceilings and walls with plasterboard, thus concealing (but also preserving) the building's wounded surfaces. It was in this condition that Christo and Jeanne-Claude first encountered the building, and, decades later, it was in this condition that it was wrapped, with the interior already veiled by these modernist additions.

Wrapped Reichstag

Baumgarten's rehabilitation, ineffectual even to his own eyes, failed to endear the building to the public.[18] His inability to create a successful synthesis between present and past resurfaced during the extraordinary parliamentary debate over Christo and Jeanne-Claude's *Wrapped Reichstag*, suggesting that what was at stake in their temporary artwork was the larger question of whether or not the building could become a symbol of unity. In this light, divergent perspectives on the meaning of the project indicate a deeper conflict at the time over the possibility of redemption, not only of the building's past, but also of the nation's past.

Despite its present-day association with the politics of reunification, the project had in fact been under development since 1971, when Michael Cullen sent Christo a postcard of the rambling, empty building and asked the artist if he would be interested

Figure 2.5 The Berlin Wall under construction to the east of the Reichstag, November 23, 1961. Bundsarchiv-Bildarchiv, Berlin.

in using it in his work. Christo, who had long aspired to complete an installation involving an entire public building, responded positively, but the Reichstag's position on the border between East and West rendered it, at least provisionally, an impossibility.[19] Although he and Jeanne-Claude would disavow specific meaning in the colorful, spectacularly scaled work for which they would later become famous, their early projects were often trenchant critiques of divisionary politics and Soviet totalitarianism. Indeed, their first work to thematize Berlin's division, titled *Wall of Barrels—The Iron Curtain*, took place in Paris, when, in June of 1962, the artists temporarily barricaded a narrow street with oil barrels to protest the construction of the Berlin Wall the preceding year. Christo and Jeanne-Claude's record of contesting Cold War politics doubtless made the wrapping of the Reichstag even more difficult to fulfill during the years of division, since the East German government had forbidden political activities to take place within the building. It seems likewise clear that the political content of their past work made their proposal to wrap the Reichstag more appealing to the Bundesrepublik after reunification, despite the artists' refusal to attach a critical agenda to the project.

Given the tensions at the border, it was only after reunification in 1990 that the work's realization became feasible, leading to intensifying emotions as that feasibility increased. It faced serious governmental opposition from powerful officials; for example, chancellor Helmut Kohl had long argued that wrapping the building ran the risk of trivializing the institution of the Reichstag as well as its architectural home, and he warned that it might therefore diminish the image of democracy in reunified Germany. Others, including Süssmuth and parliamentarian Peter Conradi of the Social Democratic Party, were equally ardent advocates who consistently underscored the centrality of culture to the image of the Berlin Republic. Interest in the project ran so high that the unusually impassioned debate in parliament over whether or not to approve the project was televised to the entire European Union.[20]

The debate itself is worth examining closely for what it reveals about the political meanings associated with advanced art and architecture at the time. Wolfgang Schäuble, the leader of the Christian Democratic Union, contended that the building's history was simply too "weighty" to undertake such an "experiment."[21] For Kohl, Schäuble, and many other politicians on the right, the wrapping of the Reichstag was a hazardous enterprise with minimal payoff. At best, Berlin would receive a somewhat redundant affirmation of being an ambitious, adventurous, and international center for the arts; at worst, the keen international gaze trained on the capital city would wonder, disapprovingly, how the Bundestag could make its future home "the object of such an act."[22] But others viewed the wrapping of the Reichstag as a crucial episode in the government's return to Berlin, a "spectacular and necessary reconsecration of an otherwise defiled historical site."[23] For supporters of Christo and Jeanne-Claude's work, only after a process of "purification,"[24] a "rite of passage"[25] that would usher in a new era of peace, stability, and true democratic rule, could the Bundestag reoccupy the Reichstag's haunted corridors. Ultimately, Conradi (who was also a vocal supporter of Norman Foster) convinced his peers during discussion preceding the vote that the wrapping of the building would translate it into a "precious gift" bequeathed to the German public: "With this act," he claimed, "we want to send a positive sign, a beautiful, bright signal, that offers courage and hope and radiates self-confidence."[26] Thus persuaded, the Bundestag voted 292 to 223 in favor of the wrapping, clearing the way for the festive display described above.

Although critics debated the import of the project without consensus, most agreed that Christo and Jeanne-Claude's wrapping—a technique the artists had used on various objects and buildings since the 1960s to great critical acclaim—was alchemical, transforming the building from a grandiloquent fossil into Berlin's most stunning (and stunningly contemporary) attraction. Paul Goldberger reported in the *New York Times* that "this immense stone hulk, a heavy, bombastic building that epitomizes German excesses of the late 19th century, is rendered light, almost delicate. It takes on an ethereal beauty, and looks as if it could float away into the silvery, cloudy Berlin sky."[27] To Goldberger, the dialogue underlying the work was one between impossibly polarized terms; and indeed, the otherworldly effect of the wrapped Reichstag turned on its ability to transform the building into its apparent opposite—from hard to soft, from permanent to ephemeral, from monumental to fragile.

However, none of these oppositions was as much discussed, or as historically significant, as the transformation from heaviness to lightness. By no means was

Goldberger the only observer who noticed the quality of lightness that Christo and Jeanne-Claude's wrapping had given the old structure. Rather, the term appears in a substantial proportion of the literature surrounding the project, and is presented as self-evident by journalists, architects, critics, and historians alike. My goal in what follows is not simply to catalog the appearance and track the movement of a single word. Rather, I intend to demonstrate the way in which lightness was used axiomatically in reference to the Reichstag's postreunification life and posed as an imperative by a variety of stakeholders in, and observers of, the building's reuse. This axiomatic movement toward lightness, as we will see, is one that permeates the global architecture of the present day.

Historian Charles Maier, for one, noted how the wrapping appeared to evaporate the mass of the building's heavy masonry. When viewing the installation, he wrote, "it seemed almost possible that the building underneath might have somehow disappeared; the package created the sense of bulk without weight."[28] For Maier, this dematerialized quality, and the transition from massiveness to buoyant volume, was a metaphor for the removal of historical freight: "The wrapped Reichstag, in effect, took a holiday from this heavy legacy."[29] Other writers noted similarly transformative effects: one journalist for *Der Spiegel* praised the work for its "lightness, symmetry, and color,"[30] while another in the *Frankfurter Allgemeine Zeitung* celebrated the "lightness, the joyful improvisation"[31] that made the project so beloved to its public. Some commentators even associated lightness explicitly with the liberalism and open-mindedness that formed the politico-cultural identity of the reunified government. In the *Washington Post*, Marc Fisher asserted: "The government's decision to allow the Reichstag wrap is an inspiring display of self-confidence and even lightness in a society forever fretting about its xenophobia and its image abroad."[32] According to Fisher, this bold artistic choice was a clear demonstration of the Bundesrepublik's commitment to culture: "(the wrapping) is also a reminder that however insular the Germans might be ... theirs is a society more comfortable with intellectual pursuits and exotic thinking than the United States has been for some time."[33]

Despite the range of specific associations that these writers attached to the term, they unanimously agreed that the wrapped Reichstag not only projected the appearance of being lightweight, but also generated a pervasive atmosphere of lightness. In other words, the way in which Christo and Jeanne-Claude had altered the glum countenance of the Reichstag building ultimately transformed the emotional condition of the people who beheld it.[34] Unconsciously, these accounts reprise the modernist, utopian faith in architecture's universal intelligibility and its consequent ability to catalyze social change. As one journalist proclaimed, the building's wrapping "imparted the lightness that Berlin so badly needed after all the years of division."[35] Whether or not the artists had intended it, catharsis seemed to be on offer for those who sought it, along with a sense of historical ease and a hopeful promise of unity. If in theory the work had run the risk of trivializing the Reichstag's past, in practice it seemed to offer just the right measure of relief from the painful events that the building had witnessed. Even if it was impossible to agree on what the work *meant*, it was difficult to deny that it *signified* lightness. Notwithstanding the presence of dissenting voices—the writer Joel Agee, for example, spotted a young man who paraded through the crowd for days on end wearing a gold shirt and carrying a sign that read "THIS IS NOT ART!"—this decorous celebration of lightness ensured the installation's overwhelmingly enthusiastic reception.[36] Even those observers who were wary of this ambiance of conviviality and consensus, such as Andreas Huyssen, nonetheless acknowledge the work's affective power, with the Reichstag's hulking form "both dissolved and accentuated by a lightness of being that was in stark contrast with the visual memory of the heavy-set, now veiled architecture."[37]

With his invocation of Milan Kundera's novel *The Unbearable Lightness of Being* (1984), Huyssen here begins to clarify what is meant by "lightness" in this context. In fact, he was not the only one to refer to Kundera's novel in discussions of *Wrapped Reichstag*; the historian Rudy Koshar likewise notes: "Transiency, provisionality, and lightness—words used to describe the visual effects of the shimmering wrapped monument—had been part of the German national identity for a long time, even at those moments when it seemed heaviest and most concerned about establishing a centuries-long lineage, a state of eternal return."[38] In their allusions to Kundera's concept of lightness, Huyssen and Koshar signal the openly metaphysical nature of the term as it was applied in discussions of the wrapped Reichstag. In the novel, Kundera questioned the Nietzschean idea of eternal recurrence—that is, that all events in history have happened before and humans are thus fated to repeat the past ad infinitum, including even the most cataclysmic historical misjudgments. Instead, Kundera depicted a historical condition in which events and situations only occur once, creating a terrifying inconsequentiality for human decisions, actions, and lives. In the entangled relationships of Tomáš, his wife Tereza, and his lover Sabina in the aftermath of the Prague Spring, Kundera illustrated the philosophical paradox at the heart of historical consciousness: that both heaviness and lightness are fundamentally unendurable states. As he wrote,

> The heavier the burden, the closer our lives come to the earth, the more real and truthful they become. Conversely, the absolute absence of a burden causes man to be lighter than air, to soar into the heights, take leave of the earth and his earthly being, and become only half real, his movements as free as they are insignificant. What then shall we choose? Weight or lightness? ... The only certainty is: the lightness/weight opposition is the most mysterious, most ambiguous of all.[39]

In the end, the novel offers no answer to the choice between lightness and weightiness, instead lingering on the enigmatic opposition itself. In so doing, Kundera's existential quandary is presented as emblematic of the historical condition in postwar Europe.

In understanding reunified Germany and the wrapping and rebuilding of the Reichstag in terms of Kundera's "lightness of being," Huyssen and Koshar have a slightly different purpose than their source. Their goal is not to meditate on the positive and negative qualities of lightness and weight, but rather to observe that the Reichstag was saddled with the task of presenting each in a manageable intensity. In its metaphysical sense, the building's performance of lightening is self-justifying and self-explanatory, demonstrating Germany's acceptance of its historical burden and yet anticipating a less encumbered future on the horizon. Beginning in the 1960s, this questioning of how to bear up under the historical baggage of two world wars became endemic to Europe's rebuilding.[40] In many ways, then, scholars and writers employ the term "lightness" so frequently because its philosophical significance is expected to be intuitive for readers. We know what lightness means historically these days.

But it is crucial to look closely at the idea that architecture itself was to be the means by which this historical lightening was attained, both in the Reichstag's wrapping and in its reuse. To achieve this sense of relief meant translating the idea of historical lightness into the visual language of the distinct, if cognate, trope of architectural lightness. Lightness, of course, stands diametrically opposed both to heaviness and to darkness, and contemporary architects (including Foster) make use of the slippage between these two antonyms. When architecture addresses matters of historical significance, it is often lightness as the antithesis of weight that is the primary point of departure for design, such that a structure's ability to contain or project light becomes a secondary function.[41] In the most fundamental sense, weight itself is necessary for architecture to perform its most basic functions and is thus, to some extent, proper to the art (as Hegel described it, architecture is first "A heavy mass subject to mechanical laws").[42] Lightness, therefore, is always a contradiction of architecture's most immanent qualities; but the movement between physical and metaphorical registers is what marks the Reichstag project—understood broadly, including Christo and Jeanne-Claude's wrapping—as a work of contemporary architecture culture.

It is possible to trace how the discourse of architectural lightness in the modern era developed in the direction of these contemporary meanings. In nineteenth-century Germanic tradition, lightness became associated with the constructional openness and soaring height of Gothic Revival buildings. For Friedrich Schlegel and others, these qualities were associated with the German national character; recalling his visit in 1806 to Cologne Cathedral, then under construction, Schlegel wrote: "As one gazes up at the choir vault of the unfinished cathedral in Cologne, the heart is filled with wonderment."[43] Schlegel praised the cathedral specifically for its "delicacy" and its "lightness with grandeur."[44] Similarly, despite his resistance to the Gothic Revival, Leo von Klenze owned that his beloved neoclassical architecture would benefit from aiming at the "lightness and transparency" of Gothic cathedrals.[45] Heinrich Hübsch claimed that the very idea of lightness began with the introduction of Gothic architecture, which he felt was authentically German in origin: "In the thirteenth century appeared the so-called Gothic or Old-German style," he wrote, "... in which all parts give an impression of lightness and extend to a remarkable height. These two qualities ... clearly set the new style apart from the old."[46] Whatever the particular nationalistic investment, therefore, this lightness was both tectonic and directional, depending not only on the leanness of the structural frame but also on the sense of an upward-striving spatial arrangement.[47]

Given this emphasis on structure, it is perhaps unsurprising that, in the twentieth century, lightness became increasingly associated with the skeleton frame and the resulting emancipation of the facade.[48] As architects and theorists explored the potential of lightweight frame construction, the term came to suggest a range of architectural implications, from the elimination of ornament and the abnegation of monumentality to the salubrious effects of physical hygiene and political progressivism. Indeed, much of modern architecture could be described as a search for lightness, not only in building, but also in design. As early as 1902, Hermann Muthesius described "our contemporary aesthetic-tectonic orientation" as aiming "to increase the amount of light and air . . . to replace the heavy and unmovable with light . . . and to strive for an overall sense of brightness."[49] In fact, Muthesius found the Reichstag to be a praiseworthy model of heavy, historically referential architecture: "every visitor to the Reichstag will be captivated by the somber, almost gloomy gravity of the south entry hall, in which the whole space and ornamentation pursue the goal of transporting the visitor into a consecrated mood that anticipates the grandeur and significance of this monument."[50] For Muthesius, the Reichstag's lack of style was a virtue, evidence of its architect's originality (though it is possible that he was not totally impartial, having worked for a time in Wallot's office); nevertheless, the building's old-fashioned ponderousness belonged to a previous generation's way of life.

Gradually, architectural heaviness came to signify a host of problems, as dense masonry architecture became the breeding ground of social torpor, political rot, authoritarianism, and militancy. At the very least, as Muthesius demonstrated, architectural weightiness was passé, and the modern architect strove instead for brightness, movement, energy, and ease. These objectives have hypertrophied in the present, taking on exaggerated proportions in contemporary architecture, whose technical flourishes often seem less about the candid expression of structure than about superseding rational apprehension altogether. The tent-like atrium of Helmut Jahn's Sony Center at Potsdamer Platz is a signature example of this tendency, as is the fluid curtain wall and interior cone of Jean Nouvel's Galeries Lafayette—and their resemblance to Foster's Reichstag dome is not coincidental. As Hal Foster has pointed out, "lightness confirms the drive, already strong in modern architecture, towards the refinement of materials and techniques, and yet now this refinement seems pledged less to healthy, open spaces and transparent, rational structures . . . than to aesthetic effects and decorous touches."[51] In some ways, contemporary architecture's brand of lightness is precisely the traversal of architecture's native weight; contemporary architecture is thus supra-architectural, attempting to realize seemingly impossible feats of lightening and pulling strands from visionary movements like expressionism for its inspiration.

By changing the Reichstag's message from heaviness to lightness, Christo and Jeanne-Claude auspiciously aligned the project with contemporary architecture's tendency toward expressionism. While wrapped, the visual character of the Reichstag altered with shifting light and weather conditions. In bright sunlight, the pleats of the fabric lent the structure a distinctly fluted appearance, defining its mass and sharpening its contours. Under overcast skies, its colors became muted and these sharp edges softened and blurred, making the building appear to float like a cloud—or to hover eerily like a monumental ghost. At night, artificial illumination provided by the city of Berlin transformed the structure into a glowing beacon. Certainly, these transitory guises were part of the duo's larger artistic project of experimenting with different effects of ephemerality. But *Wrapped Reichstag*'s particularly expressionistic quality seems to be more coincidental than calculated.[52] It resulted from its position at a conjunction of contexts: geographically, in the country of expressionism's birth, and temporally, within contemporary architecture's fascination with lightness. The ungainly Reichstag had effectively been turned into a light frame building, with translucent fabric walls supported by a slender metal armature that smoothed away its cumbersome ornament. In its wrapped form, the building appeared somehow both crystalline, suggesting Taut's prismatic glass fantasies or Wassili Luckhardt's 1920 project for a cinema (Figure 2.6), and plastic, evoking the sculptural curves of concrete expressionist architecture, like the crisp creases of Rudolf Steiner's 1919 Goetheanum in Dornach, Switzerland (Figure 2.7). In an article written in 1914, the critic and expressionist champion Adolf Behne praised the use of glass in architecture for its "wondrous color ... liveliness ... and unique beauty," encouraging the public to forgo "heaviness and elephantine massiveness" in favor of glass's "freedom, fresh lightness, and cheerfulness."[53] Though of course Christo and Jeanne-Claude's Reichstag was not wrapped in glass, Behne's words help us string together the expressionistic chain of associations that begins with architecture and ends with collective lightheartedness. They also help us see how expressionism established a dual identity for glass as a material that persists into the present, including in Foster's work—on the one hand, a transparent, efficient, and lightweight spatial container; on the other, a powerful generator of expressive, emotional lightness.

On July 7, 1995, after a run of only two weeks, Christo and Jeanne-Claude—refusing to extend the exhibition, despite exhortations from the public and latecomer

Figure 2.6 Wassili Luckhardt, project for a cinema, c. 1920. Watercolor on cardstock, 43.5 x 76.5 cm. Akademie der Künste, Berlin.

Figure 2.7 Rudolf Steiner, Goetheanum, Dornach, Switzerland, 1919.

encouragement from Kohl—disassembled the polypropylene and the steel skeleton that supported it, leaving the work to circulate in their trademark ephemera of drawings, photographs, and videos. The following day, demolition began on Baumgarten's interiors to clear the way for Foster's renovation. To be sure, Christo and Jeanne-Claude's installation was a highly appealing interlude in the life of a building with a persistent public image problem. By anyone's estimation, it was wildly successful; while the Bundestag had hoped that it might attract 500,000 visitors, ultimately over 5 million people came to see the work. Looked at closely, however, this project constitutes more than simply a popular art event that was auxiliary to the renovation. Rather, *Wrapped Reichstag* crystallizes the stakes attending the reuse of the Reichstag building after reunification and offers a clear look at the techniques of contemporary architecture that this reuse would need to engage. To become a viable representation of the transparent democracy of the Berlin Republic, it had to approach the architectural condition established in Bonn, or what Conradi termed a "Bonn-like lightness of being."[54] This lightening had to take the form both of an amelioration of its perceived historical burden and an easing of its stern architectural manner. In other words, to become "lighter" required both official and public demonstrations of the government's commitment to transparency and globalism and key visual alterations to the building's form. Only then could the stage be set for the unveiling of Foster's radiant, undeniably contemporary cupola, hovering ethereally over the building like a beacon of democracy.

"The Big Roof"

Understanding Foster's own interpretation of lightness requires us to backtrack. Before the Reichstag's wrapping, and before the construction of Foster's now-iconic dome, came his winning proposal for the competition for the building's reconstruction held in 1992. Though it is strikingly different from the final building, Foster's proposal nevertheless reveals many of the strategies of global contemporary architecture on view in the Reichstag as it was constructed. In fact, taken together, the designs produced by the international cast of architects who submitted proposals serve as a snapshot of high-profile, headline-making architecture from the 1990s. The competition was open to all architects living and practicing within the boundaries of the Bundesrepublik, and the Bundestag also solicited proposals directly from fourteen internationally renowned luminaries, including past and future Pritzker Prize laureates such as Fumihiko Maki, Aldo Rossi, and I. M. Pei. (Foster would be awarded the Pritzker in April of 1999 at a ceremony in Berlin, a week before the official opening of the Reichstag.) Scholars have read the eighty responses to the competition brief as having proposed an exceptionally varied range of solutions to the thorny problem of national identity and to the historic building's dubious aesthetic quality. But from a distance of a quarter-century, various consistencies of approach have become apparent, and the proposals contain many attributes that are paradigmatic of architecture at the end of the twentieth century. For the purposes of understanding contemporary architecture, therefore, it is useful to note what the responses have in common as well as observing their differences.

In fact, the strategies displayed in many of the competition entries share important conceptual ground with *Wrapped Reichstag*. That is, the new interventions proposed by these architects were intended to reframe the historical building, thus prompting the viewer to reconsider its history and future. The initial competition guidelines had called for a sweeping 33,000 square meters of accommodation, which was twice as much as the frame of the old building could realistically contain. The brief made no assumption that Baumgarten's 1961 interiors would be retained in the renovation, freeing architects essentially to gut the Reichstag and use it as a shell into and around which they could insert new construction. Therefore, most of the projects submitted to the competition proposed dramatic new structures lying outside the existing building as well as offering recommendations for its future use. Whether or not their designers did so consciously, these entries are frankly museological in the gaze they solicit from the viewer. That is, they place the historical building on display, treating it as a work of art—and in this reification, they obviate the question of the original object's value. Rather than the building's architectural merit, its salient feature becomes its very historicity. The reinscription of authenticity and singularity anchored in historic architecture is a tactic common to global contemporary architecture (discussed further in Chapter 4), meant—in Douglas Crimp's definition of the museological—to "enhance the art work's aura, to designate the work of art as separate, apart, inhabiting a world unto itself."[55] In the case of the Reichstag, this meant an implicit recategorization of the historical structure's aesthetic value, its original lack of distinction reevaluated by new virtuoso architecture. Wallot's creation, once derided as "heavy-handed," "of terrifying

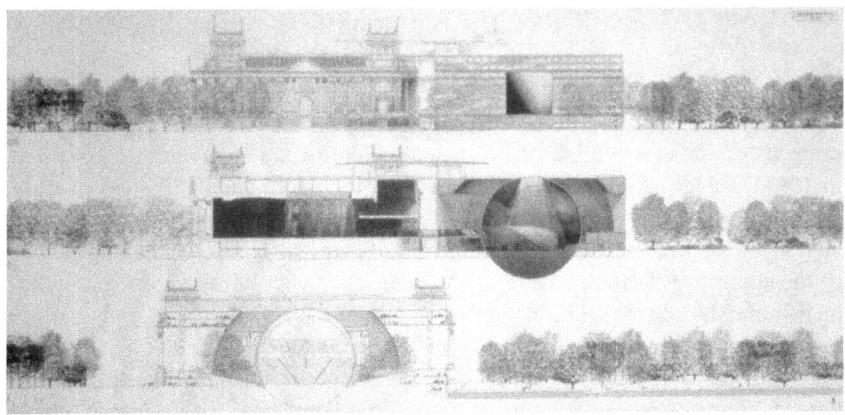

Figure 2.8 Jean Nouvel, Emmanuel Cattani & Associés, proposal for the Reichstag, Berlin, 1992. © 2020 Artists Rights Society (ARS), New York / ADAGP, Paris.

insensitivity and clumsiness," and "a first-class hearse," was now to be venerated as first-class art.[56]

For example, Jean Nouvel and Emmanuel Cattani suggested in their proposal (Figure 2.8) that a cubic, glazed building with the same footprint as the Reichstag be built alongside it to the east, connected by skybridges and a glass roof that partially sheltered both structures. Though free from applied ornament, the glazed panels of the new building were subtly detailed, creating a visual delicacy reminiscent of Nouvel's earlier Institut du Monde Arabe that stood in intentional contrast to the graceless ornament of the historical building. According to the architects, the solution to the problem of the building was "to build a 'double', a twin to the existing Reichstag, as a modern working place for elaborating the laws of the nation."[57] The curved contours of the plenary chamber, itself encapsulated in glass, would be visible through niches puncturing three of the "twin's" four facades. Chapel-like, the plenary chamber would be illuminated from an oculus overhead, adhering to the theme of lightness and easing the "darker times and bitter lessons" to which the building had borne witness.[58] Like other competitors, Nouvel and Cattani conceived their proposal in terms of dualities—old and new, most significantly—and their project sought to provide an alternative Reichstag alongside the existing structure that would place its troubled past at a comfortable distance. Bundestag members were confused and even disturbed by the idea of this uncanny doppelgänger, and Nouvel and Cattani's project was never seriously considered. However, Nouvel would later reinvigorate some of its elements in the floating glass screens of the European Patent Office in The Hague and the Fondation Cartier in Paris.

Other proposals projected the image of a futuristic Germany that would visually supersede the historical building and place new and old architecture into a contrapuntal relationship. With characteristic iconoclasm, the German architect Gottfried Böhm, in cooperation with his son Peter and Friedrich Steinigeweg, presented a vividly rendered

Figure 2.9 Gottfried Böhm, *Wettbewerb Umgestaltung des Reichstags*, Berlin, 1992. Charcoal on transparent paper. Deutches Architekturmuseum, Frankfurt am Main. © Gottfried Böhm-Archiv Deutsches Architekturmuseum, Frankfurt am Main; Foto: Uwe Dettmar, Frankfurt am Main.

cupola in which interlocking segments of concrete appear simultaneously space-age and archaic (Figure 2.9). The interaction of these leaves, they argued, "with their penetrating, individual shapes and articulated movements, present(s) a unified body."[59] This cupola developed a proposal that had been privately solicited by the Bundestag in 1988 for the restoration of the historic dome. In both projects, Böhm radically envisioned the dome as a space for the public, first in encircling viewing platforms and then in helical ramps. Though both these bids were unsuccessful, they left a significant impression: the 1988 design had been included in the competition packet sent to architects in 1992, and it was to Böhm's 1992 design that the Bundestag directed Foster's attention as his project developed, since it worked within the contours of the existing building while still presenting a contemporary dome. Once Foster had amended his proposal, critics in the know found it impossible to ignore that Foster's circular ramps for the public seemed to be direct quotations of Böhm's, both in form and concept. Though Böhm had been awarded the Pritzker in 1986, he lacked Foster's international profile; and despite his long-standing insistence on incorporating the public into the dome, his vision for its form might have seemed too private and idiosyncratic. According to Wolfgang Voigt of the Deutsches Architekturmuseum, "In the end, the Bundestag wanted both: Foster as architect and the dome filled with visitors."[60] Despite this shunting, Böhm continued to issue his public support for the construction of a dome.

Another inventive concept came from the Vienna office of Wolf Prix and Helmut Swiczinsky of Coop Himmelb(l)au (Figure 2.10), fresh off their inclusion in the landmark exhibition *Deconstructivist Architecture*, which had opened at the Museum of Modern Art in New York in 1988 and provided a now-infamous shot of energy to the careers of many future starchitects.[61] Though Coop Himmelb(l)au was not among the competition's prizewinners, deconstruction's emphasis on the undecidability of

Figure 2.10 Coop Himmelb(l)au, proposal for the Reichstag, Berlin, 1992. © Coop Himmelb(l)au.

meaning was nonetheless a sympathetic fit with the Reichstag's history, comparable to Christo and Jeanne-Claude's insistence on suspending interpretation. In Prix and Swiczinsky's design, an orthogonal glazed volume seems to emerge from within the historic building, fracturing and opening the roof. This volume would act as a "cut" through the Reichstag, "setting free" the southern part of the building, which would be completely reconstructed and function solely as a monument.[62] A twisting, off-center roof protruded from above the plenary chamber, irresistibly recalling the spiral of Vladimir Tatlin's Monument to the Third International (and resurfacing in Coop Himmelb(l)au's 2011 competition-winning proposal for the parliament of Albania in Tirana). This vertical coil would serve as a visual complement to the "media wall" they envisioned for the west facade, projecting local, national, and international news around the clock and acting as an information kiosk much like the Vesnin brothers had envisioned for the Leningrad Pravda tower in 1924. These references to constructivism, including the Proun-like form of the glass addition, provide the discontinuity and fragmentation that characterized the work of those architects labeled (however imprecisely) as "deconstructivist."

Out of these many proposals, three projects—all by foreign architects—were initially awarded a joint first prize. The winners, Pi de Bruijn, Santiago Calatrava, and Norman Foster, each proposed radical solutions to the Reichstag, all of which would have the effect of placing the historical building inside a viewing frame. These proposals also would have uniformly marked the building as an ambitiously contemporary work

Figure 2.11 Pi de Bruijn, proposal for the Reichstag, Berlin, 1992. © Pi de Bruijn, de Architekten Cie.

of architecture. Pi de Bruijn, of the Amsterdam group de Architekten Cie, offered a project (Figure 2.11) that drew openly on Oscar Niemayer's National Congress for Brasília, in which a bowl-shaped plenary chamber rested on a podium in front of the Reichstag like a piece of public sculpture. Along the northern perimeter of the site, a horizontal strip would house the presidential wing, appearing almost as though one of Brasília's twin parliamentary towers had been turned on its side and cut open for pedestrian traffic. The historical Reichstag was partially submerged in the raised podium, thus becoming another object in this catalog of historical references. As in de Architekten Cie's addition to the Dutch national parliament in The Hague, which had opened the previous year, forms taken from architectural history (particularly the heroic modernism of mid-century capitals) were treated as abstract motifs to be reassembled in new compositions.

The Spanish-Swiss engineer and architect Santiago Calatrava's competition entry (Figure 2.12) likewise invoked modernist precedents, but with a lyrical expressionism absent from de Bruijn's cerebral modernist citations. In his proposal, the emphasis on visual dynamism on which Calatrava had hitherto built his career was transformed into actual motion. Calatrava proposed to rebuild the Reichstag's interior in crystalline glass and reconceive the dome as four segmented glass shells floating above the plenary hall. These shells would open and close slowly like the petals of a flower, a concept in

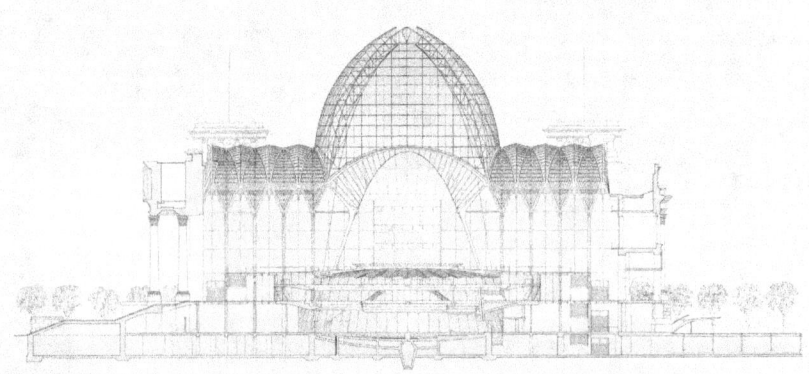

Figure 2.12 Santiago Calatrava, *Realisierungswettbewerb Umbau des Reichstagsgebäudes zum Deutschen Bundestag Ein 1. Preis, Regierungsviertel, Schnitt*, Berlin, 1992. Berlinische Galerie, Berlin. Markus Hawlik/Berlinische Galerie.

line with his later designs at the Milwaukee Art Museum's Quadracci Pavilion and the main building at Florida Polytechnic University in Lakeland (among others). In the economy of the starchitect, Calatrava's gestural, techno-poetic designs have become his signature. In his Reichstag proposal, he hoped that this organic metaphor of growth and renewal would negate the building's painful history, projecting instead a sense of openness, airiness, and naturalness. Calatrava's submission documents emphasized the idea that the building should "retain its identity" by hewing closely to the existing contours of Wallot's design.[63] Of the three finalists, Calatrava most restricted his interventions to within the walls of the extant structure. Yet no less than the others, his proposal reframes and re-presents the historical building, overlaying its deficiencies with a gauzy mantle of emotionalism and nostalgia. Calatrava's design seems less to present Berlin's particular history in clear terms than to offer a poignant lens through which to view the past. This ruin-gazing lens is elegiac but nonspecific, romantically juxtaposing the old and the new in a treatment of historic architecture that is common in contemporary architecture culture.[64] According to Calatrava, these interventions would give the building a "new inner life, and therefore a new meaning for contemporary dome construction."[65] The jury was positively disposed to Calatrava's design, praising it for its elegance, its introspective demeanor, and its creative contemporary rethinking of the ancient form of the dome. In later stages of the competition, Calatrava was unique in his commitment to remaining within the contours of the historical building, garnering substantial support among Bundestag members and experts. Among others, Michael Cullen vocally supported Calatrava's approach, deeming it to be the most graceful response to the complicated historical condition of the building.

Yet it was the third finalist, Norman Foster, to whom the Bundestag would eventually award the commission. Describing his proposal for the Reichstag (Figure 2.13), Foster

Figure 2.13 Foster + Partners, proposal for the Reichstag, Berlin, 1992. Foster + Partners. Photo by Richard Davies.

proclaimed that the building "could not shed the weight of its past associations but it had to be lightened symbolically," and this drive for lightness infused his response to the competition brief.[66] Rather than enhancing the existing Reichstag building with major flourishes, Foster's proposal conceptualized the old structure as the anchoring element of a raised plinth that created an area for public gatherings and reduced the bulk of the building from the ground-level view. Around the Reichstag, the grade of the earth would be elevated so that the building would appear to be partially buried in the ground. From the Platz der Republik, the base of the building would be invisible, shortening the facade by about one quarter and making the historic structure appear longer and lower in elevation. Seen one way, the elimination of the rusticated base made the building appear more *modernist*—horizontally disposed, sleeker, and with ample fenestration now oriented to the eye level of a pedestrian. The visual impact was similar to Christo and Jeanne-Claude's wrapping of the building, as these changes had the effect of lightening the materiality of the stone and smoothing the bulky ornament. Further lightening was to occur on the interior: a glass vitrine would be inserted into the building's historical shell, a "house within a house," as Foster described it, replacing Baumgarten's plaster and drywall interiors with exquisitely layered transparent surfaces.[67]

Though access to the building's interior spaces would be necessarily secure and restricted for official business, Foster's proposal, more noticeably than the other prizewinners', emphasized the need for vital public spaces in the new government area

Figure 2.14 Norman Foster (Architect) and Helmut Jacoby (Artist), *Wettbewerb Umgestaltung des Reichstags*, Berlin, 1992. Colored ink and photograph on cardboard. Deutsches Architekturmuseum, Frankfurt am Main. © Helmut Jacoby-Archiv Deutsches Architekturmuseum, Frankfurt am Main; Foto: Uwe Dettmar, Frankfurt am Main.

(Figure 2.14). A viewing platform on the roof (retained in the final design) would offer viewers a panoramic view of the city and permit visitors to the government district to stand symbolically above the elected representatives. A translucent roof covered the circular plenary chamber, allowing visitors on the roof to peer inside during parliamentary debates, and an interior atrium surrounding the plenary chamber would create further publicly accessible space. Furthermore, the historical building itself was sited asymmetrically within the plinth and was intended to be just one component in an entire urban ensemble that would include theaters, cinemas, galleries, bookshops, riverside cafes, schools and daycares, and abundant underground parking for public use. Indeed, inspired by recent popular gatherings at the Platz der Republik—concerts by the likes of Genesis, the Eurythmics, and David Bowie; fireworks, festivals, and protest rallies; and spontaneous celebrations of the fall of the Wall and eventually of reunification—Foster conceived the plinth as a true public space. Throughout the competition proceedings, he referred to it as a "forum" that would provide a space of leisure and activity relevant to the contemporary *flâneur* as well as to the government workers in the Reichstag's inner offices. Unlike other entries, the models, renderings, and drawings that Foster created for the competition are dynamized by the presence of human figures, no doubt encouraging the Bundestag to imagine the then-moribund Reichstag as instead a venerable and benevolent witness to the activities of everyday life. Although his proposal predated the actual wrapping of the Reichstag, the resonances in the atmosphere Foster intended to create around the building and those resulting from Christo and Jeanne-Claude's installation are conspicuous.

This lively public forum would be sheltered beneath what Foster termed "the big roof"—an immense, translucent canopy 250 meters long and 160 meters wide, intended to serve both practical and symbolic purposes.[68] Functionally, the canopy would have played a crucial role in making the building ecologically sustainable, since its square panels would be implanted with photovoltaic cells to harvest solar energy and would permit diffused natural light into the building's interiors. Each panel of the canopy would contain intersecting diagonal apertures of clear glass to admit light into the space below. Because of the pillow-like design of the panels, which were supported by steel trusswork, these slashes seem at one to reference the rib vaults of Gothic architecture (from above) and the folds of a fabric tent (from below). The canopy was supported by twenty-five lithe stainless steel columns, each 50 meters tall and tapering to a fine point at the top.[69] At the northeast corner, one of the columns, according to Foster, "dipped its toes in the River Spree, the former border between East and West, thus acknowledging the reconciliation that had made the project possible."[70] Symbolically, Foster and supportive Bundestag members believed that the canopy effectively united the old with the new, as well as lightening the mood of the existing building. The historical Reichstag would abide tranquilly beneath this high-tech umbrella, its antique interiors gutted and its base sunken into the earth, "visible from afar," as the philosopher Wilhelm Vossenkuhl described it.[71]

By now, the "big roof" technique has become such a staple of Foster's work that it, like many formal stratagems of contemporary architecture, has become largely taken for granted. But it is worth lingering on the canopy for a moment in order to unpack the revealingly museological qualities of this competition proposal, many of which persist in the built Reichstag. Architectural theorists writing in the eighteenth and nineteenth centuries, such as Marc-Antoine Laugier and Gottfried Semper, had characterized the roof as possessing a quasi-mystical ability to gather together the space and human activity beneath it.[72] Like much of modern architecture, the roof as a unifying element derived from the twin poles of craft and engineering in the 1800s, finding its most fully realized expressions in the draped roofline of the Shingle Style and the vast glazed enclosures of exhibition buildings like London's Crystal Palace and railway sheds like Berlin's own Friedrichstrasse Station. In both cases, the designers of these roofs prized their ability to synthesize disparate parcels into a cohesive and therefore modern space, acting as an element of what Sigfried Giedion called "decisive tectonic importance."[73] Yet these immense roofs also brought with them a distinctly modern euphoria of ascending, liberating space. This unifying roof has found its contemporary realization most significantly in museums, stadia, retail facilities, and airports—many of them credited to Foster himself, such as the Great Court of the British Museum, the mirrored Vieux Port Pavilion, and many projects completed for Apple, including the Steve Jobs Theater Pavilion.[74]

In the German context, the canopy of Foster's Reichstag proposal was the offspring of a genealogy of the "big roof" that includes Mies's Neue Nationalgalerie in Berlin and Behnisch's Bundeshaus (which was ironically not quite complete at the time of the Reichstag competition).[75] Yet it is also clearly related to the early museum projects that established Foster's reputation. The Sainsbury Centre for the Visual Arts on the campus of the University of East Anglia (Figure 2.15), designed with his then-wife and partner Wendy Cheesman, gathers the different functions of a museum of world art under a vast double-layered arch that terminates in diaphanous curtain walls at both ends.[76]

Figure 2.15 Foster Associates, Sainsbury Centre for Visual Arts, the University of East Anglia campus, Norwich, UK, 1978. (The Sainsbury Centre is to the left; Denys Lasdun's Norfolk Terrace student accommodation is to the right.) Countrywide Images / Alamy Stock Photo.

The roof of the Carré d'Art in Nîmes (Figure 2.16) is more varied in surface across the top of the building, but nevertheless suggests an enveloping canopy. Half of the contemporary art museum and library's nine stories are buried underground; yet as with the "big roof" of the Reichstag, natural light floods the interior from the transparent roof covering the airy atrium. A louvered portico projects from the building's glazed entrance, supported by slender steel columns. This portico creates an intentional dialogue with the Maison Carrée, the first-century BCE Roman temple that lies near the museum across a small square.[77] The temple's stepped base, slender columns, and pitched roof all recur in Foster's design, inspiring the critic Francis Rambert to declare that the "grandeur" of Foster's work was "in the true manner of the Romans."[78] Sunken halfway into the ground, the Carré d'Art implies its own excavation, framing a history of art that culminates in the contemporary collection inside its walls.

As in Foster's proposal for the Reichstag, the roofs of both of these buildings serve important ecological functions, decreasing their carbon footprint and thus representing a different form of "lightness"—sustainability—in a manner that is paramount for Foster. In his view, the sense of ecological lightness resulting from minimalistic, environmentally high-tech architecture is both ethical and humanistic. His mentor Buckminster Fuller, a pioneer of lightweight tensile structures and passive sustainable

Figure 2.16 Foster + Partners, Carré d'Art, Nîmes, France, 1993. © Carré d'Art (musée).

designs, once famously inquired of him, "How much does your building weigh, Norman?"[79] To Fuller, the calculation of the weight of a building involved its consumption of resources, the overall mass of its materials, and the stress it exerted on fragile ecosystems. But alongside these hard calculations, Fuller also contemplated the poetics of sustainability, investigating the metaphysical conditions under which humans could exist in harmony with their natural surroundings. Under Fuller's influence, Foster continued to investigate the potential of high-tech design to actualize ecological lightness, and this green approach to design has been a hallmark of his career.

But despite its centrality to the international branding of Foster's work, this environmental definition of lightness is not the only one at work in his thinking. In fact, especially in the past three decades, his philosophy of historical lightening has, perhaps, gained equal footing with his environmental approach. In both the Sainsbury Centre and the Carré d'Art—as in many of Foster's projects—lightness is achieved through a juxtaposition of a high-tech vocabulary with existing historical fabric, often in the form of classicizing masonry architecture. In the case of the Sainsbury Centre, the distinction between the historic and the contemporary is announced via the contrast between the collection and the high-tech architecture that shelters it. However, here the originary architectural object is implicit rather than present. The University of East Anglia's postwar campus means that the customary neoclassical museum building exists as an imaginary, rather than specific, reference point, but the Sainsbury Centre creates provocative visual tension with the primitive ziggurats of Denys Lasdun's adjacent university complex. In the case of the Carré d'Art, Foster not only creates a building that would seem "light" in most contexts, but also reframes and activates the "heaviness" of its ancient neighbor. For both museums, therefore, the viewer is encouraged to view architecture as a synthesizing force that unifies the disturbances and interruptions of history. Whether intentionally or not, the gaze that Foster inscribes in these buildings suggests the romantic idea that architecture can serve both as an authentic record of a history long past and as a harmonizing element in the present: *ars longa, vita brevis*.

In fact, Foster is conscious of how his treatment of the Reichstag collapses several meanings of the term "lightness" into one persuasive visual image. As he says:

> In lectures, from time to time, I talk a great deal about the importance of natural light and its humanising significance in architecture. I also wax lyrical about the properties of physical lightness and sense of uplift I get from elegantly pared-down high-performance structures. In the case of the Reichstag the distinction between these two themes becomes blurred in the quest to lighten the physical burden of the building—to transform it to meet today's needs and social attitudes, but to accept its past.[80]

This romantic pursuit of lightness infuses Foster's Reichstag, which is overtly museological both in proposal and in built form. In the proposal, the elevated plinth of the forum and the delicate materiality of the canopy give the historical building the appearance of a precious object raised on a socle and encased in glass. Indeed, the canopy has the ultimate effect of isolating the Reichstag from its surroundings and placing it on display. As Brigitte Werneburg noted in *Art in America*, Foster's "original glass roof made the Reichstag seem like a museum piece in an oversized vitrine."[81] At the same time that the elimination of the bottom of the facade made the building look sleeker, more horizontal, and more modern, it simultaneously had the effect of making the building seem yet more like an ancient ruin whose base had sunk into the sands of time. In so doing, Foster increased the aesthetic value of both his design and the Reichstag itself, using the lightness of the roof to offset the weight of the historical building. This delicate state of visual and historical equilibrium—or, rather, its lack—might also reveal why Baumgarten's earlier renovation had failed, having sought to achieve lightness by merely obscuring the building's encumbrances. Foster's museological approach, in contrast, balanced a sense of gravity and stateliness that was lacking in Bonn's official architecture with a dignified exuberance absent from Baumgarten's repackaging of the Reichstag.

It was not to be. Despite its enthusiastic reception, Foster's "big roof" was slated for the cutting-room floor. In the first place, it conflicted spatially with Axel Schultes and Charlotte Frank's master plan for the government district (see Chapter 1), whose monumental Band des Bundes also made it superfluous to expand the usable space of the Reichstag. Furthermore, economic pressures nationwide forced the Bundestag to reduce the budget for the building's reuse by a drastic percentage and to condense the necessary space from 33,000 square meters to between 9,000 and 12,000. But maybe the decisive factor in the Bundestag's decision to jettison the "big roof" was the increasing pressure from many quarters to top the historical Reichstag with a contemporary dome—a measure that Foster had flatly refused to take during the first phase of the competition.

In response to this pressure and the ensuing public controversy over reconstructing the dome, Foster fired off a volley of solutions for topping the building that stayed within the contours of the existing fabric and yet avoided the fraught issue of the dome (Figure 2.17). After several more design phases, and under particular duress from right-wing politicians, Foster began to examine possible forms for a new dome. Eventually, the Bundestag officially approved the renovation plans, whose primary exterior alterations included the glazed entrance facade and the now-acclaimed cupola, a transparent, ovoid volume whose steel oculus and ribs support the dynamic curl of the spiral ramp. Inside the cupola, a fountain-like mirrored cone issues from above the plenary chamber before cascading into the glass panels that comprise the dome's exterior.[82] The cupola's reminders of the liquid properties of glass, along with its lambent transparency, conjure the expressionist ancestry described above. Foster's redesign thus flows upwards from the heaviness of the historical building, culminating

Figure 2.17 Foster + Partners, models for Reichstag cupola, 1993. Photo by Richard Davies.

in the visually light, radiant cupola. After the original proposal, the form of the renovation changed utterly, but the essential strategy of lightening remained consistent throughout.

Interestingly, Foster's discarded proposal has become the subject of its own filmy nostalgia, often cited by critics eager to condemn Berlin's recent architecture as tamed and commercialized. For these critics, the Bundestag's failure to realize the original scheme is typical of Berlin's more general squandering of architectural vision in the 1990s and early 2000s, caused by an excess of caution regarding the new capital's international image and reunified Germany's bottom line. The architect Sebastian Schmaling characterized the abandonment of Foster's roof in favor of the cupola as a move from "radical design" to "token avant-gardism," while critic Martin Filler lamented the change as one piece of evidence that Berlin's new architecture amounted to a "lost opportunity."[83] The "big roof" has also featured prominently in popular recent exhibitions of never-constructed projects for Berlin and their accompanying catalogs, whose generally wistful tone heightens the oneiric quality of the designs within.[84] Foster's proposal has thus become part of a set of Berlin urban apocrypha that includes unrealized buildings and urban plans, joining Mies's glass skyscrapers for Friedrichstrasse, Ludwig Hilberseimer's landscape of high-rises to the west of the Gendarmenmarkt, and even Speer's north–south axis and titanic dome for Germania as the subject of a nostalgic, museological gaze.

The Faith of Graffiti

Since the process of amending Foster's plan began, most critical and popular attention has remained focused on the vexed question of the dome. Yet for all the literal and figurative high visibility of the cupola, perhaps the aspect of Foster's project that more fully reveals its strategy of reframing the Reichstag as a model of contemporary lightness has received little sustained scholarly treatment: his insistence on conserving the graffiti left by Soviet soldiers passing through the Reichstag during the Battle of Berlin (Figure 2.18). After the demise of the canopy scheme, it was these graffiti that provided the necessary pendant weight to accomplish Foster's sought-after lightening, allowing him to pronounce the Reichstag a "living museum of German history."[85] Though Foster's decision to preserve and exhibit the graffiti initially stirred public controversy, the outcry generally subsided as the project progressed and the overall narrative of lightness, with the cupola as climax, came into view. Yet we need only step back slightly to recall how peculiar the display of this graffiti truly is. Though accentuating the marks of history is by now a common strategy normalized in the architecture of the present day, the preservation of the graffiti is a genuinely startling choice that marks this project as distinctly *contemporary* rather than merely an extension of modernism. In the first place, the chance to maintain these inscriptions reiterated Foster's original impulse to mark the historical building as a ruin; second, it positioned him again in the role of historian, assembling fragments into a cogent story. Ultimately, the preservation of the graffiti shores up the museological gaze established

Figure 2.18 Reichstag corridor with conserved graffiti, 2017.

in Foster's competition entry and underscored by Christo and Jeanne-Claude's wrapping.[86]

The Reichstag itself was a significant strategic location for the Soviets—who misunderstood it to be "Hitler's lair," despite the fact that Hitler had never ruled from the building—and its conquest on April 30, 1945 signaled the imminent end of the war.[87] In Yevgeny Khaldei's well-known (and carefully staged) photograph, a soldier heroically hoists the hammer-and-sickle flag above one of the Reichstag's towers to symbolize metonymically the victory of the Red Army over the Germans (Figure 2.19). The conquered building sags beneath him, and his form is mirrored by the bulky allegorical sculptures that had attracted such mockery in earlier days. At the time of this photograph, and for several days afterwards, soldiers occupying the building used chalk, pencil, and charcoal to record their presence on every mangled surface that they could touch. The result was a frenetic skein of Cyrillic writing that visually overpowered Wallot's awkward shields, heroes, and swags (Figure 2.20). Most of these marks were erased during Baumgarten's renovation (unfortunately, in Foster's view). Today, only 202 distinct pieces of graffiti remain, but historical photographs suggest that every reachable wall was once virtually covered with text.[88]

In his seminal 1974 essay on the aesthetics of urban graffiti, Norman Mailer interviewed a young street artist who declared, "The name is the *faith* of graffiti."[89] What the artist meant, and what Mailer argues, is that the marking of one's name on the wall is the most condensed and potent affirmation of historical presence in the

Figure 2.19 Yevgeny Khaldei, *Soviet Flag over the Reichstag*, 1945. Shawshots / Alamy Stock Photo.

Figure 2.20 Reichstag stair with graffiti, Berlin, 1945. INTERFOTO / Alamy Stock Photo.

visual world, a ratification of human existence that demands the viewer's faith in response. This assertion of presence is everywhere on view in the Reichstag's graffiti. Most of the inscriptions were written with fragments of charcoal or chalk, and the vast majority simply record the writer's name: "O. Shilova," "I was here/Sherbakov," or "L. N. Borodinov was here."[90] Others take the form of messages to families, sweethearts, and other troops: one soldier inscribed "Galina and Anatoly" within a cupid's heart, and another wrote "On the day of victory over fascism we send battle greetings to all soldiers in the glorious Red Army!"[91] Others record the distances traveled by their company, and a scant few lob obscenities toward Germany and its army, such as "Serves them right sons of bitches."[92] Like the other participants in the 1992 Reichstag competition, Foster was unaware of the graffiti during the competition, and no mention was made of it in the brief. In fact, it was only unearthed in 1995, soon after Christo and Jeanne-Claude "unwrapped" the building, when demolition workers began to remove Baumgarten's plaster paneling from the building's interior in yet another unveiling to prepare the building for its new life. Foster describes this unveiling in the language of the archaeologist: "The Reichstag, as we found it in 1992, gave few clues as to what we might eventually discover."[93] According to him, Baumgarten's renovation had efficiently obscured the building's evocative "secrets": "In fact the interior of the building reminded me of nothing so much as a convention centre or a municipal baths. It had been so sanitised by reconstruction in the 1960s that it was impossible to imagine anything of interest ever having happened there."[94] With the discovery of the graffiti, the building seemed to possess the emotional intensity necessary to support the lightness that Foster had sought from the beginning and that had been displaced from the canopy to the cupola.

According to Foster, his conviction that the graffiti must be preserved was more or less immediate upon its discovery. His reasoning was straightforward: to erase or cover these marks, he argued, would be to obfuscate the historical events that the Reichstag building documented. Parliamentarians voiced vehement positions that, once again, typically broke along party lines, with left-leaning MPs supporting Foster's belief in the necessity of presenting history objectively, and many on the right arguing that it was humiliating and even borderline cruel to showcase inscriptions with no aesthetic value and with such vulgar content. At first, the Bundestag decided to document and then remove the inscriptions. But Foster himself intervened and, after a series of debates, a narrow majority voted to preserve nearly all the remaining graffiti. In consultation with the Russian embassy, the most inflammatory inscriptions were documented and removed, though one remaining inscription does say, "I fuck Hitler in the ass."[95] Today, the embassy closely guards the text of the erased graffiti, acutely aware of its potential to strain German–Russian relations.[96]

The decision to maintain the inscriptions came at considerable expense, especially at a moment in which the Bundestag was cutting budgets for building projects across the capital city. With no real precedent available, Foster's team had to improvise the technology necessary for the graffiti's conservation. Stabilizing the fragile marks meant going over each line with a fixative (thus uncannily recreating the original gestures of inscription), then cleaning the negative space by tracing the area around each letter with a minuscule sandblaster. Photographs documenting the process of conservation show hard-hatted and goggled workers in front of the walls with pencil-sized implements in their hands, contemplating the graffiti like artists poised to make the first brushstroke of a masterpiece painting. Other images show workers on ladders or scaffolds, like conservators tending the frescoed interior of a church. Foster himself noted with pride that those responsible worked "with almost watchmakerly precision to protect the fragile graffiti."[97] This fetishistic level of detail—the artisanal slowness of the process of conservation, in contrast to the speed with which the graffiti were originally scrawled—imparts a sense of handcraft to Foster's otherwise high-tech renovation. Like much of contemporary architecture, the Reichstag reveals a surprising nostalgia for the bodily intimacy of craft as manifested in ornament.

In "Ornament and Crime," Adolf Loos's 1908 polemic against the decorative, he characterizes graffiti as the most debased form of expression. For Loos, graffiti records a failure of sublimation; as he says, "The urge to ornament one's face and everything within reach . . . is the baby talk of painting. All art is erotic."[98] Loos judges that the act of making graffiti is both pathological and uncivilized, reflecting not only the subject, but his entire milieu: "the man of our day who, in response to an inner urge, smears the walls with erotic symbols is a criminal or a degenerate . . . A country's culture can be assessed by the extent to which its lavatory walls are smeared."[99] Several generations of architects had taken seriously this cry for the removal of ornament from the surfaces of buildings, and they developed the modern architecture that would, in its later days, be a visible analogue to democracy in the Bundesrepublik as represented by the transparent government architecture in Bonn. Yet in Foster's Reichstag, not only does ornament reappear after its forced exile, but it does so in its most degraded form; even more than just its return, the graffiti seem to represent the triumph of the repressed. As with much of contemporary architecture, Foster's apparently straightforward desire not to conceal the historical record belies the acts of selection that occur in the process of design.[100] For example, his fervor regarding the graffiti was matched by his disdain for Baumgarten's renovation, which was arguably no less a part of the building's history; nor did he seriously contemplate restoring Wallot's lost ornament or preserving the dirt and grime that had accumulated throughout the building's life.[101] Foster's "living museum," like all museums, presents a limited and carefully curated view of historical events in a disrupted narrative that is no less linear for that fact.

The controversy surrounding the graffiti's political implications, as well as the more general ongoing debate around graffiti's status qua art, has tended to obscure the specific work it does in Foster's renovation. Though it lacks the media presence of the cupola, it is the most "authentic" evidence of the building's historical weight and the necessary anchor to the cupola's pristine lightness—and as such, it is the crucial element in Foster's transformation of the Reichstag into a "living museum of German history." Its ability to add auratic value to the building, while at no point suspending its meaning as marks of defacement, has everything to do with graffiti's unsettled cultural position. Rosalind Krauss has described graffiti as "the dirtying of the clean wall" with significant implications for art: "the destructive, performative character of graffiti . . . acts against the high, neutralized, cultural form to lower it."[102] In fact, graffiti has long been felt to be art's "low," debased other, necessary to shore up the category of art, but also believed to be more spontaneous, authentic, and transgressive than art could ever be. Graffiti seems to retain its ability to circumvent expected visual regimes, largely due to its multiplicity: it is at once text and image, destructive and artful, a cancellation (of property) and an affirmation (of presence). Even with the continued absorption of "street art" into the art market and the visual language of contemporary architecture, graffiti maintains its alterity and its ability to trouble categories. Perhaps it is best understood as an *operation*—an operation of "lowering," to use Krauss's language, that becomes both literal and figurative in Foster's Reichstag.[103]

Consider, for example, Foster's romantic description of the completed renovation, in which the graffiti's "lowering" function becomes clear:

> We have worked within the discipline of the old shell, respecting the historical floor levels and their expression in the facades. Where Wallot's ruined corridors have been retained, you can feel the history of the place particularly strongly. The corridors leading to the east lobby feel almost sepulchral, like an ancient Egyptian catacomb. Great cyclopean boulders of stone around the newly reopened doorways are all that remain of once ornate architraves. As you rise through the building, however, its history is less evident, and there is instead an unfolding sense of lightness, growth and change.[104]

Foster's words are those of a talented architect delighted to have found historical affect there for the taking. But they also reveal the program of lightening at the heart of his renovation, whose success depended on establishing the meaningful, auratic gravity of the old structure. Despite the building's relatively young age, his description of his renovation—and the new architecture itself—treat the historical Reichstag with the same esteem afforded the Maison Carrée. Convinced of the Reichstag's weight, the viewer is thus prepared for the upward lift of the lightening to follow.

Then, too, there is the way in which the graffiti act to validate the Reichstag's historical significance, positioning the building as a reliable and objective eyewitness to the events of the past. The renovated building bears these inscriptions along with other emblems of its age, such as fragments of original moldings, mason's marks, and even bullet holes. These "scars of damage and disruption," in Theodor Adorno's words, act as a "seal of authenticity," corroborating the building's narrative of a trauma overcome.[105] In fact, it is the corporeal intimacy of the graffiti, the way in which each mark supposedly retains the indexical power of human touch, that allows it to fulfill this authenticating function. The role of architecture, then, is to facilitate this closeness, allowing the audience to "experience" the marks of history on view. Many critics, and Foster himself, have noted that the details of the renovated Reichstag call for the viewer to touch the graffiti, a haptic invitation that Christo and Jeanne-Claude's *Wrapped Reichstag* issued as well.[106]

In the wake of the Bilbao Effect and the ongoing ascendance of the starchitect-designed museum building, the Reichstag—the seat of reunified Germany's parliament—nonetheless becomes a museum worth seeing. The building's various iterations, especially the three discussed here, all serve the purpose of reinscribing "weight" into lightness; but the strategies common to global contemporary architecture allow that weight to become bearable by investing architecture with a unique ability to knit time together without dooming us to eternal return. Using "authentic" elements of the past, the historian-architect makes a claim to objectivity that is in itself a romanticizing narrative of history. That story then forms the basis of a new national myth, emphasizing cultural rather than political unity and soft power as gentle as *Wrapped Reichstag*'s billowing fabric. But perhaps this fusion of objectivity and romanticism is one of contemporary architecture's most important functions, fostering the belief that glass walls and steel frames can make history tangible, knowable, and ineradicable. If we believe such buildings, they will tell us the truth; if we believe in them, then the past will remain ever-present—in other words, the faith of contemporary architecture.

Notes

1. Rudy Koshar, *Germany's Transient Pasts: Preservation and National Memory in the Twentieth Century* (Chapel Hill: University of North Carolina Press, 1998), 329.
2. I use "Foster" throughout this chapter to refer both to the individual architect and, synecdochally, to the sprawling international firm Foster + Partners, which employees nearly 1,500 people worldwide and is currently at work on projects in no fewer than twenty countries.
3. Quoted in Cathleen McGuigan, "Vision of the Capital," *Newsweek*, April 19, 1999, 60.
4. See, in particular, Deborah Ascher Barnstone, *The Transparent State: Architecture and Politics in Postwar Germany* (New York: Routledge, 2005), Lutz Koepnick, "The Nation's New Windows," in *Framing Attention: Windows on Modern German History* (Baltimore: Johns Hopkins University Press, 2007), 240–62, and Eric Jarosinski, "Architectural Symbolism and the Rhetoric of Transparency: A Berlin Ghost Story," *Journal of Urban History* 29 (November 2002): 62–77.
5. Transparency remains a powerful metaphor for democracy in global contemporary architecture culture; recent examples include the Bordeaux Law Courts by Rogers Stirk Harbour + Partners, the United States Courthouse in Phoenix, AZ by Richard Meier & Partners, and the MOdA Headquarters of the Paris Bar Association by Renzo Piano Building Workshop.
6. Barnstone and Koepnick both note this connection. Kathleen James-Chakraborty also explores the renovated Reichstag's expressionist antecedents in *Modernism and Memory: Building Identity in the Federal Republic of Germany* (Minneapolis and London: University of Minnesota Press, 2018).
7. Citing Fredric Jameson, Elie Haddad and David Rifkind describe this misunderstanding, observing, "The attraction of the new characterizes much of what has been produced under the label of 'contemporary' architecture, which in Jamesonian terms may be nothing more than the revival of the 'modern' under new guises." See Haddad and Rifkind, "Introduction," in *A Critical History of Contemporary Architecture: 1960–2010*, eds. Haddad and Rifkind (Farnham: Ashgate, 2014), 24. I also discuss this pseudo-"newness" in the introduction to this book.

8 For a discussion of the role of historical research in contemporary art more broadly, see Mark Godfrey, "The Artist as Historian," *October* 120 (Spring 2007): 140–72.
9 Daniela Sandler discusses the recent ascendance of adaptive reuse, especially in Berlin, in *Counterpreservation: Architectural Decay in Berlin since 1989* (Ithaca: Cornell University Press, 2016), 28–32.
10 Several comprehensive histories of the Reichstag have been written, most notably by the most well-known scholar of the building, Michael S. Cullen. See Cullen's *Der Deutsche Reichstag: Geschichte eines Monumentes* (Berlin: Frolich and Kaufman, 1992), *Der Reichstag: Denkmal, Symbol, Geschichte* (Berlin: Be.Bra, 1995), and *Der Reichstag: Parlament, Denkmal, Symbol* (Berlin: Be.Bra, 1999). See also Heinrich Wefing, "*Dem Deutschen Volke.*" *Der Bundestag im Berliner Reichstagsgebäude* (Bonn: Bouvier, 1999).
11 "Berlin Houses of Parliament Competition," *The Architect: A Weekly Illustrated Journal of Art, Civil Engineering and Building* 7 (January 27, 1872): 42.
12 The form of the dome was allegedly inspired by Herman J. Schwarzmann's Memorial Hall at the 1876 Centennial Exposition in Philadelphia.
13 Cullen, *Der Deutsche Reichstag: Geschichte eines Monumentes*, 38.
14 According to Peter Chametzky, "The problem was (how) to design a building to represent a nation that hardly existed, and to house and represent a democratic body in what was essentially an imperial oligarchy." In Chametzky, "Rebuilding the Nation: Norman Foster's Reichstag Renovation and Daniel Libeskind's Jewish Museum Berlin," *Centropa* 1 (2001): 251.
15 Cullen, *The Reichstag: German Parliament between Monarchy and Federalism* (Berlin: Be.Bra, 2004), 36.
16 Albert Speer, *Inside the Third Reich*, trans. Richard and Clara Winston (New York: Simon & Schuster, 1970), 151–2.
17 The most significant manifestations of this anticipatory planning were the Hauptstadt Berlin competition of 1957–8 and the ongoing IBA (Internationale Bauaustellung, or International Building Exhibition), initiated in 1957. See Florian Urban, "Recovering Essence through Demolition: The 'Organic' City in Postwar West Berlin," *Journal of the Society of Architectural Historians* 63 (September 2004): 354–69.
18 Architects, politicians, and critics roundly criticized Baumgarten during the 1990s Reichstag colloquia for what was deemed his insensitive renovation of the building, yet he claimed that his approach had been largely dictated by his government client. As late as 1982, he stated: "It isn't my Reichstag any more. My ideas are no longer recognisable. When I describe my design concepts, for instance the idea of space inside the ruin and then someone goes to look, they say: 'but it's simply not true.' I then have to start talking of disfigurement and then there's a great fuss again." Quoted in Cullen, *The Reichstag: Germany Parliament between Monarchy and Federalism*, 62.
19 Christo and Jeanne-Claude were not the only artists of this moment who were interested in the Reichstag's iconic silhouette; Andy Warhol depicted the building in one of his trademark silkscreen paintings in 1982, now in the collection of the Yale University Art Gallery.
20 Interview with Christo, *Perspecta: The Yale Architectural Journal* 47 (2014): 95.
21 Quoted in Cullen and Wolfgang Volz, eds., *Christo—Jeanne-Claude: Der Reichstag "Dem Deutschen Volke"* (Bergisch Gladbach: Gustav Lübbe, 1995), 247.
22 Ibid.

23 James E. Young, "A City's Ritual of Renewal," http://www.waterfire.org/impressions-waterfire/citys-ritual-renewal-james-e-young.
24 Francesca Rogier, "Growing Pains: From the Opening of the Wall to the Wrapping of the Reichstag," *Assemblage* 29 (April 1996): 66.
25 Both Mayor Eberhard Diepgen and Bundestag President Süssmuth identified the wrapping as a "rite of passage," according to Brian Ladd in Ladd, *The Ghosts of Berlin: Confronting German History in the Urban Landscape* (Chicago: University of Chicago Press, 1997), 92.
26 In *Deutscher Bundestag: Verhüllter Reichstag—Projekt for Berlin* (Bonn: Deutscher Bundestag Referat Öffentlichkeitsarbeit, 1995), 18276. The transcript of this 70-minute debate documents a notably wide-ranging discussion about the nature of contemporary art and its effect on urban politics. Burkhard Hirsch of the Free Democratic Party objected to making the Reichstag the center of a "PR campaign" via its wrapping (18278). Freimut Duve of the Social Democratic Party argued for the wrapping, rhetorically pointing out that if Schäuble's objections held water, then the Bundestag should not consider rebuilding the Reichstag at all, but rather maintain it as a ruin, "a symbol of the wounds of our history" (18287). Other parliamentarians on the right expressed exasperation with the amount of attention and energy being expended on the subject of art and wonder why the discussion is being had in the first place, calling for renewed focus on economic issues.
27 Paul Goldberger, "Christo's Wrapped Reichstag: Symbol for the New Germany," *The New York Times*, June 23, 1995, C3.
28 Charles S. Maier, *Dissolution: The Crisis of Communism and the End of East Germany* (Princeton: Princeton University Press, 1997), 330.
29 Ibid., 331.
30 "Schaut auf diese Stadt," *Der Spiegel*, July 23, 1995, 25.
31 Werner Spies, "Christo and Jeanne-Claude: Der Weg zum Widerstand," *Frankfurter Allgemeine Zeitung*, June 13, 2005, 29.
32 Marc Fisher, "Germany 1995: A Riddle Wrapped in an Aluminum Enigma," *The Washington Post*, June 4, 1995, C3.
33 Ibid.
34 In the architecture critic Michael Kimmelman's assessment, "it was a celebration of art as a galvanizing and transformative, even magical, experience. After all, it was the strange, and ambiguous, gesture on the part of Christo and Jeanne-Claude that drew everyone together in the first place. And that, for a while, somehow changed the character not just of the building but also of the city. The wrapped Reichstag looked fine, handsome even, but it wasn't the look of the wrapping that makes it stick in the mind. It was the spirit of it: upbeat and embracing." Kimmelman, "Art '95; A Wrapped Reichstag: That's the Spirit," *The New York Times*, December 31, 1995, 37.
35 Lothar Heinke, "Glitzerglanzstück der Demokratie," *Der Tagesspiegel* (June 24, 2015): https://www.tagesspiegel.de/kultur/20-jahre-reichstagsverhuellung-von-christo-und-es-war-sommer/11958304.html.
36 Joel Agee, "Wrap Session," *Harper's Magazine* 292 (February 1996): 61.
37 Andreas Huyssen, "Monumental Seduction," *New German Critique* 69 (Autumn 1996): 186. Though Huyssen concludes that the wrapping of the Reichstag was too transitory and critical to be simply categorized as monumental, Jean Baudrillard argued that it amounted to an entrancing cover-up job: "Five million visitors came to

celebrate this aesthetic laundering of history. An ambiguous collective jubilation: if Nazism thrived on the aestheticization of politics, our new democracy thrives on the aestheticization of the end of history." Baudrillard, "'Lost from View' and Truly Disappeared," in *Screened Out* (London: Verso, 2014), 124.
38 Koshar, 330.
39 Milan Kundera, *The Unbearable Lightness of Being*, trans. Michael Henry Heim (New York: HarperCollins, 2004), 5–6.
40 See, for example, Italo Calvino's investigations of lightness in *Invisible Cities* (1972) and the first of his *Six Memos for the New Millennium* (1988).
41 Structures that demonstrate this contemporary drive toward dematerialization include Diller + Scofidio's Blur Building at the 2002 World Expo on Lake Neuchâtel in Switzerland and BIG's 2016 SKUM Pavilion at the Roskilde Festival in Denmark.
42 G. W. F. Hegel, "On Art," in *On Art, Religion, and the History of Philosophy: Introductory Lectures*, trans. J. Glenn Gray (New York: Harper & Row), 119.
43 Quoted in Hanno-Walter Kruft, *A History of Architectural Theory from Vitruvius to the Present*, trans. Ronald Taylor, Elsie Callander, and Antony Wood (New York: Princeton Architectural Press, 1994), 296.
44 Ibid.
45 Quoted in Kruft, 306.
46 Heinrich Hübsch, "In What Style Should We Build?," in *In What Style Should We Build? The German Debate on Architectural Style*, trans. Wolfgang Hermann (Santa Monica: Getty Institute for the History of Art and Humanities, 1992), 91.
47 From the seventeenth to the nineteenth centuries, the term was used throughout Europe to describe the Gothic style, whether the associations therein were positive or negative. In France, the lightness of the Gothic is cited by Claude Perrault, Jacques Gabriel Soufflot, and Marc-Antoine Laugier, and in England by William Chambers, Thomas Rickman, and Robert Willis (among others).
48 Sigfried Giedion described the effects of new metal construction, apparent as early as the Crystal Palace: "Even at this primitive stage of construction the meaning of the new material is sensed. Openness instead of spatial enclosure. Light. Lightness." Giedion, *Building in France, Building in Iron, Building in Ferroconcrete*, trans. J. Duncan Berry (Santa Monica: Getty Institute for the History of Art and Humanities, 1995), 122.
49 Hermann Muthesius, *Style-Architecture and Building-Art: Transformations of Architecture in the Nineteenth Century and its Present Condition*, trans. Stanford Anderson (Santa Monica: Getty Institute for the History of Art and Humanities, 1994), 80.
50 Ibid., 74–5.
51 Foster identifies this lightness as a hallmark of Renzo Piano's work. Foster, "Designing a Second Modernity?", in *The Political Unconscious of Architecture: Re-opening Jameson's Narrative*, ed. Nadir Lahiji (Abingdon: Routledge, 2016), 106.
52 For more on expressionist architecture's engagement with its viewership, see Kathleen James-Chakraborty, "Spectacle," in *German Architecture for a Mass Audience* (London: Routledge, 2000), 70–94.
53 Adolf Behne, "Das Glashaus," *Arbeiter-Jugend* 6, no. 20 (September 26, 1914): 293. Quoted in Kai Gutschow, "The Culture of Criticism: Adolf Behne and the

Development of Modern Architecture in Germany, 1910–1914" (PhD dissertation, Columbia University, 2005), 232.

54 Peter Conradi, "Impulse für die Architektur von Parlament und Regierung in Berlin," in *Kunst, Symbolik und Politik: Die Reichstagsverhüllung als Denkanstoß*, eds. Ansgar Klein, Ingo Braun, Christiane Schroeder, and Kai-Uwe Hellman (Opladen: Leske + Budrich, 1995), 154. See also Norman Foster, who refers to Conradi's idea of a "*Rheinische* Lightness of Being" in *Rebuilding the Reichstag*, ed. David Jenkins (New York: Overlook Press, 2000), 132.

55 Douglas Crimp, "The Art of Exhibition," in *On The Museum's Ruins* (Cambridge, MA: MIT Press, 1993), 253.

56 Cullen, *Symbol Deutscher Geschichte* (Berlin: Be.Bra, 2016), 45, 54.

57 Jean Nouvel and Emmanuel Cattani, "Reichstag Berlin," *Architectural Design* 114 (1995): 65.

58 Ibid.

59 Gottfried Böhm, Peter Böhm, and Friedrich Steinigeweg, "Reichstag Berlin," *Architectural Design* 114 (1995): 67.

60 Wolfgang Voigt, "Kuppel, Mauer, Hülle: Berlins 20. Jahrhundert in Zeichnungen aus der Sammlung des Deutschen Architekturmuseum," in *Berliner Projekte: Architeckturzeichnungen 1920–1990*, ed. Nadejda Bartel (Berlin: Tchoban Foundation Museum für Architekturzeichnungen), 20.

61 Curated by Mark Wigley and Philip Johnson, the show also included work by Peter Eisenman, Frank Gehry, Zaha Hadid, Rem Koolhaas, Daniel Libeskind, and Bernard Tschumi.

62 Coop Himmelb(l)au, "Reichstag Berlin," *Architectural Design* 114 (1995): 66.

63 Michael S. Cullen, *Calatrava Berlin: Five Projects* (Berlin: Birkhäuser, 1994), 135.

64 I discuss this "ruin gaze" more fully in Chapter 3. See Andreas Huyssen, "Authentic Ruins: Products of Modernity," in Julia Hell and Andreas Schönle, eds., *Ruins of Modernity* (Durham, NC: Duke University Press, 2010), 17–28.

65 Santiago Calatrava, "Reichstag Berlin," *Architectural Design* 114 (1995): 64.

66 Norman Foster, "The Reichstag as World Stage," in *Rebuilding the Reichstag*, ed. David Jenkins (New York: Overlook Press, 2000), 23.

67 Ibid., 30.

68 Norman Foster, "Architecture and History," in *Rebuilding the Reichstag*, 60.

69 The number of columns is often misidentified as twenty. This miscount seems to originate from an error in *Rebuilding the Reichstag*, 25.

70 Foster, "The Reichstag as World Stage," 25.

71 In Sir Norman Foster and Partners, *Reichstag Berlin* (Berlin: Aedes Galerie für Architektur und Raum, 1994), exhibition catalog, 3.

72 See Marc-Antoine Laugier, *An Essay on Architecture*, trans. Anni Hermann (Los Angeles: Hennessy & Ingalls, 1977) and Gottfried Semper, *The Four Elements of Architecture and Other Writings*, trans. Harry Francis Mallgrave and Wolfgang Hermann (Cambridge: Cambridge University Press, 1989). For Laugier, the classical pitched roof was the decisive expression of tectonics as defined by the "primitive hut." Semper considered the roof to be among the four crucial elements of architecture, in addition to the hearth, the mound, and the enclosure, signifying architecture's primordial task of sheltering and protecting human life.

73 Giedion, 12.

74 Another noteworthy example of Foster's "big roof" appears in Berlin at the Philological Library of the Freie Universität.
75 For an analysis of Behnisch's project and its relationship to the timing of the Reichstag renovation, see Barnstone, 138–74.
76 One of the founding partners of both Team 4 and Foster Associates, Wendy Cheesman Foster died of cancer in 1989.
77 Laugier himself considered the Maison Carrée to be among the most perfect buildings in antiquity, specifically noting its timeless expression of tectonics: "everything here accords with the true principles of architecture: a rectangle where thirty columns support an entablature and a roof . . . that is all; the combination is of a simplicity and a nobility which strikes everyone." Laugier, 13.
78 Francis Rambert, "Nîmes: Foster City?," *D'architecture* 35 (May 1993): 12–13.
79 Norman Foster, "Richard Buckminster Fuller," in *Buckminster Fuller: Anthology for the New Millennium*, Thomas T. K. Zung, ed. (New York: St. Martin's Press, 2001), 4. Fuller's question was also used as the title of the 2010 documentary *How Much Does Your Building Weigh, Mr. Foster?*, written by director of London's Design Museum and Foster biographer Deyan Sudjic.
80 Foster, "Introduction: The Living Museum," in *The Reichstag Graffiti*, ed. David Jenkins (Berlin: Jovis, 2003), 12.
81 Brigitte Werneburg, "Rebuilding Berlin," *Art in America* 83 (November 1995): 84.
82 When the design for the cupola was unveiled, Calatrava protested that it was all too obviously derivative of his project for the 1992 competition, but his outcry gained little traction.
83 Sebastian Schmaling, "Masked Nostalgia, Chic Regression: The 'Critical' Reconstruction of Berlin," *Harvard Design Magazine* 23 (Fall 2005/Winter 2006): 28. Martin Filler, "Berlin: The Lost Opportunity," *The New York Review of Books* 17, November 1, 2001, 28–31.
84 These exhibitions include *City of Architecture, Architecture of the City: Berlin 1900–2000* at the Neues Museum in 2000, *The Unbuilt Berlin* at Café Moskau in 2010, *Das Neue Berlin: Internationale Entwürfe seit 1990* at the Berlinische Galerie in 2013, and *Berlin Projects: Architectural Drawings 1920–1990* at the Tchoban Foundation in 2017. A section model of the Reichstag proposal was also displayed in *Building with History*, an exhibition of Foster's work held at Hearst Tower in 2016–17.
85 Foster, "Architecture and History," 77.
86 This museological quality has only been emphasized by recent plans to add an official visitor's center on the Platz der Republik; a temporary pavilion has already been set up to accommodate tourist demand.
87 One piece of graffiti in the southwest stairwell reads, "We made it to the Reichstag, Hitler's lair!" *The Reichstag Graffiti*, 80.
88 Helmut Engel, "The Marks of History," in *Rebuilding the Reichstag*, 118.
89 Norman Mailer, "The Faith of Graffiti," *Esquire* (May 1974): 79.
90 Ibid., 42, 100, 101.
91 Ibid., 106.
92 Ibid., 77.
93 Foster, "Introduction: The Living Museum," in *The Reichstag Graffiti*, 11. Barnstone likewise notes the archeological quality of his approach on 190.
94 Ibid.

95 George Packer, "The Quiet German," *The New Yorker*, December 1, 2014, 48.
96 In one interview, Rita Süssmuth, who oversaw the removal of the most offensive inscriptions, suggested that they referenced Russian "sabers" stabbing German "sheaths" or "vulvas," which would have been a too-graphic and painful reminder of the rapes of countless German women by Soviet soldiers after the end of the war. Andreas Kluth, "The Graffiti That Made Germany Better," *The Atlantic* (July 3, 2014), https://www.theatlantic.com/international/archive/2014/07/the-graffiti-that-made-germany-better/373872/. Susan Stewart discusses the erotics of graffiti, especially implicit in the act of "'getting up' one's name," in "Ceci Tuera Cela: Graffiti as Crime and Art," in *Crimes of Writing: Problems in the Containment of Representation* (New York: Oxford University Press, 1991), 224.
97 Foster, "Architecture and History," 77.
98 Adolf Loos, "Ornament and Crime," in *Programs and Manifestoes on 20th-Century Architecture*, ed. Ulrich Conrads (Cambridge, MA: MIT Press, 1964), 19.
99 Ibid.
100 For more on the many acts of "selection" in Berlin's contemporary architecture, see Rolf J. Goebel, "Berlin's Architectural Citations: Reconstruction, Simulation, and the Problem of Historical Authenticity," *PMLA* 118 (October 2003): 1268–9.
101 As Jorge Otero-Pailos has written, "preservation is a process of interpreting objects in such a way as to create history of a very special kind … Without buildings … there is no preservation. But conversely, without preservation those buildings cannot achieve their status as history." Otero-Pailos, "The Contemporary Stamp of Incompleteness," *Future Anterior: Journal of Historic Preservation, History, Theory, and Criticism* 1 (Fall 2004): iii.
102 Rosalind Krauss, "Jeu Lugubre," in Krauss and Yves-Alain Bois, *Formless: A User's Guide* (New York: Zone Books, 1997), 115.
103 The graffiti covering the western side of the recently disassembled Berlin Wall would have offered Foster an inescapable example of this operation. Indeed, instances of graffiti's claims to authenticity can be found throughout Germany, such as Berlin's destroyed Kunsthaus Tacheles, Jochen Gerz and Esther Shalev-Gerz's Monument against Fascism in Hamburg, and the former Gestapo prison, now a museum, at the EL-DE Haus in Cologne.
104 Foster, "Architecture and History," 77.
105 Theodor Adorno, "Situation," in *Aesthetic Theory*, trans. Robert Hullot-Kentor (London: Athlone Press, 1997), 23.
106 As Christo noted, visitors seemed compelled to touch the wrapped building: "when it was finished, they came up to stroke the fabric." In Oliver Wainwright, "How We Made the Wrapped Reichstag," interview with Christo and Wolfgang Volz, *The Guardian*, February 7, 2017, https://www.theguardian.com/artanddesign/2017/feb/07/how-we-made-the-wrapped-reichstag-berlin-christo-and-jeanne-claude-interview. Agee observed a similar response among viewers: "People are touching the cloth—with curiosity, and with a gentleness that seems out of keeping with the sturdy material. 'Like the apes in 2001,' someone near me remarks." Agee, 62.

3

Monumental Modernism—The Chancellery as Future Ruin

In W. G. Sebald's novel *Austerlitz*, the title character, an architectural historian, devotes his career to exploring the singularly affective power of monumental architecture. In a conversation with the narrator, Austerlitz reflects that it only seems possible to feel at peace in the presence of small-scale domestic architecture—for example, the cottage, the hermitage, the garden pavilion, or the child's playhouse. On the other hand, he observes, monumental structures arouse in the viewer "a kind of wonder which is itself a form of dawning horror."[1] This admixture of wonder and horror results from the viewer's instinctive knowledge that "outsize buildings cast the shadow of their destruction before them, and are designed from the first with an eye to their later existence as ruins."[2] Through the character of Austerlitz, Sebald articulates a central premise of his oeuvre: that in the very grandness of its gesture, all monumental architecture will eventually provoke an equal and opposite politico-historical force. According to this principle, monumental architecture can thus be understood to offer a glimpse forward in time by forecasting its own demise. Its imposing form, in other words, contains both the seed of a future ruin and a premonition of disaster.

In this passage, Sebald takes part in a centuries-old tradition of contemplating monumental architecture in which its ruins are envisaged as the platform for imaginative flight. Especially since the eighteenth century, ruins have figured in art, literature, and philosophy as repositories of universal truths, bespeaking such themes as the hubris of empire, the relentlessness of time's passage, and the endurance of human creation against the transience of human life. In almost every case, ruins point both backward and forward in time, offering nostalgic views of history while also making reassuring claims to its steady onward march. As with ruin-gazers throughout modern history, Sebald argues that ruins possess a kind of authenticity and insight not readily available in the visible world. But his essays and novels suggest that the wisdom engendered by ruins is bleak, drained of romantic edification. In our contemporary moment, monumental architecture remains oracular, but its prophecies offer no comfort—only the certain knowledge of destruction and decay.

Published in 2001, *Austerlitz* would be Sebald's final novel.[3] In the same year, at the official opening of Berlin's new Federal Chancellery (Figure 3.1), chancellor Gerhard Schröder addressed the crowd of officials and journalists assembled in front of the building's dramatic concrete-and-glass facade. As press cameras surveyed the vast

Figure 3.1 Schultes Frank Architekten, Federal Chancellery, Berlin, 1994–2001.

edifice, Schröder gave a strangely ambivalent speech, repeatedly insisting that the Chancellery conveyed a sense of political and urban unity and assuring the viewers that, contrary to its burgeoning reputation, it was "not a place of grand gestures."[4] Rather, he lauded the Chancellery's architects—Axel Schultes and Charlotte Frank, with Christoph Witt—for their sensitivity to history and their courage in expressing Germany's new self-confidence through the structure's bold forms. Throughout his remarks, Schröder praised the building for its "openness" and "transparency," and sternly declared that its architecture did not speak the authoritarian language of "Sanssouci or Neuschwanstein."[5] This tacit rebuke was aimed to quell criticism of what had become an especially contentious project in the construction of the new capital. Yet in point of fact, Schröder himself had been an outspoken critic of Schultes and Frank's design for the Chancellery throughout its realization. Despite the support he voiced at its opening, a few journalists reminded him of his initial, sardonic reaction to the building at its topping-out ceremony in 1999: "Don't you have it in a smaller size?"[6]

Schröder's quip, and his belated enthusiasm for the new residence and offices of the chancellor, offer a concise summary of the controversy surrounding the project. Since winning the design competition in 1994, Schultes and Frank's Chancellery has been the target of anxious concern from architects, politicians, and members of the public that it is, bluntly stated, too monumental. With its raised central cube, its extending wings, and its rhythmic sequence of bays in white concrete and aquamarine glass, the building stretches Sphinx-like along the western curve of the Spreebogen. Semicircular glazed windows puncture its broad surfaces and towering columns adorn its facades. At 12,000 square meters, it is the largest government headquarters in the world, dwarfing homologous structures like the White House, the Élysée Palace, and 10 Downing Street.[7] In contrast to its peers, the Chancellery's appearance is not of a government center at the scale—however grand—of a domestic building. Instead, it inverts this order, embedding a residence for the chancellor into an otherwise manifestly monumental government complex.

On the surface, then, the debate over the Chancellery turned on questions of scale, proportion, and decorum, with critics wondering how a structure this immense could possibly be an appropriate representation of a nation still making amends for its devastating past. Though some critics praised the building's audacious design, negative public sentiment and unfavorable press coverage accelerated as costs mounted and the government began the process of moving from Bonn to Berlin. In the months before the building's opening, it was beleaguered by a spate of bad reviews asserting that its architecture sent the wrong political message. "Size and massiveness characterize the impression of the new Chancellor's office, and size and massiveness have grown unfamiliar during the long decades of the old Bundesrepublik," wrote one journalist in the *Berliner Zeitung*.[8] Unable to resist the juvenile pun, the *Telegraph* announced: "Size does matter for Germany's grandiose Chancellery."[9] And Schultes himself expressed misgivings over the scale of the building's anchoring cube, leading the *Los Angeles Times* to declare: "Even the architect thinks Germany's Chancellery is too big."[10] Thus, the debate that played out in the popular media, both nationally and internationally, was often reduced to a simplistic dispute over architectural and political brawn—and over Germany's right to assert such *bigness*.

However, as with much of the discourse surrounding Berlin's new government architecture, the polemics into which the debate over the Chancellery has settled obscure more than they illuminate. For the core concern was, in fact, far more complex than whether size alone amounted to architectural monumentality—and, by extension, whether the building might therefore expose dubious political intentions on the part of reunified Germany. Looked at more closely, the questions raised by the Chancellery's design were subtle and difficult, engaging a number of the architectural dilemmas that remained most unsettled at the end of the millennium. The category of monumentality stands at the center of a web of associated problems—including the struggle for authenticity, the viability of the classical tradition, and the persistence of the trope of the ruin—that troubled much of Berlin's new architecture. Indeed, these anxieties, often repressed or sublimated, preoccupied architects across the world at the end of the twentieth century and still form an invisible crux of global contemporary architecture culture today. This cluster of problems reveals contemporary architecture's secret fascinations, both with monumental architecture's ability to survive across time and with the simultaneous inevitability of its eventual disintegration—what Walter Benjamin, in his discussion of ruins, characterized as the "irresistible decay" of history.[11] Moreover, these questions point to an unresolvable paradox for a discipline that has not abandoned its aspirations toward permanence, but that must confront ever clearer evidence of its own ephemerality in the form of climate crisis, geopolitical upheaval, and rapacious global development.[12]

The Future Ruin in Berlin and Elsewhere

How, then, might we clarify both the architecture of the Chancellery and the network of contemporary problems that it activates? And how, given Sebald's warnings about the future collapse of such architecture, might we come to terms with the specific mode of monumentality that the building embodies? We might begin by attending closely to an oft-mentioned but rarely explored presence in the government district at the Spreebogen: the architecture and philosophy of Louis I. Kahn. Schultes openly declares himself a "disciple" of the mid-century master and regularly cites Kahn's dictum, "Architecture is the thoughtful making of spaces. It is the creating of spaces that evoke a feeling of appropriate use."[13] In citing Schultes's many writings and interviews and allowing him to play the role of loquacious spokesperson, I follow the firm's lead, with misgivings about my own role in reproducing asymmetries of recognition and value, both in terms of gender and in terms of the inherently collaborative nature of work within any firm.[14] Nevertheless, all three principles continually cite Kahn as the most significant source for their work for the Bundesrepublik, both in the master plan for the area and in the design for the Chancellery. Scholars have followed suit, routinely observing Kahn's palpable impact on Schultes and Frank's government projects.[15] Furthermore, Kahn's work is also the most frequently mentioned precedent for the other buildings comprising the Band des Bundes: the Paul-Löbe-Haus, opened in 2001 (Figure 3.2), and the Marie-Elisabeth-Lüders-Haus, opened in 2003 (Figure 3.3), both

Figure 3.2 Stephan Braunfels, Paul-Löbe-Haus, Berlin, 1997–2002. West facade.

Figure 3.3 Stephan Braunfels, Marie-Elisabeth-Lüders-Haus, Berlin, 1998–2003. chrisdorney / stock.adobe.com.

designed by the Munich-based architect Stephan Braunfels. In interviews, Braunfels has repeatedly pointed to Kahn as the most important influence on his work for demonstrating how a modern architect might deal with history—and, additionally, to the example of Axel Schultes, as a contemporary "model of how to deal with Louis Kahn."[16] Overall, Kahn (supported by the late-career Le Corbusier) hovers like a beneficent spirit over the New Berlin's government architecture, and these repeated invocations of his oeuvre suggest that it modeled something quite specific to architects working in the reunified city.

In fact, Kahn's spectral presence at the Spreebogen speaks to his unusual place in contemporary architecture more generally, especially in projects that must address the entwined problems of monumentality, classicism, and ruination described above. Despite his idiosyncratic career—he was the consummate late bloomer, and his mature work has little in common with the technophiliac vocabulary cultivated by so many contemporary architects—and despite ongoing resistance to the brutalist idiom to which his name is often (imprecisely) attached, Kahn's star has risen steadily over the past three decades. In particular, the dignified grandeur of his work has provided many contemporary architects with an example of how one might embody communal values in built form without resorting to historicism or bombast.[17]

For many historians and critics, citing Kahn as an antecedent for Berlin's new government architecture would seem to be self-explanatory, endowing these buildings with eloquence, stateliness, and restraint. But it is my suggestion in this chapter that merely invoking Kahn's name does not sufficiently explain his peculiar ascendance in Berlin or in the broader culture of global contemporary architecture. Rather, I propose here to focus on one aspect of his work in order to clarify what might truly lie behind his pervasive recent influence. Specifically, I argue that significance can be found in Kahn's striking description of the strategy of "wrapping ruins around buildings," formulated most clearly in his monumental projects of the 1960s and 1970s. For Kahn, as we will see, the metaphor of the ruin was a means by which to restore qualities to architecture that he had come to believe formed its very essence: timelessness, solemnity, and the human search for meaning, all of which had been eroded by modernism's obsession with functionalism. For more recent architects, I argue, ruin-thinking has metastasized; no longer a metaphor, it is instead an inescapable future that can be experimentally, sometimes even playfully, figured in the present.

Thus, a careful consideration of how Kahn's concept of "wrapping ruins around buildings" is expressed in the Chancellery illuminates more than just its architects' devotion to an influential master and more than just the curious nostalgia permeating the Spreebogen. It also helps make sense of the multifarious ways in which the trope of the ruin runs through recent architecture in Berlin, and through global contemporary architecture more generally. In Berlin, this trope obviously characterizes the haunting forms of war-ravaged buildings that have been preserved in their ruined form, sometimes framed by new interventions. Such structures include Norman Foster's Reichstag, of course, but also the "hollow tooth" of the Kaiser Wilhelm Memorial Church and the evocative church and belfry built by Egon Eiermann in 1959–63; the stalwart shells of the Franciscan Monastery Church and the Anhalter Bahnhof, stabilized after the war, with the latter soon to foreground the new Exilmuseum by Dorte Mandrup; and the patchwork of David Chipperfield's Neues Museum, pieced together from remaining fragments and opened to great acclaim in 2009. Decay and collapse also plainly attend the intentional grit and grime of squatters' "house projects," like the defunct Kunsthaus Tacheles and Brunnenstrasse 183.[18] Likewise, on ready view around the city is the appropriated decay and manufactured patina that has become synonymous with the recent aesthetics of chic consumerism in many global capitals.[19] This manageable level of decrepitude appears as well in the crumbling walls and appealing "street art" of Haus Schwarzenberg near the upscale Hackescher Höfe, and in the studied dishabille of the shops and cafes of newly gentrified areas in Mitte, Prenzlauer Berg, and Kreuzberg. Finally, ruin imagery is easy to detect in what critic Sophie Lovell has termed Berlin's "post-industrial ruin aesthetic," apparent in notoriously edgy clubs like Berghain (a former power plant) or Sisyphos (an abandoned dog biscuit factory).[20] These sites do not disguise their fascination with the ruin, instead celebrating a particularly *Berlinische* form of urban memory that has, so to speak, gone global.

But seen through this Kahnian lens of ruin-wrapping, a discourse of future ruination also comes to encompass less obvious contemporary structures, both in Berlin and beyond. It can be seen in the tactile rammed-earth walls of the Chapel of Reconciliation at the Berlin Wall Memorial on Bernauer Strasse (Rudolf Reitermann and Peter Sassenroth, 1999–2000) (Figure 3.4); it can be seen in the inscribed concrete boxes of the Tchoban Foundation Museum for Architectural Drawing (Sergei Tchoban and Sergey Kuznetzov, 2009–13) (Figure 3.5); and it can be seen in the arched brick carapace encasing the former hospital building at the Forum Museumsinsel (Chipperfield again, 2010–present) (Figure 3.6).[21] These structures' powerful massing and textured surfaces exemplify a tendency toward the creation of anticipatory ruins that winds its way through contemporary architecture. Internationally, we might find it in such structures as Toyo Ito's Tama Art University Library in Tokyo (2004–7) (Figure 3.7), Michael Photiadis's Venus Marble Headquarters in Athens (2010) (Figure 3.8), and Vo Trong Nghia's Stacked Planters House in Ho Chi Minh City (2017).[22] In these and other buildings, that which makes contemporary architecture insistently and

Figure 3.4 Rudolf Reitermann and Peter Sassenroth, Chapel of the Reconciliation, Berlin, 1999–2000.

Figure 3.5 Sergei Tchoban and Sergey Kuznetzov, Tchoban Foundation – Museum for Architectural Drawing, Berlin, 2009–13.

visibly *new*—digital technology, irregular morphologies, and the thinness of glass-and-steel construction—remains present, but subjugated to a logic of architectural permanence. In a contemporary ruin-wrapped building, a materially up-to-date structure, usually transparent, is effectively enclosed in an archaic shell. Thus, these buildings appear both stable *and* transient, solid *and* fragile, current *and* antiquated.

Figure 3.6 David Chipperfield Architects, Forum Museumsinsel, Berlin, 2010–16. © Ute Zscharnt for David Chipperfield Architects.

Figure 3.7 Toyo Ito, Tama Art University Library, Tokyo, 2004–7.

Figure 3.8 Michael Photiadis, Venus Marble Headquarters, Athens, 2010.

It is not simply that multiple temporalities are folded into these designs; rather, an impending future presses upon them, anxiously and intractably.

To be sure, this practice of ruin-wrapping is a present-day architectural coping mechanism, signaling an awareness of past trauma or a presentiment of catastrophe. At the same time, however, it offers contemporary architects a means of reengaging an age-old architectural imaginary. For the architecture of many cultures across time and space has been animated by a speculative mode that envisions the future appearance of its built environment and reflects on its life span. This ruinophilia, as Svetlana Boym has termed it, permeates Berlin's new government architecture, though it is always masked by contemporary narratives of penance and progress.[23] If, as I argued in Chapter 2, Norman Foster's renovated Reichstag reveals how contemporary architecture shows a romanticist obsession with the scars of the past, then the Chancellery reveals an equally romanticist fascination with how the ravages of the future might appear. The monumentality and weight of the Chancellery, then, stands in contrast to the lightness sought by the Reichstag; Norman Foster pursued a means of dealing with a painful history, while Schultes and Frank offered a vision for posterity—a building that might endure as a monument to reunified Germany's highest aspirations, even, potentially, in a state of collapse.

Therefore, understanding the Chancellery (and the other structures comprising the Band des Bundes) means that we must also explore in parallel the web of architectural problems I introduced above. Though each node in this intricate network is equally complex in its own right, here I will look at these issues as they have arisen in the context of this much-debated building. Throughout the Chancellery's development, construction, and use, these problems have surfaced repeatedly, creating tensions and contradictions within its critical reception. Since 1994, some of these tensions have been laid out in explicit terms, but other, more painful discourses have remained buried in subtext. Though many of these dilemmas remain unresolved today, it is revealing at least to point to the pressures they exert on contemporary architecture. Hence, despite Kahn's centrality to the architecture of the Chancellery, we must leave him aside for now as we examine the context that framed his "arrival" on the scene.

The Competition

Given the intensity of the debates over the Chancellery's expression of monumentality, it is perhaps ironic that the controversy at the competition stage was centered not on Schultes and Frank's proposal, but rather on the designs of the other two finalists. The limited 1994 competition was open only to architects based within Europe and drew applications from 254 firms, fifty-one from which the Bundesrepublik ultimately solicited full proposals.[24] At the close of the competition, just forty-one entries had been received, and a mere twelve of these had come from outside Germany.[25] Sharp-eyed critics took note, comparing this lethargic turnout to the 835 designs submitted to the open Spreebogen competition and the eighty high-quality proposals entered in the limited competition for the Reichstag.[26] From the beginning, then, even during its most nascent stage, the project for the Chancellery seemed to be characterized by a higher degree of control from its government client and a lower level of enthusiasm from the profession. The prevailing reaction to the competition announcement from architects had been one of trepidation, and it was understood that only someone of rare mettle could see through a project as historically burdened as Germany's new seat of executive power. Therefore, some firms avoided the competition altogether, believing that the project would prove too charged to hazard their involvement. In general, architects frankly acknowledged (despite the government's protestations to the contrary) that the project was likely to be hemmed in by prohibitively severe restrictions.

In fact, a distinct and widely acknowledged sense of wariness—and weariness—permeated the entire proceedings. Only two years after the first competitions were held to determine the form of the new capital, the global euphoria over Berlin's boundless sense of possibility had already begun to wither, and no longer did the city's architectural prospects seem quite so bright. Increasing financial pressure from investors, the logistical strain of the deadline to move the government to Berlin by 1998, and the stylistic constraints imposed by Senate Building Director Hans Stimmann's "Critical Reconstruction" dampened the previous feeling of creative exhilaration. This peevish atmosphere spread citywide: the private-sector competition for Potsdamer Platz produced results that its sponsor, Daimler-Benz, disparaged as "provincial," despite the expense and high-profile talent involved.[27] Meanwhile, critics derided the proposals for the 1993 Spreeinsel government competition (see Chapter 4) as "tired," "lackluster," and "old-maidish," as journalists declared that Berlin's chances of becoming a world capital of architecture were tanking in an environment that was somehow both hurried and squeamish.[28] Alongside these others, the air of cynicism attending the Chancellery competition stood in stark contrast to the excitement surrounding the 1992 competitions for the Spreebogen and the Reichstag. In the brief years intervening, a sense of exhaustion and doubt had infiltrated the government district that would dog the Chancellery project from beginning to end. In terms of Berlin's architectural future, as one writer put it, "the mood is worse than ever."[29]

Given its risks, the government had embarked on the Chancellery project with well-publicized caution. Following the model of transparency and open-mindedness established in earlier competitions, officials assembled a jury that they hoped would represent a range of political and architectural positions. Thus, jurors ranged from the Milan-based architect Aldo Rossi, whose ideas of collective memory had already proven widely influential in Berlin's rebranding, to the Viennese Gustav Peichl, who had served on the jury that controversially selected Carlos Ott to design Paris's Opera de la Bastille in 1983. The logic was that both traditionalists and latter-day avant-gardists would contribute an informed voice during deliberations. To safeguard against political steamrolling, the Bundesrepublik granted delegates from then-chancellor Helmut Kohl's office a minority vote. The governmental watchfulness evident in the Bundesrepublik's jury selection was mirrored by a corresponding tentativeness from the competition's applicants. Ultimately, most of the forty-one proposals hewed closely, both in appearance and rhetoric, either to the transparency doctrine of Bonn's government architecture or to the historicism of Critical Reconstruction.

Noteworthy exceptions came from the Parisian architect Francis Soler and from the father-and-son team of Gottfried and Stephan Böhm. Soler proposed an expressionistic Chancellery in which billowing layers of glass veiled a compact building, intentionally small in scale so as not to compete with the nearby Reichstag. Media screens would be deployed across the surface, which would also be wrapped in a veil of steel arabesques. Soler described his proposal as a "crystal lantern" whose "flickering light" and "poetic qualities" would express the new harmony at the center of Berlin.[30] Though Soler's proposal did not move forward in the Chancellery competition, its filigreed surface reappears in the facades of his Ministry of Culture and Communication in Paris, completed in 2005. With admirable forbearance, Gottfried and Stephan Böhm submitted yet another recapitulation of the ramp idea at the basis of their several unsuccessful bids for the Reichstag. In their scheme for the Chancellery, auxiliary offices were housed in four block-like buildings running along the northern edge of the site, while the chancellor's office took the form of a centrally planned, glass-domed building to the south. Beneath the dome, a curved ramp unfurled like a ribbon through the soaring atrium, irresistibly recalling both their 1988 and 1992 Reichstag proposals. Indeed, both of these unusual designs seemed to have wandered into the Chancellery competition from out of the multitude of Reichstag concepts presented two years earlier. Soler was awarded seventh prize in the Chancellery competition; the Böhms did not crack the top ten. Outside of a small handful, original solutions for how to express the executive heart of Germany's new political identity seemed thin on the ground.

Contested Legacies

As in the other competitions held to determine the form of Berlin's new government architecture, an artificial binary between tradition and innovation emerged as jurors debated which proposals bore the most merit. Yet even more explicitly than in these other discussions, the outcome of the Chancellery competition seemed to hover precariously between the Scylla of history and the Charybdis of modernism. Many of the participating firms understood these stakes, feeling themselves to be struggling with two equally complicated legacies: on the one hand, the diffidence of Bonn's transparent government buildings, and on the other, the pomp and bluster of Nazi architecture. These two troublesome ancestors had colored discussions of both the Spreebogen and the Reichstag—and by 1994, for different reasons, each was equally taboo.

In the first place, West Germany's unassuming and abstract federal buildings felt entirely too vague to offer a usable precedent for the new Chancellery. Executive functions in Bonn were at first contained in the neoclassical Palais Schaumburg, but eventually a residence and reception space for the chancellor was constructed in the humbly named Kanzlerbungalow, designed by Sep Ruf and opened in 1964 (Figure 3.9). Comprising two interlocking transparent pavilions of glass and steel topped by a flat, overhanging roof, the building's clear antecedent was Ludwig Mies van der Rohe's German Pavilion at the 1929 World Exhibition in Barcelona.[31] In 1976, this modest structure was supplemented by a Chancellery that was larger in size but no more monumental in expression, bearing all the distinction of a suburban office park.

As with the other government buildings constructed in the provisional capital, the Kanzlerbungalow made high-minded claims as to progressive architecture's ability to body forth democratic ideals.[32] At the end of the century, however, Bonn's lack of

Figure 3.9 Sep Ruf, Kanzlerbungalow, Bonn, 1964.

architectural pretension could easily read instead as a nearly pathological avoidance of state representation. The first chancellor of the Bundesrepublik, Konrad Adenauer, had lamented satirically that the Kanzlerbungalow "wouldn't even burn," a mordant allusion to its lack of monumentality.[33] Moreover, by 1994, Bonn's perceived architectural timidity risked coming across as disingenuous for a country with as much economic might as Germany's. Therefore, during the Chancellery competition, architects proposing to work in a simplistically modernist language of form were summarily dismissed. Among such proposals were those from Swiss architect Max Dudler, who referred to the "openness and accessibility" of his glass facades, as well as to the scheme's overall "reduction and considered simplicity"; and Berlin-based Hilde Léon + Konrad Wohlhage, whose proposal the jury critiqued for conveying a "reserved impression," "reinforced by the neutrality of the grid façade."[34]

But if "modernism" seemed inadequate to the task of embodying the New Berlin's political values, it proved nowhere near as offensive as "classicism," likewise reduced to a few visual characteristics. For one aspect of the darkening mood surrounding the competition was the realization of how tormented Berlin's architectural tradition remained by its unresolved Nazi past. Just as Norman Foster had been required to negotiate a contested legacy in the Reichstag's Wilhelmine architecture, it was likewise necessary for the architects of the Chancellery to confront and come to terms with an historical building. However, this building, Albert Speer's Reich Chancellery, existed only as a specter, having been destroyed half a century before (Figure 3.10). The Chancellery was only one building in Hitler's grandiose plans for the Welthauptstadt Germania, but it was a critical player in the ensemble. This single building had to symbolize both Hitler's individual power and, synecdochically, the might of the National Socialist empire. As he described it:

> When one enters the Reich Chancellery, one should have the feeling that one is visiting the master of the world. One will arrive there along wide avenues containing the Triumphal Arch, the Pantheon of the Army, the Square of the People—things to take your breath away! It's only thus that we shall succeed in eclipsing our only great rival in the world, Rome. Let it be built on such a scale that St. Peter's and its Square will seem like toys in comparison!
>
> For material we'll use granite. The vestiges of the German past, which are found on the plains to the North, are scarcely time-worn. Granite will ensure that our monuments last for ever. In ten thousand years they'll be standing, just as they are, unless meanwhile the sea has again covered our plains.[35]

Though Hitler required that the Chancellery project a visual and material aura of permanence, he also demanded that it be executed with remarkable speed: construction began in early 1938 and the building was completed by January 1939. Although both Speer and Hitler forbade the use of modern materials, industrial construction techniques helped accomplish the staggering feat. At the same time, however, Hitler believed that it was crucial to place manpower itself on public view; on any given day, over 4,000 people worked to complete the building in a spectacle of imperial labor that

Figure 3.10 Albert Speer, Reich Chancellery, Berlin, 1937–9. Bundsarchiv-Bildarchiv, Berlin.

Hitler associated with Roman precedents. This muddle of past and present was equally visible in the form of the building itself, which Hitler envisioned as a hybrid of specific models (the Domus Aurea, the Aula Palatina) and general types (the urban palace and rural villa).[36]

Stretching for more than 400 meters along Voss-Strasse, the building was plainly intended to overwhelm and subdue the viewer. The tripartite street facade, surmounted by a hefty cornice, concealed a labyrinthine sequence of open courtyards, vast hallways, and cavernous rooms, all of which were ornamented with classical details. Fluted pillars, Doric pilasters, and eagles clutching wreathed swastikas in their talons abounded throughout as Arno Breker's figurative allegorical sculptures representing the Wehrmacht and the "spirit" of the Nazi Party kept watch.[37] As Dietmar Schirmer observes, the Reich Chancellery's "representational rooms and their spatial arrangement show the strategic use of oversized details to literally dwarf the viewer."[38] Hitler took special pleasure in the fact that the so-called Marble Gallery was even larger than the Hall of Mirrors at Versailles.[39] In general, the complex demonstrates Hitler's broader architectural obsessions with exaggerated scale, relentless repetition, and extravagant materials. In fact, this lavish building was only a temporary encampment to accommodate Hitler and his entourage until the yet more distended Führer-Palast could be completed at the northern terminus of the new north–south axis, facing off against the Reichstag inside the Spreebogen.

The Pleasure of Ruins

As one of the few monuments of the Welthauptstadt Germania that was actually built, the Reich Chancellery afforded an opportunity in Berlin to work through what Speer termed his *Theorie vom Ruinenwert*, or theory of ruin value. Speer's theory, which became central to Nazi architectural ideology, held that buildings should be made with an eye toward their own destruction so that they would maintain their beauty and dignity even in a state of collapse. To this end, stone of different varieties was the prized material; iron and ferroconcrete were to be avoided, since in a ruined state they looked merely pitiful rather than appropriately melancholy.[40] Indeed, according to Speer, the development of the "theory" was partly precipitated by an encounter with industrial decay. During the construction of the Zeppelinfeld in Nuremberg, a streetcar station was blown up to clear the way for the new buildings. Speer remarked later on how the "dreary sight" of the rusting iron rebar shaped his views:

> The idea was that buildings of modern construction were poorly suited to form that "bridge of tradition" to future generations which Hitler was calling for. It was hard to imagine that rusting heaps of rubble could communicate these heroic inspirations which Hitler admired in the monuments of the past. My "theory" was intended to deal with this dilemma. By using special materials and by applying certain principles of statics, we should be able to build structures which even in a state of decay, after hundreds or (such were our reckonings) thousands of years would more or less resemble Roman models.[41]

To illustrate his vision, Speer presented Hitler with a drawing of the tribune of the Zeppelinfeld in ruins, its columns fallen and its surfaces overgrown with ivy; Hitler received it with enthusiasm.

Speer presented his view of ruins as both theoretical and original, yet in reality it was neither. In fact, to formulate his "theory," the well-read architect drew on long-standing ruin tropes, some of which had been in circulation for hundreds of years.[42] Though buildings in various states of collapse possessed some artistic interest during antiquity and throughout medieval and Renaissance Europe, it was not until the eighteenth century that ruins became a distinct visual category with clear characteristics. In fact, the development of modernity was undergirded by a corresponding fascination with ruination, both natural and man-made. Codified in part by their frequent appearance in academic art, ruins came to represent silent witnesses to the mysterious movement of nature and history. Denis Diderot defined the aesthetic role of ruins in his well-known reflections on the Salon of 1767, in which the critic set the terms for much ruin-gazing that followed: "The ideas ruins evoke in me are grand. Everything comes to nothing, everything perishes, everything passes, only the world remains, only time endures. How old is the world! I walk between two eternities."[43]

Against modernity's grand narratives of progress, ruins thus became both objects of contemplation and subjects able to testify to the world's enigmas, especially those that seemed most resistant to scientific explication. In the eighteenth and nineteenth centuries, the Romantic impulse to grant special significance to ruins found expression in many cultural outlets, from Schelling's *Naturphilosophie* to Piranesi's fanciful and seductive visions of collapse. In painting, poetry, and music, ruins came to function as augurs of unknowable futures and tellers of invisible truths.[44] In all realms, the architecture that counted as a ruin was limited to the antique, especially structures referencing the classical past of Greece and Rome. Key to the modern ruin trope—and its present-day guise as well—is the idea that ruined buildings have been divested of their former function, and thus are able to be instilled with new meaning by a contemporary audience. As the art historian Michael Roth has argued, "When we frame an object as a ruin, we reclaim that object from its fall into decay and oblivion and often for some kind of cultural attention and care that, in a sense, elevates its value ... But (ruins) can never belong fully to the present without losing their status as ruins."[45]

This ambivalent temporality helps explain the strange survival of ruinophilia in the twentieth century, whose epic violence left ruination that would at first seem too real for the pleasurable metaphor to persist. During the 1900s, the trope developed in two directions: first, toward a fascination with the man-made ruins of mechanized warfare, and second, in the expansion of the scope of the ruin to include the by-products of industrial decay. In England, the novelist Rose Macaulay—who had survived the Blitz, but saw her Marylebone flat and all her worldly goods reduced to rubble—authored a 1958 treatise titled *Pleasure of Ruins*, in which she explored the wide-ranging history of what she termed "ruin lust." Her phrase was carefully chosen; throughout the book, she points to the drives, both erotic and thanatic, behind the satisfaction found in classical ruins. Like Speer, Macaulay considered industrial landscapes to fall well beneath the elevated aesthetic category of the ruin. But only nine years later, while on a "suburban Odyssey" through his birthplace of Passaic, New Jersey, the artist Robert Smithson could plainly discern the appeal of these scenes—even as he noted their toxic environmental effects.[46] During his tour, Smithson encountered a series of what he termed "monuments" (including a bridge, a derrick, a parking lot, and a sandbox), arguing that they were evidence of modernity's "ruins in reverse"—all the industrial structures yet to be built, in which "the buildings don't fall into ruin after they are built but rather rise into ruin before they are built."[47] At the place where Macaulay's "pleasure" meets Smithson's "ruins in reverse," the twenty-first century struggles to confront the sublime satisfaction we take in images of catastrophe. In views from 9/11 and Hurricane Katrina, in the bombing of Baghdad and the destruction of UNESCO World Heritage Sites, we experience what Dora Apel has described as "the paradoxical appeal of ruin imagery: the beauty of ruins helps us to cope with the terror of apocalyptical decline."[48]

Classical Controversies

Speer's own romanticist ruin-gaze and preference for classical architecture, therefore, was by no means simply a matter of politics, but was rather a common strain of modern aesthetics. In developing his "theory," Speer supposedly also drew on the writings of

Gottfried Semper, who argued that relics made from natural materials more readily translated cultural significance across time.⁴⁹ Yet the calculated future projected in Speer's idea of ruin value evidenced the cult of death at the heart of the National Socialist worldview. Speer's theory, and Hitler's embrace of it, reveal clearly the Reich's macabre headlong drive toward a new world order. Indeed, the massive scale of Nazi architecture remains noteworthy, even though other versions of "stripped classicism" were simultaneously constructed to express a range of political views.⁵⁰ Ultimately, the Reich Chancellery was reduced to rubble by Allied bombing and disassembled by Russian soldiers after the war's conclusion so that its valuable stone could be used to fashion Soviet memorials around the city. In fact, East Germany developed a socialist realist version of stripped classicism that guided the first phase of postwar reconstruction in Berlin.⁵¹ Though this application of classicism went largely unremarked during the Chancellery competition, it had important features in common with Nazi projects—chiefly the vastness of some of the structures involved, such as Hermann Henselmann and Richard Paulick's monumental project for the Stalinallee (Figure 3.11). And as global contemporary architecture culture has developed, democracies have remained demonstratively skeptical of that variety of "classicism" in which classical motifs are layered onto buildings of turgid scale, as critical reaction to much official architecture from the regimes of Nicolae Ceaușescu, Vladimir Putin, and

Figure 3.11 Hermann Henselmann and Richard Paulick, Stalinallee, Berlin, begun 1949. Jean-Pierre Dalbéra / flickr.

the Kim dynasty attests. Sebald's "dawning horror" of the ruination to come remains apposite if unarticulated in relation to such buildings, veiled by our disdain for the bad taste on view.

However, in reaction against the perceived homogenizing effect of modernism, this same global contemporary architecture culture has witnessed a renewal of interest in local and regional architectural traditions, which in Berlin took the form of a fresh look at the classical past.[52] At the same moment in the 1990s during which designs remotely resembling Nazi precedents were being publicly denounced, Berlin's "authentic" classical legacy—the neoclassicism of Friedrich Gilly, Friedrich August Stüler, and especially Karl Friedrich Schinkel—was receiving unparalleled attention.[53] These architects' creative but restrained use of the classical vocabulary was viewed historiographically as a corrective to the excesses of the Baroque, helping to fashion Berlin into an elegant Prussian arcadia for the bourgeois subject. Extended from the ideals of the French Enlightenment as manifest in the stereometric forms of Ledoux and Boullée, this line of classicism allowed its historians to include in their purview later "autonomous" investigations of classical tectonics, such as Peter Behrens's and Heinrich Tessenow's rigorous geometry and Mies's pavilion-like volumes.[54] At colloquia, roundtables, and public meetings, a family tree was thus constructed in which certain uses of classical antiquity came to be seen as intrinsically democratic and others as intrinsically totalitarian—evidence of how Schinkel has often been used, as Kurt Forster observes, as "a decoy for contemporary arguments."[55]

Thus, the sinister kitsch of Nazi architecture came to be played off against the venerability of a classical lineage that included the plastic imagination of Gilly, the synthetic virtuosity of Schinkel, and the quiet discipline of Mies. The tacit assumption was that in these designs, democratic Enlightenment ideals inhered in a way that had then been perverted by fascist aesthetics—Adorno and Horkheimer's dialectic notwithstanding.[56] But the lines between these two constructed genealogies remain unclear to this day. Often, the division of classicism into benign and suspect categories in the 1990s unwittingly suggested the logic that bolstered the Nazi vilification of modernism as "degenerate." In discussions of the New Berlin, Schinkel and his circle were presented as Berlin's native sons, producing a homegrown classicism that expressed a wholly natural local culture; Hitler and Speer, on the other hand, had imported a radicalized, foreign classicism that debased this idyllic landscape. In his memoirs, first published in 1969, Speer himself aided this selective understanding of the classical legacy by muddying its architectural terms: "I did not call (my work) neoclassicist, but neoclassical, for I thought I had derived it from the Dorian style. I was deluding myself ... Terms like "classical" and "simple" were scarcely consonant with the gigantic proportions I employed."[57] By the end of the twentieth century, conversations over Berlin's architectural patrimony had become mired in confusion. Exactly what constituted classical architecture in Germany, and what aspects of the tradition as a whole remained usable? Had regularity, symmetry, and proportion been made permanently grotesque by their abuse in fascist architecture? Did classicism constitute an entire architectural order and system of ornament, or merely a loose set of decorative motifs? The various answers—which seemed inconsistent, if not entirely arbitrary—obscured rather than clarified the stakes of the debate.

Therefore, by the time of the Chancellery competition, anxiety over a resurgent architectural conservatism in Germany was already in full swing—and the flames were further fanned by the international movement toward historical revival known as postmodernism. Several flashpoints of historicist postmodernism heightened this fear and coalesced into what Gavriel Rosenfeld has termed the "Architects' Debate," a parallel to the Historians' Debate over how to cope with the Nazi past.[58] First among them was James Stirling's addition to the Staatsgalerie in Stuttgart, in which decontextualized classical elements and motifs were rendered in travertine, sandstone, and vividly painted steel (Figure 3.12). In plan, the building wrapped around a vast rotunda in homage to Schinkel's Altes Museum; yet Stirling's rotunda was open to the sky, reading as an absence at the heart of the building rather than as an anchor. With its ironic deployment of classical forms in inventive juxtapositions, the Neue Staatsgalerie quickly became a foundational work of postmodernism, and by now is a familiar exemplar of this historicist tendency.[59] But when Stirling's proposal was announced as the winner of the 1977 competition, many German architects and critics objected passionately to what they saw as a resurrection of Nazi architecture. Despite its clever deconstruction of Schinkel and the classical tradition, Frei Otto declared that Stirling's addition was "inhuman," Günter Behnisch decried it as "totalitarian," and Peter Bürger labeled it outright "fascist."[60] The fact that—as in many postmodern buildings—the Neue Staatsgalerie not only made use of a classical idiom, but in an

Figure 3.12 James Stirling, Neue Staatsgalerie, Stuttgart, 1977–84.

already fragmented and ruined state, was by no means beside the point. Stirling's formal approach would recur in his partner Michael Wilford's British Embassy in Berlin, completed after Stirling's death in 1992.

As with Schultes and Frank's Chancellery nearly two decades later, Stirling's Neue Staatsgalerie and postmodernism in general raised a complicated knot of questions from which no single strand could be easily extricated. Chief among them was whether, in the wake of National Socialism, architectural style bore inherent meaning—a problem taken up by Léon Krier in his controversial 1985 monograph on the architecture of Albert Speer, to which the subject himself had written the preface before his death in 1981. In *Albert Speer: Architecture 1932-42*, Krier lobbied for the return of classical ideals to architecture, claiming that it was hypocritical to demolish Nazi buildings and the tradition that undergirded them while leaving the autobahns and the factories of Porsche and Krupp untouched. In fact, Krier argued, any censure of classical architecture was the result of unsound logic:

> There has been much dispute in professional circles on the question of "democratic" and "authoritarian" architecture. This is done by tirelessly reiterating a false syllogism:
>
> "Hitler loved Classical Architecture
> Hitler was a tyrant
> Hence classical architecture is tyrannical."[61]

He concluded, "*Architecture is not political. It is an instrument of politics, for better or for worse.*"[62]

Krier's claim was an acutely polemical instance of a debate unfolding internationally, pitting tradition against technology as the wellspring of architectural design. In Berlin, this debate had played out in part through the ongoing International Building Exhibition (Internationale Bauausstellung, or IBA) and the rival camps that formed within it. After all, Stimmann's totalizing impact on Berlin's architecture after he assumed the position of Senate Building Director in 1991 (as described in Chapter 1) was only the culmination of years of architectural conflict in Berlin regarding the appropriate place of history in the creation of new buildings. The "New Simplicity," a term that included the architecture of Josef Paul Kleihues and Hans Kollhoff and concomitant theoretical support from Fritz Neumeyer and Vittorio Magnano Lampugnani, emphasized conventional expressions of permanence and the use of local typologies.[63] Uniform perimeter block buildings with heavy cornices and classical facades (however reduced) reflected the geometric rigor of the square, which critics saw as ominously strict and even martial in appearance. The art historian Heinrich Klotz, formerly the director of the Deutsches Architekturmuseum in Frankfurt, described this order thus: "there is a block, the eternal block, and once again the block ... This language includes a power stance that we have not encountered since 1945 and that we have clearly rejected."[64] By 1991, debates over how to deal with Berlin's architectural birthright had become so tense that Klotz could only lament, "For God's sake, not this kind of a capital!"[65]

The anxieties swirling around the contemporary use of the classical language reached a boiling point during the Chancellery competition, in part because the building was to house the first chancellor to govern from Berlin since Hitler. That the chancellor in question was the conservative Helmut Kohl did little to alleviate the angst. By December of 1994, the jury had selected three prizewinners out of the proposals under consideration. Yet one, from the office of O. M. Ungers, caused such an uproar that it was nearly instantly shelved (Figure 3.13). Ungers's design took as its starting point the importance of maintaining the ambiguity he saw as inherent to the site and its fraught history. He thus proposed to surround the site's perimeter with an "urban colonnade," into which a free-standing volume in the shape of a truncated oval would be inserted. This oval would be clad in a gridded stone facade and mirrored by

Figure 3.13 O. M. Ungers, proposal for Chancellery, Berlin, 1994.

Figure 3.14 Ludwig Ruff, Congress Hall, Nuremburg, 1934–8.

an elliptical *cour d'honneur* at the complex's entrance. Though Ungers had derived these forms from his career-long investigation of archetypes and urban typologies, his design prompted immediate condemnation from those who saw it as appallingly reminiscent of Nazi architect Ludwig Ruff's Congress Hall at Nuremberg (Figure 3.14). Among others, a writer for the *Tageszeitung* assailed the proposal's severe appearance, saying that this "chancellor-fortress" would be "just the thing for Kohl."[66] (It remains surprising that, around the same time, the Bundesrepublik settled on a tense black ellipse for the Office of the President, designed by the Frankfurt architect Martin Gruber.)

In their remarks on Ungers's proposal, the jury noted: "there was controversial discussion ... as to whether the author was seeking to articulate a 'pretension to power' in architectural terms and whether the architectural formulation of state representation was appropriate."[67] But Ungers was no stranger to controversy at that point, nor to accusations, veiled or otherwise, of totalitarian inclinations. Earlier that very year, his residence for the German ambassador to the United States had debuted in Washington, D.C., to great international consternation over the building's classical massing and imposing colonnades, as well as its acropolis-like siting atop a hill overlooking the city (Figure 3.15). For example, Kenneth Frampton saw in Ungers's "open admiration of Karl Friedrich Schinkel" an unseemly drive toward monumentality and suggested that the building's obsessive repetition of the square "seems to evoke in the name of reunited Germany the dreams of a lost imperial past."[68]

Monumental Modernism—The Chancellery as Future Ruin   143

Figure 3.15 O. M. Ungers, residence for the German Ambassador, Washington, D.C., 1994. ncdinc / flickr.

Sensing that the selection of Ungers's proposal for the Chancellery would be imprudent, to say the least, the jury hurriedly set it aside. But the contentious response to Ungers's design was only one obstacle to their decision, as deliberations circled bootlessly around Berlin's contested architectural heritage. Unable to decide among themselves on a clear winner, jurors found themselves at an awkward stalemate, eventually awarding a joint first prize to two proposals.[69] The first came from a team of East Berliners called Krüger Schuberth Vandreike (KSV), and the second was from the office of Schultes and Frank, who had already won the commission for the master plan of the Spreebogen (Figure 3.16 and Figure 3.17). After selecting these two proposals, the jury then punted the ball to Helmut Kohl, who was left to make the final decision on his own. Kohl was known to skew conservative in his architectural tastes as well as in his politics, and the Bundestag's initial efforts during the jury selection to minimize his input were thus ironically undone by the jury itself. In the absence of an obvious frontrunner, the jury seemed eager to dodge personal accountability should the project fail to win popular support.

To aid his deliberations, Kohl requested that large models of the two first-prizewinning designs be installed in his office for him to contemplate. Furthermore, he enlisted the help of a seventeen-member committee made up of prominent cultural and political figures, including Goethe-Institut president Hilmar Hoffmann, art historian Tilmann Buddensieg, and conservative Third Reich scholar Klaus Hildebrand (himself at the center of the Historian's Debate), as well as a range of journalists from publications across the political spectrum.[70] The course of this consultation reflects exactly how tortured the process had become; Kohl announced that he would not

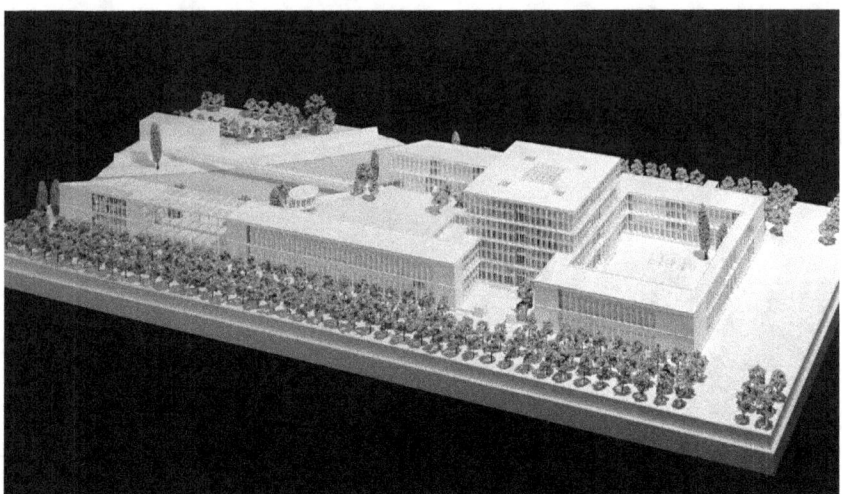

Figure 3.16 Krüger Schuberth Vandreike (KSV), proposal for Chancellery, Berlin, 1994. Architecture/model: © KSV Krüger Schuberth Vandreike, Berlin. Photo: © Antonia Weiße.

Figure 3.17 Schultes Frank Architekten, proposal for Chancellery, Berlin, 1994. Photo: Antonia Weiße, Berlin.

speak about the proposals until both teams had presented their projects and each committee member had weighed in, telling him how the designs might read to an international audience.[71] The public was also solicited for its feedback, including at an exhibition on the two proposals held in January and February of 1995.[72] At Kohl's behest, the ARD television network aired a segment about the decision in March 1995 during the program "Bericht aus Bonn," echoing the broadcasting of the Bundestag debate over Christo and Jeanne-Claude's *Wrapped Reichstag* several years earlier. This program, however, took transparency one step further: the hosts showcased both large-scale models and drawings and asked viewers to telephone in their preference.

Almost 43,000 people voted, with 79 percent in favor of KSV's design and only 21 percent supporting Schultes and Frank's.[73] Nevertheless, Kohl remained unable to make a decision, and postponed the official announcement of the winner from March to April, and then again to an unspecified date.

Though they would eventually come to be seen as stark opposites, the two proposals remaining in contention shared important ground. In the first place, both came from young firms with few major projects under their belts. KSV's principals had completed their training in various East German institutions and had only founded their firm in 1990—so by the time of the Chancellery competition, they naturally had little on their vitae. Though also early in their careers, Schultes and Frank had gained international visibility in the Spreebogen competition. Furthermore, Schultes had completed one monumental building that well demonstrated the team's concept for the Chancellery— the Bonn Kunstmuseum, which had opened to general praise in 1992 for its "sensitive mediation between monumentality and intimacy."[74] Nevertheless, the relative inexperience of both firms meant that their records, so to speak, were fairly clean. Neither came burdened with the past projects that followed many older European architects seeking to leave their mark on the New Berlin.

The two first-place proposals also had in common some important visual and formal strategies. In plan, both took the form of a rudimentary extended H, accessible to the Spree on the west and the Bürgerforum on the east. Both likewise took similar approaches to the basic parti of the building, with a central cube flanked by elongated administrative wings. However, the treatment of the facades, especially in the renderings and models presented to the jury, appeared radically different. Depicted in evocative hand drawings and a refined wooden model, KSV's Chancellery was frankly classicizing, defined by rigorous geometry and regimented two-story colonnades surrounding a raised anchoring block. These colonnades, which would serve as ambulatories open to the public along the *cour d'honneur* between the Bürgerforum and the Chancellery, were meant to present a relaxed grandeur that the architects characterized as "Alhambra and Sanssouci in the middle of the city."[75] In their proposal, KSV explicitly summoned Berlin's classical heritage and invoked the genealogy described above, positioning their Chancellery as the newest synthesis of classical ideals:

> If you go upriver from the Chancellery, after a few hundred meters you will reach an island in the river—the place where Berlin started. The Spreeinsel bears the "old" museum, built by the young Schinkel, with a mighty front facing the Lustgarten and the Schloss. Looking south from the Chancellery, you can intuit the National Gallery behind the Tiergarten. Mies van der Rohe removed steel and glass from the stone and turned the "old" museum into the "new" National Gallery. If only it were possible to unite these virtues....[76]

Like the general public, the committee initially favored KSV's design, which they felt was a more easily readable statement of Germany's new self-image. Kohl was also attracted to the opportunity to improve strained inter-German relationships by electing architects from the former German Democratic Republic to represent the reunified nation, since he was frequently criticized for failing to address the economic and cultural concerns of the East. But though opinion seemed to favor this classicizing proposal, the backlash against it was thunderous. Among other publications, the architectural journal *Bauwelt* ran an editorial stridently objecting to KSV's design, proclaiming that—despite the obvious talent on view—"As an expression of pluralistic, democratic politics, this work is simply unacceptable."[77] The editors concluded that, instead, "Schultes and Frank's proposal must be built."[78] In *Die Zeit*, the architecture writer Rudolf Stegers granted that the ancestors of KSV did indeed include Schinkel's Altes Museum and Behrens's German Embassy in St. Petersburg, both venerated exemplars of how the classical tradition could remain relevant across time. But, he argued, "The younger (ancestor) is the awful one: no, one cannot avoid remembering the Führer-Palast, which Albert Speer wanted to build a little further south."[79] Stegers was nonplussed at the unapologetic monumentality of the building, exclaiming: "As if, after the disasters of the century, monumentality were not atavism!"[80] The parliamentarian Peter Conradi (of the Social Democratic Party) even took the dramatic measure of juxtaposing photocopies of KSV's design with Speer's drawings for the Führer-Palast and distributing the leaflets around Bonn.[81]

In the face of this condemnation, Torsten Krüger, one of the founders of KSV, did his best not only to defend his proposal but also to encourage an evenhanded look at Berlin's architectural history. In an interview with *Der Spiegel*, he recalled that one of his architecture professors in Weimar claimed to hear the heavy tread of marching armies every time he saw more than three columns in a row. He shrugged, "But that's his life experience, not mine ... we have a different biography."[82] Besides, he argued of the proposal's orderly facade, "Those are supports, not columns"; his partner Bertram Vandreike helpfully chimed in, suggesting "pillars" instead.[83] From a distance of a quarter-century, it is easy to perceive a somewhat surreal contrast between such semantic nitpicking and the grave history it sought to address. In fact, this kind of architectural hypervigilance had become a sort of hobby among Berliners of all backgrounds during the 1990s. As the journalist Jane Kramer described it:

> They check [architecture] out for improvident design, as if some unpleasant, ideological DNA might be lurking inside it. They look for Hitler in the details ... They are all, suddenly, amateur semiologists, tracking the signs of a terrible Zeitgeist that they worry will replace their own ... The irony of Albert Speer's legacy is that Berliners seem finally to believe in the power of architecture as much as he did."[84]

Indeed, despite Krier's efforts to prise the two apart, the alignment between politics and architectural style remained firmly in place. Interestingly, what seemed to be troubling about KSV's proposal had nothing to do with its artistic value, its feasibility, or its responsiveness to the Bundesrepublik's demands. Though many critics noted the design's high quality, this fact only made it more dangerous and served as further evidence that it should be jettisoned. In other words, the proposal's detractors did not question its architects' claim to Berlin's classical patrimony; the problem, rather, was that they expressed their inheritance too well. As debate over the two remaining proposals intensified in the popular press, only rarely did journalists note that the similarities between them might be as significant as their differences—though one writer did observe: "Terms such as force, dignity, monumentality, and representation can be used to describe the models of both applicants."[85] Given the vehement resistance to KSV's proposal, it is perhaps of little surprise that Kohl proclaimed Schultes and Frank the competition winners on June 28, 1995. Stating that their design "radiate(d) confidence, modesty, and dignity," he declared that theirs was the proposal which was best suited to usher Germany into the twenty-first century.[86] It is tempting, therefore, to conclude that Schultes and Frank's proposal prevailed as much for what it *wasn't* as for what it *was*.

"The temple becomes the factory"

But although Schultes and Frank's design emerged in the last stages of the competition as the modernistic alternative to both KSV's and Ungers's perceived classicism, the architects had always been candidly interested in architectural monumentality. Schultes's Bonn Kunstmuseum provided a clear demonstration of how this monumentality might appear; as with Norman Foster's Reichstag, the DNA of the Chancellery comes from cultural rather than governmental architecture (Figure 3.18). No less a ruin-wrapped building than the Chancellery, the museum presents a visually impenetrable surface along most of its two street facades, but then these concrete walls cleave to display an airy courtyard of delicate columns and transparent glass walls.

Figure 3.18 Axel Schultes/BJSS, Kunstmuseum Bonn, 1992.

Poised around a majestic rotunda-stairwell and cut through with a massive diagonal axis, the building is another translation of Schinkel's Altes Museum. In Schultes's reading of the classical tradition, unexpected juxtapositions abound; the slender concrete columns appear not quite to meet the ceiling, and the concrete of the sturdy street facades folds over into a light, sail-like canopy facing Peichl's Bundeskunsthalle across a broad piazza. By creating this interplay between solid and void, Schultes sought to create a "Domus Lux" ("house of light") rather than a "Domus Aurea" (which he translated as "temple of art"). This use of light, according to the architect, would foster a spatial experience "beyond the tricks of the glass box and its illusion of freedom."[87] Upon its opening, the building was nearly universally praised—and critics seldom failed to mention that it proffered a relaxed monumentality that was in short supply in the self-conscious city of Bonn. Critic Dieter Bartetzko praised the building's "aura of archaic and ancient dignity," pointing out that the way in which concrete wall enclosures opened suddenly to large expanses of glass gave the building a pleasing temporal ambiguity: "the temple becomes the factory, from which the temple soon emerges again."[88]

Here and in later projects, such as the Crematorium Baumschulenweg in Berlin (completed in 1998), Schultes and Frank's investigation of a new monumentality was one that had deep roots in architectural modernism. Indeed, notwithstanding the anxiety that the subject of monumentality produced at the end of the twentieth century, architects had never ceased their exploration of one of architecture's most cherished values—despite Lewis Mumford's 1937 declaration that "the very notion of a modern monument is a contradiction in terms," and therefore societies should learn to "travel light."[89] During the years of World War II, modernist architects publicly debated how to forge a path toward a new monumentality in order to restore a sense of permanence and impressiveness that much avant-garde architecture had rejected. Sigfried Giedion's essays on the question, "Nine Points on Monumentality" (1943) and "The Need for a New Monumentality" (1944), were among the most influential tracts read by young architects on the subject. In both, Giedion dismissed the "pseudo-monumentality" of vapid historicism and promoted novel architectural expressions of human emotional life (including pyrotechnic displays).[90] As with the trope of the ruin, the category of monumentality (stemming from the Latin verb *monere*, meaning "to remind" or "to warn") points both backward and forward in time, and thus presents a temporality at odds with modernism's often compulsive focus on the right now. Although the subject was debated in journals, treatises, and symposia, no consensus over the appropriate architectural expression of communal sentiment resulted, and the question remained open-ended and overburdened.[91]

Yet as the century wore on, a kind of architectural monumentality developed around which critical approval began to accumulate. Originating in the 1930s in a complex transnational exchange between Europe and South America, and growing through the intertwined careers of Lúcio Costa, Oscar Niemeyer, and Le Corbusier, the buildings constructed in this vein often sought to capture emergent national identities, especially those stemming from grassroots revolutions.[92] In new capital cities like Brasília and Chandigarh, the use of frankly exposed concrete satisfied modernism's

Figure 3.19 Louis Kahn, National Assembly Building, Dhaka, Bangladesh, begun 1962.

requirement for honest materiality while also lending monumental gravity to this novel democratic architecture. Light itself, whether filtered through stained or transparent glass or admitted directly into interiors without intervention, did much of the narrative work formerly achieved via applied ornament. Between the archaic massiveness of concrete and the dematerialized beauty of light, this mode of architecture sought to embody democracy's evolution and the primeval power of human agency—reaching its apex, for many, in Kahn's designs for the new Bangladeshi capital of Dhaka. The impact of Kahn's National Assembly Building and other exemplars of this new monumentality results from concrete's double temporality, its ability to appear both modern and nonmodern, or even anti-modern (Figure 3.19). One oft-invoked anecdote claims that Kahn's Assembly was spared from aerial bombing during the Indo-Pakistani War of 1971 because its powerful massing and the geometric apertures in its exterior walls gave the impression of an ancient building that was *already in a ruined state*.[93]

"Wrapping ruins around buildings"

In order to understand Schultes and Frank's idea of monumentality and its manifestation in the Chancellery, we might now return to Kahn's own ruin-gaze and how it became formative in the architecture of the Spreebogen. Kahn's eccentric path through the twentieth century has made him one of modern architecture's most legendary figures.[94] If Philip Johnson was its gadfly, Kahn was its guru, known for his quasi-mystical proclamations and earnest faith in human institutions. As the profession began its long turn away from a rapidly ossifying international style after the middle of the century, Kahn undertook a deeply personal consideration of how one might think of modernism and monumentality as parallel rather than antagonistic pursuits. Though he explored the problem of monumentality alongside Giedion in an essay of 1944, it was not until his career-altering sojourn at the American Academy in Rome in 1950 that his contemplations began to translate into solid architectural form.[95] For Kahn, monumentality was the natural outcome of the search for order that had preoccupied him since his early years; monumentality, in other words, would be the answer to a properly formulated architectural question. As he famously declared, "Design demands that one understand the *order*. When you are dealing, or designing in brick, you must ask brick what it wants, or what it can do ... If you're dealing with concrete, you must know the order of nature, you must know the nature of concrete, what concrete really strives to do."[96] Kahn's search for monumentality was moreover a "quest for beginnings," an inward investigation of form, material, and human custom rather than the outward imposition of the architect's will.[97] This quest for architectural beginnings was inextricable from an exploration of endings, and in ruins Kahn found poignant evidence of the endurance of human enterprise.[98] Ruins, then, were not grim remains, but rather the heart of architecture's own desire for the *longue durée*. To use Kahn's own terms, ruins were what all architecture ultimately wants to be.

In a 1961 interview with *Perspecta*, Kahn explained the technique that would ultimately become a signature of his monumental architecture: that of placing a heavy fenestrated wall a few feet in front of the glass wall concealed behind it. As Kahn described it, "I thought of the beauty of ruins ... the absence of frames ... of things which nothing lives behind ... and so I thought of wrapping ruins around buildings; you might say encasing a building in a ruin so that you look through the wall which had its apertures by accident."[99] The structure under discussion was the (ultimately unbuilt) United States Consulate and Residence in Luanda, Angola, which Kahn was designing at the time of the interview. Though he had contemplated the idea since the early 1950s, Kahn's strategy of ruin-wrapping was one that matured as his practice began its global expansion. In some ways, it was a response to the challenges presented by the tropical and subtropical climates of the Indian subcontinent, Israel, and Texas.[100] Indeed, the technique was particularly well-suited to hot climates like Luanda's, in which the mitigation of sun and wind was a paramount concern.[101]

But for Kahn, the "beauty of ruins" and the device of wrapping went far beyond practical questions of climate and ventilation.[102] More importantly, it allowed the architect to imbue buildings made from modern materials and for modern purposes with a primal, elemental force. In the unbuilt meeting house at the Salk Institute in La Jolla, California (1959–62), as well as in more obviously monumental structures like the Kimbell Art Museum in Fort Worth, Texas (1966–72) and Dhaka's National Assembly Building (begun 1962), Kahn explored the expressive potential of this heavy exterior screen. In particular, ruin-wrapping allowed Kahn to control the qualities of light and the effects of shadow that were so central to his concept of monumentality. For Kahn, beauty was not to be superficially applied to architecture, but to be drawn from deep within human history, so that a building could express "closer and closer the desire and the existence will of aspirations."[103] The archaic screen, therefore, was not decorative, but rather essential to the building's authentic self-expression.

Shored up by the metaphor of the ruin, Kahn's idea of authenticity differed in fundamental ways from other modernist architects. In particular, as his concept of monumentality developed, he became less and less enchanted with the modernist conceit of the "honest" expression of structure. He addressed this issue in a speech at the last meeting of the *Congrès internationaux d'architecture moderne* (CIAM) at Otterlo in 1959, taking aim at Ludwig Mies van der Rohe's recently completed Seagram building as evidence: "She is a beautiful bronze lady but she is all corseted inside. She wears corsets from the first to the fifteenth story, but you can't see the corsets. She is a beautiful bronze lady, but she is not true."[104] According to Kahn, the Seagram building's hidden steel cross-bracing, designed to make the building resistant to wind, was precisely the problem: "the building is not honest, because the wind forces are not being expressed . . . If this building expressed the force of the wind, I am sure that when an ordinary man passed by he would look at it. . . . even if it were done brutally."[105] The ruin also allowed Kahn to explore architectural truth beyond simply the modernist fixation on function. As he wrote, "The quiet ruin reveals again the spirit out of which it once stood as a proud structure. Now it is free of its bonds . . . The quiet ruin now freed from use welcomes wild growth to play joyously around it and is like a father who delights in the little one tugging at (his) clothes."[106] In some ways, then, Kahn's ideas perpetuated the romanticist ruin trope of earlier centuries—establishing a building's autonomy beyond function, or "function transcending into awe," as Vincent Scully described the results of his ruin-wrapping technique.[107]

In Kahn's idea of "wrapping a ruin around a building," glass becomes secondary, hidden, or even altogether absent. At the Salk Institute, panes of glass are recessed deep into the concrete walls; at the Exeter Library, the glass windows read as voids punched out of the brick facade. At Dhaka and in Ahmedabad, geometric apertures are left entirely open to the elements. Here and elsewhere in Kahn's later work, walls often draw apart at corners or extend above parapets, perforated to show the lack of a glass shell behind them. These buildings convey the impression that their glazed surfaces could collapse, but the concrete or masonry shell would remain. As Kahn described his unbuilt Hurva Synagogue in Jerusalem (Figure 3.20), perhaps the purest expression of his ruin-wrapping technique, "The new building should itself consist of two buildings—an outer one which would absorb the light and heat of the sun and an inner one, giving the effect of a separate but related building."[108]

In Berlin, as in the rest of contemporary architecture culture, glass is the *sine qua non* of materials, signifying a range of meanings from environmental sustainability to consumerist luxury. Yet the contemporary future ruins inspired by Kahn likewise subordinate glass within materials of greater heft and durability, such as brick, stone, concrete, or rammed earth. The metal framework of these buildings, if it exists, tends to be hidden entirely rather than exuberantly exposed. Kahn's recent popularity is

Figure 3.20 Louis Kahn, project for Hurva Synagogue, 1968. Louis I. Kahn Collection, University of Pennsylvania and Pennsylvania Historical and Museum Commission.

evidence that his weighty contemplation of architecture's life span has resonated with contemporary architects around the world, including an international network of students and colleagues, such as Denise Scott Brown, Moshe Safdie, Peter Zumthor, and Balkrishna Doshi; an old-guard cadre of starchitect devotees, like Frank Gehry, Norman Foster, and Robert A. M. Stern; and younger figures like Alejandro Aravena and Sou Fujimoto, more known for their explorations of ephemerality than their reflections on eternity.[109] Yet Fujimoto in particular has described the impact of Kahn's ruin-thinking on his own work, leading him to contemplate both endings and beginnings: "For me the ruin is one of the sliding points of architecture which is not yet architecture."[110] It is not that Kahn's architecture has showed these architects that the ruin can be a relevant, generative metaphor; it is that his works reveals the ruin as an inescapable future phase of architecture, no matter how lightly a building might seek to tread.

"A warming-up exercise for us all"

Among these others, Schultes expresses his devotion to Kahn in such plain terms—and his discipleship is so well-known—that he seems almost like a Renaissance architect declaring his loyalty to a master that he never had the opportunity to meet. In fact, he claims to have patterned his drawing style after Kahn's for the purposes of more fully understanding the master's method.¹¹¹ For years, Schultes's love of Kahn seemed to be his most salient characteristic. In a letter from Peichl to Schultes and Frank upon the opening of the Chancellery, Peichl wrote: "Charlotte, please make sure that Axel carries on wearing those towering shirt collars, revering Louis Kahn and resisting the seductions of architectural know-it-alls with their fashionable foibles, be they glass crates or steel bubbles!"¹¹² And when Schultes was recognized as the honoree of the Konrad Adenauer Foundation's annual "homage" to German culture, the widely acknowledged highlight of the evening was an emotional reading of Kahn's essays—not Schultes's—by the actor Otto Sander.¹¹³ It is difficult to imagine a high modernist architect acknowledging his or her influences with such openness, yet Schultes's dedication to Kahn possesses a kind of sincerity that likewise puts it at odds with postmodernism's clever appropriations. Rather, Schultes and his partners seem to embrace Kahn not only as an individual artistic forebear, but also Kahn-ism as a mode of architectural thought, especially useful for working through the problem of monumentality.¹¹⁴

Indeed, Schultes and Frank began the text accompanying their competition entry by quoting Kahn and informing the jury that they had studied Chandigarh and Dhaka as background for their own design. Their graceful concrete Chancellery, presented in sleek models and computer renderings, was meant to inspire "sympathy at the first glance."¹¹⁵ Rather than offering the chilly, formal monumentality of Versailles or Schönbrunn, the architects claimed to have based their concept on the idea of the urban villa, with its casual interpenetration of public and private spaces and its tranquil interspersing of architecture and nature. From the beginning, Schultes spoke of the project as part of an interdependent spatial ensemble, in which the necessarily closed executive building was counterbalanced by the openness of the Bürgerforum and the visual penetrability of the *cour d'honneur*. As in Schinkel's concept of environmental planning, no one structure existed in stern isolation; rather, every dimension of the urban setting was to work in concert to produce a milieu of congenial monumentality. As Schultes put it, "I would like to give an example, a warming-up exercise for us all: the Chancellery has every right to be the central focus of the second power, located at a strategic location in the Spreebogen, to express its significance in architectural and urban spatial terms."¹¹⁶ For Schultes and Frank, monumentality was not an interdiction, but rather the poignant locus of collective yearning.

But the wistful beauty that characterized their design in renderings and models was immediately eroded by government demands. While the architects had originally intended all of the individual buildings within the Band to reach a uniform height of five stories, thus reflecting the idea of a spatial ensemble rather than individual monuments, Kohl insisted that the central volume be raised so that the nearby Reichstag would not visually dominate the area.¹¹⁷ An agonistic relay between Kohl, the architects, the media, and the public ensued that lasted for a year and a half. Though some critics objected to this perceived aggrandizement of the chancellor's role, Schultes and Frank eventually complied, following Kohl's claim that such an increase would more accurately reflect the balance of power between the executive and legislative

Figure 3.21 Schultes Frank Architekten, proposal for Chancellery, Berlin, 1995.

branches of the government. To fit these new recommendations, the architects gathered the central volume, which had previously been dissolved into smaller elements distributed along a diagonal axis, into an immense nine-story central cube (Figure 3.21). This cube would house the chancellor's executive offices and cabinet meeting rooms, flanked by the two five-story wings for staff offices. As they rambled west, the lateral wings would be interspersed with a series of glass-covered atria that Schultes and Frank termed "winter gardens."

The winter gardens were not the only measure that the architects took to relieve the executive building's new massiveness. The taller central cube would essentially be made up of two elements: a glass box, and then a concrete screen in front of the surface of the glass, broken at the corners and perforated with enormous circles on each facade. The architects saw the circles as Kahnian apertures that would preserve a sense of openness and transparency in this newly expanded central form. But the apertures instantly created alarm in Berlin when computer-generated images of the altered proposal were circulated in the summer of 1995. Rather than exposing the chancellor to the public in compliance with Bonn's transparency doctrine, the apertures were instead interpreted as lenses through which the chancellor could keep watch over the public. Eberhard Diepgen, the mayor of Berlin, called them "the eyes of the Chancellor," solidifying the public sense that they were an authoritarian symbol of government surveillance.[118] Journalists hastened to preach caution against this revised Chancellery and its version of monumentality. "No, it's not that our democracy should grovel before itself," argued Manfred Sack in *Die Zeit*. "But a little more composure would serve the political community quite well."[119]

Schultes and Frank hastily submitted a series of revisions. In one version, the circular apertures on the northern and southern facades were reshaped into flattened semi-ovals to maintain the allusion to Bonn's transparency but remove the uncomfortable disciplinary implications. In another, the architects experimented with a double-door entry surrounded by irregularly shaped pillars (derived from Le Corbusier's dog-bone pilotis) that rose the full nine stories of the central cube. These colossal columns predictably provoked a public outcry, and Kohl himself expressed discomfort with the design. In yet another scheme, the entrance on the east was festooned with an abstract concrete tree, whose trunk, roots, and branches wove their way up the facade. Schultes presented a blue foam model of the tree concept during a press conference in June 1996, but even he did not seem convinced; later, he wrote that it was "too naïve (oh God, a tree!)" and risked turning the Chancellery into "nothing more than kitsch."[120] However, the firm would use the motif of the tree in the symbolic "key" to the building that they handed over to Schröder in 2001. It would also reappear, this time as pure sculpture, in their proposal for a Monument to Freedom and Unity to be placed on the Schlossplatz (2009–10).

An Archaic Modernism

In the design on which Kohl and his advisors ultimately settled, the executive building is thus a distinct cube contained between significantly lower wings. As built, the inflated profile of the core structure, as well as its semicircular apertures, create what Wolfgang Sonne has described as "iconic recognizability on the television screen."[121] The main facade is similarly photo-ready: two tiers of sinuously shaped concrete columns, some 14 meters high, adorn the entryway and its counterpart on the western face of the cube (Figure 3.22). But to assuage the building's new magnitude, metaphors of natural growth and lightness abound throughout; though the iconography of the tree was abandoned on the facade, live olive trees emerge romantically from atop the freestanding columns on the lower level, while ivy spreads over the surfaces of the side wings. Throughout, references to antiquity blend freely with modernist citations. In plan, the architects layered elements not only of Kahn's National Assembly Building, but also the Hagia Sophia in Istanbul, the hypostyle hall at the temple of Amun-Re at Karnak, and the Ali Qapu in Isfahan.[122] An upturned white canvas panel shelters the entrance, suggestive both of the stateliness of Le Corbusier's sweeping concrete roofs and the provisional lightness of Frei Otto's tensile structures.[123] The panel's free-form silhouette is echoed in the roof over the portico, whose curvilinear apertures create the appealing illusion of a sun-bleached, Mediterranean ruin. Similarly, in the so-called Kanzlerpark at the complex's western edge, a canopy supported by slender columns and a tall screen, all rendered in fair-faced white concrete, slices to the edge of the site. With its vast square and circular openings, the screen reads as a remainder of a

Figure 3.22 Schultes Frank Architekten, Chancellery, Berlin 1994–2001. Entrance facade.

structure that once existed; the contents of this imaginary building seem to have crumbled away. Overall, Kahn's concept of ruin-wrapping, however unnamed, appears throughout. As Schultes described it:

> I remember, for instance, Exeter Library, where Kahn was creating space to the outside by means of cutting the edges and space on the inside by means of mass. He had these non-carrying walls with these big holes. For me, it was showing space by means of mass and mass by means of space. This led us to making a façade without a façade.[124]

This commingling of modern and archaic references continues throughout the building. Behind the facade's columns, a flat glazed wall and a raised glass cylinder are simultaneously visible, thus suggesting Bonn's transparent architecture but complicating easy "glass box" allusions. Both on the main facade and along the side wings, with their rhythmic rectangular apertures, the impression is of a transparent, open building contained within a concrete shell. Visitors ascend the foyer's vast staircase beneath an undulant coffered ceiling, heightening the structure's antique air, and the glass cylinder holds a massive amphitheatrical "Skylobby," similar to the round stairwell at the Bonn Kunstmuseum. The diminutive guardhouse outside the north wing punctuates the Chancellery's entry with its curved concrete facade, whose smooth surfaces, ribbon windows, and glazed entry level are intentionally resonant with the

Figure 3.23 Schultes Frank Architekten, Chancellery, Berlin 1994–2001. View from west.

streamlined modernism of J. J. P. Oud's worker's housing at the Hook of Holland (1924–7), or—closer to home—Erich Mendelsohn's 1928 Universum-Kino in Berlin. The aerodynamic curve of the "Chancellor's Bridge" as it leaps across the Spree conjures Berthold Lubetkin's concrete Penguin Pool at the London Zoo, completed in 1934. The eclectic revivalism of the 1970s and 1980s even appears in the facade at the bridge's terminus, whose fenestration, in the shape of Doric capitals, recalls the semiotic games of Robert Venturi and Denise Scott Brown (Figure 3.23). Perhaps inadvertently, Schultes and Frank's version of monumentality at the Chancellery is one that gestures somewhat frantically outside itself, in contrast to the surpassing self-possession of Kahn's ruin-wrapped buildings.

Monumentality in the Band

Opposite the Chancellery, across the road that now runs through what Schultes and Frank intended to be the Bürgerforum, lie the other two buildings comprising the Band des Bundes: Stephan Braunfels's Paul-Löbe-Haus and Marie-Elisabeth-Lüders-Haus, containing additional office space for MPs and committees as well as housing the parliamentary library, archives, and research services. Braunfels's designs have largely escaped the laser-sharp criticism trained on the Chancellery, and his buildings are most often critiqued in the larger context of the Band des Bundes. Yet these structures help us understand the Chancellery in important ways, as they were intended to be visually continuous with their imposing neighbor and are likewise buildings wrapped in ruins, in the Kahnian sense.

In addition to the 1994 Chancellery competition, the Bundestag also held a closed competition for the Alsenblock, named for the historical neighborhood that the two buildings would occupy.[125] As well as forming the eastern section of the Band, the structures would perform crucial symbolic repair to the urban fabric, bridging the former border along the Spree between East and West Berlin and cutting across Speer's phantom north–south axis (Figure 3.24). Schultes and Frank's master plan strictly dictated the contour of the buildings at a width of 100 meters and a height of 22 meters. Though some of the competition entries tried to circumvent these constraints—for example, the German firm of Hübner/Blanke/Forster inserted a glazed skyscraper into their scheme to balance the high-rises already under construction at the nearby Potsdamer Platz—these projects lacked a government champion and generally went unremarked. Overall, the Alsenblock competition attracted far less notice than the earlier design contests held for the government district. Only a small, select group of German architects was invited to participate, with a much smaller set of proposals requiring consideration and debate. Furthermore, the bureaucratic function of the buildings made them much less controversial at the competition stage than either the Reichstag or the Chancellery. Although some critics objected to the perceived "neo-Nazi" quality of a few submissions, they seemed to be more opposed to Schultes and Frank's master plan, which had already determined their general organization.[126]

Figure 3.24 Stephan Braunfels, Paul-Löbe-Haus and Marie-Elisabeth-Lüders-Haus, Berlin. Aerial view. dpa picture alliance archive / Alamy Stock Photo.

In fact, Braunfels emerged as an early favorite in the competition precisely because his design seemed to mitigate the monumentality of the Band. As with Schultes and Frank, Braunfels's most important work to predate his government commissions was an art museum—the Pinakothek der Moderne in Munich, for which Braunfels had won a well-publicized competition in 1992 (Figure 3.25). Braunfels credited Schultes's Bonn Kunstmuseum for inspiring his own design, and the overall appearance of the two museums is strikingly similar. Like the Kunstmuseum, the Pinakothek der Moderne is rendered in stretches of white concrete punctuated by expanses of glass, and the entry lies beneath a concrete canopy supported by lissome columns. In plan, the core of the building is another classical rotunda slashed through with a diagonal cut, such that two triangular sections seem to slide against each other. But whereas Schultes's round stair forms a peaceful interregnum in the building's massing, Braunfels's segmented, spoke-like rotunda at the Pinakothek der Moderne gives the interior a sense of layered and transparent space. As with Schultes's museum, the Pinakothek der Moderne received widespread praise upon its opening in 2002 for how its subtle proportions and light-flooded interiors made it both stately and approachable; Peter Schjeldahl gave it a rave review in the *New Yorker*, noting: "it is a big but self-effacing, 'invisible' building," while Ulrike Knöfel in *Der Spiegel* congratulated Braunfels for expressing "not just a provocative avant-gardism, but rather a solemn, smooth, and friendly monumentality."[127]

Figure 3.25 Stephan Braunfels, Pinakothek der Moderne, Munich, 1992. dpa picture alliance archive / Alamy Stock Photo.

In other words, as in his design for the museum, Braunfels's proposal for Berlin seemed to radiate the kind of decorous confidence that had initially buoyed Schultes and Frank's Chancellery to its competition victory. As in the Chancellery, the references to Kahn's work are proudly obvious. A five-story central atrium runs the length of the Paul-Löbe-Haus, and offices and committee rooms are contained in glazed cylinders to each side, suggestive of the monumental volumes of the National Assembly Building. Though the atrium is topped by a glazed roof, it is supported by a dropped concrete grid that extends to the canopy on the entrance facade to the west. This grid irresistibly recalls the luminous concrete ceilings of both of Kahn's buildings for Yale University, the Art Gallery (1951–3) and the Center for British Art (1969–74). As Braunfels described it:

> I am returning increasingly to the simple, elementary forms adopted by Le Corbusier, Mies van der Rohe, and Louis Kahn ... Firstly, the material: the only option that came into question was exposed concrete. Secondly, the attempt to work without frivolous ornamental trickery and only use architectural techniques, to create effects through the contrast between closed, heavy elements and open, light elements ... And then of course the elementary forms of the square and the circle, as they were used by Kahn. This is particularly clear on the Spreeplatz, where the new design deploys the basic forms cube, circle, and cylinder.[128]

Throughout both the Paul-Löbe-Haus and the Marie-Elisabeth-Lüders-Haus, the architecture suggests a formerly closed volume in the process of elegant collapse. The relentless length of the two buildings is relieved by open, inset courtyards—much like Schultes and Frank's "winter gardens"—thus breaking up the expanses of concrete along the exterior. In the space that the river slices through the Band, the two buildings terminate unevenly in response to the curve in the Spree that they abut. In this cut, the concrete screen seems sharply to outline the stereometric forms that Braunfels describes above, and the correlating shapes of the two buildings' canopies—one curved, one receding—eloquently suggest the longing for unity across this former border. Yet the glass curtain walls of its eastern and western facades seem oddly unsure next to these monumental gestures, and the overly genteel portico facing the Chancellery seems only to heighten the contrast with the buildings' archaic elements. It is partly this awkward combination of confidence and uncertainty that has made the Band less a compelling form in reality than it was on paper, as well as the fact that it has stopped well short of its destination, despite its extension to Luisenstrasse in 2017 and the addition of a visually extraneous entrance canopy.

While the free play of signifiers and quotations within the Chancellery and its neighbors makes it possible to align them with other works of historicist postmodernism, the buildings aimed at an overall impression that superseded such individual references. Even in its compromised form, the Chancellery was intended to be the synthesis of a modern monumentality and the creation of an environment as a whole. For Schultes and Frank, the point was not for the viewer to delight in citational games or provocative juxtapositions, nor simply to appreciate the architects' freedom to experiment with history. Far from it—the irony of postmodernism, or even its complexity and contradiction more generally, is countered by the Chancellery's heartfelt attempt to express a powerful collective idea. In fact, the architects' hope was to propose an alternative to postmodernism's relentless metanarratives by offering a Kahnian synthesis of form and meaning. After Schröder's remarks at the building's opening, Schultes offered his own interpretation of his creation: "The undeniable generosity of the Chancellery breathes an archaic modernity that might also be interpreted as a release from jail after the period of architectural punishment that we have been inflicting on ourselves for decades, especially in Berlin."[129]

But we already know that the reception of the building disappointed its architects' lofty hopes. After the government began working from its new executive center, negative international publicity ran rampant; one writer warned that the building represented Germany's "increasing assertiveness," proclaiming "Bigfoot Berlin steps on European toes."[130] In the *New Yorker*, Paul Goldberger christened it "Das Big Haus," and lamented the lost opportunity to radiate the "confidence, modesty and dignity" at which its architects had aimed.[131] As did many other critics, Goldberger linked the Chancellery's excessive scale directly to the politics of the leader who had demanded it, despite Kohl's retirement from politics in 1998. Indeed, Kohl's insistence on scaling up the central cube above the rest of the Band has caused the building's, and its architects', ongoing association with the conservative head of state. As recently as 2017, the *Berliner Morgenpost* referred to Schultes as Kohl's "favorite architect" and his most famous building as a "snow-white Trutzburg" (or "counter-castle"); and Berliners often refer to the building as the *Kohllosseum*.[132] Schröder's attempt to distance himself from the building was also, therefore, an effort to distinguish his government agenda from his predecessor's. Signaling his liberal bona fides in matters of both taste and politics, Schröder made it known when he was elected chancellor that he would have requested something "more Bauhaus."[133]

Even those critics who well understood the references to Kahn found little to love in the new Chancellery. Sebastian Schmaling characterized the building as a "strange collage of Louis Kahn's late work," while Martin Filler argued that its architects' "approximations" of classicism placed it among the least successful architectural projects of the New Berlin.[134] As Filler said, "Schultes and Frank somehow imagined they were channeling the spirit of Louis Kahn in this scheme. But their amalgam of superscale geometric forms, portentous voids, and evasive classical references are the antithesis of Kahn's stirring evocations of Roman prototypes."[135] A few critics stepped forward to fight back against the onslaught, arguing that the building was, in fact, a wholly modern expression of monumentality. In the *Berliner Zeitung*, the architecture critic Michael Mönninger (who would later author a monograph about the building in collaboration with Schultes and Frank) defended the Chancellery, claiming: "It will take years for the German public to accept this architectural wonder of the world."[136]

Despite its architects' aim to confer the dignity of a future ruin upon Germany's new Chancellery, its reputation remains uncertain and its legacy unclear. As opposed to the overwhelmingly positive international reception of Norman Foster's Reichstag, criticism of the Chancellery has been ambivalently split between praise and sometimes scalding disapproval. Yet by now, the vitriol has become somewhat muted and the building's detractors seem more or less reconciled to its presence (in contrast to the ongoing high tempers running at the Schlossplatz; see Chapter 4). This tired ambivalence has an air of resignation to it, as though the Chancellery's failure to garner general acclaim was nearly inescapable given the complex problems underpinning it of monumentality, classicism, and the buried discourse of catastrophe. Initial critiques of its bigness have given way to comments on its strange blankness of message, and the building is now often treated as an awkward but inevitable Goliath. On the tenth anniversary of its opening, one journalist wrote: "It has become familiar to us … however, the largest building that was constructed for the Berlin Republic still stands for nothing."[137]

In a controversial decision that some critics saw as a blatant attempt to boost the building's standing, it was awarded the German Architecture Prize in 2003. Before Schultes, Frank, and Witt could claim their award, Gerhard Schröder spontaneously bounded onto the stage and took the podium. In his brief impromptu speech, he claimed that only at that moment, during the evening's celebratory speeches and analyses of the building, had he come to understand its architectural significance. With the building as a backdrop, in a scene reminiscent of his initial speech at its opening, he addressed the crowd while press cameras flashed. But this time he also spoke directly to the architects, expressing his personal, if overdue, gratitude for their contribution: "Thank you for this lesson!" he pronounced, with trademark gusto.[138] Though Schröder's criticism of the building had been unstinting in the interim years, at this gala event he presented himself as a student transformed by Schultes's "warming-up exercise."

In early 2019, the Bundesrepublik announced that Schultes and Frank had won approval for a six-story, 400-room extension to the complex that would effectively complete the western segment of the Band des Bundes (Figure 3.26). The number of employees in the chancellor's office has nearly doubled since 2001—a number that reflects the governmental growth industries of cybersecurity, anti-terrorism, alternative energy research, and immigration management—and currently, many employees work in offsite facilities around the city.[139] The expanded square footage will allow employees of the chancellor's office to work under one roof and will provide a photogenic event space and dramatically cantilevered helipad for the chancellor's use. A new pedestrian bridge will securely channel employee foot traffic from the original building to the extension. The extant semicircular edge of the Band, currently limned only by a narrow concrete wall, will be articulated more assertively in an arc of offices and winter gardens; the firm's computer renderings show these concrete walls already overgrown with the ivy that has made its home on the rest of the building's surfaces. Yet the Bürgerforum has stayed unbuilt, and the traffic passing in front of the Chancellery is painful evidence that it is likely to remain so. By breaking the Band des Bundes, Axel Schultes asserted in 2018, "the Bundestag is breaking its promise."[140] With the new extension, the Chancellery will become larger—but perhaps no more monumental in the way that its architects envisioned.

Monumental Modernism—The Chancellery as Future Ruin

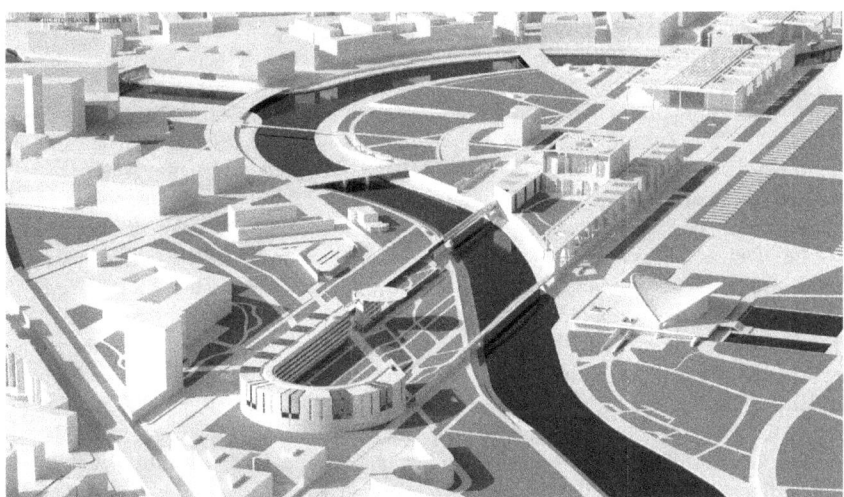

Figure 3.26 Schultes Frank Architekten, project for the extension of the Chancellery, Berlin, 2019.

At a projected cost of 460 million euros, the new building, currently scheduled to open in 2027, will cost nearly twice as much as the original structure.[141] Though critics continue to debate the architectural significance of the Chancellery with no resolution, there is meaning in this growth itself. Germany's decade-long economic boom has made it the largest national economy in Europe, a position that has given it disproportionate political might against the backdrop of profound global turmoil. And along the way, the country outgrew its oversized Chancellery: "Only 18 years old and already too small," declared the *Berliner Morgenpost* after the Bundesrepublik announced the new extension, wryly inverting years of the building's usual criticism.[142] Kahn's monumental architecture, as Scully described it, stands in perpetual equanimity, "avoid(ing) gestures in favor of utter quiet."[143] But the anxious noise of growth and instability, in postreunification Berlin and in contemporary architecture more broadly, tends to drown out quiet statements of posterity. What legacy should we leave, both political and architectural, to be found generations hence? Not only do we not know the answer; more to the point, these days, we're even uncomfortable with the question.

Notes

1   W. G. Sebald, *Austerlitz*, trans. Anthea Bell (New York: Random House, 2001), 18.
2   Ibid., 19.
3   *Austerlitz* was released shortly before Sebald's death in December 2001.
4   Gerhard Schröder, "Rede von Bundeskanzler Gerhard Schröder bei der Schlüsselübergabe im neuen Bundeskanzleramt am 2. Mai 2001 in Berlin," Presse- und

Informationsamt der Bundesregierung, http://gerhard-schroeder.de/2001/05/02/neues-bundeskanzleramt/.
5   Ibid.
6   Bernd Kammer, "Nur bei Möbeln und Kritik wird gespart," *Neues Deutschland*, October 23, 1999, https://www.neues-deutschland.de/artikel/786138.nur-bei-moebeln-und-kritik-wird-gespart.html. Though the building's structure was completed in 1999, it did not officially open until the ceremony described above, known as the *Schlüsselübergabe* (or key handover). The monumental interiors of the building, as well as the implementation of elaborate security measures, prolonged its construction beyond initial estimates. Schröder continued to distance himself from the building throughout his terms as chancellor.
7   Journalists and scholars often claim that the Chancellery is either eight times or ten times the size of the White House. Both figures are incorrect; at 5,110 square meters, the White House is slightly less than half the size of the Chancellery. For an example of this frequent error, see Holger Schmale, "Einblick ins Bundeskanzleramt: Angela Merkels Zimmer mit Aussicht," *Berliner Zeitung*, November 24, 2015, https://www.berliner-zeitung.de/berlin/einblick-ins-bundeskanzleramt-angela-merkels-zimmer-mit-aussicht-23339286.
8   Nikolaus Bernau, "Das Kanzleramt ist Architektur gegen die westdeutsche Staatsbautradition," *Berliner Zeitung*, February 1, 2001, https://www.berliner-zeitung.de/das-kanzleramt-ist-architektur-gegen-die-westdeutsche-staatsbautradition-monumentaler-abschied-von-bonn-16514996.
9   Toby Helm, "Size Does Matter for Germany's Grandiose Chancellery," *The Telegraph*, March 14, 2001, https://www.telegraph.co.uk/news/worldnews/europe/germany/1326364/Size-does-matter-for-Germanys-grandiose-Chancellery.html.
10 Carol J. Williams, "Even the Architect Thinks Germany's Chancellery is Too Big," *Los Angeles Times*, February 6, 2001, https://www.latimes.com/archives/la-xpm-2001-feb-06-mn-21692-story.html.
11 Walter Benjamin, *The Origin of German Tragic Drama*, trans. John Osborne (London: New Left Books, 1977), 178.
12 The necessity for contemporary architecture to confront environmental and political instability has been addressed in many recent symposia, exhibitions, and publications. See, for example, the symposium *Democracy in Retreat?: Master Planning in a Warming World*, cohosted by the Temple Hoyne Buell Center at Columbia University and the ByWater Institute at Tulane University in March 2019. See also the 2016 Venice Architecture Biennial, titled *Reporting from the Front* and curated by Alejandro Aravena of Santiago-based firm Elemental, as well as the exhibition *Creation from Catastrophe: How Architecture Rebuilds Communities*, held at the Royal Institute of British Architects in London in 2016.
13 One such example occurs in Axel Schultes, "Observations on Bonn and Berlin," *The Journal of Architecture* 2 (Summer 1997): 103–11. Schultes begins the article with Kahn's maxim, restating it as "a careful creation of spaces which can convey a sense of usefulness." Kahn repeated this basic formula in many texts and interviews throughout his later career, including in "Form and Design," *Architectural Design* 31 (April 1961): 114–21.
14 The firm presents Frank as a reticent, "almost archaic Stoa figure, guiding ideas with cool precision," and Witt as the "worldling," in opposition to Schultes, the vocal

"romantic pessimist." See Schultes Frank Architekten and Michael Mönninger, *Kanzleramt Berlin* (Stuttgart: Edition Axel Menges, 2002), 218.

15 Among the many examples are Kathleen James-Chakraborty, *Modernism and Memory: Building Identity in the Federal Republic of Germany* (Minneapolis and London: University of Minnesota Press, 2018), 141; Christoph Asendorf, "Berlin: Three Centuries as Capital," in *Power and Architecture: The Construction of Capitals and the Politics of Space*, ed. Michael Minkenburg (Oxford and New York: Berghahn Books, 2014), 147; and Giovanni Rizzoni, "Political Architecture and the Seduction of Place: The Form of Parliaments and European Identity," in *The Essence and the Margin: National Identities and Collective Memories in Contemporary European Culture*, eds. Laura Rorato and Anna Saunders (Amsterdam and New York: Rodopi), 188.

16 "Stephan Braunfels, Architekt der Pinakothek der Moderne in München," interview by Dr. Michael Schramm, *Bayerischer Rundfunk*, September 16, 2002.

17 For example, we might see Kahn's influence in Pei Cobb Freed's United States Courthouse in Hammond, Indiana (1994–2002), whose design and construction were coeval with the Chancellery's and which shares some superficial visual characteristics with it.

18 For more on these *Hausprojekte*, see Daniela Sandler, "Living Projects: Collective Housing, Alternative Culture, and Spaces of Resistance," in *Counterpreservation: Architectural Decay in Berlin since 1989* (Ithaca: Cornell University Press, 2016), 47–89.

19 We might also think of the weathered interior surfaces of much new development in Brooklyn, the exposed brick and salvaged furniture of London's newer cafes, and the vintage boutiques and coffee shops in the fashionable neighborhood of Samcheongdong in Seoul.

20 Sophie Lovell, "Becoming Berlin," *The Architectural Review* 242 (November 2017): 80.

21 In some cases, these structures incorporate actual fragments of former buildings into new fabric. Chipperfield's design for the Neues Museum incorporates both fragments and rubble into the new building, assembling the whole like a vast jigsaw puzzle. The walls of Reitermann and Sassenroth's chapel contain pieces of glass and stone from the original Church of the Reconciliation that stood on the site before it was destroyed in 1985 by the East German government.

22 Photiadis's and Bernard Tschumi's Acropolis Museum, as well as Renzo Piano's Stavros Niarchos Foundation Cultural Center, combine ruin-wrapping with the "big roof" strategy described in the second chapter.

23 Svetlana Boym, "Ruinophilia," in *The Off-Modern* (New York and London: Bloomsbury Academic, 2017), 43–8.

24 Annegret Burg and Sebastian Redecke, eds., *Kanzleramt und Präsidialamt der Bundesrepublik Deutschland* (Berlin: Bauwelt/Birkhäuser, 1995), 116.

25 Ibid. Of these twelve, five were submitted by Vienna-based practices; therefore, only seven proposals came from outside German-speaking countries.

26 Most of the participating firms had regional or national profiles. A few were internationally known, and had submitted proposals to several competitions in the New Berlin. They included Gottfried and Stephan Böhm, Hans Hollein, Hilmer and Sattler, Gerkan, Marg & Partners, Stephan Braunfels, and Franco Stella. Unlike the Reichstag competition, the project for the Chancellery did not attract notice from celebrity architects outside its limited ambit, and this low level of professional fanfare

was conspicuously different from the international enthusiasm greeting the Spreebogen competition.

27 "Die verlorene Mitte," *Der Spiegel*, May 23, 1994, 196.
28 Ibid. The Swiss art historian Kurt Forster was responsible for the latter insult, referring to the architectural strategies invading Berlin overall. As well as an expert on Berlin's architecture, Forster was also a juror for the Potsdamer Platz competition. For more on this competition and its legacy, see Hans Stimmann, Hilde Léon, et al., "Wettbewerb Potsdamer Platz vor 25 Jahren," *Bauwelt* 40 (December 2016): 54–7.
29 "Die verlorene Mitte," ibid.
30 See Burg and Redecke, 77. Soler's design was included in the exhibition *Das Neue Berlin: Internationale Entwürfe für Regierungsbauten und Botschaften seit 1990*, held at the Berlinische Galerie in 2013. Soler also submitted a proposal to the 1994 Bundesrepublik-sponsored Alsenblock competition that was ultimately won by Stephan Braunfels.
31 A number of scholars have linked Ruf's "bungalow" to Mies's pavilion, including Deborah Ascher Barnstone, *The Transparent State: Architecture and Politics in Postwar Germany* (New York: Routledge, 2005), 57 and Michael Z. Wise, *Capital Dilemma: Germany's Search for a New Architecture of Democracy* (New York: Princeton Architectural Press, 1998), 28. Carola Ebert points out that the affinity was reinforced by the publication of *Der Bungalow* in 1967, containing forty-four photographs of the Kanzlerbungalow and a brief essay by Erich Steingräber that cites the German Pavilion as a model. Since it had been demolished shortly after the exhibition and had yet to be reconstructed, the German Pavilion was, at the time, only knowable through photographs. See Ebert, "Private Vistas and a Shared Ideal: Photography, Lifestyle and the West German Bungalow," in *Camera Constructs: Photography, Architecture, and the Modern City*, eds. Andrew Higgott and Timothy Wray (London: Routledge, 2016), 85.
32 This alignment of architectural style and politics was not without its controversy, and the Kanzlerbungalow faced criticism even at the time for being too retiring for a contemporary head of state. For more, see Samuel Sadow, "Provisional Capital: National and Urban Identity in the Architecture and Urban Planning of Bonn, 1949–79" (PhD dissertation, CUNY Graduate Center, 2016), 139–42.
33 Quoted in Wise, 28.
34 Burg and Redecke, 86, 90. Some of Dudler's later work, such as the City Library in Heidenheim, shares characteristics with the ruin-wrapping concept described in this chapter.
35 Adolf Hitler, "Table Talk (1941)," in *Metropolis Berlin: 1880–1940*, eds. Iain Boyd White and David Frisby, (Los Angeles and Berkeley: University of California Press, 2012), 609.
36 For more on this welter of precedents and Hitler's appropriation of antiquity, see Alexander Scobie, *Hitler's State Architecture: The Impact of Classical Antiquity* (University Park, PA: Pennsylvania State University Press, 1990), 97–106.
37 Breker's sculptures originally stood in the courtyard. Confiscated as trophies by the Russians after the war and sold on the black market after 1989, they were rediscovered in the warehouse of a collector in Bad Dürkheim in 2015. Also stashed away were other sculptures from the Reich Chancellery: a pair of female nudes by Fritz Klimsch, a large relief by Breker, and Josef Thorak's massive bronze "Walking Horses," which flanked the entrance of the building's garden facade.

38 Dietmar Schirmer, "State, Volk, and Monumental Architecture in Nazi-Era Berlin," in *Berlin – Washington, 1800–2000: Capital Cities, Cultural Representation, and National Identities*, eds. Andreas W. Daum and Christof Mauch (New York: Cambridge University Press, 2005), 133.
39 Robert R. Taylor, *The Word in Stone: The Role of Architecture in the National Socialist Ideology* (Berkeley: University of California Press, 1974), 136.
40 For more on the way that stone—granite and limestone for exteriors, and marble for interiors—figured in the Nazi economy, see Paul Jaskot, "The Interest of the SS in the Monumental Building Economy," in *The Architecture of Oppression: The SS, Forced Labor and the Nazi Monumental Building Economy* (New York: Routledge, 2000), 11–46.
41 Albert Speer, *Inside the Third Reich*, trans. Richard and Clara Winston (New York: Simon & Schuster, 1970), 56.
42 I offer here only a brief look at this long history. For more comprehensive explorations, see Brian Dillon, "Fragments from a History of Ruin," *Cabinet* 20 (Winter 2005/2006): 55–9; Robert Harbison, *The Built, the Unbuilt, and the Unbuildable* (Cambridge, MA: MIT Press, 1991), 99–130; and Dillon, ed., *Ruins* (Cambridge, MA and London: MIT Press and Whitechapel Gallery, 2011).
43 Denis Diderot, *Diderot on Art, Volume II: The Salon of 1767*, trans. John Goodman (New Haven: Yale University Press, 1995), 198.
44 For a discussion of how the ruin-gaze related to modern visual technologies, see Sophie Thomas, *Romanticism and Visuality: Fragments, History, Spectacle* (New York and Abingdon: Routledge, 2008).
45 Michael Roth, "Irresistible Decay: Ruins Reclaimed," in Roth, Claire Lyons, and Charles Merewether, eds., *Irresistible Decay: Ruins Reclaimed* (Los Angeles: Getty Research Institute, 1997), 1, xi.
46 Robert Smithson, "A Tour of the Monuments of Passaic, New Jersey," in Jack Flam, ed., *Robert Smithson: The Collected Writings* (Berkeley and Los Angeles: University of California Press, 1996), 72.
47 Ibid.
48 Dora Apel, *Beautiful Terrible Ruins: Detroit and the Anxiety of Decline* (New Brunswick, NJ: Rutgers University Press, 2015), 5.
49 Semper's theory of *Stoffwechsel*, it should be noted, is far more complex than Speer's reductive reading of it. See Gottfried Semper, *Style in the Technical and Tectonic Arts; or, Practical Aesthetics*, trans. Harry Francis Mallgrave and Michael Robinson (Santa Monica: Getty Research Institute, 2004).
50 Robert A. M. Stern used the phrase "stripped classicism" to describe the modern, international use of the classical language in official state architecture that cut across the political spectrum. See Stern, "The Rise of Modern Classicism," in *Modern Classicism* (New York: Rizzoli, 1988), 9–56.
51 See Virag Molnar, "Building Socialism on National Traditions: Socialist Realism and Postwar Reconstruction," in *Building the State: Architecture, Politics, and State Formation in Post-War Central Europe* (New York: Routledge, 2013), 30–68. Importantly, East Germany claimed Schinkel in ways that anticipated reunified Berlin's embrace of "heritage"; the year 1951, which marked the 170th anniversary of Schinkel's birth, saw a flurry of publications in his honor, some of which claimed that his work had been heavily influenced by Russian classicism.

52 We can see evidence of this "rediscovery" of the local in Kenneth Frampton's theory of Critical Regionalism and the subsequent response by Alexander Tzonis and Liane Lefaivre. It is also on view in the new interest in "typologies," as well as the investigations of place in the work of Juhani Pallasmaa and Christian Norberg-Schulz.

53 Among other symptoms of this new interest was the flurry of English-language monographs and exhibitions about Schinkel that appeared in the 1990s, including *Karl Friedrich Schinkel: A Universal Man*, ed. Michael Snodin (New Haven and London: Yale University Press, 1991), published to coincide with an exhibition at the Victoria and Albert Museum in London; *Karl Friedrich Schinkel, 1781–1841: The Drama of Architecture*, ed. John Zukowsky (Chicago and Tübingen: The Art Institute of Chicago and Wasmuth, 1994), published in conjunction with an exhibition at the Art Institute of Chicago; and Barry Bergdoll, *Karl Friedrich Schinkel: An Architecture for Prussia* (New York: Rizzoli, 1994). Gilly likewise received fresh attention, as evidenced in the publication of *Friedrich Gilly: Essays on Architecture, 1796–1799*, trans. David Britt (Santa Monica: Getty Center for the History of Art and the Humanities, 1994.)

54 We can see this genealogy constructed, among other places, in Stanford Anderson, "The Legacy of German Neoclassicism and Biedermeier: Behrens, Tessenow, Loos, and Mies," *Assemblage* 15 (August 1991): 62–87. As I mentioned in my introduction here, this "family tree" would eventually come to encompass Norman Foster as well.

55 Kurt W. Forster, *Schinkel: A Meander through his Life and Work* (Basel: Birkhäuser, 2018), 7.

56 Max Horkheimer and Theodor W. Adorno, *Dialectic of Enlightenment*, trans. Edmund Jephcott (Stanford: Stanford University Press, 2002).

57 Speer, 62.

58 Gavriel D. Rosenfeld, "The Architects' Debate: Architectural Discourse and the Memory of Nazism in the Federal Republic of Germany, 1977–1997," *History and Memory* 9 (Fall 1997): 189–225. Rosenfeld argues that the architectural debates taking place in Germany toward the end of the century should be viewed against the backdrop of the *Historikerstreit* taking place in Germany in the late 1980s. Both discussions centered on the complex issue of how to assimilate the Third Reich into German history; some historians argued that the Nazi era continue to be seen as exceptional, while others argued that it should be assimilated into the narrative of German history and normalized in German consciousness and identity. As Rosenfeld points out, both debates were partisan and political in ways that bore directly on the architecture of the present day.

59 The postmodernist critic Charles Jencks argued that Stirling's design "epitomized the first stage of Post-Modernism in much the way the Villa Savoye and Barcelona Pavilion summarized early Modernism." Jencks, *The New Paradigm in Architecture: The Language of Post-Modernism* (New Haven: Yale University Press, 2002), 110. For an insightful analysis of Stirling's design, see also James-Chakraborty, "An Architecture of Fragmentation and Absence: West German Museums," in *Modernism as Memory*, 81–137.

60 Quoted in Anthony Vidler, "Losing Face: Notes on the Modern Museum," *Assemblage* 9 (June 1989): 53. The modernist Behnisch was particularly insulted by the design, as he had also been a finalist in the competition. He ultimately won the third prize.

61 Léon Krier, "An Architecture of Desire," in *Albert Speer: Architecture 1932–42* (Brussels: Archives d'Architecture Moderne, 1985), 224. A new edition of the book was released by the Monacelli Press in 2013 with a foreword by Robert A. M. Stern.

62 Ibid., 227. Emphasis in original.
63 For a more detailed discussion of the "Neue Einfachheit," see Naraelle Hohensee, "Building in Public: Critical Reconstruction and the Rebuilding of Berlin after 1990" (PhD dissertation, CUNY Graduate Center, 2016), 156–69. This loose movement is occasionally classified as "Rationalism," "Berlinische Architektur," or simply "kritische Rekonstruktion," and its adherents sometimes characterized as the "Berlin School."
64 Heinrich Klotz, Nikolaus Kuhnert, and Angelika Schnell, "For God's Sake, Not This Kind of a Capital: Heinrich Klotz in Conversation with ARCH+," trans. Tamara Domenrat, *Arch+* 122 (June 1994): 87.
65 Ibid.
66 Rolf Lautenschläger, "Dem Kanzler eine steinerne Landmarke," *Die Tageszeitung*, December 15, 1994, 2.
67 Burg and Redecke, 61.
68 Kenneth Frampton, "In the Name of the Father," *Domus* 766 (December 1994): 22.
69 There seems to have been a slight preference among the jurors for KSV's design, but the chairman, the Munich-based architect Kurt Ackermann, made it clear that he favored Schultes and Frank's proposal. After many hours and very late at night, the jury made the decision to award two prizes.
70 Hermann Funke, "Was hinten herauskam," *Jungle World* 33, August 13, 2003, 4. Hildebrand faced off against Jürgen Habermas in the *Historikerstreit* over what Habermas termed "apologetic tendencies" in right-wing intellectual approaches to National Socialism.
71 Heinrich Wefing, *Kulisse der Macht: Das Berliner Kanzleramt* (Stuttgart: Deutsche Verlags-Anstalt, 2001), 136–40. Wise also offers a summary of some aspects of the controversy, 65–72.
72 Funke, 4. The guest book was handed over to the committee so they could review the comments therein.
73 Wefing, 132.
74 Dieter Bartetzko, "Das Bewußtsein des Menschen für sich selbst. Das Erbe des postmodernen Museumsbau der achtziger Jahre," in *Vom Elfenbeinturm zur Fußgängerzone: Drei Jahrzehnte deutsche Museumsentwicklung versuch einer Bilanz und Standortbestimmung* (Wiesbaden: VS Verlag für Sozialwissenschaften, 1996), 86. Schultes completed the building under the firm auspices of BJSS (Dietrich Bangert, Bernd Jansen, Stefan Scholz, and Schultes), of which Charlotte Frank was also a member.
75 Burg and Redecke, 55.
76 "Bundeskanzleramt, Germany, Berlin, 1994, 1. Prize," Krüger Schuberth Vandreike, https://www.ksv-network.de/en/project/bundeskanzleramt/. As would recur in the Spreeinsel competition, KSV naturalized the alignment of the historic core of the city with historical "Berlinische" meaning.
77 "Wettbewerb Bundeskanzleramt," *Bauwelt* 1–2 (January 13, 1995): 62.
78 Ibid.
79 Rudolf Stegers, "Drang zum Monumentalen," *Die Zeit*, December 23, 1994, https://www.zeit.de/1994/52/drang-zum-monumentalen.
80 Ibid.
81 Jürgen Leinemann, "Rückkehr nach Hause," *Der Spiegel*, May 25, 1998, 66.

82 Leinemann, "Auf vergiftetem Boden," *Der Spiegel* 8 (February 20, 1995): 64. Wise points out that Behnisch expressed similar sentiments, 67.
83 Ibid.
84 Jane Kramer, "Living with Berlin," *The New Yorker*, July 5, 1999, 54.
85 Leinemann, "Auf vergiftetem Boden," *Der Spiegel* 8 (February 20, 1995): 64.
86 Helmut Kohl, "Einleitende Erklärung zur Pressekonferenz von Bundeskanzler Dr. Helmut Kohl," Berlin, 28 June 1995. Presse- und Informationsamt der Bundesregierung.
87 Axel Schultes, *Axel Schultes: Kunstmuseum Bonn* (Berlin: Ernst & Sohn, 1994), 35.
88 Bartetzko, 86.
89 "If it is a monument, it cannot be modern, and if it is modern, it cannot be a monument." Lewis Mumford, "The Death of the Monument," in *Circle: International Survey of Constructive Art*, eds. J. Leslie Martin, Ben Nicholson, and Naum Gabo (London: Faber & Faber, 1937), 264, 268.
90 As examples of empty historicism, Giedion uses both Paul Ludwig Troost's Haus der Deutschen Kunst in Munich and Benno Janssen's Mellon Institute in Pittsburgh, crossing political ideologies rather than dividing them into "good" and "bad" classicism. Sigfried Giedion, "The Need for a New Monumentality," in *New Architecture and City Planning: A Symposium*, ed. Paul Zucker (New York: Philosophical Library, 1944), 549–68.
91 For more on this context, and Kahn's place within it, see Sarah Williams Goldhagen, *Louis Kahn's Situated Modernism* (New Haven: Yale University Press, 2001), 24–40.
92 On the relationship between the material of concrete and these nascent identities, see Adrian Forty, "National Concretes," in *Concrete and Culture: A Material History* (London: Reaktion Books, 2012), 119–44. On the discourse of authenticity that surrounds these concrete capitals, see William Curtis, "Authenticity, Abstraction and the Ancient Sense: Le Corbusier's and Louis Kahn's Ideas of Parliament," *Perspecta* 20 (1983): 181–94.
93 Among other places, this story is recounted in Lawrence Vale, *Architecture, Power and National Identity* (New Haven: Yale University Press, 1992), 242.
94 Kahn's periodicity has long been debated, as has his relationship to modernism. Vincent Scully read him as a transition figure between modernism and postmodernism who laid the groundwork for later critics of the modern movement, such as Aldo Rossi and Robert Venturi. See Vincent Scully, "Louis I. Kahn and the Ruins of Rome," in Neil Levine, ed., *Modern Architecture and Other Essays by Vincent Scully* (Princeton: Princeton University Press, 2003), 312–15. Sarah Williams Goldhagen has insisted that Kahn remained a committed modern architect throughout his career, and has chafed against the idea that his journey to Rome was a "single, epiphanic moment" in which "with singular heroism and prescience, (he) realized the inadequacies of modernism and the self evident value of history." See Goldhagen, 205. I agree with Goldhagen that to exile Kahn from the modern movement is to misunderstand his career. But I am likewise inclined to agree with David B. Brownlee that "Kahn's work did change in the 1950s, not solely under the influence of his Roman sojourn, but certainly not in spite of it. As the most serious and successful architect of his generation to resuscitate the muse of history, he must be assigned a role in the historicist tendency of recent decades, although he cannot be blamed for all the mauve porticos of the suburban strip." See David B. Brownlee, review of *Louis Kahn's Situated Modernism* by Sarah Williams Goldhagen, *Journal of the Society of Architectural Historians* 61 (June 2002): 240.

95 Louis Kahn, "Monumentality," in *New Architecture and City Planning: A Symposium*, ed. Paul Zucker (New York: Philosophical Library, 1944), 577–88. As James-Chakraborty has observed, it is difficult to connect this essay, which celebrates the lightness and flexibility of skeletal metal frames, to the gravity of Kahn's mature work. See Kathleen James-Chakraborty, "Louis Kahn's Monumentality: Theory and Practice," *Mythos Monument: Urbane Stragien in Architektur und Kunst*, ed. Carsten Ruhl (Bielefeld: Transcript, 2014), 77–97. However, he does articulate several positions that remained fundamental in his later career, including a belief in institutions and the idea that monumentality is a "spiritual quality inherent in a structure which conveys the feeling of its eternity."

96 Louis I. Kahn, "I Love Beginnings," in *Louis I. Kahn: Writings, Lectures, Interviews*, ed. Alessandra Latour (New York: Rizzoli, 1991), 288.

97 Kahn first refers to "beginnings" in a letter to Anne Tyng of January 8, 1954, while the latter was abroad in Rome to avoid the scandal of her pregnancy with their daughter Alexandra. See *Louis Kahn to Anne Tyng: The Rome Letters 1953–54*, ed. Anne Griswold Tyng (New York: Rizzoli, 1997), 89. In a speech in Tel Aviv in 1973, Kahn spoke evocatively of his search for "Volume Zero," the non-existent "book" of human history that would precede and preempt current knowledge. As he said, "every time I start to read Volume I, I linger on Chapter One, and I re-read it and re-read it and always feel something else in it. Of course my idea is probably to read Volume Zero...." See Louis I. Kahn, *What Will Be Has Always Been: The Words of Louis I. Kahn*, ed. Richard Saul Wurman (New York: Rizzoli, 1986), 245. As Stanford Anderson has pointed out, Kahn's obsession was not so much with recovering "history" in any empirical sense, or with establishing unbroken continuity within it; rather, his notion of Volume Zero is "reciprocally critical and creative between the present and that imagined time immemorial." Stanford Anderson, "Public Institutions: Louis I. Kahn's Reading of Volume Zero," *Journal of Architectural Education* 49 (September 1995): 21.

98 Kahn's idea of the cyclicality of time is often expressed in his aphorism, "what was has always been, and what is has always been, and what will be has always been." See, for example, his lecture at Pratt Institute in 1973, reprinted as "1973: Brooklyn, New York," *Perspecta* 19 (1982): 98.

99 Louis Kahn, "A discussion recorded in Mr. Kahn's Philadelphia office in February 1961," *Perspecta* 7 (1961): 9.

100 The projects to which I refer here are the Indian Institute of Management in Ahmedabad, India (1962–74); the National Assembly Building in Dhaka, Bangladesh (begun 1962); the unbuilt Hurva Synagogue in Jerusalem (begun 1968); and the Kimbell Art Museum in Fort Worth, Texas (1966–72).

101 That this primitivizing aesthetic is not neutral and that it has particular meaning in a postcolonial context has not gone unremarked. As Rebecca M. Brown has noted, for example, Kahn's architecture at Ahmedabad (and that inspired by his followers) manifests "constructed decay," appearing "like a ruin rising out of an ancient platform." This Kahnian ruin-wrapping thus allows a building to filter "its antiquity through the colonial episteme of India-as-ruin, an episteme employed to justify the intervention of a colonial power in order to rehabilitate both the building and the culture overall." Rebecca M. Brown, *Art for a Modern India, 1947–1980* (Durham, NC: Duke University Press, 2009), 88, 93.

102 Kahn, "A discussion," 9.
103 Ibid., 11. Elsewhere, Kahn argues that the human ability to perceive beauty is itself a "beginning," emerging as a child's intellect forms: "The first feeling is that of beauty. Not the beautiful, just beauty." See Kahn, *What Will Be*, 151.
104 Louis Kahn, "Talk at the Conclusion of the Otterlo Congress," in *New Frontiers in Architecture: CIAM '59 in Otterlo*, ed. Oscar Newman (New York: Universe Books, 1961), 212.
105 Ibid., 214.
106 From a letter written by Kahn to Harriet Pattison in 1964. In Alexandra Tyng, *Beginnings: Louis I. Kahn's Philosophy of Architecture* (New York and London: Wiley, 1984), 166.
107 Scully, 315. For more on Kahn's use of the ruin metaphor at Dhaka, see Maryam Gusheh, "Louis Kahn in Dhaka: Ruin as Method," (PhD dissertation, University of New South Wales, 2013).
108 Kahn, letter of July 1968, quoted in *Louis I. Kahn: Complete Work 1935–1974*, eds. Heinz Ronner and Sharad Jhaveri (Basel: Birkhäuser, 1987), 363.
109 All of these architects spoke to Kahn's influence in interviews for the panoramic recent retrospective of his work, *Louis Kahn: The Power of Architecture*. We might think of Peter Zumthor's design for the documentation center at the Topography of Terror, the remains of the former Gestapo headquarters in Mitte, as the inverse: a building wrapped around a ruin. Construction on Zumthor's competition-winning proposal was halted in 2004 after a series of devastating budget cuts; it was replaced by a new building by Ursula Wilms, which opened in 2010.
110 Interview with Sou Fujimoto, in *Louis Kahn: The Power of Architecture*, eds. Mateo Kries, Jochen Eisenbrand, and Stanislaus von Moos (Weil am Rhein: Vitra Design Museum, 2012), 261.
111 Christian Welzbacher, "Postmodernism Devours Its Own Children: Marginal Notes on the Bundeskanzleramt in Berlin by Axel Schultes," *Archis* 5 (2001): 113.
112 In *Kanzleramt Berlin*, 25.
113 Bernhard Schulz, "Ehrung für Kanzleramts-Architekt Axel Schultes," *Der Tagesspiegel*, January 14, 2010, https://www.tagesspiegel.de/kultur/konrad-adenauer-stiftung-ehrung-fuer-kanzleramts-architekt-axel-schultes/1664996.html.
114 To my knowledge, the value of Kahn's architectural legacy itself was never questioned, by any party, during the Chancellery competition proceedings.
115 Axel Schultes, "Ich will einen Ort des Gleichgewichts," *Frankfurter Allgemeine Zeitung*, June 29, 1995, 29.
116 Axel Schultes, "Spreebogen," in *Kanzleramt Berlin*, 57.
117 The height had also initially been capped by the guidelines of Critical Reconstruction. Kohl was generally supportive of Stimmann, but drew the line at what he perceived as an excessively humble representation of the chancellor's role. The Reichstag remains slightly taller than the Chancellery; as a writer for *Der Spiegel* put it, "The difference in height should remind you (the chancellor) whom you serve." Jan Fleischhauer, "Im Kanzleramt," *Der Spiegel*, September 17, 2005, 23.
118 Dankwart Guratzsch, "Eine Vision für das 21. Jahrhundert aus Stein und Glas," *Die Welt*, June 29, 1995, https://www.welt.de/print-welt/article659864/Eine-Vision-fuer-

das-21-Jahrhundert-aus-Stein-und-Glas.html. Kohl griped back that Diepgen must have been thinking of the eyes of the Lord, as described in the Bible.
119 Manfred Sack, "Mehr Gelassenheit!," *Die Zeit*, July 7, 1995, https://www.zeit. de/1995/28/Mehr_Gelassenheit_.
120 Schultes, "The Intimacy of the Monument," in *Kanzleramt Berlin*, 80.
121 Wolfgang Sonne, "Specific Intentions—General Realities: On the Relation between Urban Forms and Political Aspirations in Berlin during the Twentieth Century," *Planning Perspectives* 19 (2004): 302. The elevation of the central mass also inevitably suggests Gilly's 1798 project for a national theater on the Gendarmenmarkt. See Karin Wilhelm, "Demokratie als Bauherr: Überlegungen zum Charakter der Berliner politischen Repräsentationsbauten," in *Das Parlament, Beilage aus Politik und Zeitgeschichte* 34–5 (August 2001): 14.
122 See Michael Mönninger, "Yearning for the Lightness of Stone," in *Kanzleramt Berlin*, 28–30.
123 We might think, for example, of Otto's design for the Music Pavilion at the Bundesgartenschau in Kassel in 1955.
124 Stanley Collyer, "Interview: Axel Schultes," *Competitions*, Spring 1997, https:// competitions.org/2017/08/interview-axel-schultes-spring-1997/.
125 During proceedings, the two buildings were described as the Alsenblock (later the Paul-Löbe-Haus) and Luisenblock (Marie-Elisabeth-Lüders-Haus). They were officially renamed for significant politicians.
126 Francesca Rogier, "Growing Pains: From the Opening of the Wall to the Wrapping of the Reichstag," *Assemblage* 29 (1996): 69, n. 46.
127 Ulrike Knöfel, "Feierliches Labyrinth," *Der Spiegel*, September 9, 2002, 178.
128 Stephan Braunfels, *Insights: A Tour of Berlin's Parliamentary Quarter* (Berlin: Deutscher Bundestag, 2006), 92.
129 Schultes, "Specifically Republican Enthusiasm," in *Kanzleramt Berlin*, 49.
130 Lucian Kim, "Bigfoot Berlin Steps on European Toes," *Christian Science Monitor*, May 4, 2001, https://www.csmonitor.com/2001/0504/p6s1.html.
131 Paul Goldberger, "Das Big Haus," *The New Yorker*, August 13, 2001, 66.
132 Jörg Quoos, "Die Nacht der Einheit war die Sternstunde von Helmut Kohl," *Berliner Morgenpost*, June 16, 2017, https://www.morgenpost.de/politik/article210935685/ Die-Nacht-der-Einheit-war-die-Sternstunde-von-Helmut-Kohl.html. The building's other cheeky nicknames include *Bundeswaschmaschine* and *Elefantenklo* (or elephant's bathroom).
133 Patrick Sisson, "Check Out Angela Merkel's Official Home, Ten Times the Size of the White House," *Curbed*, December 10, 2015, https://ny.curbed. com/2015/12/10/9892324/check-out-angela-merkels-official-home-10-times-the-size-of-the-white.
134 Sebastian Schmaling, "Masked Nostalgia, Chic Regression: The 'Critical' Reconstruction of Berlin," *Harvard Design Magazine* 23 (Fall 2005/Winter 2006): 30; Martin Filler, "Berlin: The Lost Opportunity," *The New York Review of Books* 17 (November 1, 2001): 31.
135 Ibid.
136 Mönninger, "Richtfest für das neue Kanzleramt," *Berliner Zeitung*, October 23, 1999, https://www.berliner-zeitung.de/richtfest-fuer-das-neue-kanzleramt--ein-grosser-

bau--ein-distanzierter-gerhard-schroeder-und-die-hoffnung-auf-eine-stimulierung-der-regierungsgeschaefte-die-furcht-vor-der-pracht-16148666.

137 Robin Alexander, "Das Kanzleramt steht immer noch für nichts," *Die Welt*, May 1, 2011, https://www.welt.de/debatte/article13308458/Das-Kanzleramt-steht-immer-noch-fuer-nichts.html.

138 Christina Tilmann, "Danke für diese Lektion!," *Der Tagesspiegel*, November 12, 2003, https://www.tagesspiegel.de/berlin/danke-fuer-diese-lektion/464578.html.

139 Bundesamt für Bauwesen und Raumordnung, "Das Bundeskanzleramt wird erweitert," press release, January 15, 2019, https://www.bbr.bund.de/BBR/DE/BBR/Presse/Pressemitteilungen/2019/190115_erweiterung-bkamt.html. The number of employees in the offices of the chancellor grew from around 410 in 2001 to 750 by 2018. Around 200 of those employees currently work offsite.

140 Bernhard Schulz, "Bürgerforum im Band des Bundes: 'Der Bundestag bricht sein Versprechen,'" *Der Tagesspiegel*, February 24, 2018, https://www.tagesspiegel.de/berlin/buergerforum-im-band-des-bundes-der-bundestag-bricht-sein-versprechen/20999562.html. Schultes has been vocally critical of his largest client and its decision to "delete" the most meaningful part of the Band.

141 The original building cost 262 million euros.

142 Isabell Jürgens, "Erweiterung am Kanzleramt: Merkel landet auf dem Dach," *Berliner Morgenpost*, January 16, 2019, https://www.morgenpost.de/berlin/article216217879/Bundeskanzleramt-in-Berlin-Erweiterungsbau-soll-rund-460-Millionen-Euro-kosten.html.

143 Scully, introduction to *The Louis I. Kahn Archive: Personal Drawings*, in Levine, 258.

4

Palaces of Doubt

By 1994, the sweeping government transformation of the Spreebogen was underway and the 60-hectare area had been transformed from a *terrain vague* into part of "Europe's largest construction site," as Berlin's energetic marketers often dubbed the city center (Figure 4.1). But despite the bustling sense of progress represented by the skyline of cranes, heated controversy over the form of the capital continued—and the feverish pace of construction seemed to be in part an effort to stifle any voices of uncertainty over the shape that the New Berlin was hastily assuming. In spite of the dizzying pace, however, countless critics both within and outside of Berlin continued to express their doubts in vehement terms, and disputes ignited like brushfires over urban sites across the city. At Potsdamer Platz, along Friedrichstrasse, and around the site of the destroyed Chancellery and bunker in which Hitler spent his last days, impassioned arguments erupted over the appropriate role of history in defining Berlin's new architectural identity. At sometimes painful length, debates unfolded over how to adapt Berlin's Wilhelmine and Weimar architecture to the city's new life, how to grapple with the visible urban traces of National Socialism and World War II, and how to ameliorate the persistent, ragged gash left by the Berlin Wall.

Less easy to voice, however, were doubts over the place of the former East, whose memory did not haunt Berlin so much as simply lived on, stubbornly occupying the most quotidian aspects of urban life like an unwelcome squatter in the rapidly gentrifying city. In the context of the reunified government's new architecture, these doubts proved especially troublesome. According to official policy, the German Democratic Republic (GDR) had been first "dissolved" and then "absorbed" by the Bundesrepublik on October 3, 1990, symbolic terms that implicitly described the erstwhile state's built remnants as well as its politics. But as architects and planners endeavored to assemble Berlin's urban fragments into a coherent cityscape, it became clear just how stubbornly these fragments could resist facile political metaphors from above. Intransigent and insurgent, Berlin's architectural ruins, splinters, and afterimages thwarted the official rhetoric of transition and assimilation. Reunification, it seemed, did not necessarily bring unity, and the fragmentation of the built environment made manifest these larger social and political uncertainties.

Perhaps the most incendiary locus of this doubt could be found 1.5 kilometers away from the Spreebogen at the eastern terminus of Unter den Linden. Situated on the island in the river known as the Spreeinsel, which had recently been reclaimed from its position in the East, was the site of two uncomfortably prominent ruins. The first was

Figure 4.1 Spreebogen construction site, Berlin, 1996. Bundsarchiv-Bildarchiv, Berlin.

the seat of the Hohenzollern dynasty known as the Stadtschloss, or city palace, which dated to the fifteenth century and which had been the home of the electors of Brandenburg, the kings of Prussia, and the emperors of the German Reichs (Figure 4.2). Heavily damaged by Allied bombing during World War II, the baroque Stadtschloss had remained in disrepair, obstinately dominating its central location throughout the first years of postwar rebuilding. In 1950, it was imploded by the East German government in a theatrical strike against Berlin's royal past that required four months of labor and 12 tonnes of dynamite.[1] In its place, the GDR erected the so-called Palast der Republik, designed by Heinz Graffunder and opened in 1976, which not only housed the East German parliament (*Volkskammer*) but also represented a Soviet "palace for the people" replete with restaurants, theaters, and discotheques (Figure 4.3). Framed in steel, edged with marble, and clad in bronze-tinted, mirrored glass, the building cut a conspicuous figure in the historic heart of the city. Though it had been closed for asbestos removal in 1990, the defunct Palast still hunkered defiantly at the focal point of one of Berlin's most celebrated vistas, disturbing the staid tranquility of its neoclassical neighbors. As the rebuilding of Berlin ramped up, fervent advocates of the Palast's preservation faced off against supporters of the Stadtschloss's reconstruction, and each faction become increasingly entrenched in their beliefs. By the mid-1990s, debates over the fate of the Schlossplatz—the location of two seemingly opposite buildings, one a ghost and the other a cadaver—had become explosive, and acceptable solutions seemed nowhere to be found.

Figure 4.2 Berlin Stadtschloss, early twentieth century.

Figure 4.3 Heinz Graffunder, Palast der Republik, Berlin, 1974–6. Sueddeutsche Zeitung Photo / Alamy Stock Photo.

As tempers ran high over the future of the site, a mysterious design surfaced at a press event for the government's urban planning competition at the Spreeinsel. This enigmatic object took the form of a small plaster model of the Schlossplatz area, rumored to have been recently discovered in an archive in Moscow after languishing there for half a century in a cache of German art looted by the Russians after World War II (Figure 4.4). The model's surface was pocked and patinated with age and its edges were convincingly yellowed, seeming to testify to its long life and its wearying transcontinental journey. The urban landscape depicted in the model was balanced and classical, yet with a radical proposal at its core: a newly elongated Lustgarten that would extend from the front of Schinkel's Altes Museum to well into the Schlossplatz, opening a public forum directly through the center of the old Hohenzollern palace. On one side, the model bore a crumbling label in handwritten Cyrillic script that read, "From the estate of K. F. Schinkel, confiscated from [a] private property, Berlin,

Figure 4.4 Schultes Frank Architekten, "Schinkel's Dream," 1994.

28 August 1945."[2] In the label's right corner, a detailed accession number appeared to corroborate the model's provenance. The widely respected art historian Tilmann Buddensieg examined the object carefully in front of the astonished press and proclaimed it—"without a doubt," in his words—the creation of Berlin's favorite architectural son Karl Friedrich Schinkel.[3] At first blush, the design seemed to offer the perfect proportions of historical awareness and future vision to allay the public's misgivings over the site's new life. Perhaps this serendipitous discovery could offer a usable concept, authentically rooted in the best of Berlin's architectural heritage, for this perplexing site and its recalcitrant past.

Or perhaps not. In fact, this apparent *deus ex machina* was the work of none other than the architect Axel Schultes, carried out in cahoots with Buddensieg to demonstrate the city's willingness to kowtow before historical authority instead of actually seeking original, timely solutions to contemporary architectural problems. According to Schultes, the prank laid bare that Schinkel seemed to be the "only authority" to which "Berlin—and Bonn—are still willing to listen."[4] In an accompanying article later published in *Der Tagesspiegel*, Schultes labeled his model "Schinkel's dream," and argued, *pace* Nietzsche, that it taught the city's builders and restorers an invaluable "lesson on the use and abuse of history for life."[5] For Schultes and his coconspirator Buddensieg, Schinkel's unquestioned authority at the turn of the twenty-first century was evidence of the widespread "unarchitectonic confusion" in which the New Berlin was floundering.[6]

The jig was quickly up: Schultes declared himself the satirical author of the plan and breathlessly awaited confirmation that his message had landed. Yet once it was revealed, Schultes's and Buddensieg's prank was swiftly brushed aside, and ultimately it left only the slightest impact on the course of the debates over the Schlossplatz. If they reacted at all, the journalists to whom it appealed regarded it as either "a kind of charming April Fool's" or a misguided effort on Schultes's part to publicize his firm's own submission to the Spreeinsel competition, which shared some characteristics with the faux-fragment of his Schinkel model.[7] Therefore, however deeply felt it may have been, their hoax has become little more than an entertaining footnote in the annals of the reunified capital.

Yet I recount the anecdote here because, much like the complicated site on which it is based, it offers a useful capstone to my examination of Berlin's contemporary architecture—while at the same time suggesting an essential truth about contemporary architecture culture more broadly. Certainly, "Schinkel's dream" was intended to highlight the nagging architectural doubts that troubled the Schlossplatz's redevelopment. Indeed, the site remained vexed by apparently unanswerable questions: how could the new capital marshal its fragmentary resources in the service of preserving and teaching historical lessons? Which layers of the city's palimpsest most authentically represented its unmanageable past? What architectural means could most effectively heal a city like Berlin, subjected as it had been to repeated historical traumas? Moreover, behind these questions lay some that are still more fundamental to contemporary architecture, and still more unsettled: in the service of historical understanding in a global context, *what* does architecture mean, what *can* it mean, and *how* does it communicate that meaning to an international public? Yet just as the Schlossplatz discloses the myriad uncertainties underlying contemporary architecture culture, it simultaneously reveals an essential and often unstated prescript of that culture: that it is not doubt, but rather *belief*, that powers today's high-profile architecture. The Schlossplatz's recent past illustrates clearly that one of global contemporary architecture's most motivating premises is not doubt, but rather a deep-seated conviction in architecture's ability to materialize elusive historical sensibilities.

It is necessary to begin this story at the end. Though the controversy continued throughout the 1990s, in 2002 the Bundestag voted in favor of what they called the "baroque solution" for the Schlossplatz—a strangely euphemistic shorthand for the demolition of the Palast and the reconstruction of one of the Stadtschloss's two courtyards and three of its four facades. After many delays, at the time of this writing, the building is soon to open as the so-called Humboldt Forum, designed by the Italian architect Franco Stella and serving as a museum and cultural center housing the collections of Berlin's Ethnological Museum and Museum of Asian Art (a function that was determined well after the decision was made to reconstruct the building). But as the Humboldt Forum nears its completion, the site of the Schlossplatz remains the target of ongoing anger, frustration, and doubt. As with the other structures examined in this book, the debate surrounding the Schlossplatz can be understood in historical terms with the benefit of a narrow retrospect. However, unlike the government district at the Spreebogen and its individual buildings, the Humboldt Forum's critical reception has not yet settled like another layer of sediment into Berlin's sandy terrain. Inadvertently, the domineering new building projects a sense of tension that is different in tone from the city's other government structures. Despite its near-finished state, the Stadtschloss reconstruction feels for many like an open wound, and the ongoing tenderness of the subject among both Berliners and general observers of the new capital remains instructive. The questions raised by the Schlossplatz are, in fact, difficult problems that continue to nettle the Hauptstadt's official claims to historical understanding and complicate its assertions of political unity.

As with Norman Foster's Reichstag renovation, the rhetoric surrounding the reconstruction of the Stadtschloss has been both triumphalist and elegiac, as the celebration of both sites' new lives required that their troubled histories be first performatively laid to rest. However, as I have argued, Foster—with an assist from Christo and Jeanne-Claude—combined the Reichstag's funeral and rebirth into one compelling architectural spectacle, such that his renovated building continually and exegetically celebrates both occasions. In addition, Foster judiciously made room for doubt in the ritualistic mode of viewership attending his renovation, while also constantly reaffirming the viewer's belief in contemporary architecture. Moreover, as I described in the last chapter, Schultes and Frank's Chancellery has settled somewhat uneasily into its life and the once-heated criticism it inspired has largely cooled. Though it failed to achieve the gravitas of a future ruin, it has nonetheless lumbered awkwardly toward its future life. The announcement in early 2019 of its expansion did not reopen a sustained discussion of whether its particular mode of monumentality risked fanning any dangerous political flames, even at a moment of intensifying far-right activity both within Germany and around the world. In fact, not quite two decades after its opening, the building seems already to be a part of Berlin's history, as accustomed to the public's tepid regard as the Reichstag has become to its continuing glorification as one of contemporary architecture's greatest success stories. Yet the story of the Schlossplatz still proves discomfiting, not only in the context of Berlin's process of reunification, but also in larger discussions of architecture's historical import.

In one sense, the reconstructed Stadtschloss will no doubt be absorbed into the landscape of the New Berlin as quickly and surely as other once-controversial sites, including OMA's apartment building at Checkpoint Charlie, Peter Eisenman's Memorial to the Murdered Jews of Europe, and the star-studded, lackluster ensemble of buildings at Potsdamer Platz. But in another sense, it appears that the reconstruction will endure as a travesty, a term I use here not for its pejorative meanings but rather for its literal ones. It is my argument here that the Humboldt Forum remains such a painful outcome for the Schlossplatz in the perspective of so many viewers not only because of the conflicted identity problems that it underscores in the reunified capital, but also because it stages an unconscious parody of modernist architecture's utopian aims for the city. To say that the reconstructed Stadtschloss travesties modern architecture is to claim that it is a rejection of modernism's most cherished tenets, including the aesthetic alignment of form and function, the renunciation of applied ornament, and the "honest" expression of the materials of everyday life. But most importantly, the reconstruction travesties the utopian sociopolitical aspirations that gave modernism its core meaning—and in so doing, exposes the utopianism that necessarily underpins the project of reunification. If modernist architects dreamed of the will of a mass public embodied in architectural form, the reconstructed Stadtschloss expresses—unintentionally, but powerfully—a concerted doubt over the social significance of today's architecture and its ability to serve an increasingly complex global public. Moreover, it highlights the anxiety attending Germany's second unification, and the diffuse if often unspoken fear that (to paraphrase Marx) history might merely be repeating itself as farce.

As was the case with the Reichstag, the standoff between the Palast der Republik and the Stadtschloss has become an overly visible episode in Berlin's history of reunification. Therefore, seeing these structures clearly entails stepping back and using other means to examine them, including the various postreunification competitions held for the site and the series of art exhibitions staged in the defunct Palast before its demolition. We can also make use of the fragments and remainders created by all three buildings that have stood on the Schlossplatz as a way to contemplate the site as a whole—not with a romanticist's imaginative gaze, but by considering these fragments as pieces of evidence testifying to the high stakes of contemporary architecture's role in shaping historical understanding for a global viewership.

History of the Site

From Berlin-Kölln's earliest days, a fortified keep marked the crossing of the Spree as a residence and stronghold for the margraves of Brandenburg. In 1443, Frederick II laid the cornerstone of a new, expanded castle and occupied it upon its completion in 1451 as part of an effort to subdue the disorderly population of Berlin (who chafed against the economic constraints of monarchical rule) under the governance of the margraves of the Holy Roman Empire. In the sixteenth century, Joachim II commissioned the Renaissance *Baumeister* Caspar Theiss to transform the castle into a more genteel palace, and its embellishment and enlargement continued under the margraves of the seventeenth century. But it was during the eighteenth century that the Stadtschloss began to assume the contours for which it would later be known. In 1702, under Friedrich I—the so-called "King in Prussia"—the architect and sculptor Andreas Schlüter expanded the palace into what would become its distinctive form of four-story wings enclosing an ornately decorated courtyard. Only a few years later, Schlüter was replaced by Johann Friedrich Eosander von Göthe, who doubled the palace's footprint by extending its wings around another vast courtyard to the west (Figure 4.5). Eosander also moved the Stadtschloss's entrance to the western facade, facing the narrow waterway of the Spreekanal. Each subsequent ruler continued the palace's adornment in accordance with his own tastes and political concerns. In the 1840s, under Friedrich Wilhelm IV (known colloquially as the "Throned Romanticist" for his enrichment of both Berlin and Potsdam with majestic new architecture for the crown), the prolific architect Friedrich August Stüler added a towering dome over the royal chapel in the palace's western wing.[8] Based on an earlier design by Schinkel, the dome was intended to link the Stadtschloss with the nearby cathedral, which Schinkel had also recently renovated in the neoclassical style. By the nineteenth century, therefore, the palace had become the urban fulcrum of the Prussian capital, its northwestern corner looming at the visual endpoint of Unter den Linden. As Brian

Figure 4.5 Stadtschloss, Berlin, aerial photograph taken between 1905 and 1925.

Ladd has observed, "While rulers came and went—and often lived elsewhere—the palace's physical presence defined the city center."⁹

Schinkel was also responsible for the urban developments that shaped the Stadtschloss's immediate surroundings. His contributions to the landscape nearby included not only modifications to its cathedral (a structure that was supplanted by Julius and Otto Raschdorff's neobaroque counterpart in 1893), but also the colonnaded Altes Museum and the elegant bridge that linked the Schlossplatz to Unter den Linden. Indeed, one of the most signature views of the Stadtschloss is Schinkel's perspective drawing through the double row of the Altes Museum's graceful Ionic portico (Figure 4.6). Furthermore, he collaborated on the design of the royal garden to the north of the palace with the landscape architect Peter Joseph Lenné, transforming it into an urban core around which Berlin's civic and cultural institutions were arrayed in Arcadian harmony.¹⁰ For its designers, then, the image of urban equipoise that unfurled around this new public Lustgarten was an effort to cater to the new bourgeois subject. As part of a larger vision of the capital city as "Athens-on-the-Spree," Schinkel's classicizing buildings were intended to instruct their viewers in the edifying powers of art.¹¹ Many late-twentieth-century historians viewed Schinkel and his circle as protomodernists, and Buddensieg even argued that the undecidability of Schinkel's

Figure 4.6 Karl Friedrich Schinkel, *Perpektivische Ansicht von der Galerie der Haupt, Treppe des Museums durch den Porticus auf dem Lustgarten und seine Umgebungen*, 1824. Published in Schinkel, *Sammlung Architektonischer Entwürfe, 1819-1840*.

treatment of the Altes Museum marked it as an early instance of deconstruction, confronting the Stadtschloss with the democratic "temple" of the *polis*.[12] For its royal patrons, however, this tranquility was a semi-explicit attempt to belie the intensifying class conflict occurring throughout Europe in the nineteenth century. In March 1848, thousands of people crowded into the Schlossplatz to send an "address to the king" inside the Stadtschloss, demanding the reform that would come with German unification and a liberal constitution. A startled Friedrich Wilhelm IV crept out from the palace long enough to acquiesce to these demands, only to renege later in a volte-face with long political consequences. This and other events solidified the later image of the Stadtschloss as a "Junker-Trutzburg," and Karl Liebknecht triumphantly declared a German Socialist Republic from its balcony on November 9, 1918 (shortly after Philipp Scheidemann made the same proclamation from the Reichstag).[13]

But though it remained an important anti-symbol during the Weimar Republic, the palace was mostly ignored under National Socialism, and Hitler primarily used it as a massive support for flags and banners during parades in the Lustgarten (Figure 4.7). During the final months of World War II, Allied bombs aimed at the city center twice struck the Stadtschloss, leaving its exterior damaged and its roof collapsed. However, it remained structurally sound, with much of its abundant interior ornament intact.

Figure 4.7 National Socialist parade on the Schlossplatz, Berlin, 1936.

After the conclusion of the war, it was briefly used as an exhibition space to showcase "degenerate" art recuperated from the Nazis as well as Hans Scharoun's *Kollectivplan* for rebuilding the devastated city. Scharoun's 1946 exhibition, titled "Berlin Plans," demonstrated a gleaming, modern capital that starkly contrasted with the wreckage of the city outside the palace walls.[14] Yet despite a widespread interest in the Schloss's fate, no compelling vision of its longer-term life materialized. Soviet discussions of its use ensued, and several possibilities were explored, including its renovation and reuse as a government seat. Indeed, as recently as 2016, a GDR feasibility report was discovered that claimed the Stadtschloss could have been repaired for the comparatively affordable cost of 32 million marks.[15] Yet in July 1950, Walter Ulbricht announced that the palace would be removed, the land beneath it smoothed and paved, and a tribune erected at the eastern end of the site made from fragments of the destroyed building.[16] The dynamite and paving stones alone would cost 8 million marks—that is, a quarter of the overall cost to preserve the ornate Schloss.

During later discussions of the Stadtschloss's fate taking place in the 1990s, those in favor of its reconstruction often argued that the act of historical demolition itself was an expression of the destructive politics of the Soviet regime. But in fact, the GDR's decision in 1950 to raze the Stadtschloss (Figure 4.8) was highly controversial in East Germany, creating a philosophical rupture within the party that endured throughout its life. Though Ulbricht's plan for demolition was supported by many who saw the

Figure 4.8 Detonation of Berlin Stadtschloss by GDR, 1950. Bundsarchiv-Bildarchiv, Berlin.

building either as mere rubble or as a symbol of the decay of imperialist power in Germany, the idea of destroying such a venerable building was denounced as "an act of cultural barbarism" by some East German art historians—a term loaded with the fear of replicating the philistinism of Nazi aesthetics.[17] Earlier that year, a delegation of East German architects had traveled to Moscow for a "study tour," returning with an official recommendation that the party should preserve or rebuild Berlin's historical buildings to the greatest possible extent.[18] Even up to the night before the first explosions, some party leaders continued their desperate efforts to persuade Ulbricht to halt the process.[19] And after the demolition was complete, the *Tägliche Rundschau*, then the official organ of the GDR, commented that Berlin would long look back "with disgust" at the "cultural shame" of the party's destruction of the Stadtschloss, aligning it with the ravages of Allied (capitalist) bombing.[20]

"A House of the People"

For those in both the East and the West who denounced the Stadtschloss's removal, it seemed especially painful that it was to be replaced only with a void. However, this void was in fact the communist heart of a utopian spatial ideal, and its interpretation was thus a matter of Weltanschauung. To emphasize the openness and accessibility of the people's state—in contrast to the aloof, fortress-like Schloss—the land beneath the former eastern wing of the royal palace was left free to serve as a sweeping public space named Marx-Engels-Platz (Figure 4.9). As Ulbricht declared, "Our contribution to progress in the area of architecture shall consist in the expression of what is special to our national culture; the area of the Lustgarten and the Schloss ruin has to become a square for mass demonstrations which will mark the will to build and to fight expressed by our people."[21] The East German pendant to Moscow's Red Square, Marx-Engels-Platz was to serve as a crucial tool of class consciousness, allowing the newly liberated proletariat to view its power en masse. (Despite a few demonstrations in the first flush of the GDR, including one in which 750,000 people arrayed in seventy-two columns paraded through the square, it must be acknowledged that the space was thereafter primarily used as a parking lot filled with phalanxes of Trabants.)

Though the Palast der Republik would later acquire a reputation as an overvisible, overbearing monument, it was never meant to appear as awkwardly isolated as it did in the 1990s. Rather, it was intended to be only one part of an urban ensemble surrounding Marx-Engels-Platz that also included the Staatsratsgebäude (Council of State Building), the Ministerium für Auswärtige Angelegenheiten (Ministry of Foreign Affairs), and the Fernsehturm (broadcast tower), the latter of which was then, as it remains today, the tallest structure in Berlin. Soviet planners placed the Palast at the site of the Stadtschloss to mark the visual boundary of Unter den Linden so that the historic city's grand boulevard containing the Brandenburg Gate, the opera house, the Crown Prince's palace, and Humboldt University would visually culminate in their own architecture. As the easternmost element in this ensemble, the Fernsehturm not only punctuated the sequence; it also provided a clear summary of the architectural

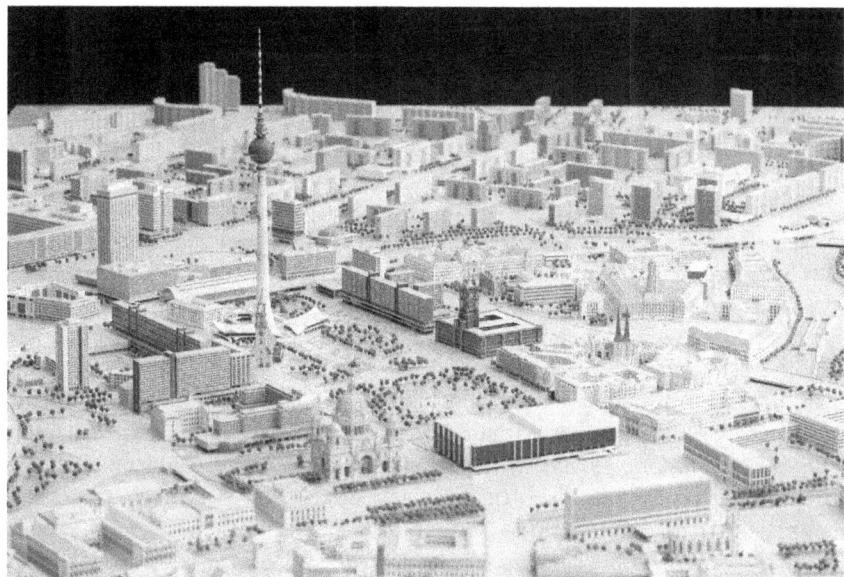

Figure 4.9 Model of East Berlin Stadtzentrum with Marx-Engels-Platz, Palast der Republik, Ministerium für Auswärtige Angelegenheiten, and Staatsratsgebäude in right foreground. Adam Eastland Art + Architecture / Alamy Stock Photo.

narrative at its base, proudly displaying the vastness of the socialist network and its technological prowess as evidence of Ulbricht's claims of a "scientific-technological revolution" occurring in the GDR during the 1960s. For the East German government, Unter den Linden thus provided a chronology of political power, as well as a chronicle of historical and architectural progress, both illustrated in legible materialist form. The process of modernization that had begun with the Brandenburg Gate in 1750 implicitly terminated in the futuristic modern architecture of the Palast and the Fernsehturm, creating a built genealogy (however tortured) that was completely unavailable to the cordoned-off West Berlin.

Though the Palast was to be the focal point of the East German capital, it was meant as a visual crux opening to the urban spaces to its east and west, and a "central building" had long been planned for the site.[22] As Emily Pugh has noted, the GDR's quest for "functionalism" was in reality less a study of practical usage than it was an exploration of the sociopolitical possibilities of architecture and urban planning.[23] In both the design of the Palast and in its urban context, East German architects attempted to illustrate the accessibility that they claimed to be absent in the "fascist" government architecture of the capitalist West. Plans for the area therefore took the form of a dynamic, abstract composition that owed much to the utopian city schemes of high modernism. To the south of the Palast, the composition was bounded by the low-rise profile and rhythmic bays of the Staatsratsgebäude, and to the west, by the enormous slab of Josef Kaiser's ministry building, built on the site of Schinkel's redbrick Bauakademie, damaged during World War II and then destroyed for the purpose. Between the Palast and the Fernsehturm, a space was cleared and transformed into a public park, named the Marx-Engels-Forum after the statue of the communist forefathers placed at its center. The mixed-use character of this urban space was intended to attract the public, invigorating the space and standing in contrast to the lifelessness and formality of the government districts of Western capitalism, populated only by officials and administrators.

Having already eradicated the Stadtschloss itself, the GDR thus both erased and superseded its historical footprint, subsuming the memory of the Schloss completely within a state-sponsored modernist ensemble. Yet fragments of the Hohenzollern building remained not only in the temporary tribune, but also as a kind of spolia in the main entrance of the Staatsratsgebäude. Here, the royal portal from which Liebknecht had made his historic 1918 declaration was incorporated into the new facade, the cartouche stripped of its Prussian eagle and decorated instead with the GDR's emblematic wreath and compass. Overall, the Marx-Engels-Platz and the three buildings defining it were envisioned as evidence of socialism's triumph displayed in architectural form. In the words of one official, they would "express in architecture and volume the victory of the socialist society and its superiority over previous epochs in social development."[24] Standing at the middle point of this ensemble, the Palast was meant to be a literal and figurative center—the cultural center of the capital of East Germany, the command center of the westernmost outpost of Soviet rule, and the communications center of the communist state. Both symbolically and urbanistically, the Palast endeavored to shift the balance of power towards the East.

While the Palast's main entrance issued a friendly invitation for passersby in the Marx-Engels-Platz to ascend its marble stairs, it was open and accessible from all of its four facades. In fact, the Palast's multipurpose, multiaudience design was an attempt to forge a new building type that united civic and government functions, and offered strong visual evidence of the ideological shift from Ulbricht to Erich Honecker's "consumer socialism." During the years of its construction, Graffunder was the head of the Institute for Residential and Commercial Buildings at the GDR's architectural academy, and the building therefore also served as a curricular tool for the academy's students. Graffunder explained that his building was to be open—both figuratively and literally—to all citizens of the GDR, saying: "the clear openness of the Palace for all citizens will be manifested through the optical transparency of the building mass and the plastic penetration of building elements."[25] This idealized description is powerfully suggestive of the utopian socialism of Germany's avant-garde, recalling Walter Gropius's first Bauhaus manifesto, accompanied by Lyonel Feininger's woodcut of the "Cathedral of Socialism," in which Gropius exhorted artists and craftsman to "join together to desire, imagine, create the new building of the future ... the crystalline symbol of the new faith to come."[26] But it is also worth recalling that Graffunder was making these utopian claims at the very moment that they were being rehearsed in strikingly similar terms in the West. Deborah Ascher Barnstone has pointed out that the rhetoric of the Palast was continuous with the ideology of architectural transparency officially supported in Bonn, arguing that Graffunder was "grappling with the selfsame questions of the representative power of architecture and the appropriate architectonic means with which to represent the state which concerned his Western counterparts."[27] Yet ultimately, Graffunder may have been aiming to outdo West German transparency, making his own structure still "*more* democratic, *more* modern, and perhaps *more* utopian."[28]

To make a clear statement of the GDR's new commitment to the happiness of its citizens, Graffunder was granted an unusually large budget of 1.2 billion ostmarks, using what was, for the efficiency-minded GDR, a lavish set of materials. Famously completed in fewer than a thousand days, the five-story building was a large rectangular volume 180 meters long and 85 meters wide, containing an 800-seat plenary hall for the Volkskammer and a vast auditorium with 5,000 seats for party congresses and larger meetings. At the building's corners, its steel and concrete structure was encased in white marble panels that visually offset its reflective, copper-colored glass skin, which was further embellished by gold-tinted framing. According to its architect, the pleasantly woozy hue of the glass gave it the visual lightness and penetrability of other modern structures, while also modulating the light filtering into the interior and creating "a certain intimacy" within the vast space.[29] The layered space of its multileveled foyer was intended as a continuation of the dynamic public zones outside its walls, functioning as a sort of interior public square (Figure 4.10). On the exterior—free of

Figure 4.10 Palast der Republik, main lobby with "glass forms." Sueddeutsche Zeitung Photo / Alamy Stock Photo.

applied ornament, save once again for the GDR national emblem—changing conditions of light would constantly generate "graphically interesting" reflections of the Palast's surroundings on its shimmering facade.[30] Inside, special pride was taken in the building's "glass forms," including its gridded constellation of globe lamps and the 5-meter-tall "glass flower" in the main lobby. Here, its designers summoned early-twentieth-century ideas of glass's social potential, making use of the material's utopian associations just as Norman Foster would do in his design for the Reichstag two decades later. Inside the Palast, the warm glow of the lamps reflecting on this abundance of glass offered a dreamlike contrast to the reality of the city outside, which remained perpetually suspended between rubble and reconstruction.

In practical terms, the Palast's official function as the seat of the rubber-stamp Volkskammer was distantly secondary to its use as a "house of the people."[31] Its elaborate lobby opened onto a dazzling array of recreational spaces, including a wide variety of cafes and restaurants, an espresso bar, a youth club, a small theater, sport facilities, two dance clubs, a billiard room and a bowling alley, and several galleries displaying regime-approved works. One corner of the building housed a post office that was open every day, a rarity in the later days of the GDR. In all of these spaces, the generous funds allotted for the building had allowed for a visual richness and ornamentation that was scant in East Berlin; in their palace, the people reclined on real leather seats, basked in the glow of exotic wood wall paneling, and danced on rotating circular platforms painted with pinwheel motifs. In its capacity as a cultural center, the Palast held regular performances of classical music as well as showcasing popular bands from throughout the communist world. However, it also hosted non-party-approved musicians, such as Carlos Santana, Harry Belafonte, and the West German pop star Udo Lindenburg, who famously performed at the Palast in 1983 (though he left his smash hit "Sonderzug nach Pankow," which brutally lampooned Honecker to the swingy tune of "Chattanooga Choo Choo," off the setlist that evening). It was also common for the building to host nongovernment events like birthday parties, anniversary celebrations, or even weddings.[32] In general, regardless of one's view of its ostentatious appearance or the politics of its sponsors, the building clearly succeeded in creating a dynamic social space for a large cross section of the public. In the *New York Times*, one Western visitor even worried that it would outdo the entertainment venues of its capitalist counterpart: "With all its attractions and its big congress hall the new center is apt to take business away from West Berlin."[33]

Overall, the Palast appeared to fulfill Graffunder's intentions for its integral use to the state. As he described it, "The multi-use building will be a house of the people . . . a building at the center of social life that—commensurate with its socio-spatial position in the center of the city—will be at the highpoint of social life in the socialist capital of the GDR."[34] Graffunder's government clients amplified his message: at the building's topping-out ceremony in 1974, Honecker associated the Schloss with the 1848 Revolution and proclaimed the Palast a fully realized "house of the people, a place of vibrant political and cultural life" that bore witness to the "industriousness and productivity of our people."[35] Receiving 12 million visitors during its first year, the Palast enacted a new phase in the regime's history in which a vital social life would motivate the public in the service of the state. Ample evidence suggests that, for many citizens of the GDR, the coppery massif hovering over Unter den Linden was a warm and reassuring presence, offering its users a kind of architectural pleasure that was scarce to be found in other parts of the country. The building proved so charismatic that it eventually earned the nickname "East Germany's largest corner bar."[36]

The Spreeinsel Competition

Not surprisingly, the Palast der Republik's aesthetic reputation in the West was somewhat different in tone, as were attitudes toward it more generally. If the Berlin Wall was by far the GDR's most iconic piece of architecture, the Palast was often presented as its somewhat hysterical sidekick, and its mirrored surfaces and ornamental verve were used as evidence of the bankruptcy—economic, ethical, and aesthetic—of the communist state. Far from its overtly utopian intentions, the building was viewed as both sinister and cynical, an exercise in Ossi kitsch that attempted to conceal the regime's deadly agenda. Therefore, on the "free" side of the Wall, witty sobriquets for the Palast during its functioning years ranged from "Ballast of the Republic" to "Palazzo Prozzo" (pompous palace) to "Erichs Lampenladen" (Erich's lamp shop). That it shared some qualities in common with West Berlin's signature architecture, such as the Internationales Congress Centrum in Charlottenburg (1976–9, Ralf Schüler and Ursulina Schüler-Witte)—from its overwhelming massing to its burnished aluminum cladding to the asbestos in its walls—usually went unremarked (Figure 4.11). By the moment of reunification, Western perceptions of the building ranged from the bemused to the skeptical, usually based in the assumption that it was a gaudy trinket meant to distract from the grim political conditions of the East.

As was also the case for the Reichstag and the Chancellery, discussions of the Schlossplatz's future were framed by a large-scale federal planning initiative. In this case, it was the second of the two major government competitions for the Hauptstadt: the Stadtmitte Spreeinsel competition of 1993–4, which encompassed the center section of the island in the Spree that still defined the eastern zone of the city center. Hence, what was at stake in this competition—stated in explicit terms—was the recuperation of Berlin's "heart," and the opportunity to repair what were viewed as the travesties committed against it by the GDR.[37] The notion of the Schlossplatz and its surroundings as Berlin's "heart" was reiterated continually throughout the 1980s and 1990s by the traditionalist architect Josef Paul Kleihues and the publisher and critic Wolf Jobst Siedler, and this corporeal metaphor infused later perceptions of the Stadtschloss and Palast as well. As we have seen, the Spreebogen site was distinctive precisely because of its marginal position, as it seemed always to occupy a border terrain at the edge of some other more unified urban parcel. In contrast, as the East Germans well understood, the area around the Schloss lay at the very epicenter of the city's urban past, forming the heart of historic Kölln and supporting many of Berlin's most important cultural resources.

Figure 4.11 Ralf Schüler and Ursulina Schüler-Witte, Internationale Congress Centrum (ICC), Berlin, 1976–9.

Stripped of the city's historic heart, the Bundesrepublik had energetically funded the construction of new, modern architecture in West Berlin to house its civic institutions, yielding some of the postwar era's most quintessential designs, including Fritz Bornemann's Deutsche Oper (1961), Hans Scharoun's Philharmonie (1963), and Ludwig Mies van der Rohe's Neue Nationalgalerie (1968). Yet undeniably, the island in the Spree remained the home of many of the city's most august buildings. On the northern tip of the island (known as the Museuminsel) lay the Bode-Museum, the Pergamonmuseum, the Neues Museum, and the Alte Nationalgalerie, all slated for individual renovation at the time of the competition. At its center lay the concrete field of the Lustgarten and Schlossplatz watched over by the Altes Museum, the Berliner Dom, and the Palast der Republik, as well as the various GDR ministries described above. To the south, a well-preserved medieval neighborhood on the so-called Fischerinsel that had survived into the twentieth century had been replaced by a covey of *Plattenbauten*, Soviet-era housing blocks made of prefabricated concrete slabs.[38] Neither the Museuminsel nor the Fischerinsel was included in the competition area, as both were to be decided in separate competitions. However, the zone defined by the program extended westward across the narrow Spreekanal to include several of Schinkel's most significant structures, including the site of Schinkel's destroyed Bauakademie (still occupied by the GDR's foreign ministry) and his likewise *Backsteingotik* Friedrichswerder Church.[39] In delineating these parcels of land as a unified area with a distinct historical character, and mounting a competition to "restore" its identity, the brief already implied that the East German architecture on the site was an aberration requiring corrective measures. Thus, an emphasis on Berlin's architectural heritage—or at least on one narrow slice of it—was built into the competition brief, and bound to condition, at least partially, the responses that it received. At the same time, however, the program called for a decidedly nontraditional combination of functions at the Spreeinsel, stipulating the addition of a city hall, conference center, library, mixed-use buildings, and transit centers, as well as two new buildings for the foreign and interior ministries. The seemingly contradictory pressures outlined in the brief—on the one hand, to preserve and restore; on the other, to develop—contributed in no small part to the Spreeinsel competition's failure.

Furthermore, the government's rebuilding euphoria, as described in Chapter 1, manifested at the Spreeinsel as a kind of hubristic expansiveness. In 1992, the Spreebogen competition had set international records; in 1993, the Spreeinsel competition blew past that contest's staggering numbers, quickly surpassing it to become the largest urban planning competition in history.[40] In the wake of the competition announcement, more than 2,000 architects from sixty countries around the world requested materials. Ultimately, the competition attracted 1,105 entries from forty-nine countries, 355 of which came from Germany alone. Almost half of the German submissions—174—came from architects and planners working within Berlin.[41] In the exultant atmosphere that still characterized the Hauptstadt excitement of the early 1990s, the Bundestag seemed to be resolved to outdo themselves in every respect, even spending a yet more staggering amount—4.5 million deutsche marks, to the Spreebogen's 4 million—on the competition.[42] The timing is significant here, as these two blockbuster competitions ran virtually simultaneously—and the Spreeinsel competiton followed close enough on the heels of its prototype that disappointment over the Spreebogen's results had yet to become clear. With investment capital still flowing in the direction of Berlin, and still buoyed by the international excitement of the other Hauptstadt competitions, the government re-upped for another round. However, the Spreeinsel was to be only the first in a series of competitions, symposia, and other events held to determine the form of the Schlossplatz. Therefore, the competition itself forms only one part of a debate that was already well underway by the time it commenced and that would continue long after it ended.

The jury comprised familiar figures, including Kleihues, Gustav Peichl, and Hans Stimmann, as well as newcomers such as Franco Stella and the architect, critic, and curator Peter Blake. Over the course of only a few days in December 1993, the jury winnowed the pile of anonymous submissions down to fifty-two finalists, nearly every one of which envisioned the demolition of the Palast and other GDR buildings on the site and the reconstruction of Schinkel's Bauakademie. By the spring of 1994, the jury had agreed, with minimal drama, on the winning submission from the anonymous applicants (Figure 4.12).[43] It came from 35-year-old Bernd Niebuhr, a Berlin-based architect, who proposed to replace the defunct Palast der Republik with a building in the dimensions of the former Schloss encompassing a large oval courtyard. In this massive new building would be gathered many of the mixed-use functions that the government envisioned for this new artificial district, including the library, conference

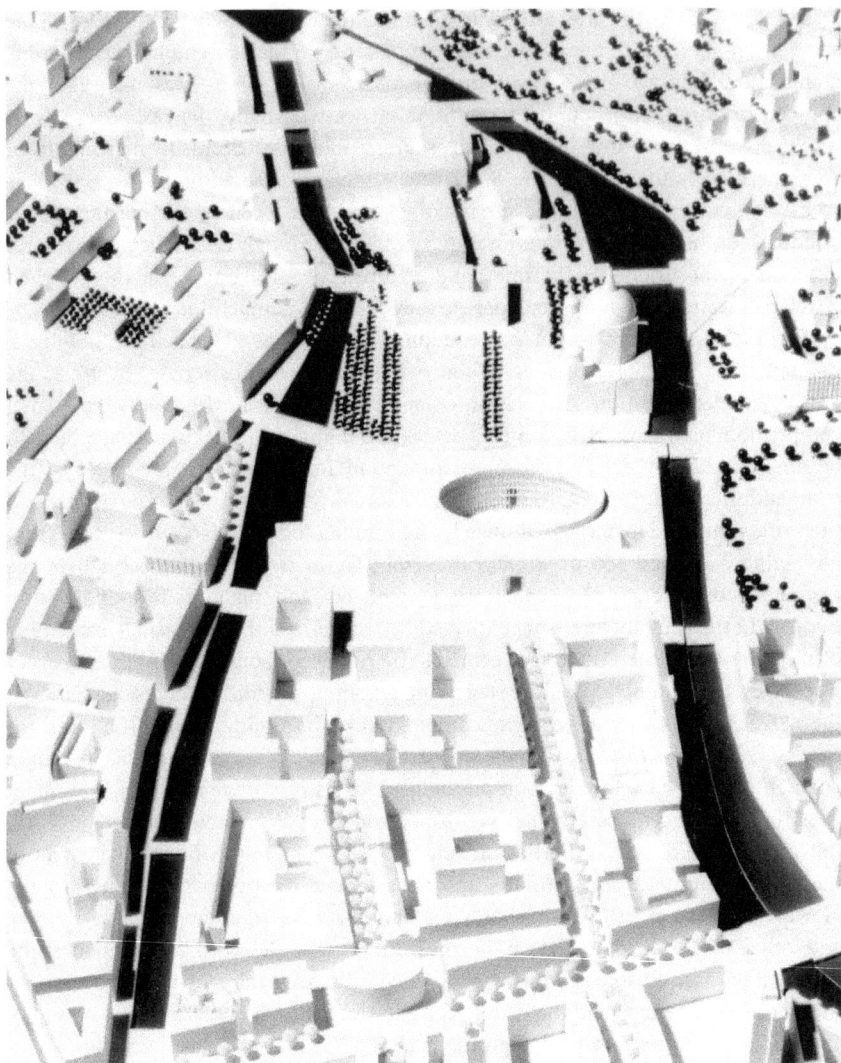

Figure 4.12 Bernd Niebuhr, proposal for the Spreeinsel, Berlin, 1994. Courtesy of Bernd Niebuhr.

center, and city hall. The new ministry buildings stipulated by the brief were contained in dignified buildings of traditional profiles and materials flanking the Spreekanal to the south of the Schlossplatz, and a stately grid of narrow block buildings filled the open area between the Schlossplatz and Alexanderplatz. In his proposal, Niebuhr echoed the notion of the Schlossplatz as the heart of the city, arguing that the Stadtschloss long functioned as the "center of society" in Berlin, and that the city's urban "spaces are senseless and meaningless without the cubature of the Schloss."[44] Though his proposal aligned well with the historicism implicit in the government brief, he faced challenges from the press over his lack of interest in the site's GDR-era architecture. Speaking with one journalist, Niebuhr vehemently resisted suggestions that his concept was nostalgic, labeling it instead "reminiscent urban planning."[45]

Despite its consensus on his plan, the jury appears to have had qualms, after the fact and behind the scenes, about the exposure of the architect himself—or, rather, his lack thereof. In contrast to the high-profile, celebrity cast of characters in competition for the Reichstag, and against the largely established finalists for the Spreebogen, Niebuhr was young and inexperienced, and had little reputation to publicize. In contrast to the other winners of the Hauptstadt competitions, he even lacked the institutional legitimacy of belonging to a firm. Government officials reacted with surprise and doubt when his name was announced as the competition winner, and the press took notice especially of the Senator for Urban Development Volker Hassemer's quick attempts to regroup for the sake of appearances. After the announcement, some journalists responded positively to Niebuhr's lack of star status. "Young Architects Surge in Open Spreeinsel Competition," announced *Architectural Record*, congratulating officials for their open-mindedness.[46] On the other hand, however, the *Tageszeitung* referred to the architect as "Nobody Niebuhr," and one jury spokesperson snidely suggested that—given the fact that Niebuhr did not even have an office—he had probably produced his plans for one of the most important sites in Berlin from "a drawing board next to the kitchen table."[47] Here, the marketability of the architect himself was explicitly at stake alongside the viability of his design.

Still, with a clear winner safely determined, the jury appeared anxious to represent a range of positions in the other premiated designs, secure in the knowledge that these plans would not be realized. Months before their first-prize standoff with Schultes and Frank for the Chancellery, Krüger Schuberth Vandreike (KSV) was awarded second place at the Spreeinsel (Figure 4.13). Their design was unapologetically nostalgic, calling for the reconstruction of the Schloss, the reconstruction of the Bauakademie, and the interpolation of various arcades and colonnades throughout the area to lend it a traditional urban character. For this team of former citizens of the GDR, the task was explicitly to return Berlin to a state that they claimed "basically already exists."[48] This state was, in their words, "a modern Athens on the Spree," which would again make Berlin "a city to remember: one of well-proportioned squares and buildings, stone and glass in a new context of meaning."[49] The jury responded approvingly to KSV's interpretation of Berlin traditionalism and—as in the case of the Chancellery—praised the high quality of the firm's contemporary take on classicism. For the selection of the third- and fourth-place winners, the jury appears to have been more experimental: in third place, the Swiss architect Rudolf Rast again recommended the rebuilding of the Bauakademie and the construction of a building with the contours of the Schloss, yet his was rendered partially in glass and steel and enhanced by an elliptical glass high-rise to the south of the site. In fourth place, O. M. Ungers, by far the biggest name among the finalists, proposed a bold approach—or at least it appeared bold in the context of the obvious historical biases on view in the government's brief. At the

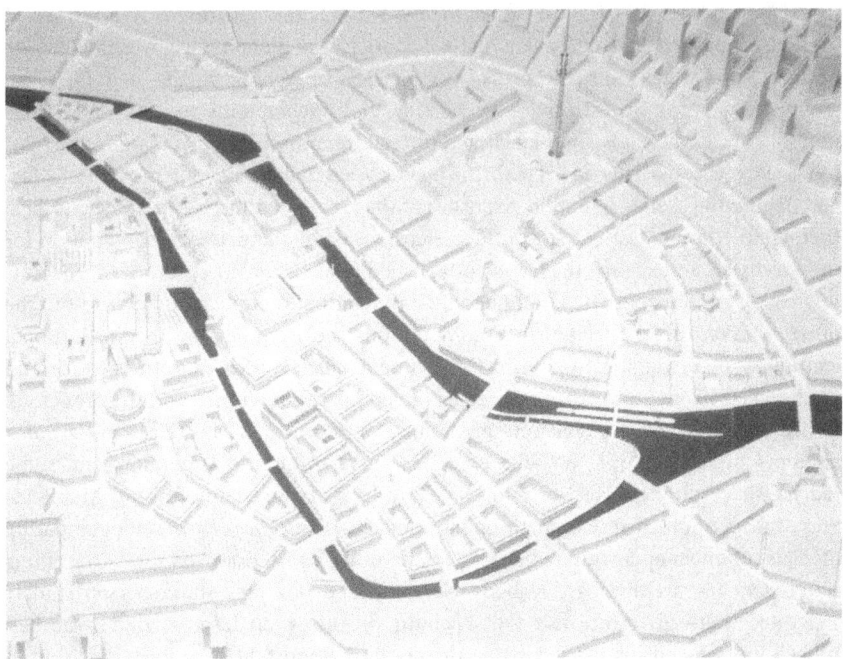

Figure 4.13 Krüger Schuberth Vandreike (KSV), proposal for the Spreeinsel, Berlin, 1994. Copyright architecture/ model: KSV Krüger Schuberth Vandreike, Berlin. Copyright photo: Antonia Weiße.

beginning of his competition statement, Ungers specified that the proposal assumed the preservation of the Palast der Republik in its original form. Moreover, he stated that funds should be allotted for "respectful restoration of the interior and exterior aesthetics."[50] However, Ungers's idea was that the Palast would be "liberated from its parade position"—in a reverberation of the idea of "liberating" urban fragments that appeared in his 1977 proposal for "Berlin as Green Archipelago"—and integrated into an enclosed urban form, with new buildings ringing the Schlossplatz and forming a courtyard in front of the Palast.[51] Thus, the old footprint of the Schloss was left mostly free, while its surrounds were built up, forming a new negative space from the site's historical layers.

Relegated to obscurity in the large pool of finalists despite the faux-Schinkel prank was the proposal from Axel Schultes and Charlotte Frank (Figure 4.14). Viewed at a slight historical distance, Schultes and Frank's proposal approaches the history of the site in a way that appears strikingly different from their methods at the Spreebogen, though both proposals thematized the urban fragment. In their competition materials, the architects took the unusual measure of preemptively scolding their evaluators: "The primary task of a critical jury would be to combat this wretched Berlin tradition, this

Figure 4.14 Schultes and Frank Architekten, proposal for the Spreeinsel, Berlin, 1994.

cramped antiquarianism," they wrote, cautioning against the "feeble strategy of fragments" that had inflected the rhetoric surrounding the Schlossplatz.[52] As with many of the other submissions, Schultes and Frank argued for the removal of the Palast and the reconstruction of the Bauakademie. But the defining element of their proposal was the addition of an enormous, u-shaped structure with flanking wings, irresistibly recalling the plan of the palace at Versailles. However, as with Ungers's project, the purpose of the structure was to shape the urban environment. What was required, in the architects' view, was "reprogramming the program" for the area, which meant the careful placement of new urban volumes that would allow for function and meaning to develop over time.[53] By opening a well-defined urban space across from the Lustgarten, Schultes and Frank's proposal sought to reinstate the atmosphere of Schlüter's courtyard, which was "the only detail in the Schloss that could lay claim to urban quality."[54] In contrast to their allegorical conception of the Spreebogen's historical fragments, they proposed the creation of an urban framework at the Schlossplatz that could flexibly contain its future use.

The heightened, nearly aggravated tone of Schultes and Frank's proposal is a further reminder that the furor surrounding the Schlossplatz was already underway by the time of the competition, and therefore that the Spreeinsel competition represented only one of its moments of peak intensity. Almost immediately after the competition concluded, the murmur of doubt about the viability of such massive government intervention at the Spreeinsel reached a roar. In the first place, predictable resistance arose to the systematic erasure of the GDR's buildings on the site. Josef Kaiser's foreign ministry, abandoned and unloved, garnered little individual support, but supporters of the Palast loudly protested the government's plans, especially during an exhibition of all 1,105 first-round proposals held at the former Reichsbank from June to September of 1994. Distressed over the general attitudes toward East Germany's built heritage on view in the government's approach to the site, a coalition of architects, architectural historians, and urban planners formed to lobby for the preservation of the Staatsratsgebäude, arguing that its comparatively historicizing architecture, as well as the historical Schloss portal itself, merited preservation. Their successful campaign marked the first of many changes to the Bundestag's plans for the Spreeinsel.[55]

However, perhaps none of the changes was more significant than the massive wave of budget cuts leveled at the Spreeinsel in February of 1995 by Federal Minster of Finance Theo Waigel. Less than a year after the end of the competition, an economic reckoning had reached Berlin as the deadline for the government to reoccupy the capital was pushed ever further into the future. Originally set for 1997, the date had been moved to sometime after the turn of the millennium, and real estate prices correspondingly plunged along with the confidence of investors. Furthermore, a 1991 study had demonstrated that, spread among existing official government buildings (formerly belonging both to East and West Germany, but "absorbed" by the reunified government), there was more than ample space available in the city for the new government functions, and that renovation of these structures could be achieved much more cheaply than new construction. Waigel thus eliminated funding for all but three government building projects: the Chancellery, the Reichstag renovation, and the office of the president. For some, these budget cuts represented a stay of execution for the Palast, and therefore were cause for celebration. For others, they meant that the dream of reconstructing the Schloss grew remote, and so other channels for supporting its rebirth needed to be pursued.

Schloss Simulacra, Schlossplatz Visions

As the Spreeinsel competition unfolded, the Stadtschloss received a helpful PR boost intended to fan up enthusiasm around its reconstruction. In 1993, a nonprofit group calling itself the *Förderverein Berliner Stadtschloss*—the "friends of the Berliner Stadtschloss," headed up by Wilhelm von Boddien, a wealthy Hamburg businessman with aristocratic ancestry—privately sponsored the installation of a full-size mock-up of two of the Stadtschloss's baroque facades (Figure 4.15). Brightly painted on canvas screens and tracing the contours of the Schloss's original footprint, the mock-up concealed the Palast behind a vivid photorealist veil.[56] The screens were mounted on an intricate system of scaffolding erected over the Palast's facade. Where the mock-up met the Palast at a right angle, another elaborate scaffold was erected, this one supporting a massive mirror to reflect the illusory "wing" of the Stadtschloss so that its bays ramified in both directions along the Schlossplatz. The surfaces of this veil eclipsed mere *trompe*

Figure 4.15 Simulation of rebuilt Stadtschloss, Berlin, 1993.

l'oeil, its coruscating ochre surfaces falling into the uncanny valley of the digital at the dawn of its ascendance in contemporary architecture. Indeed, its sponsors referred to the mock-up as a "Schloss Simulation," unconsciously suggesting the astounding level of artifice that the entire project of reconstruction would require. The flat screen achieved a haunting dimensionality, with faux-shadows cast by its segmental pediments, corner quoins, and crowning baluster. Standing at the end of Unter den Linden, the mock-up functioned like an eerie billboard advertising not only the reconstruction of the Stadtschloss itself, but of "historic Berlin" more generally. Inside the courtyard created by the scaffolding, a small exhibition titled *Das Schloss? Eine Ausstellung über die Mitte Berlins* narrated the Stadtschloss's history, including its inglorious fate at the hands of the GDR, and proposed suggestions for its restoration. As with the Spreeinsel competition itself, the simulation and exhibition explicitly conflated the Stadtschloss with Berlin's urban heart. The mock-up was to be the first of many simulations of the Stadtschloss staged in the years to come.

After reunification, the strategy of urban simulation was not uncommon in Berlin. Indeed, as Claire Colomb has observed, simulation was central to the city's rebranding, and screens, mock-ups, and billboards were the key to "selling the cityscape of the future Berlin."[57] Throughout the 1990s, the city was screened in a variety of ways; large-scale mock-ups were erected at Leipziger Platz and the Bauakademie, and the InfoBox at Potsdamer Platz and the so-called *Schaustelle*, a series of exhibitions held at construction sites around the city, offered ample opportunities for what marketers came to label "Architainment."[58] To these more glaring examples of Architainment, we would do well to add the *Berlin Tomorrow* initiative of 1991, unfolding in the architecture feuilletons and museums of Berlin but no less an example of urban simulation for that fact. As the purpose of this urban simulation was to allow viewers to imagine a new future for the structures in question, whether they existed currently as ruins or did not exist at all, we should also remember that Christo and Jeanne-Claude's *Wrapped Reichstag* might represent the *ne plus ultra* of this form of picturing the city, permanently etched as it now is on the memory of the Reichstag.

However, several characteristics separated the Stadtschloss simulation from other of Berlin's city-imaginary initiatives. In the first place, it was a highly unusual instance of a privately funded project appearing on state-owned land and property. In this case, of course, the building in question had only recently changed hands from one state to the other. Yet individual members of the Förderverein, who were nearly all significant members of Berlin's business community, had long had the ear of the government and were able to promote their architectural concerns through channels that were unavailable to most members of the public. They were aided by sympathetic members of the press, in particular Siedler and the journalist Joachim Fest (the culture editor for the *Frankfurter Allgemeine Zeitung*), both of whom published seminal articles arguing for the reconstruction of the Stadtschloss. In his long career, Siedler had been critical both of modernism and historicism as urban methods, seeing both as destructive to the character of the city. Therefore, it was with self-professed "resignation" that he concluded: "The Schloss wasn't *in* Berlin—Berlin *was* the Schloss."[59] In other words, for Siedler, the question of rebuilding the Stadtschloss was "not as much about the Schloss as it was about the classic center of Berlin ... The point was less a single edifice than the entire city image."[60] Fest's "plea" for the palace's reconstruction was more candidly nostalgic, romanticizing the public role of the building and characterizing it as an open and accessible structure whose loss had been keenly felt throughout Germany.[61]

In 1996, the *Berliner Tagesspiegel* sponsored an "ideas competition" for the future of the city center, in part to diversify the range of architectural responses to the Schlossplatz and reorient them away from the endless standoff between Schloss and Palast. Over the course of the next few months, the newspaper published the proposals of more than twenty architects, including projects both from local figures and internationally renowned luminaries. Schultes submitted the plan for "Schinkel's dream" described above, accompanied by an essay by Buddensieg reminding readers of the progressive public mission behind Schinkel's architecture and planning. In his submission, the Berlin-based architect Hinrich Baller praised the Stadtschloss as "the highest quality building Berlin had ever managed to build," but argued that its "terrifying size" made a straightforward reconstruction untenable.[62] Instead, he proposed that fragments of the castle be arranged within a modern, glazed facade that would radiate openness and permeability, thus creating a new Stadtschloss with "a place for everyone."[63] Indeed, the concept of a visibly contemporary "glass house" concept for the site was a recurring theme in the competition entries; Stuttgart-based Michael Walker submitted a luminous, high-tech frame building with approximately the same dimensions as the Stadtschloss, while the Berlin architect Wolf-Rüdiger Borchardt's design inserted a vast glass cube within the Schloss's reconstructed facades.

As with *Berlin Tomorrow*, the premise of the "competition" was to gather ideas unbounded by practical concerns, thus revealing new insights on how the site's past might inform its future. Some proposals focused less on constructing new architecture for the Schlossplatz than on creating environments that might force a reconsideration of its history. Titled "Berlin Mitte Falls into the Water," Bernd Kühn's scheme called for geometric, recessed reflecting pools in the contours of the Stadtschloss. This gesture, in line with other contemporary countermonuments (to adopt James Young's term), was meant to highlight that democracy created instability and complexity that was nonetheless preferable to the false consensus of authoritarianism.[64] After their unsuccessful bid for the Chancellery, Hilde Léon + Konrad Wohlhage proposed reconstructing the shell of the Schloss and filling it with a Ferris wheel and rollercoaster, using the "funfair as a symbol for the void."[65] They were not the only ones who imagined a festival atmosphere. Strikingly, Norman Foster reinvigorated the "big roof" concept that had won his firm the Reichstag competition four years before, placing a vast canopy (50 meters by 50 meters) over the Schlossplatz made up of individual umbrellas that could be folded and lowered into the earth when desired. Underneath, Foster envisioned the Schlossplatz as a vital public "forum" (echoes again of the Reichstag concept) for sports, festivals, and other events; his rendering displayed the square filled with sand and framed by grandstands for a lively game of beach volleyball presided over by the decorous Altes Museum. Frei Otto extended this idea of ephemerality and impermanence yet further, arguing that a tent-like pavilion constructed over the Schlossplatz would be sufficient architectural intervention for the next thirty years, allowing tempers to cool and the future of the site to come naturally into view. As he said, "Anyone who is definitively planning the space now is blocking the future. First, the space has to be brought to life."[66] (As we shall see, this concept of interim use would reverberate years later in the Palast der Republik's life.) Still other proposals wittily punctured the air of high stakes attending the Schlossplatz debate; Amsterdam-based Matthijs Bouw/Joose Meuwissen suggested that the square be lined with monumental statues of dachshunds, poodles, and terriers to show that Berlin had finally "gone to the dogs."[67]

The Stadtschloss mock-up of 1993 was thus only one instance of a dreamed future for the Schlossplatz, hovering somewhere between private concern and public statement. However, there was a quality of literalness to the mock-up that stood in contrast to the imaginative exercises of other experiments to determine the Schlossplatz's new form. If one category of picturing the city involved summoning the viewer's imaginative faculties, the simulation did the viewer's work for her, providing a full and hyperdetailed image that—depending on perspective—was either visually stimulating or almost bizarrely banal. In any case, it is clear that both sides of the Schlossplatz debate believed that their adversaries were supporting kitsch, and that the unwished-for outcome would be, in effect, a travesty of Berlin's history. Though others, including Buddensieg, argued passionately for a new solution on the site—a novel solution that could navigate Berlin out of the cul-de-sac of the Stadtschloss-vs.-Palast standoff—historical nostalgia had become the default, and doubt had been cast on contemporary architecture's ability to negotiate the heart of the city in any novel way.

Advocates for the reconstruction of the Stadtschloss consistently expressed their position as a form of national, collective longing—an avowedly nostalgic position that gained a surprising amount of traction over the years. As Claudia Breger has noted, over the course of the debate, the position of von Boddien and his cohort moved from reactionary to mainstream, from a sort of fringe sentimentality to a legitimate and legitimized longing for the restoration of losses dealt during illegitimate reigns.[68] With the government district officially established in the West, at stake was the symbolic heart of the city—implicitly believed to be beyond politics, but in fact among the most highly politicized sites in the country, and in the grips of what Ladd has termed "rival nostalgias."[69] As Ladd points out, even the "third way"—clearing the slate and starting anew—was a form of nostalgia for the heroic modernism of the 1920s.[70]

On July 4, 2002, the Bundestag convened to decide the fate of the Schlossplatz once and for all during a parliamentary debate that recalled the discussion of Christo and Jeanne-Claude's *Wrapped Reichstag* eight years before. The decision to be made was whether to approve the reconstruction of three of the Stadtschloss's four facades—the "baroque solution"—or to hold a new competition to explore further alternatives. As with the earlier debate, the discussion largely broke along party lines, with left-leaning members of parliament advocating for a new, modern building on the site and those on the right supporting the reconstruction of the Stadtschloss. However, it is worth noting that the terms of the Reichstag session had been explicitly binary; the vote was whether or not to move forward with the proposal to wrap the building. In contrast, the Schlossplatz debate *became* binary as it ran its course, lapsing into the back-and-forth of traditionalism versus modernism that had characterized earlier discussions of Berlin's new government architecture. By 2002, this false binary had become seemingly inescapable, having been especially evident in its stymying effect during the Chancellery's development. The Bundestag's choice seemed to lie between privileging the East German past and protecting the true heart of the city. The scales were helpfully tipped by Gerhard Schröder. From his temporary office in the Staatsratsgebäude overlooking the Schlossplatz, Schröder declared the abandoned Palast der Republik languishing outside his window "monstrous" and averred his preference for a new Stadtschloss. The subsequent Bundestag vote overwhelmingly favored reconstructing the Stadtschloss, with 384 in favor and 133 opposed. The press quickly dubbed the vote "Schlüter's Victory."

Zwischennutzung

If von Boddien, Fest, and other Stadtschloss supporters could argue that the building's destruction in 1950 had been an act of cultural barbarism for political ends, the opposite claim could be marshaled as well: that is, that the decision to tear down the Palast was a politically motivated hit job against East German memory. In Andreas Huyssen's words, the vote to demolish the Palast "was not just tinkering with the communist city text. It was a strategy of power and humiliation, a final burst of Cold War ideology, pursued via a politics of signs."[71] In the oddly prolonged liminal moment between the sealing of the Palast's fate and its ultimate removal, artists and architects took the opportunity both to underscore the politics of its demolition and to present alternative views of both its past and its potential futures. As with many of the "visions" presented by architects in the earlier *Tagesspiegel* ideas competition, these artists imagined a revivified Palast that would be "for the people" in much the same the way its creators had intended in its former life. Notably, these interventions took place within the hulking carcass of the building, shifting the focus from the facade, which had dominated the politicians' debate. In 2004, the organization Urban Catalyst applied for and received approval to use the Palast as the frame for a series of exhibitions, performances, and actions that began later that year. These events became known collectively as the *Initiative Zwischenpalastnutzung*, making use of a postreunification marketing term meant to signal a building's provisional use for a purpose other than that for which it was constructed. As Simon Ward has described it, the term *Zwischennutzung* describes a "model of cultural activities in an intermediate space and time," and also characterizes the use of many of Berlin's other "transitional" spaces, such as the Kunsthaus Tacheles, the former Schultheiss brewery in Moabit, and the Mengerzeile, a disused piano factory in Alt-Treptow.[72] The ambiguity of the preposition *zwischen* in this case—it can signify *between*, *interim*, or *temporary*, depending on the context—was useful for leaving open the possibility of a new outcome for the Palast.

What followed the 2004 approval were months of events that ranged from motocross demonstrations to film screenings to experimental dance performances. Political debates and theater performances were held inside the ruined shell; a traveling exhibition of China's terracotta army even made a brief appearance. Though some of the programming of the Zwischennutzung took advantage of the building's abandoned warehouse atmosphere to stage political rallies or standard-issue large-scale parties and raves, other events took their cues from the architecture itself, amounting to surprisingly thorough and revealing analyses of the building's modernist form.

For the organizers of the Volkspalast, the Palast der Republik was not a fixed symbol of an authoritarian regime but rather a slippery signifier whose meaning could be altered along with its historical circumstances. To that end, the first order of business was the renaming of the building as "Volkspalast." According to Amelie Deuflhard, the project's artistic director, the name itself acted as a magnet, drawing the public to the exciting "new" building and encouraging viewers to perceive it as a vital space instead of a rotting pile: "instead of asking for the Palast der Republik, everybody on the street asked, 'Could you show me the way to the Volkspalast?'"[73]

In retrospect, the Zwischennutzung is significant partly in its canny move away from the stultifying dead ends of the reconstruction debate and toward the questions of public use that had been sidelined in elite discussions of the Schlossplatz's future use. The festive, communal memory of the building's past prompted a series of cultural events and installations held in the Palast between 2004 and 2006. The Bundestag had reluctantly consented to the Volkspalast venture under increasing pressure from a broad cross section of the public, aided by a vocal group of journalists who repeatedly accused the government of acting solely on its phobic relationship to history and thus repressing the East German past. Numerous articles appeared in the popular press encouraging the Volkspalast project and criticizing the Bundestag's decision to demolish the Palast, suggesting that instead it be converted to a cultural center like the Centre Pompidou in Paris. Sympathetic journalists pointed out that the government's insistence that there was no money in its coffers to rehabilitate the Palast lacked merit given the expense it was willing to incur to reconstruct the Stadtschloss. Summoning the same popular notion of "Schinkel's Dream" earlier invoked by Axel Schultes, the critic Niklas Maak wondered:

> Doesn't Berlin already have the castle of its dreams? ... There is no consensus that the Palast der Republik is ugly and a reconstructed castle is beautiful. The melancholy of the Schlossplatz is not that the Palast der Republik is ugly but that nothing is going on there. Instead of dreaming of a castle that will never come to exist, Berlin could transform its greatest ruin into a popular stage for public life. In contrast to the monies for a castle, the energies for reinterpreting the palace are freely available. They need only be recognized and supported by politics.[74]

An examination of the Volkspalast events themselves reveals their ongoing emphasis on the building's use and a continued reorientation from the facade to the interior. The first Volkspalast event took place on September 3, 2004, with the opening of the so-called "Fassadenrepublik," a collaboration between the art collective raumlabor Berlin and Peanutz Architekten. In the Fassadenrepublik, a performance-cum-installation, a snaking 400-meter-long "facade" of painted plastic tarps was installed in the main hall of the Palast. The hall was then flooded knee-deep with water from the Spree. Upon arriving at the Palast, visitors were greeted by rubber-booted hosts who escorted them into inflatable boats. Other guides led the boats on a tour of the new "city," providing commentary on the proposals. Most of the images—of houses, storefronts, and city squares—were the result of a public "call for facades" that solicited proposals of up to 3 meters by 3 meters to be created by "amateur architects" (meaning the public) and then sent to raumlabor's offices for painting.[75] The facades represented a persuasive sample of standard city images while also revealing the desires of those who created them. There was a Facade-Academy, a Facade-Parliament, a Facade-Workshop, and even a Facade-Red-Light-District close to the Facade-Harbor. The installation was insistently participatory: visitors could propose policies to parliament, analyze the architecture of the facades in the academy, or even apply for and be granted a license to drive one of the inflatable boats. Throughout, participants were encouraged to discuss and critique the proposed facades, in mock-serious mimicry of official discussions of land use and policy—what the artists hoped would be a productive "role-play."[76] If so moved, visitors could alter, deface or even destroy facades.

Certainly, the Fassadenrepublik was akin to the relational art prevalent in the larger art world at the time. But as a specific intervention into Berlin's architecture culture, it also served as a vital space for architectural critique at a time when avenues for such critique had grown scarce. By offering a provisional, interactive space for debates on urban planning, the Fassadenrepublik pointedly ironized what had by then become a common sight in Berlin: the temporary recreation of the facades of historical buildings to signal public hopes for their reconstruction. At the same moment in which visitors slogged through the flooded Palast, a printed plastic facade of Schinkel's Bauakademie was installed across the Schlossplatz. The goal of that project was to encourage public support for the building's actual, brick-and-mortar reconstruction, yet it also served as a handy surface on which to advertise its sponsor, Mercedes-Benz. Indeed, by 2004, such printed facades had become ubiquitous and thus largely unnoticed, and so it was left to the artists of the Volkspalast to point out their phantasmal strangeness. The Fassadenrepublik deliberately evoked the so-called "plastic facades" of the reunified city, pointing up the tensions, erasures, and conflicts inherent in reconstruction. Overall, the Fassadenrepublik gave spatial form to many of the doubts plaguing the Schlossplatz—and Berlin more generally.

In some cases, the artistic interventions into the empty Palast shell of the early 2000s suggested opportunities for new social structures to coalesce between its walls. One such case was the installation *Der Berg* ("the mountain"), the work of the self-described "performing architect" Benjamin Foerster-Baldenius in collaboration with raumlabor (Figure 4.16). Inside the Palast, the artists erected a crystalline steel and fiberglass mountain that spilled out of the top and sides of the building. Upon arriving, visitors were asked to select one of three paths to follow on the journey through the landscape—the way of the pilgrim, the philosopher, or the mountaineer. Amid drawings, architectural models, and video installations, the mountain spread rhizomatically through the interior of the hall, "suck(ing) up" its obsolete meaning (according to Foerster-Baldenius) and infusing it with new energy.[77] The words "Ceci n'est pas une montagne" appeared in cursive concrete script at the base of the mountain, detourning Magritte's "Ceci n'est pas une pipe" and suggesting the installation's anchor

Figure 4.16 Benjamin Foerster-Baldenius and Raumlabor, *Volkspalast: Der Berg*, 2005. Installation, Palast der Republik, Berlin. 360b / Shutterstock.

in the practices of the historical avant-garde. Certainly, it would have been difficult to miss the installation's surrealist use of the outmoded building and the way in which it embodied the continuous return of the repressed East German past. However, much like the *Wrapped Reichstag*, in context *Der Berg* took on an expressionistic quality, unavoidably suggesting Bruno Taut's drawings for *Alpine Architektur* in which the grimly utilitarian modern world would be reconfigured with crystalline glass architecture.

To underscore *Der Berg*'s atmosphere of play, an international congress was convened in mid-October 2004 to discuss the Palast's future in light of Cedric Price's famous "Fun Palace" of 1961. Price's influential vision brought together a theater, a museum, and a university in a large temporary and mobile structure, the uses of which would adjust, machine-like, according to various needs. Organizers Hans Ulrich Obrist, Stefan Rethfeld, Philipp Oswalt, and Philipp Misselwitz sought to draw provocative parallels between Price's cultural structure and the Palast der Republik in its current state and to question whether the hull of the Palast, threatened with destruction, might not better function as such a place. Called Fun Palace 200X, the symposium was an opportunity for artist, architects, and critics to air their views, and they unilaterally condemned the dismantling the Palast, with Rem Koolhaas calling the action "kind of insanely ahistorical."[78]

While the Volkspalast activities were taking place, doubts intensified in the larger German public sphere about the Palast's demolition and the Stadtschloss's reconstruction. This heightened atmosphere provided the backdrop for the most famous and visible Volkspalast work: the Norwegian artist Lars Ø. Ramberg's blankly corporate sign atop the Palast that simply declared *Zweifel*, or "doubt." Rendered in chunky, three-story-tall aluminum letters lit with neon tubes, the word appeared like a logo within the palace's split roofline (Figure 4.17). The sign instantly became a press sensation when it appeared in January of 2005, drawing the interest of Palast proponents and the ire of critics irritated by what they saw as special pleading on behalf of a building that had never been as popular as when it was threatened. According to Barry Bergdoll, the word shone "like the letters above a permanently closed department store for which someone still pays the electricity bill."[79] Ramberg used the very inescapability of the site for effect, and his sign was visible from many points within the city, parodying Berlin's triumphalist urban marketing strategies. In April of 2005, *Der Spiegel* used a photograph of the work to accompany an article titled "A Nation in Search of Itself," which reflected on Germany's inability during the sixty years since the end of World War II to forge a cohesive political identity. On the same day that the issue hit the shelves, Ramberg printed and circulated what he christened the *Zweifel Allgemeine*—a simulated newspaper made up exclusively of headlines containing that single provocative word, a sampling of the 350 "Zweifel" headlines that he had gathered in four short months. Ramberg titled this multiplatform project PALAST DES ZWEIFELS, and it has become another tenacious fragment of the Palast's brief life. Even after the sign was dismantled, tags began appearing around the city in Ramberg's trademark font, using the project's invitation cards as stencils.[80]

Figure 4.17 Lars Ø. Ramberg, *PALAST DES ZWIFELS (PALACE OF DOUBT)*, 2005. Installation, Palast der Republik, Berlin. © Lars Ø. Ramberg.

Highly visible, Ramberg's work seemed to encapsulate Germany's troubled politics of reunification, of which the Palast's fate had become a distillate. Ongoing political, economic, and social tensions between East and West had cast doubt even on the choice to knock down the Berlin Wall, given that the *Mauer im Kopf*, or "wall in the head" (the invisible, notional division first articulated by writer Peter Schneider) had proven more durable than its built manifestation.[81] For some, Ramberg's skepticism got to the heart of the contradictions endemic to reunification. Jennifer Allen's *Artforum* review of the installation observed that uncertainty is at the heart of the entire project of democracy, which must make room for debate and dissent, while a dictatorship suspends such deliberations with a false veneer of consensus.[82] For others, the prosaic corporate vernacular of Ramberg's signage was taken to be evidence of the misgivings many felt at turning post-Wall Berlin into a compulsively commercial tourist playground, of which the decision to reconstruct the royal palace seemed emblematic.

If the 1993 Schloss simulation had been a surprise success, so too was the Volkspalast. Its various activities proved enormously popular among Berliners and visitors; between August and November of 2004 alone, 55,000 guests swept through the shell of the Palast. Artists maintained the festival atmosphere around the Palast until the last possible moment. An exhibition called *Fraktale IV* was held in September and October of 2005, requiring the construction of a "white cube" gallery outside the Palast financed by a donation of 950,000 euros from art collector and entrepreneur

Dieter Rosencranz. After the exhibition closed, the "Temporary Kunsthalle" remained, prompting organizers to ask what else might be accomplished as the Palast's hourglass ran out. In a nineteen-day stretch in December 2005, Berlin-based artists—including the blue-chip art stars Tacita Dean, Thomas Demand, and Olafur Eliasson, who shared a studio space at the time—rallied around the cause and mounted the exhibition *36x27x10*, titled after the dimensions of the pristine gallery space. Open for only a week, the exhibition has now become apocryphal, described in reverential tones as one of the most authentically contemporary of contemporary art shows—in the words of one reviewer, as "tragic and beautiful as art seldom can be."[83] The work on view shared an elegiac tone: Rirkrit Tiravanija lovingly encased the well-worn towel that he had used since moving to Berlin in a glass vitrine, while Eliasson's *Inverted Berlin Sphere*—akin to a decommissioned disco ball—placed one of the artist's characteristic phenomenological investigations in the context of the city's storied underground dance scene, already moving into the mainstream at the time.

Eliasson's work did more than recall Berlin's raucous recent club history. Displayed like a luxury good in the center of the pristine white-cube gallery, the sphere functioned in context as a fragment, inescapably evoking the chromed 1970s allure of the ruined building that had occasioned the work's existence. Spontaneous dance parties erupted underneath Eliasson's lamp, leading Berlin newspapers to compare the work to the discos the Palast had contained in its heyday. In fact, *Inverted Berlin Sphere* unconsciously pointed to one of the most deeply buried problems of the Palast: namely, its unsettling glamor. While the Palast and its amenities had been popular among its East German users, it edged even in its prime toward a modernism that seemed false—too vulgar, too expressionistic, too concerned with visual effect. This was the thread that its post-*Wende* critics took up when they maligned the building as an "aesthetic monstrosity." The early-2000s proponents of demolition accused the building—standing inert, unused, and defenseless at that point—as a mere "prestige object," more garish glitz than social substance, an illusion that projected a false image of affluence and freedom in a society that lacked both.[84] This thread was taken up by critics across the Atlantic, as when *New Yorker* critic Jane Kramer described the Palast as "immense and incontestably ugly." Critical pronouncements such as these gave Gerhard Schröder the cover he needed, and the very language he adopted bore the traces of modernist good taste—as in his identification of the Stadtschloss reconstruction as "a choice of the beautiful over the ugly."[85] The Palast's aesthetic quality—or lack thereof—has, in fact, become part of reunified Berlin's official architectural self-image, and its uncouth gaudiness is still ritually invoked as a cautionary tale for the new Hauptstadt. Thus, vehement public support for the Palast has been consistently dismissed as mere *Ostalgia*, a kitschy and superficial nostalgia for the "bad modernism" of the East German past. In this, the Palast stands as a model of the way East German architecture *tout court* has played the role of kitschy bad object to the good taste of West Germany's avant-garde—evidence of the unresolved problems of modernism and its relationship to capital on both sides of the Wall.

As the Zwischennutzung actions drew to a close in 2005, the magazine *Super Illu* published the results of a poll conducted of more than 1,000 people in eastern Germany.

Over 60 percent opposed the demolition of the Palast, as it would "destroy a part of the GDR's history."[86] In a last-ditch effort to save the building, the Left and Green Parties staged protests in December of 2005 that temporarily forestalled the demolition crews at the ready. These measures were met with irritation by the Bundestag, most of whose members had come to see the demolition—and the Stadtschloss reconstruction—as a fait accompli, despite the lack of available funding or timeline for the latter. Repeatedly, and in the face of evidence to the contrary, the Bundestag presented the clear government consensus as a popular consensus that did not exist in reality. When pressed on the unpopularity of the decision, Bundestag vice president Wolfgang Thierse impatiently declared, "I see no truly persuasive reasons to overturn this decision."[87] His colleagues in the Bundestag were willing to make yet stronger statements. The conservative MP Wolfgang Börnsen said that the Palast defaced the city; it was nothing more than "architectural debris ... whose ruins are just too ugly."[88] In 2006, official banners appeared across the ruined building, reminding passersby that its demolition was "Eine demokratische Entscheidung"—a democratic decision.

Indeed, the burst of creative effort at the Volkspalast did little to stall the Palast's demise and plans for its demolition moved forward in an uncanny parallel of the artistic activities on the site. The removal of the ruined building commenced in April of 2006, slowly unfolding over the following years in a process that the government euphemistically termed "Dismantling, Not Demolishing." Bundestag signs surrounding the Palast assured the public in oddly upbeat tones that what seemed to be a painfully drawn-out ritual was, in fact, "good for the environment and the city." Protesters continued to haunt the site, proclaiming that this slow demolition was a "symbolic act of revenge or triumph," a public show of torture performed on the body of the building itself.[89] Critics continued to declare the removal of the palace as the realization of a violent fantasy, a wish fulfillment cloaked in the pretense of the common good. As Daniela Sandler has noted, the performative slowness of the building's disaggregation was difficult not to interpret in ideological terms as an echo of the implosion of the Hohenzollern palace with the ideologies reversed.[90] The art historian Khadija Carroll La has described the prolonged process of removal as a painful kind of "demolition theater."[91]

By 2007, the center section of the Palast containing the lobby between the split rooflines had been entirely removed, in an unintentional parody of Schultes's faux-Schinkel Schlossplatz plan. By 2008, the dismantling concluded, dramatically revealing the foundations of the Stadtschloss. In 2011, the Stadtschloss foundation retained KSV to design the so-called Humboldt Box for the site, a massive cube containing a viewing platform for the reconstruction project, complete with rooftop cafe, and an exhibition about the historical Stadtschloss, with entry fees supporting the reconstruction. Intended as a new iteration of the bright red Infobox at Potsdamer Platz meant to raise interest in the city's rebuilding, the Humboldt Box was a futuristic fantasy of angular steel and turquoise glass (Figure 4.18). Critics noted that, under the circumstances, KSV's exoskeletal design seemed to be a disjointed surface appropriation of the visual language of global contemporary architecture; yet in fact, it points to the historical contradictions at the very core of this culture.[92] To offset the costs of the Palast's

Figure 4.18 KSV, Humboldt Box, Berlin, 2011.

demolition, the city sold some of its materials, so that 22,500 tonnes of its steel now forms part of the skeleton supporting the Burj Khalifa in Dubai. East Germany's largest corner bar, therefore, has now become the world's tallest building. The ideological irony of this particular instance of fragmentation was not lost on one journalist for *Bild*, who proclaimed: "The Burj Khalifa is an Ossi."[93] Other pieces of the building's frame have been sold to Volkswagen, and granite slabs from the interior now form the smooth surfaces of a skatepark at Tempelhof.[94]

The building's fragmentation goes yet further; in addition to being sold for parts, a somewhat robust market for its decor developed over the course of its demolition. The lobby chandeliers went on sale in 2009, available for purchase from the government for between 2,000 and 3,000 euros.[95] American institutions, including the Getty Center and the Wende Museum, were quick to buy up pieces of furniture, flatware, and stationery from the Palast, as well as architectural plans and models.[96] Furthermore, many artists either bought or salvaged pieces of the Palast for use as raw material in their own work. One of the chandeliers forms part of the Israeli artist Amir Fattal's 2011 work, *The last time you fell, who was there to catch you?*, hovering above a mold of a baroque carving from the Stadtschloss displayed on a stainless steel medical cart. The Palast's bronze glass can be found in Benjamin Bergmann's *The Dream of Something Big* (2008) and in Fred Rubin's 2003 work *Palast-Transfer*, a reconstructed miniature version of the Palast against a crumbing stone wall in the southern French city of Bandol. A small online vendor now sells "authentic" fragments of the Palast's marble at a premium for those in the market for aura; they can be found next to pebble-sized pieces of the Berlin Wall.

In 2008, with only one concrete stair tower remaining before the demolition was complete, the government held a small, limited competition for the reconstruction of three of the Stadtschloss's facades, leaving the fourth to the designer's imagination. The process was quiet and notably subdued, in contrast to the hype surrounding the government-sponsored competitions of the early 1990s; as *New York Times* architecture critic Michael Kimmelman noted, "Few serious architects bothered to apply."[97] Eventually, the Bundestag announced that it had selected the little-known Italian architect Franco Stella to reconstruct three of the Stadtschloss's facades in order for it to become the Humboldt Forum (Figure 4.19). The forum would include the Humboldt collection of "non-European art" along with various commercial services. According to the Berliner Stadtschloss Initiative, "The castle/palace is planned to be the biggest tourist attraction in Berlin, with a wide range of quality shops, restaurants and even a Business Centre ... Overall, the building will boast an aura of opulence and style that will be the envy of Germany."[98] Stella, a former juror for the Spreeinsel competition and a follower of Aldo Rossi, claimed that his role as architect was purely cultural rather than political: "I don't ask myself about political issues, whether the person who built the building was a king," he said in 2008. "The Schloss was important for the German nation and because Berlin is disjointed, not homogeneous, it's all the more important to recover its history. Memory is what distinguishes Europe from America."[99] The

Figure 4.19 Franco Stella, Humboldt Forum, Berlin, 2008–20.

difference in tone in the reception of the commission from the 1990s and early 2000s was sharp. In 2001, *Der Spiegel* had called the proposed Stadtschloss reconstruction "a beautiful, crazy dream, an enticing illusion, a Fata Morgana."[100] Upon the selection of Stella as architect, and with the illusion becoming all too real, Kimmelman declared that Berlin is "a city forever missing the point of itself."[101]

After several false starts, and under the auspices of a continuously powerful lobby from its wealthy champions, by 2013 the Humboldt Forum had secured sufficient funding from a combination of federal and city governments and private corporate and individual donations to commence construction.[102] At the time of writing it is nearing completion, with three of its four facades rebuilt and much of its ornate decoration recreated from photographs and drawings by traditionally trained artisans, aided anachronistically by sophisticated digital visualizations. The so-called Eosander Portal has been reconstructed at the Schloss's traditional entrance and now faces onto the Schinkelplatz, still bereft of the Bauakademie.[103] Left to Stella's imagination, the fourth facade is an almost parodically disciplined grid of stone with deeply inset windows, suggestive more of the stripped classicism of the 1930s than of recent architectural innovations (Figure 4.20). Icily formal, this eastern facade trains a warning gaze on the avuncular statues of Marx and Engels still standing in the forum across the Spree.

In the end, what is contemporary about the Stadtschloss reconstruction is, precisely, its lack of apparent contemporaneity. Public projects like Foster's Reichstag and Chipperfield's Neues Museum brought history into a subtle contrapuntal relationship

Figure 4.20 Franco Stella, Humboldt Forum, Berlin, 2008–20.

with the present, thus leaving room (at least theoretically) for doubt; yet the Humboldt Forum makes its case for public belief in architecture's historical power in surprisingly coarse terms. The reconstructed Schloss seems less real, somehow, than its 1993 simulation in canvas and paint—and for many Berliners, it is far less pleasurable. Furthermore, many have critiqued the use of the Humboldt Forum as a showcase for "non-western" art as less a premise than an alibi supporting its construction. Even as the opening date of September 2020 draws near after several setbacks, a dark cloud attends the institution amid charges from historians and activists that its directors have not adequately pursued issues of the provenance of its objects—or their possible repatriation.[104] Doubts over the "absorption" of the architectural fragments of the former East have only amplified as unresolved problems surrounding Germany's colonial past rise to the surface. These doubts extend, sometimes tacitly, to whether the products of global contemporary architecture culture function only as opulent containers presenting their contents as consumable goods on display—whether in the case of luxury shopping or looted artifacts.

Around the Schlossplatz, embattled architectural traces of East German history continue to struggle with the monumental forms of official memory. Owned by the federal government, the East German Haus der Statistik on Otto-Braun-Strasse will be renovated and reused after a successful grassroots campaign against its demolition. In front of the Humboldt Forum, ground has been broken on the official memorial to reunification, a massive, kinetic platform designed by architects Milla & Partner that Berliners have nicknamed the "seesaw." Meanwhile, despite its removal, the Palast der Republik's remnants continue to force themselves into view. From May to October of 2019, the Kunsthalle Rostock (itself housed in a GDR-era building) hosted an exhibition titled *The Palast der Republik: Utopia, Inspiration, Politics*. The exhibition showcased art from the Palast, as well as decor and furniture drawn from collections around the world and gathered together for a strange reunion tour. Inside the exhibition's walls, the artists Nina Fischer and Maroan el Sani reconstructed a section of the dance floor inside the Palast's youth hall, a black-and-white pinwheel that raised and lowered along with the beat of the music. Elsewhere, the Palast's chairs, tables, and lamps were placed in front of wall-sized photographs of the building's interiors. Whether one perceives the display of these objects as mere Ostalgia, with its lingering implications of kitsch, or as the traces of an authentic longing for an irretrievable past, the Palast's fragments remain nonetheless uncomfortably present. In fact, these persistently material fragments seem to refuse to disappear, resurfacing in ways that challenge the Humboldt Forum's capacity to draw a broadly affectionate audience to its sumptuous walls.

It would be easy to see the elimination of the Palast der Republik and the reconstruction of the Stadtschloss as evidence only of the Bundesrepublik's repression of East German identity and the violent amnesia of the digital age. Yet this interpretation fails to account for the impassioned belief in architecture's historical significance that lay on both sides of the debate, and for the poignant hoarding of the Schlossplatz's fragments, tinged with the fear of a permanent loss of historical consciousness. As in Norman Foster's preservation of the Reichstag graffiti, at the heart of the still-unsettled Schlossplatz debate is faith—a sincere belief that contemporary architectural interventions can either repress or summon forth the most crucial events of the past. For better or for worse, Axel Schultes's frustration over the Spreeinsel competition seems to have been justified. However imagined, illusory, spectacularized, partisan, misconstrued, or misrepresented, "history" still seems to be the only authority to which Berlin—and contemporary architecture more broadly—will listen.

Notes

1 "Späte Rache an den Barbaren," *Der Spiegel*, December 14, 1992, 192.
2 "Из наследства К. Ф. Шинкеля / конфискирован из частной собственности / Берлин, 28 августа, 1945."
3 Quoted in Lars Krückeberg, Wolfram Putz, and Thomas Willemeit, "Unheard(-of) Ideas," in *Unbuilding Walls: From Death Strip to Free Space* (Basel: Birkhäuser, 2018), 139.
4 Quoted in ibid.
5 Axel Schultes, "Schinkels Traum: Das Verhältnis des preussischen Generalbaumeisters zur Berliner Mitte," *Der Tagesspiegel*, September 8, 1996, https://www.tagesspiegel.de/wirtschaft/immobilien/schinkels-traum/5444.html.
6 Ibid.
7 Benedikt Hotze, "Der Architekt Axel Schultes," *ZEIT-Punkte*, June 24, 1999, http://www.hotze.net/schultes.htm.
8 Arthur Venner, "Along the Havel," *Harper's New Monthly Magazine* 56 (December 1877–May 1878): 854.
9 Brian Ladd, "Old Berlin," in *The Ghosts of Berlin: Confronting German History in the Urban Landscape* (Chicago: University of Chicago Press, 1997), 52.
10 The classic source on Schinkel's urban planning is Hermann G. Pundt, *Schinkel's Berlin: A Study in Environmental Planning* (Cambridge, MA: Harvard University Press, 1972). For the ways in which Lenné integrated technology into his landscape plans, see Michael Lee, "Infrastructure as Landscape Embellishment: Peter Joseph Lenné in Potsdam and Berlin," in *Technology and the Garden*, eds. Michael Lee and Kenneth I. Helphand (Washington, D.C.: Dumbarton Oaks, 2014), 169–97.
11 Friedrich I was the first to use this phrase to describe his cultural ideal for Berlin. Yet it was in Schinkel's era that the idea gained traction under the auspices of Friedrich Wilhelm III and his successor and the output of philosophers, artists, architects, and scholars from Hegel to the Humboldts. For more on Schinkel's role in defining this "Athens," see Can Bilsel, "No Place Like Greece: Berlin's Museum Island and the Architectures of History," in *Antiquity on Display: Regimes of the Authentic in Berlin's Pergamon Museum* (Oxford: Oxford University Press, 2012), 29–88.
12 Tilmann Buddensieg, *Berliner Labyrinth, neu besichtigt: Von Schinkels Unter den Linden vis Fosters Reichstagskuppel* (Berlin: Wagenbach, 1999), 176–86. According to Buddensieg, Schinkel "respected the Schloss, this 'monument of the founders of the royal house,' as 'inviolable,' but only truly admired Schlüter's contribution as a work of art" (177). See also Buddensieg, "Von Schinkel zur Moderne—Berlin als Stadt des Wandels," in *Neue Berlinische Architektur: Eine Debatte*, ed. Annegret Burg (Berlin and Basel: Birkhäuser, 1994), 43–61.
13 The demolition of a row of burghers' homes along the Spreekanal in 1892 at the behest of Wilhelm II was a particularly incendiary action. Walter Ulbricht and others would

later refer to the Stadtschloss as a "Junker-Trutzburg" (patrician fortress) and a symbol of "feudalist-capitalist autocracy" during their deliberations over its demolition. Klaus Gehrke and Cornelia Rabitz, "Stadtschloss-Wettbewerb in Berlin entschieden," *Die Welt*, November 28, 2008, https://www.dw.com/de/stadtschloss-wettbewerb-in-berlin-entschieden/a-3820415.

14 This ambitious approach to rebuilding was typical in the West, in which planners often tended to ignore (or repress) the actual, ruined condition of the city. See Harald Bodenschatz, "Berlin West: Abschied von der 'steinernen Stadt," in *Neue Städte aus Ruinen: Deutscher Städtebau der Nachkriegzeit*, ed. Klaus von Beyme et al. (Munich: Prestel, 1991), 58–77.

15 Hildburg Bruns, "Geheimes Gutachten: Krimi um die Sprengung des Berliner Schlosses," *Berliner Zeitung*, August 3, 2016, https://www.bz-berlin.de/berlin/mitte/geheimes-gutachten-krimi-um-die-sprengung-des-berliner-schlosses.

16 Anke Kuhrmann, *Der Palast der Republik: Geschichte und Bedeutung des Ost-Berliner Parlaments- und Kulturhauses* (Petersberg: Michael Imhof, 2006), 15.

17 Richard Hamann, among others, was a vocal advocate of maintaining the Schloss. Rainer Haubrich, "Niemand hatte die Absicht, ein Schloss zu errichten," *Die Welt*, October 16, 2013, https://www.welt.de/kultur/kunst-und-architektur/article116991551/Niemand-hatte-die-Absicht-ein-Schloss-zu-errichten.html.

18 On this study tour and its West German counterpart, see Greg Castillo, "Design Pedagogy Enters the Cold War: The Reeducation of Eleven West German Architects," *Journal of Architectural Education* 57 (May 2004): 10–18.

19 On the complex role of the art historian Gerhard Strauss in this negotiation, see Simone Hain, "Berlin, 'schöner denn je': Stadt ideen im Ostberliner Wiederaufbau," DAM *Architektur Jahrbuch* (1992): 9–21.

20 Quoted in "Späte Rache an den Barbaren," 192.

21 Quoted in Svetlana Boym, "Berlin, the Virtual Capital," in *The Future of Nostalgia* (New York: Basic Books, 2001), 182.

22 For a thorough and insightful discussion of the site's development, see Emily Pugh, "The Dreamed-of GDR: Public Space, Private Space, and National Identity in the Honecker Era," in *Architecture, Politics, and Identity in Divided Berlin* (Pittsburgh: University of Pittsburgh Press, 2014), 155–99. For an analysis of the GDR's politics of preservation in Berlin more generally, see Florian Urban, *Neo-historical East Berlin: Architecture and Urban Design in the German Democratic Republic 1970–1990* (London: Routledge, 2016).

23 Ibid., 168.

24 SED Fifth Convention, quoted in William J. V. Neill, "Memory and Identity II: Erasing the Past in the City of the Victors," in *Urban Planning and Cultural Identity* (London and New York: Routledge, 2004), 99.

25 Quoted in Deborah Ascher Barnstone, *The Transparent State: Architecture and Politics in Postwar Germany* (New York: Routledge, 2005), 233.

26 Walter Gropius, "First Bauhaus Manifesto," in Hans Maria Wingler, *The Bauhaus: Weimar, Berlin, Dessau, Chicago*, ed. Joseph Stein (Cambridge, MA: MIT Press, 1969), 31–3.

27 Barnstone, ibid.

28 Barnstone, "Transparency in Divided Berlin: The Palace of the Republik," in *Berlin Divided City, 1945–89*, eds. Philip Broadbent and Sabine Hake (New York and Oxford: Berghahn Books, 2010), 110.

29 Heinz Graffunder and Martin Beerbaum, *Der Palast der Republik* (Leipzig: E. A. Seemann, , 1977), 9.
30 Ibid.
31 On the evolution of the Volkskammer as a governing body, see John O. Koehler, "East Germany: The Stasi and De-Stasification," in *Dismantling Tyranny: Transitioning Beyond Totalitarian Regimes*, eds. Ilan Berman and J. Michael Waller (Lanham, MD: Rowman & Littlefield, 2006), 48.
32 Thomas Beutelschmidt and Julia M. Novak, *Ein Palast und seine Republik* (Berlin: Bauwesen, 2001), 157.
33 "East Berlin Gets Vast Civic Center," *The New York Times*, May 9, 1976, 18.
34 Quoted in Pugh, 166.
35 Graffunder and Beerbaum, 7.
36 "New Book Reveals Last Photographs of Berlin's Palast der Republik," *Der Spiegel*, September 21, 2010, https://www.spiegel.de/international/germany/memories-of-east-germany-s-showcase-new-book-reveals-last-photographs-of-berlin-s-palast-der-republik-a-717697.html.
37 As historian Geoffrey Broadbent put it, "West Berlin is a city with no heart," and only through reunification and reconstruction could the city be made whole again. See Geoffrey Broadbent, *Emerging Concepts in Urban Space Design* (London and New York: Taylor & Francis, 1990), 370.
38 The medieval houses in this settlement, known as the Fischerkiez, were cleared in the late 1960s to make way for modern construction. As in the destruction of the Stadtschloss, these aggressive planning politics were a source of controversy and division within the party.
39 On the use of the *Backsteingotik* (redbrick Gothic) style in Schinkel's work, see M. Norton Wise, "Altes Museum, University, and Bauschule," in *Aesthetics, Industry, and Science: Hermann von Helmholtz and the Berlin Physical Society* (Chicago and London: University of Chicago Press, 2018), 41–4.
40 Michael S. Falser, "Scheinplausibilität und ihre destruktive Kraft—Berliner Neomythen für den Stadtumbau nach 1990," in *Stadt als Erfahrungsraum der Politik: Beiträge zur kulturellen Konstruktion urbaner Politik*, ed. Wilhelm Hofmann (Berlin: LIT, 2011), 52.
41 These official numbers are recorded in *Hauptstadt Berlin: Stadtmitte Spreeinsel-Internationaler Städtebaulicher Ideenwettbewerb 1994*, ed. Felix Zwoch (Berlin: Bauwelt/Birkhäuser, 1994), 7, 16.
42 Francesca Rogier, "Growing Pains: From the Opening of the Wall to the Wrapping of the Reichstag," *Assemblage* 29 (April 1996): 62.
43 The minutes of each of the several jury sessions are documented in Zwoch, 184–97.
44 Ibid., 49.
45 Matthias Oloew, "Schlossplatz: Für immer der Erste," *Der Tagespiegel*, November 27, 2008, https://www.tagesspiegel.de/berlin/schlossplatz/schlossplatz-fuer-immer-der-erste/1381654.html.
46 Peter Blake, "Young Architects Surge in Open Spreeinsel Competition," *Architectural Record* 7 (July 1994): 11.
47 Rolf Lautenschläger, "Nostalgie vom Küchentisch," *Die Tageszeitung*, May 13, 1994, 5.
48 In Zwoch, 52.

49 Ibid., 54. As in the Chancellery competition, KSV's proposal suggested that the Spreeinsel be conceived as a "new Alhambra," their shorthand for an architecture that is simultaneously relaxed and grand.
50 In Zwoch, 60.
51 Ibid.
52 Ibid., 116.
53 Ibid.
54 Ibid., 118.
55 After the Bundesrepublik approved its preservation, the Staatsratsgebäude functioned as an information center for new urban planning initiatives in the late 1990s, then as the interim seat of the chancellor from 1999–2001, and now as the European School of Management and Technology. A subtle renovation by the architect H. G. Merz, who was also responsible for updating the Alte Nationalgalerie, the Staatsbibliothek, and the Staatsoper, has made it one of the preservation success stories of GDR-era architecture.
56 The screen was the work of Parisian artist Catherine Feff and a team of her students. These large-scale *trompe l'oeil* screens are Feff's stock-in-trade; she was also commissioned to cover the Arc de Triomphe in a red, white, and blue cover during its restoration in the late 1980s and to complete a large mural of horses at Versailles. Von Boddien encountered her work at the Church of the Madeleine in Paris in 1992.
57 See Claire Colomb, "Staging Urbanism: Construction Site Tourism and the City as Exhibition," in *Staging the New Berlin: Place Marketing and the Politics of Urban Reinvention Post-1989* (London: Routledge, 2012), 188–221.
58 Ulrike Zitzlsperger, "Filling the Blanks: Berlin as a Public Showcase," in *Recasting German Identity: Culture, Politics, and Literature in the Berlin Republic*, eds. Stuart Taberner and Frank Finlay (Woodbridge: Camden House, 2002), 47.
59 Wolf Jobst Siedler, "Das Schloss lag nicht in Berlin," in Förderverein Berliner Stadtschloss, *Das Schloss? Eine Ausstellung über die Mitte Berlins* (Berlin: Ernst & Sohn, 1993).
60 Ibid.
61 Joachim Fest, "Plädoyer für den Wiederaufbau des Stadtschlosses," in Michael Mönninger, ed., *Das Neue Berlin* (Frankfurt: Insel, 1991).
62 Quoted in Christian van Lessen, "Der Luftschlossplatz," *Der Tagesspiegel*, November 27, 2008, https://www.tagesspiegel.de/berlin/schlossplatz/gedankenspiele-der-luftschlossplatz/1381652.html.
63 Quoted in van Lessen, "Viel Raum fürs Volkshaus," *Der Tagesspiegel*, September 13, 1996, https://www.tagesspiegel.de/wirtschaft/immobilien/viel-raum-fuers-volkshaus/5458.html.
64 See James Young, "The Countermonument: Memory against Itself in Germany," in *The Texture of Memory: Holocaust Memorials and Meaning* (New Haven and London: Yale University Press, 1993), 27–48.
65 Monika Zimmermann, ed., *Der Berliner Schlossplatz: Visionen zur Gestaltung der Berliner Mitte* (Berlin: Argon, 1997), 88.
66 Ibid., 96.
67 Ibid., 112.
68 Claudia Breger, "Royal Imaginaries and Capital Architecture: Berlin's Hohenzollern Palace and the Palace of the Republic," in Leslie Adelson, ed., *The Cultural After-Life of East Germany: New Transnational Perspectives*, AICGS Humanities 13 (2002): 111.

69 Ladd, 59.
70 Ibid., 60.
71 Andreas Huyssen, "The Voids of Berlin," in *Present Pasts: Urban Palimpsests and the Politics of Memory* (Stanford: Stanford University Press, 2003), 49–71.
72 Simon Ward, "Reconfiguring the Spaces of the 'Creative Class,'" in *Cultural Topographies of the New Berlin*, eds. Karin Bauer and Jennifer Ruth Hosek (New York and Oxford: Berghahn Books, 2018), 114. See also Holger Lauinger *Urban Pioneers, Berlin: Stadtentwicklung durch Zwischennutzung* (Berlin: Jovis, 2007).
73 Amelie Deuflhard and Sophie Krempl-Klieeisen, "Volkspalast: History of an Interim Usage: Art-Intervention-Activism-Transformation," *Monu: Magazine on Urbanism* 4 (2006): 80.
74 Niklas Maak, "Palast der Republik: Schaut in dieses Haus," *Frankfurter Allgemeine Zeitung*, October 19, 2004, 35.
75 A smaller group of facades were erected on the spot by visitors to the performance.
76 Raumlabor Berlin, http://raumlabor.net/fassadenrepublik/.
77 Quoted in Geeta Dayal, "Berlin's Indoor Mountain of Art and Protest," *The New York Times*, August 25, 2005, E1.
78 Quoted in Dayal.
79 Barry Bergdoll, "Reconstruction Doubts: The Ironies of Building in Schinkel's Name," *Harvard Design Magazine* 23 (Fall/Winter 2005): 33.
80 Ramberg vows that he had no involvement in this copycatting, attributing it instead to an invisible bulwark of "underground" guerilla support for the Palast.
81 Peter Schneider, *Der Mauerspringer* (Darmstadt: Hermann Luchterhand, 1982).
82 Jennifer Allen, "Lars Ramberg: Palast der Republik," *Artforum International* 43 (May 1, 2005): 358.
83 Katherine Koster, "TKH: White Cube or White Elephant?," *Exberliner*, September 1, 2010, https://www.exberliner.com/whats-on/art/tkh-white-cube-or-white-elephant/.
84 Beutelschmidt and Novak, 11.
85 Jane Kramer, "Living with Berlin," *The New Yorker*, July 5, 1999, 50.
86 "Palast der Republik wird abgerissen," *Die Welt*, January 19, 2006, https://www.welt.de/politik/article192404/Palast-der-Republik-wird-abgerissen.html.
87 "Berlin's Palace of the Republic Faces Wrecking Ball," *Die Welt*, January 20, 2006, https://www.dw.com/en/berlins-palace-of-the-republic-faces-wrecking-ball/a-1862424.
88 Ibid.
89 Robert Halsell, "GDR Architecture and Town Planning in Post-Unification Germany: 'Geschichtsaufarbeitung' or Aesthetic Autonomy," in *The GDR and its History: Rückblick and Revision*, ed. Peter Barker (Amsterdam and Atlanta: Rodopi, 2000), 207.
90 Daniela Sandler, "Destruction and Disappearance," in *Counterpreservation: Architectural Decay in Berlin since 1989* (Ithaca: Cornell University Press, 2016), 204.
91 Khadija Carroll La, "The Very Mark of Repression: The Demolition Theatre of the Palast der Republik and the New Schloss Berlin," *Architectural Design* 207 (2010): 116–23.
92 For example, Lothar Heinke referred to it as "an architectural monster in galactic proportions." Heinke, "Der Großklotz vom Schlossplatz," *Der Tagesspiegel*, June 11, 2011, https://www.tagesspiegel.de/berlin/humboldt-box-der-grossklotz-vom-schlossplatz/4276574.html.

93 "Der Burj Chalifa ist ein Ossi," *Bild*, January 5, 2010, https://www.bild.de/reise/2010/palast-der-republik-ossi-wahnsinn-projekte-architektur-10991870.bild.html.
94 "Zombie Palace: The Afterlife of the Palast der Republik," *Uncube Magazine*, September 5, 2013, http://www.uncubemagazine.com/blog/10642637.
95 Sara Richards, "Palast Lights Go On Sale," *National Public Radio*, July 28, 2009, https://www.npr.org/templates/story/story.php?storyId=111174408.
96 Maciuka, 28.
97 Michael Kimmelman, "Rebuilding a Palace May Prove a Grand Blunder," *The New York Times*, January 1, 2009, https://www.nytimes.com/2009/01/01/arts/01iht-01abroad.19025085.html.
98 Stadtschloss Berlin Initiative, http://www.stadtschloss-berlin.de/englisch.html.
99 Quoted in Kimmelman. Stella first proclaimed that he was Rossi's student, but then later clarified that he meant the term in a general sense, as he had never actually met Rossi. See Christoph Stölzl, "Aldo Rossi und die unvergängliche Macht der Geometrie," *Berliner Morgenpost*, December 4, 2008, https://www.morgenpost.de/kolumne/stoelzl/article103377178/Aldo-Rossi-und-die-unvergaengliche-Macht-der-Geometrie.html
100 Mathias Schreiber, "Das verrükte Traumbild," *Der Spiegel*, January 15, 2001,185.
101 Kimmelman.
102 Over the years, von Boddien and his partner Kathleen King von Alvensleben successfully gained the support of Henry Kissinger and George H. W. Bush, among others.
103 At the time of writing, the Bauakademie will be reconstructed beginning in 2021 to function as a national forum for architecture and urbanism. To facilitate the process, the state of Berlin sold the property to the federal government in 2017. According to Senator for Building Katrin Lompscher, the reconstruction will follow the motto "as much Schinkel as possible."
104 Thomas Rogers, "Berlin's Troubled Museum Delays Its Opening," *The New York Times*, June 15, 2019, C3.

Conclusion

No One Intends To Open an Airport

No matter one's position on the individual buildings in question, it would be difficult to deny that the controversial reconstruction of the Stadtschloss and the problems still plaguing the Humboldt Forum have sounded a decidedly downbeat note at the end of Berlin's long process of rebuilding. Although the fervid debate surrounding the Schlossplatz's development testified to the underlying faith in architecture's power that in part fueled the Hauptstadt's building boom, the process also revealed an increasingly widespread understanding that architecture alone—at least on the terms of the global contemporary architecture culture I have described here—was insufficient to address the accelerating challenges of the twenty-first century. In Berlin, the pressures of historical memory and the demand for architecture to reinforce one of the most crucial political tenets of reunification, the official imperative to "never forget," created an obsessive focus on the past, perhaps at the expense of a clear recognition of the present. Three decades after reunification, the heroics of the starchitect system and its resulting iconic buildings—a system that has been challenged in recent years, but by no means dismantled—often appear powerless to address the most pressing issues of the day, both national and global. The theatrical milieu in which Berlin's gleaming new cityscape was constructed, with renowned architects laboring to wrest forth and materialize historical meaning in impressive and novel buildings, seems far removed from Germany's actual material conditions today, including the capital city's mounting debt, the persistent economic disparities between East and West, the alarming resurgence of far-right extremism, and the increasing fragility of the European Union. These internal problems, of course, relate inextricably to matters of global scale—the ascendance of nationalism and authoritarianism worldwide; the constant threat of cyber insecurity and cyberterrorism; the rapid acceleration of the climate emergency; the newly complex problem of global public health; and the human cost of ongoing conflict and its resulting refugee crisis. Berlin's new government architecture aimed to convey openness, transparency, and accessibility. But perhaps its makers, both politicians and architects, underestimated the preeminence of questions related to *safety* that the new millennium would pose for public architecture.

By the mid-2000s, as the Palast der Republik faded slowly from view and the reconstruction of the Stadtschloss gathered steam, many began to declare the architectural experiment that had taken place in Berlin's "laboratory" to have been a resounding failure.[1] Not surprisingly, much like the frenzied celebration surrounding Norman Foster's 1999 Pritzker win with which I began this study, these subsequent proclamations of failure were exaggerated and sometimes hyperbolic. Nonetheless, the architectural targets of this widespread sense of disappointment accumulated in the city center, and its most glaring examples were the sites, both public and private, whose design had been zealously controlled by government oversight. The truncated Band des Bundes with its overlarge Chancellery projecting from one end; the withholding black oval of the Office of the President; Potsdamer Platz's expensive, ill-conceived transformation; and the stone enfilade of offices, embassies, and hotels flanking Pariser Platz, whose dutiful conformance to the guidelines of Critical Reconstruction created an oddly inert environment broken only by the translucent facade of Günter Behnisch's Academy of Arts—all of these projects, directed by official interests, became symbolic of Berlin's widely perceived failure to rise to its own historical occasion. For many critics, the root of the problem lay with the government itself, whether local, state, or federal, and whether acting as sole client or within one of the many "public–private partnerships" forged with private-sector corporations during the capital city's rebuilding. Some committed progressives accused the Bundesrepublik of not going far enough to define a clear, assertive vision for reunified Germany's official architecture. On the other hand, free-market fanatics blamed government meddling and mismanagement for stifling architectural creativity and dampening the potential of individual projects to enliven key areas of the city. As one journalist described it, the problem was "too much government money, too much top-down planning, and too great a desire to build a tourist attraction masked as a symbol. So far, the top-down planning model has produced what is at best a tourist trap, at worst an outright failure."[2] The city's luminous examples of adventurous architecture, of which Foster's Reichstag was emblematic, seemed to have been realized in spite of these forces rather than having been auspiciously guided by the government's big plans and heroic aspirations.[3]

However, as I stated in my introduction, my aim in this project has not been to assess the success or failure of these buildings, but rather to situate them meaningfully within the larger tendencies that characterize global contemporary architecture. In this framework, the category of "failure" itself opens interesting and revealing views beyond the blind spots of contemporary architecture culture.[4] By deflating the iconicity of monumental signature projects, the concept of failure prompts us to look instead to the infrastructure that supports and subtends what is ordinarily identified as significant government architecture. Therefore, I conclude here with a brief look at two publicly funded architectural projects that lie beyond the representative, monumental government center of the Hauptstadt, but that make plain some of the fundamental challenges confronting architecture today. It is by no means a coincidence that these projects are both airports, whose critical significance as a type has shifted away from iconic terminal designs, designed by starchitects and embodying various positivist associations with technology, national identity, and economic mobility, and toward what the sociologist Manuel Castells has characterized as a "space of flows," regulating the movement of bodies and capital.[5]

Conclusion 223

Ghost Airport

Much like the central railway station that formed a crucial node of the master plan for the government district, the eventual construction of a new airport was understood to be essential to the success of the Hauptstadt. After reunification, the city maintained three functioning airports: Tempelhof, the city's original airfield, and Schönefeld and Tegel, which had served East and West Berlin, respectively. In 1991, the federal government, along with the states of Berlin and Brandenburg, formed a limited liability partnership (known as Berlin Brandenburg Flughafen Holding GmbH, or BBF) to fund the construction of a new facility, supplanting the existing three and realizing the "single airport concept" proposed during reunification. However, as with many other projects throughout the city, the momentum of the early 1990s slowed as the decade wore on. By 1996, BBF had resolved to site the new airport on a parcel of land adjacent to the existing Schönefeld and to incorporate some of its intact infrastructure. Furthermore, it had farmed the project out to a private investor, retaining the Hochtief consortium to own, construct, and operate the airport. In the first of many setbacks, Hochtief's competition in the bidding process, the rival firm IVG, filed a successful lawsuit alleging that the government review process had been biased. By the end of 1999, the construction contract had been annulled and the project seemed to be back to square one.

In the wake of what was widely viewed as a conspicuous failure of privatization, officials changed tack, deciding in 2003 that the new airport would instead be publicly owned and operated.[6] BBF rebranded itself as FBB (Flughafen Berlin Brandenburg GmbH), with ownership shared by Berlin, Brandenburg, and the federal government. Throughout the early 2000s, the project was thwarted by numerous delays and setbacks. In 2004, around 4,000 residents of the neighborhoods around Schönefeld filed suit against the government in objection to the noise pollution that the new airport would cause. The residents eventually lost a protracted court battle with no possibility of appeal, but the legal proceedings slowed the project considerably.[7] After a decade and a half of planning with little forward motion, ground was finally broken in 2006 on the future Willy Brandt Berlin Brandenburg International Airport (BER), named for the Nobel-Peace-Prizewinning former mayor of West Berlin (Figure 5.1). The terminal buildings were designed by Meinhard von Gerkan, whose firm gmp (Gerkan, Marg & Partners) had previously completed both the vast new railway station in the government district and, some forty years earlier, Tegel's famously idiosyncratic hexagonal terminal building—both widely regarded as successes.[8] With its futuristic glass-and-steel facades, polished marble floors, and soaring, multileveled interiors tastefully warmed with faux-walnut paneling, the architecture of the new airport would speak the global vernacular of international air travel at the turn of the new millennium (Figure 5.2).

The design circulated widely in 2007–8, as the government attempted to revive national enthusiasm for this vital symbol of the capital's growing touristic popularity. This time, the optimism seemed warranted, at least in terms of the nation's financial outlook. While the European economy reeled from the 2008 global financial crisis, Germany's GDP proved relatively resilient; in the face of teetering economies in

Figure 5.1 Berlin Brandenburg Airport, Terminal 1. Exterior view. Arne Müseler / www.arne-mueseler.com.

Figure 5.2 Berlin Brandenburg Airport, Terminal 1. Interior view. Arne Müseler / www.arne-mueseler.com.

Greece, Spain, and Italy, the *Wall Street Journal* wondered, "Is Germany Europe's Safest Bet?"[9] The answer, according to the international corporate development magazine *Site Selection*, was a resounding yes. The country's economic strength was due in no small part to its capital city's grand new airport, as *Site Selection* stated: "Some have suggested that taking on such a massive project during a global recession was unwise, but in truth not one single German state recorded growth of less than 3.2 percent in the first half of 2011, a rather startling and remarkable feat."[10] It was thus clear, the magazine concluded, that the new mega-airport would undoubtedly have a long-term positive economic effect, not only in the capital but throughout the country, making it the "safest investment spot" in the eurozone.[11] On track to open in March 2012, the airport's future finally looked rosy, while its contributions to national security—from an economic perspective, that is—seemed assured.

Yet once again, the optimism proved unfounded, as costs, delays, and scandals mounted. Beginning in 2012, it became clear that major problems with the building's fire protection and alarm system, constructed by the European technology company Imtech, would demand many years and millions of euros to repair. This would be only one of numerous structural and technical flaws to hamper the airport's progress in the coming years. Meanwhile, charges of corruption surfaced in the press, including the bribery of an airport construction official by an Imtech manager in 2012.[12] Perhaps most embarrassingly, an official 2013 study revealed that the airport, as it had been conceived, would already be operating at the limit of its capacity when it opened, necessitating a total redesign well after construction was underway.[13] When von Gerkan objected, his contract was unceremoniously terminated.[14] Later that year, the opening of the airport was postponed indefinitely, prompting *Schadenfreude*-laden quips about "German efficiency" from the international press.[15] In a particularly hard blow, the director of the Willy Brandt Foundation publicly stated that he regretted giving permission to attach Brandt's name to such a disastrous project.[16] The following year, Berlin mayor Klaus Wowereit resigned, in part due to his role in the mismanagement of the airport.

By 2018, yet more money had been spent but the airport seemed no closer to completion. The BBC reported that the so-called "ghost airport" "looks exactly like every other major modern airport in Europe, except for one big problem: more than seven years after it was originally supposed to open, it still stands empty."[17] Despite the fact that no movement of people or planes was transpiring through this Brobdingnagian space of flows, the structure was nonetheless filled with ghostly motions and gestures. At a nearby airport hotel, a small staff reported to work in an empty building, regularly mopping floors, airing linens, and checking taps for the nonexistent clientele. At one point, a glitch in the computer system made it impossible to turn off the lights in the terminal for a stretch of several months, skyrocketing energy costs and making the airport appear eerily occupied from a distance. In a tunnel below the terminal, Deutsche Bahn conductors piloted passengerless trains once every weekday at precisely 10:26 a.m. to the airport's new, vacant railway station in order to keep air moving through the tunnels and prevent the tracks from rusting. Empty luggage carousels rotated spectrally to prevent their belts from atrophying. Expensive monitors parasitically displaying information for flights at Schönefeld eventually burned out; all 750 were recently replaced at a cost of 500,000 euros. Tourists—some of them German citizens keen to see exactly how their taxes were being spent at this now-infamous money pit—arrived in double-decker buses to survey the construction site from an observation platform, gazing over a windswept landscape of dormant runways, desolate parking lots, and empty terminals. Along Unter den Linden, souvenir shops sold postcards blazoned with the facetious phrase "No one intends to open an airport," an ironic appropriation of Walter Ulbricht's notorious dissimulation in June 1961— "No one intends to build a wall"—only weeks before the first coils of barbed wire were laid. A pair of locals designed and sold a board game called "UnberechenBϵR," the objective of which was to waste the most taxpayer euros possible.[18] The sardonic slogan on the front of the box read, "Building an airport—it's not child's play!"

If the Reichstag circulated internationally as the signature image of Germany's postreunification optimism, the new airport became the face of its humbling denouement. By 2016, a decade after ground was broken, the only way for the public to experience the airport was from a 32-meter-tall "InfoTower," housing an observation deck and a gift shop ingenuously selling a variety of souvenirs embellished with the airport logo. As Claire Colomb has noted, this last gasp of reunification euphoria was part of a larger trend: "while the 'spectacularization' of the built environment faded away with the completion of Berlin's largest urban development projects, it did not disappear."[19] The skeletal, decommissioned quality of the airport construction site uncannily echoed the city of cranes that defined the city's euphoric rebuilding, yet the ceaselessness of construction on the site now read as farce. Thus, the airport became an odd pendant to the Palast der Republik, an indolent theater of construction rather than of demolition. This slowness, both in the "disassembling" of the Palast and the prolonged construction of the airport, still felt foreign to a city recovering from the whiplash of rapid post-Wende change, and the failure of contemporary architecture seemed endemic. "Germany's long-awaited Berlin airport falls short of expectations— such as opening," declared the *Los Angeles Times* satirically in May 2019.[20] In November of that year, officials announced, with minimal pomp, that the airport would open on October 31, 2020, at a final cost of 7.3 billion euros—an astronomical sum nearly four times the original estimate.[21] Journalists wondered cynically whether the announcement truly marked "the beginning of the end, or merely the end of the beginning."[22] At the time of writing, the date of the grand opening remains in place—while over the course of only a few months, the future of air travel itself has been thrown into turmoil by a global pandemic whose final human and economic toll will likely remain unknown for years to come.

"The only benefit is safety"

In 2008, about 3 miles due south of the Brandenburg Gate and 10 miles northwest of the new international airport, planes were grounded at Tempelhof Airport in premature anticipation of BER's opening, prompting a contentious discussion of the old airfield's

Figure 5.3 Johannn Heinrich Hintze, *Blick vom Kreuzberg*, 1829. Oil on canvas, 48 cm × 66 cm. Alte Nationalgalerie, Berlin.

future. As one of Germany's oldest airports, with infrastructure dating to 1923, it was also firmly embedded in both the urban fabric and the history of the city. Constructed at the southern edge of Kreuzberg, Tempelhof was one of Europe's largest pre-World War II airports, built in the very earliest days of civilian air travel. The site, a wide-open green plain on the Teltow Plateau unfolding south of the city, had originally served as military drilling and parade grounds for the Berlin garrison (Figure 5.3). Its proximity to the city center made it useful to the National Socialists when they took power, while its dramatic alignment with Karl Friedrich Schinkel's neo-Gothic Prussian National Monument for the Liberation Wars atop the Kreuzberg appealed symbolically to Nazi hubris. Albert Speer's planned north–south axis for the city would have been anchored at its southern terminus by the expanded airport, intended to serve as the international gateway to the Welthauptstadt Germania.

Between 1935 and 1936, a massive terminal building was constructed from a design by the architect Ernst Sagebiel, fresh off his successful completion of the Ministry of Aviation along Wilhelmstrasse. Consistent with the "Luftwaffe modern" style Sagebiel developed for Hermann Göring's headquarters, the airport was characterized by a disciplined grouping of architectural volumes, in this case a series of curved, slab-like segments that responded to the adjacent circles of a ceremonial entry plaza and the Tempelhof Field.[23] From the plaza, a sight line would be opened northward through Speer's gargantuan (and never-built) triumphal arch, visually connecting the airport to

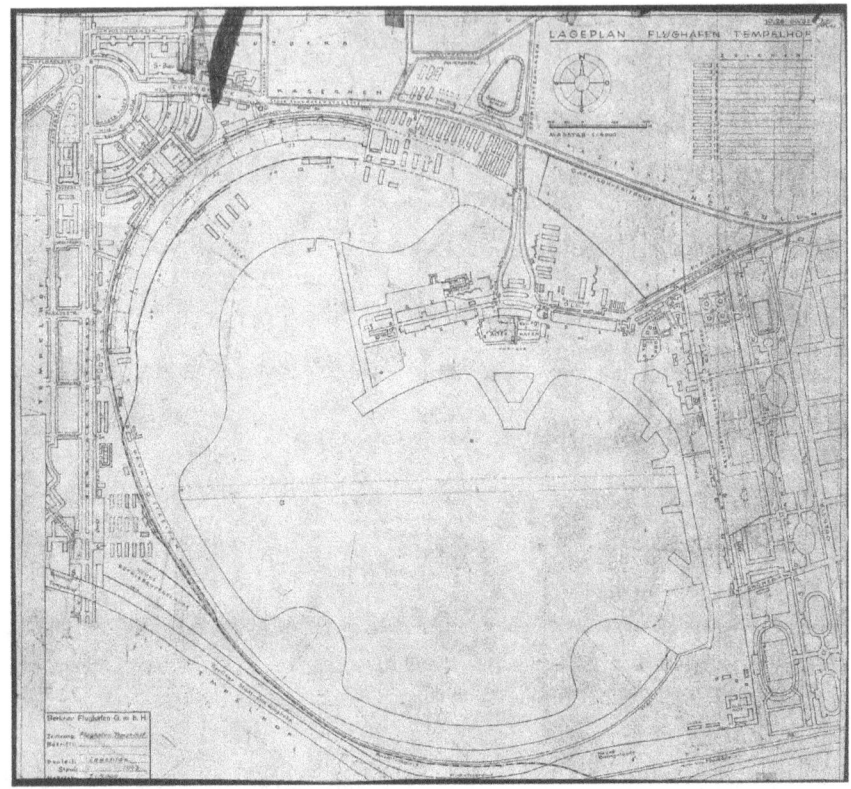

Figure 5.4 Ernst Sagebiel, *Flughafen Berlin-Tempelhof*, c. 1935–45. Blueprint, 60.0 × 66.4 cm. Architekturmuseum der Technischen Universität Berlin.

other symbolic structures testifying to the Third Reich's world conquest. The facades were treated with Sagebiel's characteristic streamlined classicism, and the terminal interiors were simplified and modern, typical of Nazi architecture in its techno-triumphalist mode (Figure 5.4 and Figure 5.5). Like the Ministry of Aviation, the airport building has remained standing into the present—both strangely intact traces of Nazism whose ongoing use is evidence of the complex intertwining of classicism and modernism in the architecture of the twentieth century.[24] Despite its unsavory political pedigree, Tempelhof's architecture remained well-regarded enough for Norman Foster, a longtime flight enthusiast and amateur pilot, to describe it in 2015 as "one of the really great buildings of the modern age"; indeed, for Foster, it is "the mother of all airports."[25] To be sure, Tempelhof had accrued positive political valence in the interim owing to its central role in the Berlin Airlift of 1948–9, when Allied planes dropped millions of tons of food and supplies to citizens blockaded in West Berlin after the Soviet Union closed land routes into the city.

Conclusion 229

Figure 5.5 Ernst Sagebiel and Adolf Kautzki, *Flughafen Berlin-Tempelhof, Perspektivische Innenansicht der Abfertigungshalle*, 1935–45. Blueprint, 61.4 × 85.6 cm. Architekturmuseum der Technischen Universität Berlin.

Upon the government's announcement in 2008 that all future air traffic would be channeled through the new main airport, thousands of Berlin residents protested, gathering signatures for a referendum to keep Tempelhof open and functioning. For many Berliners, especially those in the city's western districts, Tempelhof's central location made it both practical and historically significant. Yet the initiative was bootless, and the final commercial flight departed from the runway on October 30, 2008, as hundreds gathered for a candlelight vigil below. Though the site would no longer function as an airport, both federal and local governments put forth ambitious plans for its use, including a Berlin Airlift museum, commercial space for startups, sports facilities, and parks. In August 2009, city officials announced that the sprawling meadowland to the south of the terminal would be transformed into a public park and dedicated 60 million euros to its conversion.[26] At the same time, the city of Berlin became the sole owner of the park, purchasing remaining shares from the federal government at a cost of 35 million euros. At over 300 hectares, significantly larger than the city's beloved Tiergarten, the park proved enormously popular, attracting bicyclists, picnickers, and plant enthusiasts eager to work in the community gardens lining its eastern edge. The undisturbed green space even became a significant habitat for rare and endangered bird species. In the meantime, the airport's hangars were used to host trade expositions and auto shows. Though the passenger hall remained empty, tenants

Figure 5.6 Eagle Square, Tempelhof Airport, Berlin.

including the Berlin police force and a male strip club and revue called "La Vie en Rose" rented office space within the terminal, supervised sternly from the Platz der Luftbrücke by the sculptor and Luftwaffe pilot Wilhelm Lemke's bronze eagle's head (Figure 5.6).

In 2011, the city proposed to sell a portion of the former airport's land to private developers for the construction of several new commercial areas, a zone of office buildings, and 4,700 homes. A citizens' initiative called "100% Tempelhofer Feld" fought back, with its supporters protesting the private acquisition of this public land and arguing that increasing privatization in the capital had been responsible for many of its failures. As part of the plan, the prospect of a major new public library—a pet project of Wowereit's prior to his resignation—did little to assuage the general attitude of skepticism. Though the Berlin Senate alleged that the new construction would be "affordable housing," the numbers told a different story—and when confronted, politicians and developers hedged. As one writer reflected, "this government hasn't built a single social apartment for 10 years—are they going to start right when parkside real estate opens up?"[27] After months of heated debate, 64.3 percent of voters elected in 2014 to maintain the public park at Tempelhof, prompting a journalist for the *Guardian* to marvel: "the people decided they didn't trust big business not to mess up the park they loved. It's a state of affairs that would be almost unimaginable in Frankfurt or Munich, let alone London or New York."[28] Other commentators were not so sanguine; Ulf Poschardt, deputy editor of the conservative newspaper *Die Welt*, grumbled: "The wonder is that Berlin still carries on ... In the Prussian capital, hippie culture has become state policy."[29]

Unfolding alongside the privatization debacle at BER, the success of Tempelhof's defenders over private interests seemed to indicate a still-vital public sphere in the rapidly gentrifying city. Yet the following year, the very character of Berlin's "public" was called into question and the fragility of the consensus surrounding the park was thrown into high relief. In September 2015, as Germany struggled to address an influx of refugees from Syria, Iraq, Afghanistan, and elsewhere, the federal government announced that it would open a center at Tempelhof to provide temporary housing for up to 1,200 of the displaced in two of the airport's hangars.[30] Over the next months, those numbers only grew as a result of Chancellor Angela Merkel's polarizing "open door" policy.[31] By the end of 2015, nearly 2,500 refugees took up temporary residence in cubicles arrayed beneath the 16-meter-high ceilings of the hangars (Figure 5.7). Sentimental media accounts quickly associated the refugee center at Tempelhof with the humanitarian feats of the Berlin Airlift. Instead of the supplies delivered by the airlift's "candy bombers," the refugees were provided with shelter and safe haven, but the narrative of international altruism seemed poignantly parallel. Rather than the city that let in the architects, Berlin had now become capital of the country that saved the refugees.

Of course, the reality was far more difficult, revealing Germany's unresolved relationship with its own past and with the very idea of "foreignness." Merkel's policies, and the new migrant populations of cities across Germany, laid bare the nation's deep political schisms and brought the simmering racial and ethnic tensions in its cities to a boiling point. At Tempelhof, officials attempted to accommodate the new population while also respecting the protective legislation forbidding changes to the building—a direct result of the 2014 victory against privatization intended to stave off the

Figure 5.7 Refugee accommodation center in a former hangar at Tempelhof Airport, Berlin, 2015. Sueddeutsche Zeitung Photo / Alamy Stock Photo.

development of the site. Little in the way of architectural intervention could be managed beyond the sterile row of cubicles, each housing up to twelve people, huddled inside the cavernous space. Some residents enlivened their limited allotments by scribbling brightly colored drawings on the wall panels, but an official ban against graffiti was put in place after offensive marks appeared in some areas.[32] Privacy was nonexistent, despite the blankets and sheets that refugees hung from their bunk beds to create tent-like enclaves. Even the smallest noises echoed from the glass-and-steel walls of the enormous hangar.[33] Amid crowding, poor living conditions, and harsh treatment from guards, as well as the relentless boredom of waiting, a mass brawl broke out in November 2015. Photographs of Berlin police struggling to subdue unruly refugees appeared in the right-wing press, presented as evidence of mass migration's dangers, while journalists on the left strained to downplay the scuffle's violence. However, what was missing from most journalistic accounts of the conflict was the central role that the architectural inadequacy of the meager shelter at Tempelhof had played. The flimsy, serial, makeshift architectural quality of the center made it just one more of the "waiting rooms" that form what the political philosophers Sandro Mezzadra and Brett Neilson have termed the "temporal borders" of the larger mobility regimes in which global migration takes place.[34] As one refugee from Baghdad stated, "We were hurting in Iraq, but now we're hurting maybe even more. We were afraid of rockets. But we were living in a stable house comfortably. Here, there's no stability; the only benefit is safety."[35]

By 2017, the refugee population at Tempelhof had largely been dispersed. Frustrated by the slowness of the asylum process, some returned to their native countries; others were relocated to "Tempohomes," somewhat more commodious temporary housing arranged around the periphery of the park. These forms, which are the very opposite of the stylish contemporary architecture for which Berlin is now famous, are no less a manifestation of architectural contemporaneity—with safety as the insufficient ethical goal of their design. In recent years, individual politicians with hardline anti-immigration policies and organizations like the far-right party Alternative für Deutschland (Alternative for Germany, or AfD) have received a groundswell of support, especially from economically disadvantaged former East German regions. Today, Germany continues to wrestle with the newly overt discrepancy between the official doctrine of openness affirmed during the process of reunification and the factious reality of politics on the ground.

Therefore, the central role of architecture itself in either inciting or assuaging these conflicts, as well as addressing the problems I described above, must become better understood. In 2013, *Der Spiegel* conducted an interview with three high-profile architects: von Gerkan, Pierre de Meuron, and Christoph Ingenhoven, whose projects in Germany have come to represent notorious failures of public architecture. The interviewer began the discussion with the adversarial assertion: "Architecture's reputation in this country is worse than ever."[36] This striking statement might serve as a judgment that resonates beyond Germany and the specific examples of contemporary architecture I have invoked here. Despite the profession's recent obsession with risk management, we seem—at a global scale—to be caught continually unawares by disaster, whether natural or human-made. In interrogating the foundations of a practice forever reconsidering its ethical purchase, we must continue to train attention on problems both structural and infrastructural, viewing the forms of contemporary architecture as useful evidence of whose safety we prioritize, and at what cost it is achieved. Berlin, the contemporary capital, might prove historically instructive in ways unanticipated by its makers, suggesting the necessity of expanding architecture's sense of public mission for the safety of us all.

Notes

1. As Simone Hain described it, to use only one example, "the characterless and monstrous architecture of Potsdamer Platz and the cold, exclusive architecture that defines the redeveloped Friedrichstrasse, indicate that such flight to the comforting past is impossible. This is so because today's roving global capital has developed its own dynamics ... the city's grandiose development project is turning into a failure." Hain, "Berlin's Urban Development Discourse: Symbolic Action and the Articulation of Hegemonic Interests," in *The Berlin Reader: A Compendium on Urban Change and Activism*, eds. Matthias Bernt, Britta Grell, and Andrej Holm (Bielefeld: Transcript, 2014), 54, 60.
2. Dave Copeland, "Poor, Sexy Berlin: The Failure of Urban Planning," *Reason* 36 (December 2004): 56.
3. A bootless effort was made in 2012 to determine the design for a visitor center to manage tourism in the government quarter, with the Reichstag by far its most popular attraction. In 2016, the Bundestag held an open, anonymous competition, which was won by the Zürich-based architect Markus Schietsch, together with landscape architect Lorenz Engster. The current timeline projects that the center, which will serve as an entrée to the entire government district, will open in 2023. After it completion, visitors will access the Reichstag via a tunnel running underneath Scheidemannstrasse. The center will also entail the construction of a new "security zone" to be built around the Reichstag with a system of trenches and fences to protect against terrorist attacks.
4. Indeed, the history of modern architecture is shot through with resonant examples of "failed" buildings or movements. See Douglas Murphy, *Architecture and Failure* (Washington, D.C. and Winchester: Zero Books, 2012).
5. Manuel Castells, "Space of Flows, Space of Places: Materials for a Theory of Urbanism in the Information Age," in *Comparative Planning Cultures*, ed. Bishwapriya Sanyal (New York and London: Routledge, 2005), 45–63. For a discussion of the "transnational capitalist class" and the role of mobility in contemporary architecture culture, see Leslie Sklair, "The Transnational Capitalist Class and Contemporary Architecture in Globalizing Cities," *International Journal of Urban and Regional Research* 29 (September 2005): 485–500. For an example of recent critical scholarship on airport infrastructure, see Max Hirsh, "Design Aesthetics of Transborder Infrastructure in the Pearl River Delta," *Journal of the Society of Architectural Historians* 73 (March 2014): 137–52.
6. "Privatisierung von Hauptstadt-Flughafen gescheitert," *Frankfurter Allgemeine Zeitung*, May 22, 2003, https://www.faz.net/aktuell/wirtschaft/berlin-privatisierung-von-hauptstadt-flughafen-gescheitert-1104085.html.

7   "Postcard from Berlin: Can a New Airport Make this City Soar?," *Der Spiegel*, March 16, 2006, https://www.spiegel.de/international/postcard-from-berlin-can-a-new-airport-make-this-city-soar-a-406321.html.
8   As the writer Thomas Friedman stated after the opening of the railway station, "If all Americans could compare Berlin's luxurious central train station with the grimy, decrepit Penn Station in New York City, they would swear we were the ones who lost World War II." Friedman, "Who Will Tell the People?," *The New York Times*, May 4, 2008, https://www.nytimes.com/2008/05/04/opinion/04friedman.html.
9   Thorold Barker, "Is Germany Europe's Safest Bet?," *The Wall Street Journal*, video, June 5, 2012, https://www.wsj.com/video/is-germany-europe-safest-bet/93BD887D-9B28-411D-A533-9A79AA9A29A2.html.
10 Adam Jones-Kelley, "Is Germany Europe's Safest Bet?," *Site Selection*, November 1, 2011, 868.
11 Ibid.
12 In August 2016, the BER manager was found guilty of accepting 150,000 euros in bribes at a 2012 gas station rendezvous with the Imtech contact. See Thorsten Metzner, "Ehemaliger BER-Manager gibt Erhalt von Schmiergeld zu," *Der Tagesspiegel*, August 23, 2016, https://www.tagesspiegel.de/berlin/korruption-am-berliner-flughafen-ehemaliger-ber-manager-gibt-erhalt-von-schmiergeld-zu/14443604.html.
13 The impetus for the redesign came partly from the desire to accommodate the A380-Airbus, with its capacity of up to 800 passengers. See Jobst Fiedler and Alexander Wendler, "Berlin Brandenburg Airport," in Genia Koste and Fiedler, eds., *Large Infrastructure Projects in Germany: Between Ambition and Realities* (London: Palgrave Macmillan, 2018), 115. Behind the scenes, the aircraft would eventually pose yet another problem for the airport, as it was announced in 2019 that production of the plane would cease in 2021.
14 Von Gerkan later published a book revealing the details of his negative experience with the airport project, describing the government's "wishful thinking, penchant for optimism, and refusal to implement reality." In his view, the project was a "self-made catastrophe." See Meinhard von Gerkan, *Black Box BER: Vom Flughafen Berlin Brandenburg und anderen Großbaustellen* (Munich: Bastei Lübbe, 2013).
15 See, for example, Nicola Clark, "Airport Delays Undermine Image of German Efficiency," *The New York Times*, September 4, 2012, B3, and Derek Scally, "New Airport Proves Not to Be Best Example of German Efficiency," *The Irish Times*, January 12, 2013, https://www.irishtimes.com/news/new-airport-proves-not-to-be-best-example-of-german-efficiency-1.957296.
16 In an interview with *Das Bild*, Wolfram Hoppenstedt stated: "The name of the former chancellor should not be associated with these failures of planning." In the same article, Sahra Wagenknecht, deputy leader of the Left Party, went still further: "This is an abject tragedy. Willy Brandt would probably turn in his grave if he knew that he's supposed to give his name to this catastrophic airport." "Verliert der Airport seinen Namen 'Willy Brandt'?," *Das Bild*, January 15, 2013, https://www.bild.de/regional/berlin/flughafen-berlin-brandenburg/verliert-der-airport-seinen-namen-willy-brandt--28103598.bild.html.
17 Emily Schultheis, "Whatever Happened to Berlin's Deserted 'Ghost' Airport?," BBC Worklife, November 5, 2018, https://www.bbc.com/worklife/article/20181030-what-happened-to-berlins-ghost-airport.

18 Ava Johnson, "Airport Delay Byproduct," *Exberliner*, November 21, 2017, https://www.exberliner.com/whats-on/insider-tips/airport-delay-byproduct/.
19 Claire Colomb, "Staging Urbanism: Construction Site Tourism and the City as Exhibition," in *Staging the New Berlin: Place Marketing and the Politics of Urban Reinvention Post-1989* (Abingdon: Routledge, 2012), 216.
20 Erik Kirschbaum, "Germany's Long-Awaited Berlin airport Falls Short of Expectations—Such as Opening," *The Los Angeles Times*, May 20, 2019, https://www.latimes.com/world/la-fg-germany-berlin-empty-airport-20190520-story.html.
21 Over the past decade, the government has spent millions of euros each month simply to maintain the building. Steven Perlberg, "Berlin's 'Ghost' Airport Might Finally Open—Billions over Budget and Eight Years Late," *Fortune*, January 26, 2020, https://fortune.com/2020/01/26/berlin-brandenburg-airport-open/.
22 Arthur Sullivan, "Berlin's New Airport: A Potted History," *Deutsche Welle*, December 12, 2019, https://www.dw.com/en/berlins-new-airport-a-potted-history/a-41813465.
23 Elke Dittrich, *Ernst Sagebiel: Leben und Werk (1892–1970)* (Berlin: Lukas, 2005), 14. In the late 1920s, Sagebiel worked in the office of Erich Mendelsohn before joining the NSDAP in the early 1930s. The modernist tendencies apparent in his later work are frequently attributed to the influence of his former employer.
24 This intertwining of tendencies is what Jeffrey Herf famously and controversially characterized as "reactionary modernism" in Herf, *Reactionary Modernism: Technology, Culture and Politics in Weimar and the Third Reich* (Cambridge: Cambridge University Press, 1984).
25 Alexandra Lange, "Seven Leading Architects Defend the World's Most Hated Buildings," *The New York Times Magazine*, June 5, 2015, https://www.nytimes.com/interactive/2015/06/05/t-magazine/architects-libeskind-zaha-hadid-selldorf-norman-foster.html?smid=fb-nytimes&smtyp=cur&_r=0. Nicolai Ouroussoff has identified Tempelhof as a precedent for Foster's terminal building at Beijing International Airport. See Ouroussoff, "In Changing Face of Beijing, a Look at the New China," *The New York Times*, July 13, 2008, A1.
26 A. J. Goldmann, "Repurposing Tempelhof," *The Wall Street Journal*, August 25, 2011, https://www.wsj.com/articles/SB10001424052702303823104576391572709176418.
27 John Riceburg, "Everyone is Lying about Tempelhofer Field," *Exberliner*, May 12, 2014, https://www.exberliner.com/features/opinion/everyone-is-lying-to-you-about-tempelhofer-feld/.
28 Ciarán Fahey, "How Berliners Refused to Give Tempelhof Airport over to Investors," *The Guardian*, March 5, 2015, https://www.theguardian.com/cities/2015/mar/05/how-berliners-refused-to-give-tempelhof-airport-over-to-developers.
29 Ulf Poschardt, "Berlin ist doch nur eine Kleingärtner-Metropole," *Die Welt*, May 5, 2014, https://www.welt.de/kultur/kunst-und-architektur/article128430318/Berlin-ist-doch-nur-eine-Kleingaertner-Metropole.html.
30 Raziye Akkoc, "Refugee Crisis: Europe's Borders Unraveling as Austria and Slovakia Impose Frontier Controls," *The Telegraph*, September 14, 2015, https://www.telegraph.co.uk/news/worldnews/europe/eu/11863246/Refugee-crisis-EU-ministers-Germany-border-control-Austria-army-live.html.
31 In June 2019, the United Nations High Commissioner for Refugees (UNHCR) reported that, at the end of 2018, there were 1.06 million refugees in Germany. Most of these individuals—nearly 1 million—arrived over the course of 2015 as part of what

Merkel termed Germany's "Wilkommenskultur." Merkel's administration tightened Germany's borders significantly in 2018.
32 Toby Parsloe, "Appropriating Buildings to House Refugees: Berlin Tempelhof," *Forced Migration Review* 55 (June 2017): 36.
33 A former journalist from Afghanistan stated in the *Washington Post* that the acoustics of the space alone had contributed to significant mental strain: "Imagine in one hangar, there are more than 500 people . . . They say one word, and it makes more than 500 echoes because the ceilings and walls are made of iron." Quoted in Luisa Beck, Rick Noack, and Joyce Lee, "Inside an Enormous Abandoned Airport in Berlin That's Coming Back to Life," *The Washington Post*, March 17, 2018, https://www.washingtonpost.com/world/inside-an-enormous-abandoned-airport-in-berlin-thats-coming-back-to-life/2018/03/16/65ca90a6-2642-11e8-b79d-f3d931db7f68_story.html.
34 Sandro Mezzadra and Brett Neilson, *Border as Method, or, the Multiplication of Labor* (Durham, NC and London: Duke University Press, 2013).
35 Quoted in Sonia Narang, "Pregnant Inside Tempelhof, Germany's Largest Refugee Camp," *Refugees Deeply*, August 16, 2016, https://www.newsdeeply.com/refugees/articles/2016/08/17/pregnant-inside-tempelhof-germanys-largest-refugee-camp.
36 Susanne Beyer and Ulrike Knöfel, "The Men Behind Germany's Building Debacles," *Der Spiegel*, June 14, 2013, https://www.spiegel.de/international/germany/de-meuron-von-gerkan-and-ingenhoven-on-german-construction-headaches-a-905472.html. As well as von Gerkan's Berlin airport, the projects in question were Ingenhoven's Stuttgart railway station (known as Stuttgart 21) and Herzog & de Meuron's Elbphilharmonie in Hamburg.

Bibliography

Abramson, Daniel M. *Obsolescence: An Architectural History*. Chicago and London: University of Chicago Press, 2016.

Akcan, Esra. *Open Architecture: Migration, Citizenship, and the Urban Renewal of Berlin-Kreuzberg by IBA-1984/87*. Basel: Birkhäuser-de Gruyter, 2018.

Apel, Dora. *Beautiful Terrible Ruins: Detroit and the Anxiety of Decline*. New Brunswick, NJ: Rutgers University Press, 2015.

Barnstone, Deborah Ascher. *The Transparent State: Architecture and Politics in Postwar Germany*. London and New York: Routledge, 2005.

Bergdoll, Barry. "Reconstruction Doubts: The Ironies of Building in Schinkel's Name." *Harvard Design Magazine* 23 (Fall 2005/Winter 2006): 31–5.

Beutelschmidt, Thomas, and Julia M. Novak. *Ein Palast und seine Republik*. Berlin: Bauwesen, 2001.

Beyme, Klaus von. "Hauptstadtplanung von Bonn bis Berlin." In *Stadt als Erfahrungsraum der Politik. Beiträge zur kulturellen Konstruktion urbaner Politik*, edited by Wilhelm Hofmann, 13–33. Berlin: LIT, 2011.

Boym, Svetlana. *The Future of Nostalgia*. New York: Basic Books, 2001.

Boym, Svetlana. *The Off-Modern*. New York and London: Bloomsbury Academic, 2017.

Broadbent, Philip, and Sabine Hake, eds. *Berlin Divided City, 1945–89*. New York and Oxford: Berghahn Books, 2010.

Buddensieg, Tilmann. *Berliner Labyrinth, neu besichtigt: Von Schinkels Unter den Linden vis Fosters Reichstagskuppel*. Berlin: Wagenbach, 1999.

Burg, Annegret, ed. *Neue Berlinische Architektur: Eine Debatte*. Berlin and Basel: Birkhäuser, 1994.

Burg, Annegret, and Sebastian Redecke, eds. *Kanzleramt und Präsidialamt der Bundesrepublik Deutschland*. Berlin: Bauwelt/Birkhäuser, 1995.

Castillo, Greg. *Cold War on the Home Front: The Soft Power of Midcentury Design*. Minneapolis: University of Minnesota Press, 2010.

Chattopadhyay, Swati, and Jeremy White, eds. *The Routledge Companion to Critical Approaches to Contemporary Architecture*. New York: Routledge, 2020.

Christensen, Peter. *Germany and the Ottoman Railways: Art, Empire, and Infrastructure*. New Haven: Yale University Press, 2017.

Colomb, Claire. *Staging the New Berlin: Place Marketing and the Politics of Urban Reinvention Post-1989*. London and New York: Routledge, 2012.

Cullen, Michael S. *Der Deutsche Reichstag: Geschichte eines Monumentes*. Berlin: Frolich and Kaufman, 1992.

Daum, Andreas, and Christof Mauch, eds. *Berlin-Washington 1800–2000: Capital Cities, Cultural Representation, and National Identities*. New York: Cambridge University Press, 2005.

Filler, Martin. "Berlin: The Lost Opportunity." *The New York Review of Books* 17 (November 1, 2001): 28–31.

Forster, Kurt W. *Schinkel: A Meander through his Life and Work*. Basel: Birkhäuser, 2018.

Galetti, Nino. *Der Bundestag als Bauherr in Berlin: Ideen, Konzepte, Entscheidungen zur politischen Architektur.* Berlin: Droste, 2008.
Gerstenberger, Katharina, and Jana Evans Braziel, eds. *After the Berlin Wall: Germany and Beyond.* New York: Palgrave Macmillan, 2011.
Gordon, David L. A., ed. *Planning Twentieth Century Capital Cities.* New York: Routledge, 2006.
Habermas, Jürgen. "Modernity—An Incomplete Project." In *The Anti-Aesthetic: Essays on Postmodern Culture,* edited by Hal Foster, 3–15. Port Townsend, WA: Bay Press, 1983.
Haddad, Elie, and David Rifkind, eds. *A Critical History of Contemporary Architecture: 1960–2010.* Farnham: Ashgate, 2014.
Harvey, David Harvey. *Spaces of Global Capitalism: A Theory of Uneven Geographical Development.* London: Verso, 2006.
Hell, Julia, and Andreas Schönle, eds. *Ruins of Modernity.* Durham, NC: Duke University Press, 2010.
Hertweck, Florian Hertweck. *Der Berliner Architekturstreit: Architektur, Stadtbau, Geschichte und Identität in der Berliner Republik 1989–1999.* Berlin: Gebrüder Mann, 2010.
Hertweck, Florian, and Sébastien Marot. *The City in the City—Berlin: The Green Archipelago.* Zürich: Lars Müller, 2013.
Hohensee, Naraelle. "Building in Public: Critical Reconstruction and the Rebuilding of Berlin after 1990." PhD dissertation, CUNY Graduate Center, 2016.
Huyssen, Andreas Huyssen. *Present Pasts: Urban Palimpsests and the Politics of Memory.* Stanford: Stanford University Press, 2003.
Jenkins, David, ed. *Rebuilding the Reichstag.* Woodstock, NY: Overlook Press, 2000.
James, Chakraborty, Kathleen. *Modernism as Memory: Building Identity in the Federal Republic of Germany.* Minneapolis and London: University of Minnesota Press, 2018.
Jaskot, Paul. *The Architecture of Oppression: The SS, Forced Labor and the Nazi Monumental Building Economy.* New York: Routledge, 2000.
Jordan, Jennifer. *Structures of Memory: Understanding Urban Change in Berlin and Beyond.* Stanford: Stanford University Press, 2006.
Kahn, Louis. "A discussion recorded in Mr. Kahn's Philadelphia office in February 1961." *Perspecta* 7 (1961): 9–28.
Klemek, Christopher. *The Transatlantic Collapse of Urban Renewal: Postwar Urbanism from New York to Berlin.* Chicago: University of Chicago Press, 2011.
Koolhaas, Rem, and Bruce Mau (Office for Metropolitan Architecture). *S,M,L,XL.* New York: Monacelli Press, 1995.
Koshar, Rudy. *Germany's Transient Pasts: Preservation and National Memory in the Twentieth Century.* Chapel Hill: University of North Carolina Press, 1998.
Kuhrmann, Anke. *Der Palast der Republik: Geschichte und Bedeutung des Ost-Berliner Parlaments- und Kulturhauses.* Petersberg: Michael Imhof, 2006.
Kunze, Donald, David Bertolin, and Simone Brott, eds. *Architecture Post Mortem: The Diastolic Architecture of Decline, Dystopia, and Death.* Farnham: Ashgate, 2013.
Kries, Mateo, Jochen Eisenbrand, and Stanislaus von Moos, eds. *Louis Kahn: The Power of Architecture.* Weil am Rhein: Vitra Design Museum, 2012.
Ladd, Brian Ladd. *The Ghosts of Berlin: Confronting German History in the Urban Landscape.* Chicago: University of Chicago Press, 1998.

Large, David Clay. *Berlin*. New York: Basic Books, 2000.
Libeskind, Daniel. "Between the Lines: Extension to the Berlin Museum, with the Jewish Museum." *Assemblage* 12 (August 1990): 18–57.
Mezzadra, Sandro, and Brett Neilson. *Border as Method, or, the Multiplication of Labor*. Durham, NC and London: Duke University Press, 2013.
Minkenberg, Michael, ed. *Power and Architecture: The Construction of Capitals and the Politics of Space*. New York and Oxford: Berghahn Books, 2014.
Molnar, Virag. *Building the State: Architecture, Politics, and State Formation in Post-War Central Europe*. New York: Routledge, 2013.
Mönninger, Michael. *Kanzleramt Berlin*. Stuttgart: Axel Menges, 2002.
Osayimwese, Itohan. *Colonialism and Modern Architecture in Germany*. Pittsburgh: University of Pittsburgh Press, 2017.
Owens, Craig. "The Allegorical Impulse: Toward a Theory of Postmodernism." *October* 12 (Spring 1980): 80.
Pugh, Emily. *Architecture, Politics, and Identity in Divided Berlin*. Pittsburgh: University of Pittsburgh Press, 2014.
Rogier, Francesca. "Growing Pains: From the Opening of the Wall to the Wrapping of the Reichstag." *Assemblage* 29 (April 1996): 40–71.
Rosenfeld, Gavriel D. "The Architects' Debate: Architectural Discourse and the Memory of Nazism in the Federal Republic of Germany, 1977–1997." *History and Memory* 9 (Fall 1997): 189–225.
Sandler, Daniela. *Counterpreservation: Architectural Decay in Berlin since 1989*. Ithaca: Cornell University Press, 2016.
Sassen, Saskia. *Globalization and its Discontents: Essays on the New Mobility of People and Money*. New York: New Press, 1998.
Scheer, Thorsten, Josef Paul Kleihues, and Paul Kahlfeldt, eds. *City of Architecture, Architecture of the City: Berlin 1900–2000*. Berlin: Nicolai, 2000.
Schmaling, Sebastian. "Masked Nostalgia, Chic Regression: The 'Critical' Reconstruction of Berlin." *Harvard Design Magazine* 23 (Fall 2005/Winter 2006): 24–30.
Schneider, Peter. *Berlin Now: The City after the Wall*. Translated by Sophie Schlondorff. New York: Farrar, Straus and Giroux, 2014.
Seidel, Martin, ed. *Architektur der Demokratie: Bauten des Bundes 1990–2010*. Ostfildern: Hatje Cantz, 2009.
Sklair, Leslie. *The Icon Project: Architecture, Cities, and Capitalist Globalization*. New York and Oxford: Oxford University Press, 2017.
Solà-Morales Rubió, Ignasi de. "Terrain Vague." In *Anyplace*, edited by Cynthia C. Davidson, 118–23. Cambridge, MA: MIT Press, 1995.
Speer, Albert. *Inside the Third Reich*. Translated by Richard and Clara Winston. New York: Simon & Schuster, 1970.
Stoler, Ann Laura, ed. *Imperial Debris: On Ruins and Ruination*. Durham, NC: Duke University Press, 2013.
Strom, Elizabeth. *Building the New Berlin: The Politics of Urban Development in Germany's Capital City*. Lanham, MD and Oxford: Lexington Books, 2001.
Till, Karen. *The New Berlin: Memory, Politics, Place*. Minneapolis and London: University of Minnesota Press, 2006.
Ward, Janet. *Post-Wall Berlin: Borders, Space and Identity*. New York: Palgrave Macmillan, 2011.

Wefing, Heinrich. *Kulisse der Macht: Das Berliner Kanzleramt.* Stuttgart: Deutsche Verlags-Anstalt, 2001.
Weiss-Sussex, Godela. "Berlin: Myth and Memorialization." In *The Cultural Identities of European Cities,* edited by Katia Pizzi and Godela Weiss-Sussex, 145–64. Bern: Peter Lang, 2011.
Wise, Michael Z. *Capital Dilemma: Germany's Search for a New Architecture of Democracy.* New York: Princeton Architectural Press, 1998.
Young, James. *At Memory's Edge: After-Images of the Holocaust in Contemporary Art and Architecture.* New Haven and London: Yale University Press, 2000.
Zimmermann, Monika, ed. *Der Berliner Schlossplatz: Visionen zur Gestaltung der Berliner Mitte.* Berlin: Argon, 1997.
Zwoch, Felix, ed. *Hauptstadt Berlin: Parlamentsviertel im Spreebogen-Internationaler Städtebaulicher Ideenwettbewerb 1993.* Berlin: Bauwelt/Birkhäuser, 1993.
Zwoch, Felix, ed. *Hauptstadt Berlin: Stadtmitte Spreeinsel-Internationaler Städtebaulicher Ideenwettbewerb 1994.* Berlin: Bauwelt/Birkhäuser, 1994.

Index

Academy of Arts, 222
Achtung: Berlin (symposium 2013), 11
adaptive reuse, 82
Adenauer, Konrad, 133
Adorno, Theodor, 15, 113
Agee, Joel, 89–90
airports, 16, 222–3, 225–32
Akcan, Esra, 45
allegory
    architectural, 60–2, 67, 68
    sculpture, 84, 109, 134
Allen, Jennifer, 207
Alsenviertel, 30, 37, 58
Alte Nationalgalerie, 192
Altes Museum, 8, 85, 139, 148, 183–4
Anhalter Bahnhof, 126
anxiety, in contemporary architecture
    culture, 4, 17, 26, 57, 123, 163
Apel, Dora, 136
architainment, 199
Architectural Association, 64
Arndt, Adolf, 42
Art Institute of Chicago, 9
ARX, 55–6, 57
authoritarianism, 92, 140, 154, 201, 221
avant-garde
    good taste, 208
    influence, 3, 15, 40, 64, 206
    rejection of monumentality, 148
    Spreebogen proposals, 15, 33–5
    transparency, 81, 188

Baller, Hinrich, 200
Band des Bundes
    as a bridge, 62–4
    design, 14–15, 23–5, 58–64, 107
    dissatisfaction with, 67–8, 162, 222
Barenboim, Daniel, 10
Barnstone, Deborah Ascher, 81, 188–9
Bartetzko, Dieter, 148
Battle of Berlin, 15, 37, 85, 108

Bauakademie
    destruction, 188, 192
    proposed reconstruction, 193, 195, 197,
    204–5, 219 n.103
Baudrillard, Jean, 116 n.37
Bauhaus, 161, 188
Baumgarten, Paul, 85, 86, 106, 109, 111,
    112
Behne, Adolf, 69 n.15, 93
Behnisch, Günter, 81, 103, 139, 222
Behrens, Peter, 138, 146
belief, in contemporary architecture
    culture, 16, 114, 180, 213–14, 221
Benjamin, Walter, 61, 68, 123
Bergmann, Benjamin, 210
Berlin Airlift, 228, 229, 231
Berlin Brandenburg International Airport
    (BER), 223–6
Berlin Cathedral, 85, 182, 183
Berlin Cube, 68
Berlin Senate, 52
Berlin Tomorrow: Ideas for the Heart of a
    Great City, 44–52, 199
Berlin Wall
    as architecture, 64–6, 68, 191
    construction, 41, 87
    fall, 4, 41, 102, 207
    former site, 4–5, 14, 43, 175
    graffiti, 120 n.103
Berlin Wall Memorial, 126
Berlin-Kölln, 26, 181
Berliner Tagesspiegel, 200–1
Berlinische Galerie, 45
"big roof" technique, 102–7, 201
Bilbao Effect, 45, 113
Blake, Peter, 193
Boddien, Wilhelm von, 198, 202
Bode-Museum, 192
Böhm, Gottfried, 96–7, 131
Böhm, Peter, 96–7
Böhm, Stephan, 131

Bohnstedt, Ludwig, 83
Bonn
  as provisional capital, 42, 43, 81, 85
  timidity of architecture, 42, 132–3
  transparency of architecture, 42, 81, 85, 94, 112, 132
Borchardt, Wolf-Rüdiger, 200
Bornemann, Fritz, 192
Bouw, Matthijs, 201
Brandenburg Gate, 28, *29*, 50, 51, 85, 187
Brandt, Willy, 223, 225
Braunfels, Stephan, 6, 67, 125, 157, 159–60
Breger, Claudia, 201–2
bridges, 157, 162, 183
Brown, John Carter, 8–9
Bruijn, Pi de, 98, 99
Brunnenstrasse 183, 126
brutalism, 125
Buddensieg, Tilmann, 143, 179, 183–4, 200, 201
Bundeshaus (Bonn), 81, 103
Bundesrat, 54, 58, 67
Bundesrepublik
  absorption of GDR, 175
  Chancellery, 130, 131, 162
  criticism of, 222
  postwar architecture, 192
Bundestag
  Bonn, 42, 43, 81, 85
  Chancellery, 143
  move back to Berlin, 2, 41–3, 123, 130
  Reichstag, 95, 96, 97, 100, 102, 107, 111
  Schlossplatz vote, 16, 180, 202, 203–4, 209
  Spreebogen, 52, 54–5, 57, 60, 68
  Spreeinsel, 193, 198
  Wrapped Reichstag debate, 88
Bürger, Peter, 139
Bürgerforum, 60, 68, 145, 153, 157, 162

Calatrava, Santiago, 98, 99–100
capitalism, 4, 45, 186, 187, 188
Carré d'Art (Nîmes), 104, 105
Castells, Manuel, 222
Cattani, Emmanuel, 96
Chancellery, *122*
  competition, 130–2, 139, 141–7
  controversy, 122–3, 141, 142–3, 146, 153, 154–5
  critical reception, 161–2, 163, 180–1, 222
  earlier buildings, 132–5, 137
  extension, 162–3
  opening, 121–2
  as part of Band des Bundes, 58, 67, 222
  Schultes and Frank design, 16–17, 122–3, 143–5, 147, 153–7, 160–2
Chancellor's garden, 58, 67
Chapel of Reconciliation, 126, *127*
Checkpoint Charlie, 181
Cheesman, Wendy, 103
Chipperfield, David, 126, 212–13
Christo, 15, 86, 87
Christo and Jeanne-Claude, *Wrapped Reichstag,* 79, *80,* 86–90, 92–4, 200
Church of the Reconciliation, 165 n.21
classicism
  contemporary, 145, 146, 195, 212
  controversy, 137–142, 146
  stripped, 137, 212
  Third Reich, 133, 134, 136–7, 227
climate change, 124, 221
clubs, 126
Cold War, 4, 38, 39, 41, 87, 202
collaborative work, 10, 124
Cologne Cathedral, 91
Colomb, Claire, 199, 226
colonialism, 13, 72 n.38, 171 n.101, 213
competitions, 43–4
  Alsenblock, 158–9
  Berliner Tagesspiegel (1996), 200–1
  Chancellery (1994), 130–2, 139, 141–7
  German Historical Museum, 41
  Hauptstadt Berlin (1958), 39–41
  Potsdamer Platz, 130
  Prussian state, 31–2
  Reichstag (1992), 95–100
  Spreebogen (1992), 23–5, 26, 52, 53–60
  Spreeinsel (1993-4), 131, 191, 192–8
  Stadtschloss, 16, 211–12
Congrès internationaux d'architecture moderne (CIAM), 39, 51, 70 n.25, 151
Congress Hall, Berlin, 38–9

Congress Hall, Nuremberg, 142
Conradi, Peter, 60, 88, 94, 146
conservatism, 53, 56, 141, 143, 161
constructivism, 98
Coop Himmelb(l)au, 55, 97–8
Costa, Lúcio, 148
COVID-19 pandemic, 226
Critical Reconstruction, 52–3, 72 n.45, 130, 172 n.117, 222
Critical Regionalism, 11
Cullen, Michael, 84, 86–7, 100
customs wall, 28

Daimler-Benz complex, 6, 10, 130
de Architekten Cie, 99
Dean, Tacita, 208
deconstructivism, 55–6, 97–8, 184
Deconstructivist Architecture (exhibition 1988), 97
Demand, Thomas, 11, 208
Deuflhard, Amelie, 203
Deutsche Oper, 192
Deutsches Architekturmuseum (DAM), 44, 45
DG Bank building, 6, *7*
Diderot, Denis, 135
Diepgen, Eberhard, 2, 60, 154
digital technologies, 53, 127, 212
Dorte Mandrup, 126
Dudler, Max, 133
Düttmann, Werner, 38

early history, 26, 181–2
Eberstadt, Rudolf, 32
Ebert, Wils, 39
ecological concerns, 9, 16, 102–3, 104–5, 136, 151
economic conditions, 199, 221, 223–4
Eesteren, Cornelis van, 32, 64
Eggeling, Fritz, 41
Eiermann, Egon, 126
Eisenman, Peter, 10, 11, 181
Eliasson, Olafur, 208
Embassy of the Netherlands, 11, *12*
European Union, 221
Europeanism, 53, 56
Exeter Library (Exeter, New Hampshire), 151, 156

Exilmuseum, 126
expressionism, 40, 81, 92, 93, 107, 206

far-right politics, 180–1, 221, 232
Fassadenrepublik, 204, 205
Fattal, Amir, 210
Fehn, Sverre, 1
Feininger, Lyonel, 188
Fernsehturm, 186–7
Fest, Joachim, 200
Filler, Martin, 6, 108, 161
Fischer, Marc, 89
Fischer, Nina, 213
Fischerinsel, 192
Foerster-Baldenius, Benjamin, *Berg, Der,* 205–6
Förderverein Berliner Stadtschloss, 198, 200
Forum Museuminsel, 126, *128*
Foster, Hal, 92
Foster, Norman, 44, 55, 228
 "big roof" technique, 102–7, 201
 Pritzker Prize, 1, 5–6, 9, 95
 Reichstag dome, 81, 92, 94, 97, 107–8
 Reichstag proposals, 95, 98, 100–8
 Reichstag renovation, 5–6, 15, 79, 81–2, 108, 111–13
 Sainsbury Centre for the Visual Arts, 103, *104,* 105–6
 Schlossplatz proposal, 201
 use of lightness, 79, 81, 101, 104–6, 113
Frampton, Kenneth, 142
Franciscan Monastery Church, 126
Frank, Charlotte, 153, 162, 164 n.14
 See also, Schultes Frank Architekten
Friedrich I, 182, 214 n.11
Friedrich Wilhelm, 26, 27
Friedrich Wilhelm II, 27
Friedrich Wilhelm III, 214 n.11
Friedrich Wilhelm IV, 182, 184
Friedrichswerder Church, 192
Fujimoto, Sou, 152
Fuller, Buckminster, 104–5
Fun Palace 200X (symposium 2004), 206

Galeries Lafayette, 7, 10, 92
Gehry, Frank, 1, 6, *7,* 19 n.28
gender, 10, 13, 124

gentrification, 126
Gerkan, Marg & Partners (gmp), 68, 223
Gerkan, Meinhard von, 223, 225, 232
German Architecture Prize, 162
German Democratic Republic (GDR)
    Berlin Wall, 41
    dissolution, 175
    government buildings, 188, 192, 198, 213
    Palast der Republik, 176, 186, 188, 189, 190–1
    Reichstag, 87
    Stadtschloss, 176, 185–6, 188
    stripped classicism, 137
German Historical Museum, 41
Giedion, Sigfried, 148
Gilly, Friedrich, 138
Glancey, Jonathan, 6
glass, 81, 93, 107, 151, 190
globalism, 94
globalization, 4
Goldberger, Paul, 2, 88, 161
Göthe, Johann Friedrich Eosander von, 182
Gothic architecture, 91, 103
Gothic Revival architecture, 91
graffiti
    Berlin Wall, 120 n.103
    Reichstag, 15, 37, 80, 82, 108–13
    Tempelhof, 231–2
Graffunder, Heinz, 176, 188, 189, 190
Grand Hyatt, 9
Gropius, Walter, 188
Gruber, Martin, 142
Guggenheim Bilbao, 1, 6
    See also, Bilbao Effect

Hadid, Zaha, 44, 46
Häring, Hugo, 33, 40
Hassemer, Volker, 10–11, 195
Haubrich, Rainer, 68
Hauptstadt Berlin competition, 39–41
Haus der Statistik, 213
Haus Schwarzenberg, 126
heaviness, architectural, 90, 92, 106, 113, 129
Heinrich, Max, 28
Hejduk, John, 49–50

Henselmann, Hermann, 137
Herzog & de Meuron, 46, 82
high-rise buildings, 33, 69 n.15, 192
Hilberseimer, Ludwig, 108
Hilde Leon & Konrad Wohlhage, 133, 201
Hildebrand, Klaus, 143
Historians' Debate, 139, 143
historicism, 131, 139, 195
    criticism of, 64, 125, 148, 200
    versus progressivism, 53, 54, 57
history, in contemporary architecture culture, 4, 26, 53–4, 62, 82, 95
Hitler, Adolf
    bunker, 175
    Reich Chancellery, 133–4
    Reichstag Fire, 35, 85
    Stadtschloss, 184
    Volkshalle plan, 37, 85
Hoffmann, Hilmar, 143
Hohenzollern dynasty, 26, 30, 31, 176
Honecker, Erich, 188, 190
Hübner/Blanke/Forster, 158
Hübsch, Heinrich, 91
Humboldt Box, 209
Humboldt Forum, 3, 11, 16, 180, 211–13
Humboldthafen, 30, 55
Huyssen, Andreas, 4, 90, 202

Ingenhoven, Christoph, 232
Initiative Zwischenpalastnutzung, 16, 203–4, 205–8, 209
International Building Exhibition, 140
Internationales Congress Centrum, 191
Ito, Toyo, 126

Jahn, Helmut, 6–7, 92
Jeanne-Claude, 15, 87
Jencks, Charles, 57
Jewish Museum, 7–8, 9, 20 n.32
Joachim II, 182

Kahn, Louis
    influence, 59, 124–6, 151–3, 156, 160, 161
    ruin-wrapping technique, 15–16, 125, 150–1, 156, 157
Kaiser Wilhelm Memorial church, 126
Kaiser, Josef, 188, 198

Kaisersaal, 7
Kanzlerbungalow, Bonn, 132
Kanzlerpark, 155–6
Kennedy, John F., 39
Khaldei, Yevgeny, 109, *110*
Kimmelman, Michael, 211, 212
kitsch
    Chancellery designs, 155
    East German architecture, 191, 208, 213
    Nazi architecture, 138
    Schlossplatz, 201
Kleihues, Josef Paul, 52, 140, 191, 193
Klenze, Leo von, 91
Klotz, Heinrich, 140, 141
Knöfel, Ulrike, 159
Kohl, Helmut
    Chancellery competition, 131, 141, 143–4, 145–6, 147
    changes to Chancellery design, 153–4, 155, 161
    views on *Wrapped Reichstag*, 88
Kohtz, Otto, 33, 70 n.20
Kollhoff, Hans, 47, 52, 140
Königsplatz, 30, 31, 33
    See also Platz der Republik
Koolhaas, Rem, 2, 11, 15, 47, 64–6, 206
Koshar, Rudy, 90
Kramer, Jane, 146, 208
Krauss, Rosalind, 112, 113
Krier, Léon, 11, 140, 146
Kroll Opera House, 85
Krüger Schuberth Vandreike (KSV), 143–7, 195, 209
Krüger, Torsten, 146
Kühn, Bernd, 201
Kundera, Milan, 90
Kunsthalle Rostock, 213
Kunsthaus Tacheles, 126, 203
Kunstmuseum Bonn, 42, 145, 147–8, 159
Kuznetzov, Sergey, 126

La, Khadija Carroll, 209
Ladd, Brian, 182–3, 202
Lampugnani, Vittorio Magnago, 11, 44, 46, 47, 52, 140
Langhans, Carl Gotthard, 85
Lasdun, Denys, 106

Laugier, Marc-Antoine, 103
Le Corbusier
    Contemporary City for Three Million Inhabitants, 33
    Hauptstadt Berlin proposal, 39
    influence, 15, 59, 125, 155, 160
    work for developing nations, 15, 148
Lemke, Wilhelm, 229, *230*
Lengen, Karen van, 57
Lenné, Peter Joseph, 30, 183
Léon, Hilde, 133, 201
Leonidov, Ivan, 64
Liberty Bell, 23
Libeskind, Daniel, 7, 8, 20 n.32, 44, 50–1, 64
Liebknecht, Karl, 184
lightness
    contemporary architecture, 91, 92
    Germanic tradition, 82, 91
    Norman Foster's use of, 79, 81, 101, 104–6, 113
    skeleton frame construction, 91–2
    Wrapped Reichstag, 79, 88–90, 92–3
Lindenburg, Udo, 190
Loos, Adolf, 112
Lovell, Sophie, 126
Lubetkin, Berthold, 157
Luckhardt, Wassili, 93
Lustgarten, 183, 184, 192

Maak, Niklas, 204
Macaulay, Rose, 136
Mächler, Martin, 35–7
Maier, Charles, 89
Mailer, Norman, 109–111
Marie-Elisabeth-Lüders-Haus, 67–8, 124, 157, *158*, 160
Marx-Engels-Forum, 188
Marx-Engels-Platz, 186
Matthijs Bouw/Joose Meuwissen, 201
Max Reinhardt Haus, 11
Mayne, Thom, 55
McHale, John, 41
Meier, Richard, 1, 57
Memorial to the Murdered Jews of Europe, 10, 181
Mendelsohn, Erich, 7, 157
Mengerzeile, 203

Merz, H. G., 217 n.55
Meuron, Pierre de, 232
Meuwissen, Joose, 201
Mies van der Rohe, Ludwig
  German Pavilion (1929 World Exhibition), 132
  influence, 9, 138, 160
  Neue Nationalgalerie, 9, 103, 145, 192
  Seagram building, 151
  unrealized buildings, 108
migration, 13, 230–2
Milla & Partner, 213
Mocken, Franz, 38
modernism
  contemporary, 56, 59, 99, 101
  criticism of, 16–17, 151, 200, 208
  monumentality, 148–9, 150
  postwar, 39, 51–2, 85
  principles, 82, 125, 151
  rejection of, 133, 181
  Weimar Republic, 32–5
Möhring, Bruno, 32
Moneo, Rafael, 1, 9
Mönninger, Michael, 44, 161
monumentality
  Chancellery, 123–4, 129, 153, 157, 160, 161
  future ruins, 121, 129
  Kunstmuseum Bonn, 145, 147–8
  modernism, 148–9, 150
  negativity towards, 57, 92, 122–3, 148
  political associations, 25, 39, 123, 142, 146, 155
Moos, Stanislaus von, 11
Morgenthau Plan, 47
Morphosis, 55, 57
Mossehaus, 7
Mumford, Lewis, 148
Muschamp, Herbert, 4
museological architecture, 15, 95, 103, 106, 108–9, 112
Museuminsel, 192
Muthesius, Hermann, 92

National Assembly Building (Dhaka), 149, 150, 151
National Socialism
  architectural ideology, 135, 136–7, 138
  architecture, 35–7, 70 n.20, 85, 132–4, 227–8
  nationalism, 39, 221
neoclassicism, 138
neoliberalism, 4, 72 n.43
Neue Nationalgalerie, 9, 103, 145, 192
Neue Staatsgalerie (Stuttgart), 139–40
Neues Museum, 85, 126, 192, 212–3
Neumann, Dietrich, 69 n.15
Neumeyer, Fritz, 140
Nghia, Vo Trong, 126
Niebuhr, Bernd, 193–5
Niemayer, Oscar, 99, 148
nostalgia, 121, 195, 200, 201–2, 208, 213
Nouvel, Jean, 7, 10, 46, 92, 96

Office for Metropolitan Architecture (OMA), 64, 181
Office of the President, 142, 222
Opera de la Bastille (Paris), 131
ornament
  contemporary architecture, 82, 112
  modernist rejection of, 92, 112, 181
  Reich Chancellery, 134
  Reichstag (1894), 84, 85, 93, 96, 101, 109
ostalgia, 208, 213
Ott, Carlos, 131
Otto, Frei, 139, 155, 201
Oud, J. J. P., 157
Ovaska, Arthur, 47

Palast der Republik, *177*
  controversy over removal, 11, 16, 176, 202–4, 206–7, 209
  criticism of, 191, 208, 209
  demolition, 209–11, 226
  design and construction, 176, 186, 187, 188, 189–91
  Volkspalast, 203, 204, 205–8, 209
Pariser Platz, 6, 50, 222
Paul-Löbe-Haus, 124, 157, *158,* 160
Paulick, Richard, 137
Peanutz Architekten, 204
Pedadogical Academy (Bonn), 42
pedestrian viewpoint, 68
Peichl, Gustav, 131, 153, 193
Pempelfort, Gerd, 41

Pergamonmuseum, 192
Petersen, Richard, 32
Philharmonie, 192
Photiadis, Michael, 126
Piano, Renzo, 1, 6, 10, 69 n.6
Pinakothek der Moderne (Munich), 159
Plattenbauten, 192
Platz der Republik, 33, 58, 67, 79, 102
  See also Königsplatz
Poelzig, Hans, 11, 33, 40
Poschardt, Ulf, 230
Posner, Ellen, 57
post-postmodernism, 54
post-structuralism, 53
postcolonialism, 15
postmodernism, 4, 61, 139–40, 160–1
Potsdamer Platz
  competition, 130
  InfoBox, 199
  renovation, 6–7, *8,* 69 n.6, 181, 222
Price, Cedric, 206
Pritzker Architecture Prize, 1–2, 5–9, 10, 95
privatization, 223, 230, 231
Prix, Wolf, 97–8
progressivism, 53, 54, 57, 81, 85, 132
Prussian National Monument for the Liberation Wars, 227
public-private partnerships, 222
Pugh, Emily, 187

race, 10, 13, 72 n.38
railway stations, 58, 68, 103, 223, 225
Ramberg, Lars Ø., *Palast des Zweifels,* 206–7
Rambert, Francis, 104
Raschdorff, Julius and Otto, 85, 183
Rast, Rudolf, 195
raumlabor Berlin, 204, 205
refugees, 221, 230–2
Reichstag (1894)
  design, 30, 83–5, 92, 95–6
  fire, 35, 85
  renovation (1961), 85–6, 95, 106, 109, 111, 112
  as a ruin, 37, 85, 126
  unpopularity, 31, 85, 86
  during World War II, 85, 109

Reichstag (1999 renovation), *2*
  competition (1992), 95–100
  contrasted with the Humboldt Forum, 212–13
  critical reception, 1, 5–6, 161–2, 180, 181, 226
  design, 15, 100–8
  dome, 81, 92, 94, 97, 107–8
  graffiti, conservation of, 15, 80, 82, 108–13
Reichstag (parliament), 83, 85
Reitermann, Rudolf, 126
representations, in urban planning, 45
reunification
  celebrations, 23, 44, 102
  challenges, 61–2, 175, 181, 207, 221, 226
  expression in architecture, 2–3, 14
  memorial to, 213
Richter, Dagmar, 56–7
Riemann, Peter, 47
romanticism, 16, 114, 129, 135–6
Rosenfeld, Gavriel, 139
Rosh, Lea, 10
Rossi, Aldo, 41, 44, 53, 131
Roth, Michael, 136
Rubin, Fred, 210
Ruf, Sep, 132
Ruff, Ludwig, 142
ruins
  Speer's theory of, 135, 136–7
  trope, 121, 123, 135–6
  wrapping, 15–16, 125–9, 150–1, 156, 157
Russia, relations with Germany, 111

Sack, Manfred, 155
safety, in architecture, 221, 232–3
Sagebiel, Ernst, 227
Sainsbury Centre for the Visual Arts, 103, *104,* 105–6
Salk Institute (La Jolla, California), 150, 151
Sandler, Daniela, 209
Sani, Maroan el, 213
Sassenroth, Peter, 126
Scharoun, Hans, 39, 192
Schäuble, Wolfgang, 88

Scheerbart, Paul, 81
Scheffler, Karl, 3
Scheidemann, Philipp, 184
Schinkel, Karl Friedrich
    Altes Museum, 8, 85, 139, 146, 148, 183–4
    Bauakademie, 188, 192
    cathedral, 182, 183
    Friedrichswerder Church, 192
    influence, 9, 41, 138, 142, 145, 178–9
    paintings, 6
    Prussian National Monument for the Liberation Wars, 227
    Schlossbrücke, 183
    urban planning, 153, 183, 200
Schjeldahl, Peter, 159
Schlegel, Friedrich, 91
Schlossplatz
    debate, 176, 178, 179–80, 201, 202
    history, 181, 183, 184
    redevelopment proposals, 191, 194–5, 197, 201
Schlüter, Andreas, 182
Schmaling, Sebastian, 108, 161
Schmettau, Samuel von, 28, *29*
Schneider, Peter, 7, 25
Schönefeld Airport, 223, 225
Schröder, Gerhard, 6, 121–2, 161, 162, 202, 208
Schüler-Witter, Ursulina, 191
Schüler, Ralf, 191
Schultes Frank Architekten
    Chancellery, 16–17, 122–3, 143–5, 147, 153–7, 160–2
    Chancellery extension, 162–3
    Crematorium Baumschulenweg, 148
    Spreebogen, 14, 23–5, 57–64, 67, 68, 106
    Spreeinsel proposal, 196–7
Schultes, Axel
    "Schinkel's dream," 178–9, 200, 214
    criticism of changes to Band des Bundes, 162
    influenced by Louis Kahn, 124, 125, 152–3
    Kunstmuseum Bonn, 42, 145, 147–8, 159
Schwippert, Hans, 42, 81

Scott, George Gilbert, 83
sculptures, 6, 109, 134, 155, 166 n.37
Seagram building, New York, 151
Sebald, W. G., *Austerlitz*, 121, 138
Semper, Gottfried, 103, 137
Serra, Richard, 10
Siedler, Wolf Jobst, 191, 200
Simmel, Georg, 60, 62, 63
simulations, architectural, 198–200, 201, 204–5
Smithson, Alison and Peter, 40–1
Smithson, Robert, 136
socialism, utopian, 188
Soler, Francis, 131
Sony Center, 7, 92
Soviet army, 85, 108, 109, 111, 137
Soviet war memorial, 38
Speer, Albert
    classicism, 138, 140
    Führer-Palast, 134, 146
    Léon Krier on, 11, 140
    north-south axis, 14, 35–7, 39, 43, 60, 158, 227
    Reich Chancellery, 133–5, 137
    Theorie vom Ruinwert, 135, 136–7
    unrealized projects, 108
    Volkshalle design, 37, 85
Spengelin, Friedrich, 41
Spreebogen
    challenge of unification, 14–15, 23–5, 31
    competition (1992), 23–5, 26, 52, 53–60
    history to 1919, 26–32
    lack of critical analysis, 11–13
    postwar period, 37–41
    Schultes and Frank design, 14, 23–5, 57–64, 67, 68, 106
    Third Reich, 35–7
    Weimar Republic, 32–5
Spreeinsel, 3
    competition (1993–4), 131, 191, 192–8
Staatsgalerie (Stuttgart), 139–40
Staatsratsgebäude, 188, 198
Stadtforum, 52
Stadtschloss, *177*
    arguments for reconstruction, 200, 202, 208
    demolition, 16, 176, 185–6

portal, 188, 198, 212
postreunification role, 181, 194–5
prewar history, 30, 31, 176, 181–3, 184
reconstruction of facades, 211–13
simulation, 198–9, 200, 201
Stalinallee, 137
starchitects, 9–10, 97, 113, 152, 221, 222
Stegers, Rudolf, 146
Steiner, Rudolf, 93, *94*
Steinigeweg, Friedrich, 96–7
Stella, Franco, 180, 193, 211, 212
Stimmann, Hans
  Critical Reconstruction, 52–3, 130
  Critical Regionalism, 11
  Europeanism, 53, 56
  regulations, 6, 20 n.32, 53, 130, 140
  Spreeinsel competition, 193
Stirling, James, 139, 140
Straube, Julius, *30*
Stridbeck, Johann, *28*
Stubbins, Hugh, 38
Stüler, Friedrich August, 85, 138, 182
Superstudio, 59
Süssmuth, Rita, 54–5, 79, 88, 120 n.96
Swiczinsky, Helmut, 97–8
Swiss Embassy, 41

Tama Art University Library (Tokyo), 126, *128*
Tatlin, Vladimir, 98
Taut, Bruno, 35, 81, 93
  Alpine Architektur, 81, 206
  Auflösung der Städte, Die, 15, 63–4
Tchoban Foundation Museum for Architectural Drawing, 126, *127*
Tchoban, Sergei, 126
Tegel Airport, 223
Tempelhof Airport, 223, 226–232
Tessenow, Heinrich, 138
Theiss, Caspar, 182
36x27x10 (exhibition 2005), 208
Thorne, Martha, 10
3XN, 68
Tiergarten, 27, 30, 37, 67
Tiravanija, Rirkrit, 208
tourism
  BER site, 225–6

infrastructure, 18 n.11, 119 n.86, 223, 233 n.3
negative influence, 207, 222
Stadtschloss, 211
transparency, architectural
  association with democracy, 81, 94, 112
  diffidence, 42, 132
  doctrine, 42, 81, 131, 154, 189, 232
  Reichstag renovations, 81, 82, 85

Ulbricht, Walter, 185, 186, 188, 226
Ungers, O. M., 15, 47–9, 68, 141–3, 195–6
Unter den Linden
  GDR, 186–7
  history, 27–28
  Liebeskind proposal, 50–1, 64
  Weimar proposals, 32, 33, 64
Urban Catalyst, 203
urban islands, 47, 48, 49
urban planning, methodology of, 44–5
utopianism
  avant garde, 81, 188
  GDR, 186, 188–9, 191
  modernism, 16, 26, 89, 181, 187
  Reichstag, 81, 190

Vandreike, Bertram, 146
Venturi Scott Brown, 44, 51, 157
Venus Marble Headquarters (Athens), 126, *129*
Vesnin brothers, 98
Vidler, Anthony, 55
Voigt, Wolfgang, 97
Volkskammer, 189, 190
Volkspalast, 16, 203–4, 205–8, 209

Wagner, Otto, 83
Waigel, Theo, 198
Walker, Michael, 200
Wallot, Paul, 83–4, 85, 92, 95, 109, 112
Ward, Janet, 60, 62
Ward, Simon, 203
Warhol, Andy, 115 n. 19
Weimar Republic, 32–5, 59, 85, 184
Weiss-Sussex, Godela, 3
Werneburg, Brigitte, 106
Wilford, Michael, 140

Wilhelm II, 7, 85, 214 n.13
Wise, Michael Z., 11–13
Witt, Christoph, 122, 164 n.14
  See also Schultes Frank Architekten

Wohlhage, Konrad, 133, 201
World War II, damage from, 137, 175, 176, 184, 186, 188
Wowereit, Klaus, 3, 225, 230

www.ingramcontent.com/pod-product-compliance
Lightning Source LLC
Chambersburg PA
CBHW062130300426
44115CB00012BA/1870